Mexican Literature as World Literature

Literatures as World Literature

Can the literature of a specific country, author, or genre be used to approach the elusive concept of "world literature"? **Literatures as World Literature** takes a novel approach to world literature by analyzing specific constellations—according to language, nation, form, or theme—of literary texts and authors in their own world-literary dimensions.

World literature is obviously so vast that any view of it cannot help but be partial; the question then becomes how to reduce the complex task of understanding and describing world literature. Most treatments of world literature so far either have been theoretical and thus abstract, or else have made broad use of exemplary texts from a variety of languages and epochs. The majority of critical work, the filling in of what has been traced, lies ahead of us. **Literatures as World Literature** fills in the devilish details by allowing scholars to move outward from their own areas of specialization, fostering scholarly writing that approaches more closely the polyphonic, multiperspectival nature of world literature.

Series Editor:
Thomas O. Beebee

Editorial Board:
Eduardo Coutinho, Federal University of Rio de Janeiro, Brazil
Hsinya Huang, National Sun-yat Sen University, Taiwan
Meg Samuelson, University of Cape Town, South Africa
Ken Seigneurie, Simon Fraser University, Canada
Galin Tihanov, Queen Mary University of London, UK
Mads Rosendahl Thomsen, Aarhus University, Denmark

Volumes in the Series
German Literature as World Literature, edited by Thomas O. Beebee
Roberto Bolaño as World Literature, edited by Nicholas Birns and Juan E. De Castro
Crime Fiction as World Literature, edited by David Damrosch,
Theo D'haen and Louise Nilsson
Danish Literature as World Literature, edited by Dan Ringgaard and
Mads Rosendahl Thomsen
From Paris to Tlön: Surrealism as World Literature, by Delia Ungureanu
American Literature as World Literature, edited by Jeffrey R. Di Leo

Romanian Literature as World Literature, edited by Mircea Martin,
Christian Moraru and Andrei Terian
Brazilian Literature as World Literature, edited by Eduardo F. Coutinho
Dutch and Flemish Literature as World Literature, edited by Theo D'haen
Afropolitan Literature as World Literature, edited by James Hodapp
Francophone Literature as World Literature, edited by Christian Moraru,
Nicole Simek and Bertrand Westphal
Bulgarian Literature as World Literature, edited by Mihaela P. Harper and
Dimitar Kambourov
Philosophy as World Literature, edited by Jeffrey R. Di Leo
Turkish Literature as World Literature, edited by Burcu Alkan and Çimen Günay-Erkol
Elena Ferrante as World Literature, by Stiliana Milkova
Multilingual Literature as World Literature, edited by Jane Hiddleston and
Wen-chin Ouyang
Persian Literature as World Literature, edited by Mostafa Abedinifard, Omid
Azadibougar and Amirhossein Vafa
Mexican Literature as World Literature, edited by Ignacio M. Sánchez Prado
Beyond English: World Literature and India, by Bhavya Tiwari (forthcoming)
Graphic Novels and Comics as World Literature, edited by James Hodapp
(forthcoming)
Feminism as World Literature, edited by Robin Truth Goodman (forthcoming)
Modern Irish Literature as World Literature, edited by Christopher Langlois
(forthcoming)
African Literatures as World Literature, edited by Alexander Fyfe and Madhu Krishnan
(forthcoming)
Taiwanese Literature as World Literature, edited by Pei-yin Lin and Wen-chi Li
(forthcoming)

Mexican Literature as World Literature

Edited by
Ignacio M. Sánchez Prado

BLOOMSBURY ACADEMIC
NEW YORK • LONDON • OXFORD • NEW DELHI • SYDNEY

BLOOMSBURY ACADEMIC
Bloomsbury Publishing Inc
1385 Broadway, New York, NY 10018, USA
50 Bedford Square, London, WC1B 3DP, UK
29 Earlsfort Terrace, Dublin 2, Ireland

BLOOMSBURY, BLOOMSBURY ACADEMIC and the Diana logo are trademarks of
Bloomsbury Publishing Plc

First published in the United States of America 2022
This paperback edition published 2023

Volume Editor's Part of the Work © Ignacio M. Sánchez Prado, 2022
Each chapter © Contributors, 2022

Cover design by Simon Levy

All rights reserved. No part of this publication may be reproduced or transmitted in any form or by any means, electronic or mechanical, including photocopying, recording, or any information storage or retrieval system, without prior permission in writing from the publishers.

Bloomsbury Publishing Inc does not have any control over, or responsibility for, any third-party websites referred to or in this book. All internet addresses given in this book were correct at the time of going to press. The author and publisher regret any inconvenience caused if addresses have changed or sites have ceased to exist, but can accept no responsibility for any such changes.

Library of Congress Cataloging-in-Publication Data
Names: Sánchez Prado, Ignacio M., 1979- editor.
Title: Mexican literature as world literature / edited by Ignacio M. Sánchez Prado.
Description: New York : Bloomsbury Academic, 2021. | Series: Literatures as world literature | Includes bibliographical references and index.
Identifiers: LCCN 2021012900 (print) | LCCN 2021012901 (ebook) |
ISBN 9781501374784 (hardback) | ISBN 9781501374807 (eBook) |
ISBN 9781501374791 (ePDF) | ISBN 9781501374814 (XML)
Subjects: LCSH: Mexican literature–History and criticism. | Mexican literature–Appreciation.
Classification: LCC PQ7119 .M48 2021 (print) | LCC PQ7119 (ebook) | DDC 860.9/972–dc23
LC record available at https://lccn.loc.gov/2021012900
LC ebook record available at https://lccn.loc.gov/2021012901

ISBN: HB: 978-1-5013-7478-4
PB: 978-1-5013-7482-1
ePDF: 978-1-5013-7479-1
eBook: 978-1-5013-7480-7

Series: Literatures as World Literature

Typeset by Deanta Global Publishing Services, Chennai, India

To find out more about our authors and books visit www.bloomsbury.com and sign up for our newsletters.

Contents

Introduction *Ignacio M. Sánchez Prado*	1
1 World-Making and the Poetics of the New World *Jorge Téllez*	7
2 Global Sor Juana *Stephanie Kirk*	23
3 World-Making in the New Spain of the Eighteenth Century *Karen Stolley*	39
4 On (Re)productive Worlds: Transpacific Materiality and Mexican World Literature *Laura Torres-Rodríguez*	55
5 World-Making in Nineteenth-Century Mexico *Shelley Garrigan*	71
6 Rethinking Mexican Modernismo and World Literature *Adela Pineda Franco*	89
7 World-Making in the Twentieth Century: The Rise of Mexican World Literary Institutions *Ignacio M. Sánchez Prado*	105
8 From Post-Revolutionary Cosmopolitanisms to Pre-Bolaño Infrarealism: Mexican Avant-Garde Literatures in/as World Literature *Sara Potter*	117
9 Beyond the Literary Field: Octavio Paz in World Literature *Manuel Gutiérrez Silva*	133
10 Brief History of an Anthology of Mexican Poetry *Gustavo Guerrero*	153
11 Juan Rulfo's World Literary Consciousness *Nuala Finnegan*	171
12 *Uno se sale de uno para verse viendo*: Mexican Countercultural Literature as Psychedelic Interventions of World Literature *Iván Eusebio Aguirre Darancou*	187
13 Carlos Fuentes and World Literature *Pedro Ángel Palou*	203
14 Neoliberalism, Distinction, and World Literature in Mexico in the Twenty-First Century *Oswaldo Zavala*	215
15 Planetary Poetics of Extinction in Contemporary Mexican Poetry *Carolyn Fornoff*	231
Notes on Contributors	247
Index	251

Introduction

Ignacio M. Sánchez Prado

A book entitled *Mexican Literature as World Literature* entails rethinking and redefining the idea of world literature. Based on concepts such as "combined and uneven development," as the Warwick Collective does, or Pascale Casanova's "World Republic of Letters" or Franco Moretti's notions of the center, the semi-periphery, and the periphery, world literature has emerged in many canonical accounts as a unified and unequal system of literary circulation and symbolic capital.[1] Even the recognition of world literature as a concept that seeks to account the movement "from the old world to the new world," to use David Damrosch's formulation, remains grounded on a canon of books that circulate outside of their national and linguistic contexts.[2] These models are not universally accepted, of course, and the idea of world literature is subject to a robust debate in terms of the very idea of the "world" that underlies it, often pitting, as theorists like Pheng Cheah or Eric Hayot have done, the geopolitical conception of the world with forms of wordling and wordliness tied to literary representation or ontological questions.[3] Yet, the predominance of models that are either spatial or focused on literary circulation in Global North markets tends to reify world literature by taking for granted its coextension of the most hegemonic of its dimensions, namely, the one that locates it in the power cores of literary markets, former and current imperial capitals, and Anglophone and Francophone academies. In other words, many approaches to world literature conceptualize it as a factually existing object that can be measured (even literally so as Moretti's computational analysis, as well as some approaches to the digital humanities do) and described.

It should not surprise anyone that Latin Americanists like myself, located in the United States and Europe and therefore exposed to these debates, have for many years contested the naturalization of the object of world literature. It is often clear to us that, in the context of the decline of old models of the discipline of comparative literature, world literature often provides a way to once again re-inscribe Eurocentrism as a master narrative of a literary field that, in the context of the dynamics of translation and circulation that have multiplied under neoliberal globalism, territorializes an unprecedentedly large number of cultural productions into a cartography that symbolically totalizes (although does not actually cover) the world at large. Latin America in general and individual countries like Mexico (or Argentina, or Colombia, or Brazil, or pretty much any nation in the region) pose a peculiar problem to world literature theory, since their respective literary fields have been historically defined by cosmopolitanism and worldliness. In his speech "Thoughts on the American Mind," Mexican humanist Alfonso Reyes noted that Latin Americans were characterized by "our innate internationalism" and suggested that "in the computation of errors or partial misunderstanding in the European books dealing with America and the American books that deal with Europe, the balance is in our favor" (it is worth underscoring for the Anglophone reader of this book that "American" always refers, in the work of Reyes, to the Latin American).[4] In other words, Latin Americans know more than Europeans, because we know their culture well, but they know our culture in a limited and poor way.

This gesture continues to carry a meaning into the present, and into world literature studies. The bookstores of Latin America are full of astounding numbers of literary works in translation, the result of the combined efforts of an ecosystem of presses across the Spanish and Portuguese language. Two Latin American authors have a plausible claim to be considered the most influential writers in the world in the second part of the twentieth century: Jorge Luis Borges and Gabriel García Márquez. And one has to take a cursory look to the writing of any major Latin American writer of today— Luiselli and Rivera Garza, Mariana Enríquez, Samantha Schweblin, Lina Meruane, Carmen Boullosa, and so on—to find the encyclopedic archive of world literature that underlies their work. And yet, one would be hard-pressed to find any major theory of world literature that does not frame Latin America as either a creative periphery or as a repository of some purported revolutionary authenticity. Even postcolonial theory, a precursor and rival to the idea of world literature, often ignored Latin America, or reduced it to a token example, notwithstanding the fact that Latin America's postcolonial experience is over two centuries old. I will not rehash these debates here, but readers can find it in a bibliography that runs from the collection I edited back in 2006 to the collective work from scholars around the world, coordinated by Gesine Müller and her research group at the University of Köln in Germany.[5]

It would be against the spirit of this collection to re-center once again our grievances against the sidetracking of Latin America in the Anglophone and Francophone academies. But it is worth remembering that the category of world literature, at least in connections to literary traditions like the Mexican one, is a concept one has to deploy, at least to a degree, against the grain. This is not to say that I advocate here for a decolonial approach that solely focuses on the knowledge produced in Latin America itself. This is a useful form of thinking in many ways, but not one that corresponds to the cosmopolitan vein this book addresses. Rather, I want to suggest here, as I do in a more elaborate way in my book *Strategic Occidentalism*, that world literature is not an object but rather a symbolic product of the ways in which institutions of concrete literary fields (regional, national, linguistic, global) and its actors practice world literature materially.[6] Which in turn means there is no such thing as a singular world literature, but rather multiple world literatures that exist and evolve according to the ways in which fields envision and imagine the world. I pitched *Mexican Literature as World Literature* to the Literatures as World Literature series at Bloomsbury because I found that the conceptualization of the series as a place to discuss "specific constellations" and to study "the polyphonic and multiperspectival nature of world literature" corresponds to my own view in this matter.[7] It is worth noting that this understanding of world literature has been a part of the concept for a long time. Richard G. Moulton famously argued in 1911 that world literature differed from universal literature in that it was seen from a standpoint, more generally the national one.[8] In the case of this book, Mexican literature is not a literature in a hegemonic position, the way English literature was for Moulton. They argue that the idea of "Mexican world literature" provides not only one counterpoint to the gleeful naturalization of Eurocentric literary fields as the places where world literature happens, but also to understand that world literature is not a unified object (the way Moulton himself tried to present it) but an effect of institutional practices that construct the world in a given literary field.

The essays included in this book follow my interest in bringing together some of the most talented scholars in Mexican literary studies writ large to reflect on the different topics that their respective scholarship has so productively studied in tension with the idea of world literature. Although both pursuits make intermittent appearances across its pages, this book is neither an attempt to justify Mexican literature's inclusion in world literary canons nor an application of world literature theory to Mexican literature. Rather, it is an overarching history of Mexican literature from early colonial literature to the present as a production that is always already inscribed in the various forms and periods of world literature, including those that have existed *avant la lettre* for centuries.

From the chronicles of the Conquest, which mapped in the European imagination the emerging world-system built by the Spanish and Portuguese empires, to the Mexican women writers—Valeria Luiselli, Fernanda Melchor, and Cristina Rivera Garza—who have positioned themselves within the hegemonic literary circuits of 2020, Mexico has been both a crucial node of world literary circuits and a place that problematizes them. The essays in *Mexican Literature as World Literature* provide a wide—though not exhaustive—range of readings from the general to the particular on this interaction. The essays are organized by a rough chronological order, because historical narrative can effectively guide readers, particularly those not familiar with Mexican literature. However, it is important to point out that there are sets of articles with specific framings. The first of these framings are overarching articles covering long-range processes of "world-making" as related to centuries or periods in Mexican literature. These chapters provide a historical backbone to the collection, based on the idea of thinking Mexican literature as a standpoint from which one can rethink and re-narrate the category of world literature at large. A second set of chapters focus on canonical writers (Sor Juana, Juan Rulfo, Octavio Paz, Carlos Fuentes) who have been historically identified as the ones more directly in circulation in the hegemonic world-literary system. These chapters, along with a case study on the UNESCO-funded anthology of Mexican poetry, underscore the ways in which, even when participating in the global circuits of world literature, Mexican literature often raises questions that problematize its conceptual frameworks. Finally, the book includes a series of chapters on specific conceptual issues—the Transpacific, counterculture, the avant-garde, the environment—to understand the ways in which Mexican literature illuminates spaces, themes, and times that intertwine with world literature.

The first three chapters engage in the matter of the New Spain, and the role that the territory that would ultimately become Mexico plays in understanding world literature. In "World-Making and the Poetics of the New World," Jorge Téllez discusses the question of world literature in the New Spain in the sixteenth and seventeenth centuries. In a dialogue with authors like Alexander Beecroft and Franco Moretti, Téllez discusses the role that literary infrastructures of the Spanish empire played in the formation of world literature and the emergence of Mexico City as a world-literary site. Stephanie Kirk writes what she calls a globalizing view of Sor Juana's writing, through concepts of globalism and planetarity. She uses this perspective to claim Mexican literature as a way to discuss the position of colonial (or peripheral) literature in world-literature canons. Finally, Karen Stolley discusses both how world literature theory enables new understandings of eighteenth-century New Spain, and the ways in which literature from this period allows to expand beyond ideas of world literature as a problem or an object, to engage it as a conversation among writers and readers of the time and beyond.

Placing the colonial period in a transhistorical framework, Laura Torres-Rodríguez discusses the way in which the Pacific and the cultural relations between Mexico and Asia continue to be illegible from the perspective of world literature theory. Her piece, "On (Re)Productive Worlds," proposes a long-duration approach that covers this relationship from colonial texts to the contemporary culture produced around China's current relationship with Latin America.

The nineteenth century is covered by two general texts roughly divided into the two distinctive periods of Mexican cultural history: the one that runs from the early independence to the triumph of the Liberal Party (1810–80) and the Porfiriato (1880–1910), identified also with the *Modernista* movement. The former period is addressed by Shelley Garrigan, who studies national institutions (academies, libraries) to engage the role of cosmopolitanism in the formation of post-Independence Mexican literature. In doing so, she shows the ways in which a focus on world-making rather than on nationalism provides a different reading of foundational national periods. The latter period is at the core of Adela Pineda Franco's piece. Pineda Franco proposes a reading of the cosmopolitan and world-literary endeavors of Mexican *modernismo* away from what she considers to be Eurocentric approaches based on notions of cosmopolitan desire (in debate with Siskind) or the purported mimesis of the European. Instead, she argues that the economic and political landscape of Porfiriato fostered the use of cosmopolitanism to render visible the limits of the discourses of progress tied to global capitalism at the time.

The twentieth century poses a more complicated challenge in this book, as there are many directions in which one can go to account the multidimensional engagements with world literature fostered by the post-revolutionary period. I opted to collect exemplary editorial cases rather than aspire to an overarching or exhaustive account. My piece frames the post-revolutionary period as a period of emergence of institutions that allows for the construction of a Mexican world literature—publishers, translators, cultural activists, and so on—to argue that world-making in the twentieth century is, first and foremost, the consequence of these institutions. Sara Potter takes the history of the Mexican avant garde, from Stridentism to Infrarrealism, to contend with the different ways in which the cosmopolitanism-nationalism debate and vanguardist forms of world literature shape the Mexican literary imagination. Manuel Gutiérrez Silva focuses on Octavio Paz, perhaps the Mexican writer most widely read beyond the country. Gutiérrez Silva focuses on the mechanics of his consecration, particularly in relation to cultural diplomacy and the institutional art world. Parallel to this, Gustavo Guerrero writes a history of UNESCO's *Anthologie de la poésie mexicaine*, edited by Octavio Paz and translated into English by Samuel Beckett. To the discussion of Paz, Guerrero provides a unique perspective on the role of poetry, as well as of the network created between the Mexican and the French cultural fields in the mid-century.

Moving toward the realm of narrative, Nuala Finnegan discusses the figure of Juan Rulfo and his epistemology of mobility and plurality. Finnegan focuses on what she calls "Juan Rulfo's world-literary consciousness," aligning him with a reading of world literature that registers the violence of world capitalism as its essential political horizon. Iván Eusebio Aguirre Darancou provides a critical account of Mexican literature from the perspective of counterculture and psychedelia. Using writers like Fernando del Paso and Margarita Dalton as case studies, he discusses the tension between the geopolitical world and wordling as a matter of consciousness. Departing from the obituaries published after his death, Pedro Ángel Palou engages the figure of Carlos Fuentes, and his late style, in relation to his standing in world literature and his world-literary engagement with Mexican politics.

The book closes with two essays dealing with the twenty-first century. Oswaldo Zavala proposes a polemic against the configuration of Mexican literature in contemporary world literature, challenging the consumerist culture it entails in terms of the tension between the figure of the politically engaged domestic writer and the ideal of the author working in an autonomous system of distinction. Carolyn Fornoff concludes the book looking to environmental and planetary questions as a new quadrant of world literature, engaging young Mexican poets like Karen Villeda and Isabel Zapata.

Through these articles, *Mexican Literature as World Literature* aims both to be a contribution to reading Mexican literature in new and original terms and to illuminate world literature debates from a tradition that is never fully accounted in its theorizations.

Notes

1 Warwick Research Collective, *Combined an Uneven Development: Towards a New Theory of World-Literature* (Liverpool: Liverpool University Press, 2016). Pascale Casanova, *The World Republic of Letters*, trans. M. B. DeBevoise (Cambridge, MA: Harvard University Press, 2007). Franco Moretti, *Distant Reading* (London: Verso, 2013).
2 David Damrosch, *What Is World Literature?* (Princeton: Princeton University Press, 2003), 110.
3 Pheng Cheah, *What Is a World? On Postcolonial Literature as World Literature* (Durham: Duke University Press, 2016). Eric Hayot, *On Literary Worlds* (Oxford: Oxford University Press, 2012).

4 Alfonso Reyes, *The Position of America and Other Essays*, trans. Harriet de Onís (New York: Alfred A. Knopf, 1950), 38–9.
5 See Ignacio M. Sánchez Prado, *América Latina en la "literatura mundial"* (Pittsburgh: Instituto Internacional de Literatura Iberoamericana, 2006). Müller's important work is gathered in the series Latin American Literatures in the World, published by De Gruyter, which has released nine books at the time of this writing.
6 Ignacio M. Sánchez Prado, *Strategic Occidentalism. On Mexican Fiction, the Neoliberal Book Market and the Question of World Literature* (Evanston: Northwestern University Press, 2018).
7 I copy these citations from the website for the series at Bloomsbury.com.
8 Richard G. Moulton, *World Literature and Its Place in General Culture* (New York: Macmillan, 1911). See also John Pizer, *The Idea of World Literature: History and Pedagogical Practice* (Baton Rouge: Louisiana State University Press, 2006), 89–91.

1

World-Making and the Poetics of the New World

Jorge Téllez

In this chapter I chart a course for reading world literature theory in relation to colonial Latin American studies, in particular with respect to scholarship on early modern poetry. To do this, I start with the idea that the necessary infrastructure to think about the production and circulation of written culture on a global scale was already present in sixteenth- and seventeenth-century New Spain. This was due not only to the arrival of the printing press in 1539 but also to the channels of circulation of knowledge that the lettered community had established on both sides of the Atlantic and the Pacific.[1] The schema I propose to support this idea has three prongs. The first is a brief demonstration of how to read New Spain in a global context, or how and where to read the world within colonial Mexico. The second focuses on the possibilities and limits of world literature theory with respect to the study of sixteenth- and seventeenth-century colonial poetry. In the third, I propose three case studies: Diego Mexía's translation of Ovid (1608); Bernardo de Balbuena's *Grandeza mexicana* [Mexican Greatness, 1604]; and two poetics—the prologue that Balbuena wrote for his epic poem *El Bernardo o Victoria de Roncesvalles* [The Bernardo, or Victory of Roncesvalles, 1624] and the *Suma del arte de la poesía* [Summary of the Art of Poetry, c. 1591] by Eugenio de Salazar.

Even before the destruction of Tenochtitlan, Hernán Cortés made clear the geographic importance of this territory in relation to the possible commercial routes between Europe and Asia.[2] Mexico City/Tenochtitlan went from being the final destination to which goods were sent to a waypoint through which the economic flow spread from Manila through the port of Acapulco and on to Spain through the port of Veracruz. Once commercial exchange between Mexico and the Philippines began in 1573, Mexico City effectively became the center of the world.[3]

This central position that is so obvious when speaking of commercial flow stands when studying intellectual flows. Serge Gruzinski, for example, begins his book on the Spanish monarchy and the process of American colonization by citing the diary of the Nahua intellectual Chimalpahin (1579–1660): "Su experiencia personal, su existencia diaria lo sumergen en una ciudad de cerca de 100 000 habitantes, México, en donde coexisten españoles, portugueses, flamencos, indios, mestizos, mulatos y negros de África, sin contar a franceses, italianos y hasta algunos centenares, incluso un millar, de asiáticos desembarcados de Filipinas"[4] [His personal experience and his daily existence immerse him in a city of about 100,000 inhabitants, Mexico, where Spaniards, Portuguese, Flemish, Indians, mestizos, mulattos and African blacks coexist; this does not include the French, Italians and even some hundreds, perhaps up to a thousand, of Asians arrived from the Philippines]. The cosmopolitanism that Gruzinski notes is an integral part of Chimalpahin's diary, where we find references to the execution of twenty-six Spaniards in Japan in February 1597 (who would later be beatified in 1627 and canonized in 1862); to the assassination of Henry IV in May 1610; and to a Japanese delegation that visited Mexico in November 1610, to cite just three examples.

Gruzinski's call to consider the history of New Spain and of Spanish colonization within a wider context resonates not only in examples like those of Chimalpahin's diary but also in considerations of the book trade and the translation of Classical works like *Aesop's Fables* into indigenous and Asian languages, or the study of Latin in the Santa Cruz de Tlatelolco School.[5] In commenting on the poem *Grandeza mexicana* (1604) by Bernardo de Balbuena, Gruzinski concludes that "México aparece en el corazón de las redes comerciales que cercan al planeta. Se vuelve el punto de encuentro de cuatro socios mundiales: al este, las grandes tierras de la Europa católica, España e Italia; al oeste, China y Japón"[6] [Mexico appears at the heart of the commercial networks that circle the globe. It becomes the meeting point of four global partners: to the east, the great lands of Catholic Europe, Spain and Italy; to the west, China and Japan].

The sentiment of relevance and centrality that Gruzinski reads in Balbuena is a leitmotif in the writing from and about the New World during the seventeenth century.[7] What is to be done, then, with the current reflections on world literature related to a period and a culture that seem infused into a global substrate from the start? In other words, is it possible to approach the abundant written corpus of New Spain using criteria that until very recently have essentially been concerned with the literature of modernity?

World Literature Epidemics

To begin to answer these questions, I would like to discuss three recent perspectives on world literature theory: Walter Cohen's *A History of European Literature*, Alexander Beecroft's *An Ecology of World Literature*, and Franco Moretti's *Distant Reading*.[8] Despite their substantial differences, both Cohen and Beecroft seem to have an interest in broadening not only the corpus of what is considered world literature but more particularly the period to which this concept is applied. In both books, they theorize the place that Antiquity, the Middle Ages, and the early modern period hold within the global literary system, but they also emphasize overcoming periodizations as units of meaning. More than simply summarizing both positions, I would like to concentrate on the importance that European expansion into the Americas has in both cases.

The opening argument of Cohen's book proposes that European literature originally emerged from world literature and that the former was reintegrated into the latter during the Renaissance. Cohen suggests that during the European expansion of the fifteenth and sixteenth centuries, literary representations of empire enabled Europe's reintegration into the global literary system. One of the main interests of this book with respect to the European colonial expansion is the idea of a global Renaissance that negatively impacts the demography of the Americas, and which, according to Cohen, has no literary correlate in Europe. Here I would like to highlight a couple of conflicts that appear when we use world literature as a tool for reading New Spain. In the first place, one might easily propose Las Casas's *Brevísima relación de la destrucción de las indias* [Brief History of the Destruction of the Indies] as a significant exception to the presence of American devastation in European letters. However, clearly Las Casas is not "doing" literature in the same way as, for example, Alonso de Ercilla in his *Araucana*. I mean by this that a problem arises from the very conception of "literary" or "literature" on which the theory of world literature is founded, which is an eminently modern concept.

Second, there is the geopolitical aspect of how we focus New World writing: With what national literature (if I may be allowed this anachronism) should we affiliate Las Casas? Is his expansive corpus a European product or an American one? Cohen suggests an answer in his discussion of the chronicles of conquest. For him, Columbus's writings and the documents of later conquistadors, such as Cortés's *Cartas de relación* [Letters from Mexico] and Bernal Díaz del Castillo's *Verdadera historia de la conquista de la nueva España* [True History of the Conquest of New Spain], are the clearest antecedents of a new genre that he calls "utopian fiction," which could not exist without the new world; but then he argues that these utopias are "constructed around the logic of nonrepresentation."[9] Ultimately, what Cohen does is study representations of empire in European letters, which he exemplifies with Camões, Shakespeare, and Cervantes. Hence, just like the American territories, American letters thus become material that makes possible and supplies Western wealth (in this case, of the literary variety).[10]

Beecroft proposes to use the category of "ecology" to perform a comparative study of world literatures and the networks through which they circulate and communicate with one another; he proposes this category as a means of overcoming restrictions based on regions and languages. This method is central to my reading of colonial poetry through the lens of the theory of world literature, since it helps with texts whose production and circulation differ radically from the way national literatures are created and circulate in the modern age. I am referring to a literary corpus based primarily on miscegenation, but also to the conflicts that reading American colonial poetry involves, given modern geographical divisions.

Beecroft proposes six types of ecologies. The literatures written in New Spain are situated, according to his schema, between the vernacular and the national ecologies, which are a product of European expansionism and the development of nationalism.[11] Beecroft rightfully asserts that Moretti's and Pascale Casanova's studies on world literature focus primarily on national ecologies. In fact, Moretti's ideas lean heavily on historical periodization. For him, the eighteenth century is the historical moment when international market forces began to exert pressure on what were until then isolated cultures, which opens the way for literatures from the center to interfere in peripheral literatures.[12] To explain this radical change, Moretti proposes the ideas of "sameness" and "diversification," which would define the way literature circulated before and after the eighteenth century. According to him, pre-eighteenth-century literature is characterized by offering a "mosaic of separate 'local' cultures; it is characterized by strong internal diversity; it produces new forms mostly by divergence; and is best explained by (some version of) evolutionary theory."[13]

However, Moretti also states that this theory is not infallible and proposes what he calls the "Petrarchist epidemics" as an example of widespread dispersion and "sameness" during the European late Middle Ages and Renaissance.[14] Moretti uses the term *epidemic* to explain the circulation of Petrarchism in Europe. I would like to follow this path and examine in more detail the idea of a Petrarchist epidemic by decentering it from its European context and thinking it in relation to the so-called New World. What happens if, for example, one takes literally the idea of epidemics to explain the circulation of poetic forms and themes?

I am interested in highlighting two curious aspects of this way of explaining Petrarchism. The first is that Petrarch wrote his poetry in the context of an actual epidemic, the bubonic plague that devastated Europe in the mid-fourteenth century. However, literary history has made clear that patient zero of the Petrarchist epidemic was not Francesco Petrarch; rather, this movement was born of the Italian humanism running rampant during the Renaissance, specifically that of the works of Pietro Bembo. He wanted to propose Petrarch as a model for the shift from Latin to the national vernacular language, and from there this epidemic spread through Spain, France, England, and Portugal.[15] In appearance, the antibodies that this epidemic generated were mainly satirical, and Petrarchism, following a somewhat flat view of literary history, was inoculated thanks to the satire and parody to which its themes were subjected during the seventeenth century.

The second point appears when we include the New World in this schematic history; that is, in how to reflect on Petrarchism in America from a global point of view, but also within the context of illness. Here the theme of epidemic is again pertinent to explaining the European invasion of American territory, á la James L. A. Webb Jr., as a "globalization of disease" that, during the period between 1500 and 1650, manifests as an "epidemiological integration of Afro-Eurasian disease into the Americas."[16] If we take Moretti's metaphor literally we would have to read American Petrarchism in parallel with what Noble David Cook has called "The Columbian Exchange" to explain the relevance of the participation of illnesses like smallpox, measles, typhus, and malaria as agents of devastation of indigenous peoples during the Conquest. Additionally, we would have to question the use of the illness metaphor as a vehicle of circulation and appropriation of literary forms, especially given the lack of agency granted to writers when it comes to considering them as infectious agents, rather than as subjects of conscious appropriation and resignification of literature.[17]

Ovid in America

We find an example of this literary appropriation in Diego Mexía's translation of Ovid's *Heroides*, which he completed during a trip between Peru and New Spain in 1596 and published years later, in 1608, as the *Primera parte del parnaso antártico de obras amatorias* [First Part of the Antarctic Parnassus: Love Poetry]. I have written elsewhere about the relevance of this work for understanding the material conditions of reading during the seventeenth century,[18] but now I would like to focus on the iconic nature of this work within the context of a possible reflection that accords with the theory of world literature.

If we use one of the many definitions of world literature, that of David Damrosch, as works that circulate "beyond their culture of origin, either in translation or in their original language,"[19] when we talk about Mexía's volume, then we would also be talking about the circulation of Ovid in the Hispanic context; however, it is also possible to invert the priorities and see in Mexía's work not so much the circulation of the Classical poet, but the translator's aspiration to introduce himself as part of a network of poetic production that surpasses colonial bounds and seeks to become a part of a Spanish—and thus European—humanist metropolitan circle. What, then, would be the culture of origin of Mexía's translation? How do we talk about a book that was written en route to Mexico by a poet affiliated with a Limeñan academy, and whose main interest was introducing the Antarctic Academy, a group of New World poets, as peers of peninsular academies? Can this assemblage of relationships and networks now be read as world literature?[20]

This idea of reading regional or national literatures as world literatures is not new. The best articulation of it to date can be found in Ignacio Sánchez Prado's recent book, in which he suggests the "worldliness" of world literature not as a "self-evident ideal nor a utopian pursuit"; rather, his book proposes it as "a concretely existing category related to specific cultural locations and material practices."[21] Despite the radically different context he discusses—Mexican literature at the turn of the twenty-first century—his idea of a "national world literature" also works for understanding the production of literature in the colonial era as a writing that springs from and appeals to the period's peninsular production in particular, and European production more generally. Read through Moretti, Mexía is one more victim of the European Petrarchist epidemics, but it is possible to suggest a different way of understanding this contagion if we pay attention to two things: the real epidemics that Mexía witnessed en route to Mexico City while reading and translating Ovid, and the relationship that exists between these epidemics and his translation of Ovid.[22]

Of all the materials included in the *Parnaso antártico*, what has received the most critical attention is the anonymous *Discurso en loor de la poesía* [Speech in Praise of Poetry], a poem that fills pages 9 to 25 of the volume and has the aim of presenting not only the Ovidian epistles, but also the works of the Antarctic Academy. Mexía's translation of Ovid in chained tercets, on the other hand, has drawn such little attention that even today there is no modern edition except for Trinidad Barrera's 1990 facsimile.[23] The prologue Mexía wrote for his translation offers a suggestive story for understanding what it meant to write poetry in the New World at the end of the sixteenth and beginning of the seventeenth centuries. A formalist reading leads us to place it within the tradition of Boscán and Garcilaso, whose introduction of the chained tercet to Spanish verse followed Italianate patterns that can be traced to Petrarch and Dante. The choice of Ovid, on the other hand, while presented as a coincidence points to the relevance of the Classical tradition in the academic training of scholars of the period. But the prologue also allows us to see beyond Mexía's Petrarchist affiliation to concentrate on the stand he takes within the colonial society of his day.

Mexía offers an image of the Americas as a hostile territory; it is a place of storms, shipwrecks, impassable rivers, swamps, and illnesses. In particular, Mexía makes reference to an epidemic of *cocoliztli* (a Nahuatl word that refers to illness, but also to plague) that repeatedly attacked Mesoamerican territories during the sixteenth century, and which, in an outbreak that began in 1576, was estimated to have killed more than two million indigenous people.[24] In the face of this climate of ailments, Mexía characterized himself as Ovid in exile, on the periphery of the empire and surrounded by barbarians:

[A] veinte años que navego mares, y camino tierras, por diferentes climas, alturas, y temperamentos, barbarizando entre barbaros, de suerte que me admiro cómo la lengua materna no se me ha olvidado, pues muchas veces me acontece, lo que a Ovidio estando desterrado entre los rústicos del Ponto, [. . .] cuando dice que queriendo hablar romano, habla sarmático.[25]

[For twenty years I have been sailing seas, and walking lands, through different climates, altitudes, and attitudes, becoming barbaric among barbarians, such that I am surprised that I have not forgotten my native language, since the same thing often happens to me that happened to Ovid during his exile among the rustics of the Black Sea, [. . .] when he says that he wants to speak Roman, but what comes out of his mouth is Sarmatian.]

This brief postal from the New Spain is one of those literary correlates of empire of which Cohen is unaware. It is also a testimony to the demographic impact on the conquered territories in America that are overlooked in a view informed only by the European canon (Shakespeare, Cervantes, Camões), as Cohen's is. Clearly of Petrarchist stock, this translation of Ovid nevertheless needs to be read with various nuances. The most important is the one that reveals what the writer's stance says about the politics that supports his poetics. Adding a translation of Ovid as one more of the symptoms of the Petrarchist contagion in America overlooks the relevance of Mexía's book for a comprehensive understanding of American literary production. Here it is worth returning to Beecroft's ideas to realize that a more in-depth study of the ways that literatures circulate is needed to understand the context in which they are produced:

In other words, rather than limit our study to specific systems within which literature circulates (Early Modern Europe, say, or East Asia, or the contemporary Anglosphere), we might want to think about how literature circulates, what sorts of constraints operate on that circulation, and how particular literary communities respond to those constraints.[26]

When, later in his prologue, Mexía complains of the isolation in which he wrote his translation, what he is underscoring is not the absence of a literary market, but, more importantly, the absence of a literary community:

> [D]emás que estas partes se platica poco de esta materia, digo de la verdadera Poesía, y artificioso metrificar, que de hacer coplas a bulto, antes no hay quien no lo profese: porque los sabios que de esto podrían tratar, sólo tratan de interés, y ganancia, que es a lo que acá los trajo su voluntad; y es de tal modo, que el que más docto viene se vuelve más Perulero.²⁷

> [The rest of these reports speak less of this matter, I mean of true Poetry, and artificial metrification, than of making couplets at first glance, because there is no one who does not practice it: because the learned men who (before) could talk about this, (now) only talk about interest, and earnings, which is what their desire brought them here to obtain; and so it is that they come here as scholars and return as *Peruleros* (*indianos* specifically from Peru).]

Again, the image of Ovid writing from the Black sea functions as a signifier of Mexía writing from the Americas, a place he never ceases to consider a land of barbarians. *Parnaso antártico*, then, cannot be read without taking into consideration at least two things: first, and most visibly, it is evidence offered to the Spanish peninsula authors of the attempt to build a literary community that Mexía so desired, in the form of the Antarctic Academy; and second, poetic writing in America in this case implies a political stance that necessarily considers all things American as inferior. Focusing only on the sphere of literate culture has the same effect, which is the ultimate message of Mexía's prologue: the devastation of the American territory and its inhabitants is merely an inconvenience that impedes or hinders poetic translation.

The choice of metric form is consequently related to the need to become involved in a broader, European dialogue, while differing drastically from that dialogue insofar as it is written under completely different circumstances. In a recent study on colonial poetry, Rodrigo Cacho Casal produced a helpful summary of the two main trends used to study the ever more abundant colonial poetic corpus. On one hand, says Cacho Casal, are the readings informed by theoretical orientations such as postcolonialism, subaltern studies, and ethnic studies, which he categorizes as "identitarian readings."[28] On the other, there is a philological trend that has been defended for years with formalist readings: the idea that colonial literary production is nothing more than an extension of the peninsular Hispanic tradition. As proof of this latter stance, one need only read Martha Lilia Tenorio's otherwise erudite studies, which make constant references to the fact that the "colonial" category is useless for understanding the poetry of the period: "En realidad," says Tenorio, "la literatura del virreinato no es otra que la literatura española de los Siglos de Oro"[29] [In fact, viceregal literature is nothing more than Spanish literature of the Golden Age].

The problem with positions like this is not only, as Cacho Casal aptly notes, that they imply an "aesthetic of continuity that often characterizes colonial texts as derivative or strongly indebted to the Peninsular tradition,"[30] but that in so doing, they imply that their point of view is strictly literary, when in fact they promote a discourse that tries to defend the idea of "the literary" as a pure, autonomous value, since it appears completely divested of any political or ideological implication. To think about "the literary" as autonomous in the sixteenth and seventeenth centuries is to deny what many scholars have already accepted in characterizing poetic writing as "arte del Estado" [art of the State], to use the name that Anne J. Cruz gives to the literary production of the early modern academies in Spain.[31]

This philological trend has always had a certain orientation toward what could be characterized as world literature; that is, it has considered this poetic production basically as part of early modern imperial European literary production. Yet the limits of this characterization seem clear to me: in assuming colonial production to be no different from peninsular Classical culture, Hispanism in the formalist tradition forgets what Mexía emphasized repeatedly during his prologue about the difficulties of writing in the New World.[32]

Mexico City in the World

The story of how a translation of Ovid came to Mexico City brings me to the next point of this chapter: the supposed contemporaneousness of colonial poetic production relative to peninsular and European poetry. The perspective that sees in colonial poetic production nothing more than an extension of the European Classical tradition constructs its argument based on the concepts of the contemporary and the modern. Tenorio begins her book on Góngora's influence on New Spanish poetry thus: "La poesía novohispana comenzó siendo 'moderna'; siempre estuvo al día; no hubo novedad que se le escapara"[33] [New Spanish poetry started out "modern"; it was always up to date; there was nothing new that escaped it].

The concept of modernity, as Casanova has demonstrated, is one of the criteria that has historically defined the struggle between artistic centers and peripheries.[34] "To be decreed 'modern,'" says Casanova, "is one of the most difficult forms of recognition for writers outside the center, and the object of violent and bitter competition."[35] Hence, for her, the development of world literature is simultaneously defined by a hegemonic space and a normative time, which interprets and assesses the works according to their contemporaneousness or anachronism relative to what is considered modern or present-day by the hegemonic cultural center. As Tenorio shows at the beginning of her book, scholars of the early twentieth century read the first signs of colonial poetic production as contemporaneous with the peninsular Italianate school.[36] This view, in turn, was institutionalized in Latin American thought around the middle of the twentieth century thanks to such influential studies in Latin America as *Literary Currents in Hispanic America* by Pedro Henríquez Ureña.[37]

Specifically responding to Henríquez Ureña's ideas, in 1983 Ángel Rama wrote a short essay titled "Fundación del manierismo hispanoamericano por Bernardo de Balbuena"[38] [Foundation of Hispanic American Mannerism by Bernardo de Balbuena]. Published the year he died, and between two of his most influential works—*Transculturación narrativa en América Latina* (Narrative Transculturation in Latin America, 1982) and *La ciudad letrada* (The Lettered City, 1984)—Rama's short essay on Balbuena has been largely ignored except by a small number of specialists on Balbuena. In it, Rama proposes a challenge to the traditional way of dealing with the aesthetic periodizations of the Renaissance, Mannerism, and the Baroque from Latin America by taking Balbuena's work as an example.

Rama's argument consists of proposing Balbuena's work not as an extension of peninsular poetics, but in parallel with it, like a process of the "plural marco evolutivo de la poesía española posterior a Garcilaso, que va apropiándose de la estética manierista italiana"[39] [plural evolutionary frame of Spanish poetry after Garcilaso, which continues to appropriate the Italian Mannerist aesthetic]. The argument that Rama developed for understanding this aesthetic appropriately evokes what would be popularized years later with Casanova's book; to wit, that Balbuena writes from the margin with the intention of showing his ability to belong to the center. However, Rama goes one step beyond and proposes three features—epigonism, fantasy, and formalism—that make Balbuena's work something unique with respect to the common conditions of Renaissance artistic production. What is special in Balbuena, for Rama, consists of the acceptance of that margin as a condition of possibility, more than as a barrier—as Mexía did see it. With his *Grandeza mexicana*, says Rama, Balbuena not only locates Mexico City at the center of the world but also turns the literary tropes of amplification, enumeration, and hyperbole into conditions of possibility of a new way of conceiving of the American territory and its literary creation. Balbuena, asserts Rama, "es el fundador de la poesía americana en aquella vertiente en que ella se reconoce desconsoladamente como nacida en América, en los márgenes de una cultura en expansión que se proyectaba en el espacio y en el tiempo y generaba un desviado circuito que le devolvía su propia energía"[40] [is the founder of American poetry in that branch in which it is recognized disconsolately as born in America, on the margins of an expanding culture that was projected in space and time and generated an oblique circuit that returned its own energy to it].

If one of the essential concepts of world literature theory is that of circulation, in Balbuena we find Mexico City to be a central point for the circulation of goods, as Barbara Fuchs and Yolanda Martínez-San Miguel brilliantly explain: "México aparece sobre todo como un *entrepôt*, un lugar al que llega y del cual sale la mercadería"[41] [Mexico appears above all as an *entrepôt*, a place to which goods come and from which they leave]. In this sense, it is possible to imagine a literature that generates its own worldliness, not because it circulates beyond its native linguistic and cultural sphere, as Damrosch would have it, but because in its context of production there is already (1) an explicit dialogue with the aesthetic discussions of the hegemonic cultural center; and more importantly (2) the creation of a new frame of reference for understanding those discursive processes. In establishing the parallel between global commerce and poetic writing, Balbuena not only reduces Spain "a poco más que ser un socio comercial dentro de una larga y variada lista" [to little more than just one trading partner on a long and diverse list] but also makes that autonomous relationship applicable to artistic creation.[42] In fact, as Rama suggested in addition to this shifting of New Spain to the center of the world, Balbuena's revelation also comes with a poetic form: the fact that the poet chose to begin his celebration of the city in octaves and later switched to tercets generates an amalgam that Fuchs and Martínez-San Miguel call "épica urbana" [urban epic], in which they read a transition between the "épica clásica y una moderna"[43] [classical epic and a modern one].

Reading Balbuena exclusively through the concept of *imitatio* implies a certain degree of astigmatism that impedes the appropriate focus on his poetic work both in relation to European, peninsular tradition and with the environment in which Balbuena wrote. But what exactly constitutes this environment? This question brings me to raise one last issue in considering world literature theories along colonial Mexican literary production. Much has been written about the oversight of certain theories of world literature when it comes to national literatures, because that concept implies uniformity in the plurality of literary expressions within nations.[44] At the moment when Balbuena writes his poem about Mexico, that territory is a place made up of various cultures and temporalities: indigenous, but also medieval European, Asian, and African.[45] Hence, considering the peninsular tradition as the only frame of reference for colonial poetic production is a biased, imperialist view of literature. This tendency is, in fact, partly to blame for the still pending primary work needed in colonial poetic studies: the abundant but as yet little-studied corpus of popular poetry that is still hidden away in archives.[46]

Poetics as Literary History

One of the concerns world literature theory has to do with the canon, and thus with the possibility of creating a literary history for that canon, as Cohen suggests in his recent book. To conclude, I would like pose the following question: Can we speak of a literary history of poetry in New Spain from a global point of view? To determine this, first we need to see what it is that the theory of world literature says in terms of literary history. In his article titled "Toward a History of World Literature," Damrosch insists on the criterion of circulation as essential for understanding certain literature as world literature, and he adds an element that up until then had not been discussed much: authorial intention.[47] Although Damrosch does not insist on this further, nor does he mention it again, it seems to me that gesture opens a window for including works—like many of those of colonial poetic production—within the global corpus. However, it remains to explain why someone would do that. More interesting still, it also remains to perform a slightly more detailed review of what Damrosch means to say regarding what for him is the "crucial stage in a work's movement from a national context to the sphere of world literature," which consists of its reception "within a different cultural and linguistic realm" (484). Perhaps the idea of linguistic spheres is less obscure than that of cultural contexts, because if we think about Damrosch's words with respect to New Spain, it seems difficult to understand what would constitute, or how we could unequivocally mark, cultural differences both inside and out of the New World. The cases I have discussed up to now—Diego de Mexía, Bernardo de Balbuena—speak to the fact that within high culture, there is a certain uniformity on both sides of the Atlantic; this uniformity, in fact, is what has allowed Hispanism to read in the verses of Balbuena or Mexía nothing more than the same early modern peninsular tradition. It is perhaps in other social spheres, in the lower, popular classes, where the cultural frames are easier to see, more legible and recognizable, as José Joaquín Fernández de Lizardi would confirm several centuries later in his *Periquillo Sarniento*, a text that from the canonical perspective uses what has been called colonial language.[48]

But if we think about Mexico in the transition between the sixteenth and seventeenth centuries, there is an element of worldliness that the writers do not hide, and which, in contrast, is explicit in their way of writing and of theorizing poetry. According to Damrosch's criterion, in their intention there is already an element of worldliness sufficient to allow us to read its production as part of a world literature, but not from the point of view of its circulation, because we are talking about texts that did not necessarily circulate between cultural and linguistic contexts, or that simply were not even circulated. I want to mention two texts that, for the reasons previously mentioned, are presented as a problem and a challenge for literary history. The first of these is the prologue to Balbuena's epic poem *El Bernardo o Victoria de Roncesvalles*, published in Madrid in 1624 but written fourteen years earlier. The second is the *Suma del arte de la poesía* by Eugenio de Salazar, whose date of original writing we do not know, but whose later date of composition has been established as 1591.[49]

Why do these represent a challenge for the periodization of literary history? In the first place, because of the vagueness of the years when they were written and published, but mostly because these are texts that, on one hand, have been read almost exclusively with respect to their Spanish/European roots, but, on the other, have the "privilege" of being considered as foundational of the Hispanic American theoretical-poetic tradition. To start with, think about Salazar's poetic treatise, until very recently unpublished and even unknown, a text that Tenorio locates in a time prior to "la revolución gongorina y posterior a la irrupción y consolidación del italianismo en España, cuando los letrados sintieron la necesidad de clarificar principalmente dos aspectos de la poesía: por un lado, sus fines y su naturaleza, por otro, las normas y preceptos para su praxis"[50] [the Gongoristic revolution and after the appearance and consolidation of Italianism in Spain language, when the literati felt the need to clarify principally two aspects of poetry: on one hand, its goals and nature, and on the other, the norms and precepts for its practice]. Despite the fact that its probable date of writing situates Salazar's text as a pioneering poetics of Petrarchism in Spanish, narrowly surpassed by Sánchez de Lima's poetics published in 1580, Tenorio herself rushes to assert that "A pesar de los escasos antecedentes españoles, demás está decirlo, Salazar no es original"[51] [Despite having few Spanish antecedents, it goes without saying that Salazar is not original]. This lack of originality is due, according to Tenorio, to the much earlier existence of an Italian tradition of poetic reflection on the nature, form, and function of poetry.

The question of what to do with these types of texts, whether to read them in light of their originality, origin, or indebtedness to Western tradition, as part of a world contagion of Petrarchist poetics, finds an answer if we turn to Balbuena's text. In both cases, we are most likely facing first texts of poetic theory written in the New World, and yet both Balbuena and Salazar clearly are inscribed in a tradition that we can trace back to the Greek and Latin classics. Perhaps, then, reading these texts from the point of view of their origin is less productive than focusing on their destination, something that I could perhaps argue with Damrosch when he asserts that the "true history" of world literature "lies in the future rather than in the past."[52] This history, for him, is inscribed in counterpoint to two critical trends: "a narrowly bounded nationalism and a boundless, breathless globalism."[53] Something similar has already been done, I think, with the concept of the American Baroque seen by José Lezama Lima as a transhistorical element for understanding the configuration and identity of Latin America.[54]

Balbuena anchors his ideas in imitating Lucan and Herodotus; his doctrine on the unities of the epic plot are nothing more than a reading of Aristotle; his way of structuring his poem comes from Homer. Salazar's doctrine on poetic style, besides being vague and abstract—with terms like the "henchimiento y majestad del verso" [majestic swells of verse], its "gala y flor" [flowery showiness], its "dulzura y donaire" [sweetness and grace]—is strongly based, as Tenorio has already shown, on an idea of artistic taste borrowed from Dante, Boscán, Ovid, and Ariosto, among many others.[55] Thus, perhaps it would be worth considering that the theory of world literature can be useful for reading texts like these beyond their classification and origin, but, rather, such that through a critique of the spatial and temporal uniformity that they propose. They might suggest other temporalities and other spaces that resist concepts so apparently clear as Damrosch's linguistic and cultural context. In their way, Latin American colonial studies have struggled with this for a long time, whether from the adaptation and construction of a *Barroco de indias* through which *criollo* and mestizo cultural production has been read, or from other theoretical constructions such as transatlantic studies, Imperium studies, and, more recently, transpacific studies.[56] In all these cases, what is highlighted is the need to create new frameworks that help us better understand the impact of the Spanish invasion on the American cultures, and the development of what would later be configured as Latin American national traditions.

Notes

1 Two studies on the degree of significance that "global" and "cosmopolitan" held in the early modern epic are Ayesha Ramachandran, "Now to Theorize the 'World': An Early Modern Manifesto," *New Literary History* 48, no. 4 (Autumn 2017): 655–84; and Roland Greene, *Five Words: Critical Semantics in the Age of Shakespeare and Cervantes* (Chicago: University of Chicago Press, 2013), 143–71.
2 José Rabasa, *Inventing America: Spanish Historiography and the Formation of Eurocentrism* (Norman: University of Oklahoma Press, 1993), 116–24.
3 Ross Hassing, *Trade, Tribute, and Transportation: The Sixteenth-Century Political Economy of the Valley of Mexico* (Norman: University of Oklahoma Press, 1985), 160–219.
4 Serge Gruzinski, *Las cuatro partes del mundo: historia de una mundialización* (México: Fondo de Cultura Económica, 2010), 39.

5   Ibid., 74–6. For the concept of "connected histories" that he draws upon, see Sanjay Subrahmanyam, "Holding the World in Balance: The Connected Histories of the Iberian Overseas Empires, 1500–1640," *The America Historical Review* 112, no. 5 (2007): 1359–85.
6   Gruzinski, *Las cuatro partes del mundo*, 124.
7   See, for instance, Carlos de Sigüenza y Góngora's *Paraíso occidental* (1684), a book in which he frames the history of the Jesús María Convent of Mexico within the most significant global events of the time; or his *Infortunios de Alonso Ramírez* [Misfortunes of Alonzo Ramirez, 1690], a book in which the life of a humbly born *criollo* becomes the pretext for visiting the far reaches of the Spanish empire and for reflecting on the position of the *criollo* subject relative to the boundaries of global trade. The most up-to-date study of Sigüenza y Góngora is Anna More's *Baroque Sovereignty: Carlos de Sigüenza y Góngora and the Creole Archive of Colonial Mexico* (Philadelphia: University of Pennsylvania Press, 2013). A recent bilingual edition of Sigüenza's text was published by José F. Buscaglia-Salgado (ed. and trans.), *Infortunios de Alonso Ramírez/The Misfortunes of Alonso Ramírez (1690): Annotated Bilingual Edition* (New Brunswick Rutgers University Press, 2010).
8   Franco Moretti, *Distant Reading* (New York: Verso, 2013). Alexander Beecroft, *An Ecology of World Literature: From Antiquity to the Present Day* (New York: Verso, 2015). Walter Cohen, *A History of European Literature: The West and the World from Antiquity to the Present* (Oxford: Oxford University Press, 2017).
9   Ibid., 292.
10 Ibid., 280–308.
11 Beecroft, *An Ecology of World Literature*, 33–6.
12 Joan Ramon Resina studies the relationship between cultural markets in Spain and the United Kingdom relative to the emergence of the novel in Europe in "The Short, Happy Life of the Novel in Spain," in *The Novel. Volume 1: History, Geography, and Culture*, ed. Franco Moretti (Princeton: Princeton University Press, 2006), 301–12.
13 Moretti, *Distant Reading*, 134.
14 Ibid., 129.
15 For a comprehensive study of the influence of Petrarchism in Spain, see Ignacio Navarrete, *Orphans of Petrarch: Poetry and Theory in the Spanish Renaissance* (Berkeley: University of California Press, 1994).
16 James L. Webb, Jr., "Globalization of Disease, 1300 to 1900," in *The Cambridge World History*, ed. Jerry H. Bentley, Sanjay Subrahmanyam, and Merry E. Wiesner-Hanks (Cambridge: Cambridge University Press, 2015), 54–75, here 63–4.
17 Noble David Cook, "The Columbian Exchange," in *The Cambridge World History*, 103–74.
18 Jorge Téllez, "Hacia una teoría de la lectura en la época colonial," *Revista Hispánica Moderna* 71, no. 2 (December 2008), 179–96.
19 David Damrosch, *What Is World Literature?* (Princeton: Princeton University Press, 2003), 4.
20 A recent study of this volume with respect to the cultural networks between Spain and America can be found in the doctoral dissertation of Víctor Sierra Matute, "*La voz partida: prácticas de escritura plural y colaborativa en la alta modernidad hispánica (1536–1695)*" [*The Split Voice: Practices of Plural and Collaborative Writing in Spanish High Modernity*] (Philadelphia: University of Pennsylvania, 2019).

21 Ignacio M. Sánchez Prado, *Strategic Occidentalism: On Mexican Fiction, the Neoliberal Book Market, and the Question of World Literature* (Evanston: Northwestern University Press, 2018), 15.
22 For a study of Petrarchism in Diego Mexía, see Trinidad Barrera, "De academias, transterrados y parnasos antárticos" [Of academies, transplanted people and Antarctic poets], *América Sin Nombre,* nos. 13–14 (2009): 15–21.
23 Diego Mejía Fernangil, *Primera parte del Parnaso Antártico,* ed. Trinidad Barrera (Roma: Bulzoni Editore, 1990). The electronic edition I consulted can be found at http://estudiosindianos.org/en/publications/primera-parte-del-parnaso-antartico-de-obras-amatorias/.
24 See Rodolfo Acuña-Soto et al., "Megadrought and Megadeath in 16th-Century Mexico," *Emerging Infectious Diseases* 8, no. 4 (2002): 360–2.
25 Mexía, *Parnaso antártico,* fol. 4r. I have modernized the spelling and spelled out abbreviations, but have respected the original punctuation.
26 Beecroft, *An Ecology of World Literature,* 25.
27 Mexía, *Parnaso antártico,* fols. 4r-4v.
28 Rodrigo Cacho Casal, "Introduction: Locating Early Modern Spanish American Poetry," in *The Rise of Spanish American Poetry 1500–1700: Literary and Cultural Transmission in the New World,* ed. Rodrigo Cacho Casal and Imogen Choi (Cambridge: Legenda, 2019), 1–27, here 2.
29 Martha Lilia Tenorio, *Poesía novohispana: antología,* vol. 1 (México: El Colegio de México, 2010), 17.
30 Cacho Casal, "Introduction," 2.
31 Anne J. Cruz, "Art of the State: The *Academias Literarias* as Sites of Symbolic Economies in Golden Age Spain," *Calíope: Journal of the Society for Renaissance and Baroque Hispanic Poetry* 1, nos. 1–2 (1995): 72–95.
32 Mexía, *Parnaso Antártico,* fol. 4r.
33 Martha Lilia Tenorio, *El gongorismo en Nueva España: ensayo de restitución* (México: El Colegio de México, 2013), 13. Roberto González Echevarría comes to the same conclusions in his essay on colonial lyric poetry regarding the synchrony of the production of Italian forms in the New World and Europe. See "Colonial Lyric," in *The Cambridge History of Latin American Literature, Vol. 1: Discovery to Modernism,* ed. Roberto González Echevarría and Enrique Pupo-Walker (Cambridge: Cambridge University Press, 1996), 191–230.
34 Pascale Casanova, "Literature as a World," in *World Literature in Theory,* ed. David Damrosch (Malden: Wiley Blackwell: 2014), 192–208.
35 Ibid., 196.
36 Tenorio, *El gongorismo en Nueva España,* 13. She is referring here to the work of Marcelino Menéndez Pelayo, for whom "los humanistas del Nuevo Mundo no andaban rezagados, y que recibieron pronto las novedades literarias que por vía de Italia se habían comunicado a nuestros ingenios" [the New World humanists were no laggards, and they quickly received the latest literary modes from Italy that had enriched our own inventiveness].
37 Pedro Henríquez Ureña, *Literary Currents in Hispanic America* (Cambridge: Harvard University Press, 1945). Although published in 1945, the book is the edition from the Charles Eliot Norton Lectures that Henríquez Ureña gave at Harvard University in 1940–1.

38 Ángel Rama, "Fundación del manierismo hispanoamericanos por Bernardo de Balbuena," *University of Dayton Review* 16, no. 2 (Spring 1983): 13–22.
39 Ibid., 13.
40 Ibid., 21.
41 Barbara Fuchs and Yolanda Martínez-San Miguel, "La *Grandeza Mexicana* de Balbuena y el imaginario de una metrópolis colonial," *Revista Iberoamericana* 75, no. 228 (2009): 675–95, here 679.
42 Ibid., 683.
43 Ibid., 686.
44 This critique is found in Helena Carvalhão Buescu, "Pascale Casanova and the Republic of Letters," in *The Routledge Companion to World Literature*, ed. Theo D´haen, David Damrosch, and Djelal Kadir (New York: Routledge, 2012), 126–35.
45 For a study of the relationship between medieval institutions and the formation of New Spain, see Luis Weckmann, *The Medieval Heritage of Mexico* (Fordham: Fordham University Press, 1992). For relationships between the indigenous world and colonial Mexico, see Georges Baudot, *Pervivencia del mundo azteca en el México virreinal* (México: UNAM, 2004). For relationships between New Spain and Asia, see Gruzinski, *Las cuatro partes del mundo*. The relationship between the African culture and colonial Mexico is currently a hotly debated topic. To begin, consult Gonzalo Aguirre Beltrán's classic book *La población negra de México, 1519-1819: un estudio etnohistórico* (México: Fondo de Cultura Económica, 1972) and Herman Lee Bennett's most recent book, *Africans in Colonial Mexico* (Bloomington: Indiana University Press, 2005).
46 On the absence of academic material on the topic, see Cacho Casal, "Introduction," 14. An example of this type of work is María Águeda Méndez and Georges Baudot's book *Amores prohibidos: la palabra condenada en el México de los virreyes. Antología de coplas y versos censurados por la Inquisición de México* (México: Siglo XXI Editores, 1997).
47 David Damrosch, "Toward a History of World Literature," *New Literary History* 39, no. 3 (Summer 2008): 481–95, here 483. Although for the Hispanic philological tradition the concept of authorial intention has long been discredited and fallen into disuse, other traditions, such as the French, have recently produced considerable theorizing on the subject. See Antoine Compagnon, *Literature, Theory, and Common Sense*, trans. Carol Cosman (Princeton: Princeton University Press, 2004), 29–68.
48 See Nancy Vogeley, "Defining the 'Colonial Reader': El Periquillo Sarniento," *PMLA* 102, no. 5 (October 1987): 784–800.
49 Bernardo de Balbuena, *El Bernardo o Victoria de Roncesvalles*, ed. Martín Zulaica López (Sierto-Asturias: Ars Poetica, 2017). Eugenio de Salazar, *Suma del arte de poesía*, ed. Martha Lilia Tenorio (México: El Colegio de México, 2010). According to Tenorio, the poetics prior to Salazar are few, and only one, the *Arte poética en romance castellano* by Miguel Sánchez de Lima, predates it in its Petrarchist affiliations. See Salazar, *Suma del arte*, 22–3.
50 Ibid., 26.
51 Ibid., 27. For a brief biography of Eugenio de Salazar, who left Spain in 1530 and held different bureaucratic posts in the New World until he became a judge of the Royal Courts, see ibid., 14.
52 Damrosch, "Toward a History," 484.

53 Ibid., 490.
54 See José Lezama Lima, *La expresión americana* (México: Fondo de Cultura Económica, 2013), and Irlemar Chiampi, *Barroco y modernidad* (México: Fondo de Cultura Económica, 2000).
55 Salazar, *Suma del arte,* 115.
56 The bibliography on this subject is vast. To begin, consult a critical reading of the term *transatlantic studies* in Jorge Cañizares-Esguerra, *Puritan Conquistadors: Iberianizing the Atlantic, 1550–1700* (Stanford: Stanford University Press, 2006), 215–33. The subject of the Imperium studies is mentioned in Fuchs and Martínez-San Miguel, "La *Grandeza Mexicana* de Balbuena," but its articulation is found in Barbara Fuchs, "Imperium Studies: Theorizing Early Modern Expansion," in *Postcolonial Moves: Medieval through Modern*, ed. Patricia Clare Ingham and Michelle R. Warren (New York: Palgrave McMillan, 2003), 71–90. The subject of transpacific studies relative to the American colonial world is studied in Ricardo Padrón, "(Un)Inventing America: The Transpacific Indies in Oviedo and Gómara," *Colonial Latin American Review* 25, no. 1 (2016): 16–34. It is probably possible to find a revised, expanded version of this article in his book *The Indies of the Setting Sun: How Early Modern Spain Mapped the Far East as the Transpacific West* (University of Chicago Press, 2020), but the book was not published yet when I finished this chapter.

2

Global Sor Juana

Stephanie Kirk

A senior colleague in English at my institution once rejected my application to participate in a seminar on early modern culture because he disputed the notion that Mexico constituted a part of the early modern world as he conceived of it. Although one of the stated purposes of the seminar was to deepen inquisitiveness around the area of humanistic inquiry, that inquisitiveness was to be limited to Northern Europe and Italy. I include this anecdote to illustrate the politics of exclusion that has operated around the term "early modern" and how this has also served to constrain and distort early modern Mexico's participation in the genre of world literature. Critiques have been leveled at approaches that have often misrepresented, underrepresented, or misunderstood contributions from the Global South within the supposedly capacious boundaries of world literature, and a genre whose goal is to further understandings has only succeeded in exacerbating differences. This is particularly acute in the area of early modern studies as the term, which emerged from the discipline of European history to benchmark the period from the Renaissance to the Enlightenment, is an awkward fit for other regions.

I do not intend here, however, to refute all the many valuable approaches and contributions that have advanced understanding within the multivalent field of world literature but rather identify some areas of concern regarding how the early modern or "colonial" Mexican nun and poet Sor Juana Inés de la Cruz has been represented in this context and approach an alternative model for understanding her global significance and her place within world literature. As a way of reorienting perspectives on at least one writer from a marginalized tradition, I offer a globalizing view of Sor Juana's writing, the city in which she wrote and the literary movement—the Barroco de Indias or New World Baroque—of which she formed an integral part. The global circuit within which I propose we study the colonial Mexican nun is not the one within which she has been traditionally viewed by both world literature and other internationalizing contexts. Using the concepts of globalism and planetarity that are themselves embedded within key world literature theories, I would like to situate her and the supposed geographical periphery from where she wrote in a different context from the transatlantic Spanish/European one and thus highlight the uneven power dynamics that existed in her time and that persist to this day. Using these global and planetary maneuvers, Mexican literature can be mobilized as a vehicle for understanding what other standards we may use for assessing questions of how colonial or "peripheral" literature may enter productively into the canon of world literature.

To first establish the necessity of this alternative model, I want to offer a brief overview of how Sor Juana has been inserted into the world literature teaching canon through her appearances in a pair of major world literature anthologies: the Longman and the Norton. The incorporation of colonial Latin American literatures and cultures into anthologies produced by US publishing houses has long been problematic. In an article published in *Early American Literature*, Lisa Voigt analyzes Sor Juana's placement in a pair of early American literature anthologies in which a handful of Latin American texts are sandwiched in unusual places to fit a logic informed by Anglo trajectories, genres, and thematics. In one anthology, Voigt explains how Sor Juana finds herself in a section between "exploration narratives and the Pueblo revolt."[1] Both anthologies she studies "remove Sor Juana from a literary genealogy proper to New Spain or the Spanish empire."[2] Something very similar occurs in the world literature anthologies that feature Sor Juana, with each volume conjuring up curious pairings and juxtapositions that emerge alongside disappointing and disconcerting errors of fact regarding her background. In the *Longman Anthology of World Literature*,[3] the editors include Sor Juana—somewhat confusingly —in three separate entries. First, and transplanted to Europe, she features in a subsection of "The Rise of the Vernacular in Europe" entitled "Women and the Vernacular" alongside Dante, Erasmus, and Catherine of Siena. Still in Europe, she makes a second appearance in "Lyric Sequences and Self-Definition" with six of her sonnets.[4] Finally, she makes it home to Mexico, and a section entitled "Perspectives: The Conquest and Its Aftermath," where her *Loa for The Auto-Sacramental of the Divine Narcissus*, in which she revisits the Conquest and Evangelization, appears alongside a heterogeneous group of authors such as Columbus, Ruiz de Alarcón, and the participants of the "Aztec-Spanish Dialogues" of 1524. The Longman should be commended for providing a robust selection of Latin American texts, including such radical world-changing Indigenous cultural artifacts as the *Popul Vuh* and Aztec poetry. What I find disconcerting, however, is the fact that Sor Juana can only be "Mexican" here if she is writing about things that are concretely identifiable as being so from a Eurocentric perspective and that comply with preconceived notions of otherness. When producing lyric poetry, she must, by definition, be understood as European. The *Norton Anthology of World Literature*[5] takes a slightly different approach. In a volume with periodization stretching from 1650 to 1800, and alongside entries from China, the Ottoman Empire, and Japan, Sor Juana makes an appearance in "The Enlightenment in Europe"—a startling geographical and chronological placement, in my opinion— in whose introduction the only countries named are England and France and where she appears alongside the male French, British, and Irish authors Swift, Pope, Voltaire, Molière, and Racine. Sor Juana's entry comprises a section of the *Respuesta a Sor Filotea* [Reply to Sor Filotea] and in the prefatory section we are immediately confronted with the periphery-enhancing words: "One hardly expects to find a spirited defense of women's intellectual rights issuing from the pen of a seventeenth-century Mexican nun."[6] Indeed. The erasure of the importance of her geographical location on her work cannot be understated as, while she may have lived most of her life cloistered in the Mexico City convent of San Jerómino, her work bears explicit and implicit hallmarks of her Americanness, her gendered coloniality, her membership in a heterogeneous New World society, and a transatlantic and global consciousness fashioned by her status as an imperial subject. Thus, the anthology strays far from its stated goal in the introduction to present texts "in the light of their own literary traditions."[7] These mistakes, missteps, and mislocations, speak to what Gayatri Spivak terms the "sea change" that occurred in the discipline of Comparative Literature during the first couple of years of the twenty-first century.[8] Spivak describes how publishing conglomerates, recognizing the market for these anthologies, presented US-based academics with "large advances" to assemble them.[9] Offering China as an example, she describes how an entire national literature is reduced to one or two of its most recognizable texts or authors, and laments how the market drives this approach, placing the "critical edge of the humanities" in danger."[10] The fudging of periodization and national tradition that we witness in these anthologies would perhaps be avoided if the teams behind them were to think of Sor Juana as part of the New World Baroque, thus making the periodization correspond to the logic of her geographic location. The Baroque as a period appears in neither the Norton nor the Longman and certainly not in association with the Americas. Relocating Sor Juana back to New Spain and anchoring her within the Baroque allow us to comprehend better her position within world literature as well as presenting us with a different vantage point from which to read the early modern global world from which this literature emerges.

In some ways, the European model evinced in these anthologies presents the easiest and most obvious angle from which to insert Sor Juana into a trajectory and corresponds to that offered by Pascale Casanova in her book *The World Republic of Letters*.[11] Sor Juana was, nominally at least, a writer from the geographical periphery who gained membership in the Republic of Letters thanks to the multiple publication of her works in Spain—the metropolis in her case.[12] In this way, we could situate her within what Casanova calls "the global structure of dependence" in which writers like Sor Juana "live as captives of the shadows of the periphery" enjoying only a "partial view" of the great Republic of Letters.[13] The internalized *criollo* consciousness of cultural inferiority in the face of imperial supremacy perhaps lent itself to what Casanova terms "the misfortunes, contradictions and difficulties faced by writers on the periphery."[14] For Casanova, these difficulties exist because the peripheral writer—those from "outlying countries"—necessarily feels marked by his or her geographical distance from the literary centers. Sor Juana herself enjoyed notable success in Spain and in other parts of Europe and a case could be made for using Sor Juana's circulation in more established transatlantic Old World literary markets as a unique measure of her success. While this model does indeed offer one way of thinking about world literature it calls forth, as critics have pointed out, a reification of power dynamics between so-called centers and peripheries and, in the case of Mexico, consigns it forever to life on the losing end of this transatlantic relationship.

The Baroque did, of course, incorporate a transatlantic component, and many critics have dedicated studies to determining just how Spanish, Latin American, or transatlantic the Baroque in Latin America really was and if the relationship of center and periphery remained intact or whether this hierarchy ceased to be operational in this case. Mabel Moraña sees the Baroque as being both Spanish and Latin American, and that its unique New World character came from the tension between the two sites of influence: "en los siglos XVI y XVII cristalizan ya una literatura, una crítica y una historia literaria a la vez dependientes y culturalmente diferenciadas de los modelos metropolitanos" [in the sixteenth and seventeenth centuries we see the crystallization of a literature, a criticism and a history that are at the same time both dependent upon and culturally differentiated from metropolitan models].[15] Juan Luis Suárez and Estefanía Olid-Peña, for their part, have emphasized the concept of transatlantic exchange in the framing of the Hispanic Baroque, explaining that "In relation to its spatial dimensions, all considerations of the Hispanic Baroque have to include both its Peninsular and American manifestations, since events on both sides of the Atlantic belong to the same political and cultural reality, at least until the second decade of the XIX-Century."[16] They believe that, although the vastness of the Atlantic Ocean mediates relationship between metropolis and colony, the two share a "dynamic cultural system."[17] This cultural system can only be shared up to a point, however, since the societal makeup that created was radically different on both sides of the Atlantic. Thus, I would like to orient the reader away from Europe, or at least suggest we look not only to Europe, and use Sor Juana's work to ground her as a citizen of a global society—one that did not need only to engage transatlantically or Eurocentrically—in order to think about how she might fit within a world literature corpus. The Baroque was, according to many, the first global movement and nowhere was it perhaps as dynamic, compelling, and complex as in the New World. I am not proposing here that Mexico stands as the origin point of the Baroque and as its only context. Colonial Latin America does, however, constitute a privileged place from which to examine the global nature of the Baroque and, moreover, it can be seen as representing the ground zero of global Baroque aesthetics. Serge Gruzinski locates the origins of globalization in the sixteenth century with the beginning of the "proliferation of links of every type between parts of the world previously unaware of each other or in only the most distant contact."[18] He frames this globalization partly in psychological terms, showing how more rapid communication and the increased commercial opportunities "impacted on the minds of many."[19] For Gruzinski, reading globalization in terms of a mutual "discovery of the infinite diversity of landscapes and peoples" opens up an alternative way of reading the Renaissance, "less stubbornly Eurocentric but probably more in tune with our age."[20] Locating the global in Mexico goes beyond the importation of exclusively Eurocentric models but instead recognizes that a global mindset was not uniquely the product of the so-called voyages of discovery nor even of the "meeting" of diverse peoples. Aztec historians Caroline Dodds Pennock and Amanda Power explain that a global cosmology preexisted the arrival of Europeans in the Americas and that conceiving of a global history of Indigenous peoples goes beyond a mere "response, on a global scale, to the shocks set off by the Iberian initiatives."[21] For these scholars, the Aztecs' globalness stemmed from two key elements: their "thought world" demonstrated by how they incorporated all with whom they came into contact, including their enemies, into their cosmology and their globalizing ambitions demonstrated by their desire to build a "hegemonic rather than a territorial empire."[22] All of which leads Dodds Pennock and Power to conclude that "this was a truly 'global' cosmos, a view which saw every part of the world, physical, spiritual and natural, individual and communal, as interdependent."[23] Their assessment challenges the assumption that only European societies were agents of globalism since scholarship has relegated "non-Western cosmologies" to "'archaic' ways of seeing and understanding the world."[24] Thus, global underpinnings, systems, and mentalities were already in place when the Spaniards conquered Mexico and established the Viceroyalty of New Spain. While, of course, the Spanish Conquest signaled the end of the Aztecs' hegemonic empire, it is safe to say that just as many other belief systems and even societal structures remained intact so too did this global cosmovision contribute to the complex and definitively global makeup of the Barroco de Indias or the New World Baroque, especially in the former imperial city of Mexico-Tenochtitlan and in the land beyond it into which this cosmovision was so deeply embedded.

The viceregal capital of New Spain, Mexico City, represented the apotheosis of the global Baroque. Stephanie Merrim explains that in the seventeenth century and "reacting to the austerity of the Reformation, the Hispanic worlds fired back with spectacle and ostentation."[25] She describes how the Spanish colonies in the New World "produced the overblown wealth that brought these spectacular proclivities to a hyperbolic peak in statecraft, religion, architecture, consumerism, daily life, and so on."[26] Manuel Lucena Giraldo also expounds on the privileged globality of Mexico City. He quotes Eugenio de Salazar, a member of the Council of the Indies, as he reflected back on his life that began with his birth in Madrid, his education in Salamanca and Alcalá, his work on the border with Portugal, then the Canary Islands, and from there Hispaniola, Guatemala, and Mexico. Using this official, autobiographical sketch as a point of departure, Lucena Giraldo writes that "the inhabitants of the Spanish American metropolises could thus build up an urban identity by proclaiming themselves the centre rather than the periphery, they placed themselves in the first globalisation as emporia of a culture built from bits and pieces from home and abroad."[27] These "bits and pieces," according to Lucena Giraldo, involved "a series of imaginary representations of specific urban spaces, nurtured by classic traditions, biblical images and counter-reformist liturgies."[28] He calls this repertoire of images "Creole urban myths" which he describes further as being stimulated by a "Baroque topology with an exuberant reading of the symbols and rhythms of its own nature, also hagiographic due to its aim of exemplifying and disciplining those inhabiting it."[29] What Lucena Giraldo does not make explicit here is the participation of non-*criollo* subjects in the creation of the imaginaries associated with Baroque cities and that constituted key components of the bricolage that gave them their character. Yolanda Martínez-San Miguel has identified a trend in criticism around the Barroco de Indias, which has designated Indigenous and Afro-Hispanic contributions to the Baroque as belonging exclusively to the categories of the plastic arts and of *criollos* as the only producers of lettered culture.[30] Martínez-San Miguel's comprehensive classifying of criticism of the Baroque helps us see just how polemical the characterization of the New World Baroque has been and how complex it proves to unravel the web of allegiances, dependencies, and relative privileges within which the white *criollo* subject was caught. In her article, Martínez-San Miguel attempts to dismantle and decolonize this standpoint so as to reveal how the makeup of colonial societies—particularly that of the cities—produced an overwhelming "colonization of the imaginary," to use Serge Gruzinski's terminology.[31] She seeks to substantiate that manifestations of Baroque cultural production cannot be divided so dichotomously or so racially. The Barroco de Indias took on an identity of its own, quite separate from the Renaissance that had transformed Europe. The latter movement never really took hold in a New World that found itself too embroiled in conquest and its aftermath to engage in the luxury of a celebration of classical literature and art. Instead, the Barroco de Indias became the first cultural movement of the conquered Americas, responding to "la complejidad de un contexto específicamente colonial—no protonacional—que produce un discurso que integra elementos imperiales y coloniales en la coyuntura de un cambio de paradigma epistémico clave" [the complexity of a specifically colonial context—not proto-national—that produces a discourse that integrates both imperial and colonial elements during a key epistemological paradigm shift].[32] Stephanie Merrim describes how the Baroque found its most fertile ground in this American environment, explaining how "the inherently tensile nature of the Baroque" would "appear to poise it for a dynamic life in the New World."[33]

Part of the dynamic nature of the New World Baroque comes undoubtedly from its centrality in global geopolitics and culture. Aníbal Quijano, one of the most important thinkers on Latin American coloniality, located the New World at the center of global happenings in the early modern world due to its protagonism in world movements at the time.[34] His theorizings help me position the literature that accompanied these moments and movements in a very different way than world literature finds itself accustomed to conceiving of colonial Mexican cultural production. Quijano declares, "What is termed globalization is the culmination of a process that began with the constitution of America and colonial/modern Eurocentered capitalism as a new global power" and he continues, "America was constituted as the first space/time of a new model of power of global vocation, and both in this way and by it became the first identity of modernity."[35] Very much in the manner of the world literature anthologies, non-Latin Americanist scholars have also recognized the epicentric value of the New World Baroque, although, disappointingly, these inclusions often contain the seeds of Eurocentric ideologies within them. For example, in his *Universal Baroques*, Peter Davidson attempts to make the case for a global Baroque that recognizes the contributions of non-European societies, reminding the reader that it is important to "remember that the traffic in energies, creativity and ideas did not flow in one direction only."[36] At the same time, however, he definitively situates Europe as the chief locus and initiator of this creative exchange, explaining how it was "the wholeness of the arts of early modern Europe, the whole cultural system prevailing in those parts of the world" that engendered a dialogue with what he terms "geographically distant parts of the world."[37] Davidson takes pains to recognize the contributions of the Americas to this Baroque landscape, explaining how, in his book, "Ibero-America will appear constantly as a point of reference."[38] However, and in what amounts to a truly bizarre collapsing of cultural differences, he almost immediately undermines this gesture explaining how the

Iberian Americas will stand in for all non-European Baroque contributors "standing pars pro toto as a representative of analogous phenomenon taking place world-wide."³⁹ Compounding this error is an ignorance of the Baroque subjects he analyzes in service of this representation of the non-European Baroque which perhaps we can attribute in part to the expansive and "universal" nature of the book which makes up in range what it lacks in specialist knowledge. However, although there is, of course, value in this approach, some of the broad strokes and basic error of facts do present themselves as off-putting for disciplinary experts. In this regard, we see how Davidson invokes the exemplary New Spanish Baroque intellectuals Sor Juana and Carlos de Sigüenza y Góngora, addressing their contributions to the New World Baroque. Yet, he attends to them in a way that bypasses a substantive engagement with the circumstances in which they produced their work. There is value too in the brief analysis of Sor Juana's *villancicos* or lyrics for carols in which Davidson praises her use of "popular hybridity and local expression" therein along with her "Baroque ingenuity" in combining both Latin and Spanish in another of her carols.⁴⁰ He praises Sigüenza for having "overlaid" the "universal language of festival and religious processes" onto American histories in both *Glorias de Querétaro* [Glories of Querétaro] (where Davidson identifies the text as honoring the Virgin without mentioning the crucial Americanist detail that the virgin in question is Guadalupian) and *Teatro de virtudes* [Theater of Political Virtues], a text written to accompany a triumphal arch and where he invokes Aztec Emperors and the god Huitzilopochtli as paradigms of good government for the incoming Viceroy.⁴¹ The visual and festive splendor, for Davidson, exemplifies a global phenomenon that flattens difference: "the festivals in Mexico City were a manifestation of an international and supra-national phenomenon."⁴² The American Baroque is thus not allowed to stand on its own two feet but is rather subsumed (much as Sor Juana was by the European Enlightenment in the Longman anthology) into a phenomenon originating in Europe. Thus, the concepts of "world," "global," "universal," and "international" become resolutely Eurocentric with dependent subjects in peripheral spaces afforded only limited agency via their ability to "decode" this phenomenon, what Davidson terms "Baroque flexibility" and which he defines as something that can "accommodate the indigenous and the locally idiosyncratic."⁴³ Very much in the same vein as Casanova, he describes the centers of the global Baroque as being "geographically distant" (from where, one might ask) but nonetheless in dialogue or "corresponding" with Europe "in the sense of the far-flung 'corresponding' members of an *accademia*."⁴⁴ While he attempts to award these distant places some measure of autonomy, the terms in which he describes them allow them no identity independent of a connection or a relation to Europe.

New Spain, however, did possess a global identity that was disengaged from its transatlantic relationship with Spain and that was instead built on encounters with other areas of the world, manifesting itself in a variety of ways. We can see this demonstration of a global identity with varying degrees of explicitness in New Spanish literature of the period. Cosmopolitan writings such as those produced by one of the most renowned international intellectuals of the time, the Bohemian Jesuit Athanasius Kircher (1602–80), circulated widely among New Spanish intellectuals such as Sor

Juana and Sigüenza y Góngora, who received his eccentric global visions with great enthusiasm. At the same time, scholars and other viceregal citizens possessed "a view of the newly global world that was not limited to information found in books like Kircher's *China illustrata*" and that came to them through commerce and the migrations of peoples from diverse locales.[45] J. Michelle Molina rightly situates the men of the Society of Jesus as conduits for some of this global mindset, explaining how this globalism extended to the realm of religious identity as, thanks to the influence of these Jesuit networks, "many citizens of New Spain imagined themselves as belonging to a world community of Catholics that included Christians in Asia."[46] Pascal Boyer addresses the presence of this global community—not exclusively Catholic, it must be said—as he explores Sigüenza y Góngora's hybrid travel narrative *Infortunios de Alonso Ramírez* [The Misfortunes of Alonso Ramírez], explaining how the text reflects a "keen awareness of the complexity of late-seventeenth-century identities, focusing less on New versus Old World permutations of cultural belonging and more in a larger emergent, and modern, understanding of global capital."[47] Once Sigüenza y Góngora's protagonist (and historical actor) Alonso Ramírez leaves New Spain bound for the Philippines, he becomes "part of a global circulation of goods and subjects."[48] Alonso's experience as a global subject demonstrates the dark side this globalism possesses. He is kidnapped by English pirates and suffers tremendous depredations, even when finally released from captivity. He does, however, profess himself spellbound by the global movement of people and goods he encounters in the Philippines, conquered by Spain in 1571. New Spain, specifically Acapulco, functions as the gateway to this new global world and the Manila Galleon was perhaps the single most effective weapon in the viceroyalty's global arsenal.[49] The galleons, known as the "Nao de China" or "Nao de Acapulco," crossed the Pacific Ocean between Acapulco and Manila for approximately 250 years beginning in 1565. They shipped New World silver from Mexico and Peru and goods from Spain and its colonies to exchange for a range of highly coveted commodities such as spices, silks, ivory, musk, copper, and porcelain. Scholars have identified this trade as an integral part of a burgeoning global economy.[50] Boyer describes this "new geography" as encountered by Alonso Ramírez upon leaving New Spain as one "in which vessels of all nations and goods of all kinds crisscross in a dizzying spectacle."[51] Literary commodities also crisscrossed this space, and, just a few years after her death, two of Sor Juana's plays were staged in Manila.[52]

In a manner less explicit than Sigüenza y Góngora, Sor Juana's work also engages with this new geography and evinces a global mindset. Sor Juana was, as has been well documented and repeatedly analyzed, a *criollo* subject. A woman doubly marginalized by gender and the geography of her birth, as a white woman with powerful patrons she nonetheless still enjoyed relative privilege in the rigidly defined hierarchy of the colonial pigmentocracy. While I am discussing Sor Juana's work as "Mexican" in terms of how Mexican literature can be understood productively as world literature, and while Sor Juana undoubtedly occupies a foundational place in the Mexican canon, she cannot, of course, be considered "Mexican" in the nationalistic sense since her identity was that of a seventeenth-century imperial/colonial subject. Nor should we view her *criollo* identity as a proto-national one that charts an unbroken line from the sentiments of

American difference to a national Mexican consciousness. Thus, her global subjectivity cannot be seen as anti-national nor anti-sovereign in the contemporary sense but rather as gesture to an early modern resistance to coloniality. Perhaps because of the great ambiguity and precarity this particular colonial subjectivity imposed upon her along with the physical confines of the cloister she chose, through her work and her studies, to become a citizen of the world. She eschewed the geographic boundaries and Eurocentric mindset that imperial logic imposed upon her and, turning her back upon the "West," she set herself to write the globe and become an early modern version of what Spivak has termed a "planetary subject."[53]

Sor Juana's poetry often reflects inward to examine the poetic voice's affective response to a variety of situations, at times summoning up the emotional perils brought about by the rigors of courtly love. Her poetry, however, also frequently assumes the opposite posture as the poetic voice scans the world for knowledge and cultural experiences creating a global poetic microcosm that somehow always anchors the poet in her Mexican *patria* or homeland, offering it up as the constant point of departure, or as a privileged vantage point. Sor Juana's globalism uses Mexico as a staging ground for cosmopolitan experiences but does so in a way that dabbles more in library-inspired global fantasies than the harsh realities that Sigüenza outlines through Alonso Ramírez's journeys. Sor Juana's poetry also reflects the type of goods and commerce that passed through New Spain as she invokes a series of highly prized commodities and artifacts that come from the circulation of goods such as those transported on the Manila Galleon and woven into her poetry we find global references to "aromas orientales" and to precious stones such as rubies, diamonds, and sapphires and to Arabia and the mysterious and unusual things one might find there.

The global also finds itself represented in Sor Juana's most famous poem, *Primero Sueño* or *First Dream*, a 975-line *silva* in which the soul embarks on a search for all human knowledge and does so by trafficking in a series of arresting images and set pieces that include mythological characters both familiar and abstruse and human limbs and organs whose descriptions invoke early modern anatomy theaters.[54] The soul's journey also takes it around the globe where it encounters and attempts to understand a series of architectural wonders that imbue the poem with a deep and engaged cosmopolitan vision of the universe and the knowledge that it offers the intellectual. The first of these global images in the *Sueño* comes in the form of a description of Egyptian pyramids—what Sor Juana terms "ostentationes/de Menfis vano/y de la Arquitectura último esmero"[55] [blazons of vain Memphis/a masterwork hard-wrought of architecture][56]—which provides the most famous of the poem's set pieces. The poet draws upon her favorite source, Kircher, to famously invoke the Egyptian pyramids, perhaps echoing how Kircher sees Egypt as "the source of both knowledge and paganism."[57] Electa Arenal views the images of the Egyptian pyramids as functioning as an allegory of Mexico.[58] She sees the famous opening lines of the poem where the encroaching shadow of night is imagined as a pyramid "Piramidal, funesta, de la tierra/nacida sombra"[59] [Pyramidal, funereal, a shadow/born of earth] as a synecdochal emblem for Mexico, but that Sor Juana then proceeds to invoke the Egyptian pyramids but not their Mexican counterparts as a way to "cover the tracks of this daring."[60] But perhaps we can see these Egyptian pyramids as a way of connecting Mexico to a wider cosmopolitan and global circuit that excludes Spain and Mexico City and Cairo, thus forging a connection that eliminates Madrid, the supposed metropolis and supposed international intermediary, where no pyramids were to be found.[61] Other architectural visual imagery provides additional global moorings for the soul's journey. Shortly before engaging with the vision of the pyramids and during the flight over the sea, the soul encounters the Alexandrian lighthouse: "Y del modo/ que en tersa superficie que de Faro/cristalino portento,/asilo raro/fué" [And just as on/ the untroubled surface, crystalline portent/of Pharos,/that uncommon refuge and port,/ in the quicksilver mirror].[62] And finally, perhaps the most global architectural image of all—the Tower of Babel—materializes, another image perhaps inspired by Kircher.[63] While the Tower of Babel might function as a cautionary tale for the global impulse—as well as for the soul's failed attempt to access total vision—it also speaks to the lure of such a vision.

Sor Juana fashions herself as a planetary poet, someone to whom the globe has entrusted its narratives. She constantly invokes the planetary system of which the Americas form part through images such as *Romance* 23's "Reinos de las estrellas" [kingdom of the stars] and the "Provincia de los Astros" [astral province] peppering many of her poems with multiple references to globes, worlds, planets, and stars providing a complete universe in which land, sea, sky, and beyond provide endless possibilities of global travel for both lyric subject and reader.[64] A strong sense also emerges from her poetry of the situatedness of this orb within a larger universe. The planetary[65] presents a framework for Sor Juana's poetry and elucidates how, from the confines of the cloister and thanks to the richness of her library, she casts an expansive eye upon the planet unbounded by imperial restrictions and the construct of the West, which, as Walter Mignolo has pointed out, should not be conceived of as a geographical designation but rather as an imperial construct which he describes as a "language-memory-conceptual apparatus" that "penetrated directly or indirectly billions of consciousness all over the world: in Greek, Latin and the six imperial modern/colonial languages."[66] If planetary time, as Wai Chee Dimock has it, is of "irregular duration and extension, some extending for thousands of years"[67] we can see how Sor Juana's poem connects the land to a nonlinear timeframe that calls forth earlier manifestations of the Anthropocene[68] and her excavations into the earth also take on a geological cast, very different from the extractive economy[69] that had come to characterize the lands colonized by Spain and that Sor Juana herself references in one of her most famous "transatlantic" poems, *Romance* 37, in which she explains that she was born "en la América abundante/ compatriota del oro,/paisana de los metales" [in abundant America/the compatriot of gold,/countrywoman of precious metals].[70] Perhaps the most important of these geological narratives occurs, once again, in *First Dream* where the soul's visionary gaze penetrates deep into the land and into oceanic profundities in a relentless search for planetary knowledge. *First Dream*, in which she details the descent of the body into sleep and the attempted ascent of the soul into the heavens as it strives for knowledge, is undoubtedly a force majeure of planetary, if not astral, literature. *First Dream* engages with the geological scope of the planet as the soul soars over the world, beginning in the depths of the earth with dusk rising from the ground like a huge pyramid, as we saw earlier. From this point on, Sor Juana details a nocturnal dreamscape mired in geological time: "del aire que empañaba/con el aliento denso que exhalaba" [air that misted in the rush/of thick dense breath exhaled by that grim shadow], evoking the "la quietud contenta/de imperio silencioso" [the soundless empire/of the mute and silent realm].[71] This is a place where only "el viento flemático echaba viento" [the phlegmatic motion of the wind] stirs the night creatures, and where human limbs move to almost corpse-like stillness as the land takes center stage.[72] To this end, the poem takes on an astral arc and details the soul's global voyage across a sometimes-rugged terrain distinguished by "los del monte senos escondidos, cóncavos de peñascos mal formados—de su aspereza menos defendidos" [hidden concave hollows of the high/mountains, those rough and cragged peaks/guarded less by ruggedness/than by their obscurity][73] and across the "azogada luna" [the quicksilver mirror] of the ocean.[74] The soul struggles to take in the planet's marvels, ranging from the "criaturas sublunares" [sublunar creatures] to those "intelectuales claras son Estrellas,/y en el modo posible/que concebirse puede lo invisible,/en sí, manosoa las representaba/y al alma las mostraba" [those clear hues that are intellectual stars/and in the manner that the invisible/can be conceived, ingeniously represents/and displays them to the Soul].[75]

Sor Juana's locates her Mexicanness in a myriad of ways and planetary time in the way that Wai Chee Dimock understands it also allows for us to fit the New Spanish nun into a tradition that allows for a continuance rather than a rupture with the cultural histories embedded in the Mexican/New Spanish landscape despite the best efforts of the imperial institutional machine to eradicate them. Emerging from *First Dream* is a profound sense of planetary engagement that, for me, evokes the representation of the land that emerges from Aztec cosmologies:

> Perpendicular to the terrestrial world (Tlalticpac, the earth, "on the land"), the vertical plane reached below to the nine underworlds of Mictlan and above through the multiple, probably thirteen, heavens. Importantly, this belief structure blended the metaphysical with the earthly. One passed through the lower levels of the clouds, moon, sun, stars and planets, before reaching the gods and finally Omeyocan, the place of duality, the extreme edge of the known universe. The physical nature these celestial realms is clear in Aztec thought: the gods lived not in a different dimension, but merely on a higher level.[76]

Reading Sor Juana's literature as a "bearer of planetarity" and as a receptacle of the early modern global, we start to see how she writes herself into world literature in a way that circumvents the colonial bonds that tie it to Spain and Europe. Instead, Sor Juana fixes her gaze first on a world beyond the transatlantic, then to the universe above, and finally to the land around and below her engaging with what Dimock has called "'deep time' understood as temporal length added to the spatial width of the planet."[77] Although Sor Juana lived her adult life as a cloistered nun, her poetry enabled her to traverse this temporal length and spatial width. From behind convent walls and from the confines of her library she assembled the poetic tools to position herself as a global and planetary subject.

Notes

1. Lisa Voigt, "'Por Andarmos Todos Casy Mesturados': The Politics of Intermingling in Caminha's *Carta* and Colonial American Anthologies," *Early American Literature* 40, no. 3 (2005): 414.
2. Ibid., 403.
3. David Damrosch and Jane Tylus, eds., *The Longman Anthology of World Literature. Volume C: The Early Modern Period* (New York: Longman, 2009).
4. The world literature anthologies are not alone in subsuming Sor Juana within the Spanish Golden Age. As Mabel Moraña has said, "la obra de sor Juana Inés de la Cruz ha sido juzgada durante mucho tiempo como un capítulo desprendido de la historia literaria española, accidentalmente situado en el contexto de la Nueva España" (Sor Juana's work has for a long time been judged as a chapter detached from Spanish literary history, accidentally located in the context of New Spain). *Viaje al silencio: exploraciones del discurso Barroco* (Mexico City: Universidad Nacional Autónoma de México, 1998), 67.
5. Sarah Lawall and Maynard Mack, eds., *The Norton Anthology of World Literature. Volume D: 1650–1800*, 2nd ed. (New York and London: W.W. Norton and Company, 2002).
6. Ibid., 403.
7. Ibid.
8. Gayatri Spivak, *Death of a Discipline* (New York: Columbia University Press, 2003), xii.
9. Ibid.
10. Ibid.
11. Pascale Casanova, *The World Republic of Letters,* trans. Malcolm DeBevoise (Cambridge, MA: Harvard University Press, 1999).
12. Sor Juana's first volume *Inundación Castálida* (Castalian Spring) was published in Madrid in 1689. The *Segundo volumen* (Second Volume) came out initially in Seville in 1692, and the third and posthumous volume, *Fama y obras póstumas* (Fame and Posthumous Works), in Madrid in 1700. All went through repeated printings on the Iberian Peninsula both during her lifetime and shortly afterward.
13. Casanova, *The World Republic of Letters*, 303.
14. Ibid.
15. Moraña, *Viaje al silencio*, 87.
16. Juan Luis Suárez and Estefanía Olid-Peña, "Hispanic Baroque: A Model for the Study of Cultural Complexity in the Atlantic World," *South Atlantic Review* 72, no. 1 (Winter 2007): 37.
17. Ibid.
18. Serge Gruzinski, *The Eagle and the Dragon: Globalization and European Dreams of Conquest in China and American in the Sixteenth Century,* trans. Jean Birell (Cambridge: Polity Press, 2014), 4.
19. Ibid., 2.
20. Ibid., 4.
21. Caroline Dodds Pennock and Amanda Power, "Globalizing Cosmologies," *Past & Present* 238 no. suppl_13 (November 2018): 94.
22. Ibid.

23 Ibid., 105.
24 Ibid., 107.
25 Stephanie Merrim, *The Spectacular City, Mexico, and Colonial Hispanic Literary Culture* (Austin: University of Texas Press, 2010), 2.
26 Ibid.
27 Manuel Lucena Giraldo, "The Creole Metropolis," in *The Transatlantic Hispanic Baroque: Complex Identities in the Atlantic World*, ed. Harald E. Braun and Jesús Pérez-Magallón (Abingdon: Routledge, 2016), 176.
28 Ibid.
29 Ibid.
30 "(Neo) Barrocos de Indias: Sor Juana y los imaginarios coloniales de la crítica Latinoamericana," *Revista de Estudios Hispánicos* 44, no. 2 (2010): 442.
31 Ibid.
32 Ibid.
33 Merrim, *The Spectacular City*, 33.
34 Aníbal Quijano, "Coloniality of Power, Eurocentrism, and Latin America," *Nepantla: View from South* 1, no. 3 (2000): 533–4.
35 Quijano's situating of Latin America is crucial to our understanding of modernity and globalization and does compensate for the exclusion of the region from influence over these world-changing mechanisms. His representation does not, of course, cast these in a positive light and he stresses the dark side of making this connection between modernity and colonial Latin America. He explains that the Spanish empire succeeded in instituting both modernity and globalization via two historical processes including the "the codification of the differences between conquerors and conquered in the idea of 'race,' a supposedly different biological structure that placed some in a natural situation of inferiority to the others" (533) and the other, also intimately connected to questions of power and dominance is that of the control of labor. Quijano explains that this "was an articulation of all historically known previous structures of control of labor, slavery, serfdom, small independent commodity production and reciprocity, together around and upon the basis of capital and the world market" (534).
36 Peter Davidson, *The Universal Baroque* (Manchester: Manchester University Press, 2008), 97.
37 Ibid., 1.
38 Ibid., 7.
39 Ibid., 94.
40 Ibid., 107.
41 Ibid., 110.
42 Ibid., 114.
43 Ibid.
44 Ibid., 1.
45 J. Michelle Molina, "True Lies: Athanasius Kircher's *China Illustrata* and the Life Story of a Mexican Mystic," in *Athanasius Kircher: The Last Man Who Knew Everything*, ed. Paula Findlen (New York: Routledge, 2004): 366.
46 Ibid.
47 Patricio Boyer, "Criminality and Subjectivity in *Infortunios de Alonso Ramírez*," *Hispanic Review* 78, no. 1 (Winter 2010): 27.

48 Ibid., 49.
49 It is important to note that Alonso's experience as a global subject is not a positive one. He is kidnapped by English pirates and suffers terrible depredations, even once released from captivity. He does, however, profess himself spellbound by the global movement of people and goods he encounters in the Philippines.
50 José L. Gasch-Tomás, *The Atlantic World and the Manila Galleons: Circulation, Market, and Consumption of Asian Goods in the Spanish Empire, 1565–1650* (Leiden: Brill, 2018); Arturo Giraldez, *The Age of Trade: The Manila Galleons and the Dawn of the Global Economy* (Lanham: Rowman & Littlefield, 2015).
51 Boyer offers an illuminating quote from *Infortunios* to demonstrate the dynamics of this "dizzying spectacle": "El concurso que allí se ve de navios de malayos, macasares, siameses, bugises, chinos, armenios, franceses, ingleses, dinamarcos, portugueses y castellanos no tiene número. Hállanse en este emporio cuantos artefactos hay en la Europa y los que en retorno de ellos la envía la Asia. Fabrícanse allí para quien quisiere comprarlas excelentes armas. Pero con decir estar allí compendiado el universo lo digo todo" (qtd. in Boyer, "Criminality and Subjectivity in *Infortunios de Alonso Ramírez*," 37) [The concourse of Malay, Macassar, Sianes (*sic*), Bugises, Chinese, Armenian, French, English, Danish, Portuguese and Spanish ships is innumerable. Any European manufacture may be found in this emporium as well as those which Asia sends back to us for exchange. And excellent weapons are produced there for any one who might care to purchase them. I might say to sum up that the entire World is encompassed in this city]. *The Misfortunes of Alonso Ramírez: The True Adventures of a Spanish American with 17th-Century Pirates*, trans. Fabio López Lázaro (Austin: University of Texas Press, 2011), 113.
52 Susan Hernández Araico, "*Los empeños de una casa*: Staging Gender," in *The Routledge Research Companion to the Works of Sor Juana Inés de la Cruz*, ed. Emilie Bergmann and Stacey Schlau (Abingdon: Routledge, 2017), 242.
53 Spivak positions the notion of the "planetary subject" against that of the "global agent." She writes, "If we imagine ourselves as planetary subjects rather than global agents, planetary creatures rather than global entities, alterity remains underived from us; it is not our dialectical negation, it contains as much as it flings us away" (*Death of a Discipline*, 73). As we can see, Spivak very much creates a dichotomous distance between the planetary and the global. Here, I am using them as complementary forces within Sor Juana's work because I feel that the globalism she imagines is different than that which Spivak finds so problematic. With her globalism, Sor Juana opens herself up to the world as she does with her planetarity. In both we find the ethics that Spivak locates in the planetary. Wai Chee Dimock for her part sees the planetary as "another axis to globalization intersecting with the horizontal but not reducible to it." She sees it as bearing, for many people of the world, "supranational" or "subnational" time. "Planetary Time and Global Translation: 'Context' in Literary Studies," *Common Knowledge* 9, no. 3 (Fall 2003): 490.
54 Licia Fiol-Matta, "Visions of Gender: Sor Juana and the First Dream," *Nepantla: Views from South* 4, no. 2 (2003): 360. Stephanie Kirk, *Sor Juana and the Gender Politics of Knowledge in Colonial Mexico* (Abingdon: Routledge, 2016), 111–18.
55 Sor Juana Inés de la Cruz, *Obras completas de Sor Juana Inés de la Cruz I: Lirica Personal*, ed. Alfonso Méndez Plancarte (Mexico City: Fondo de Cultura Económica, 1997 [1951]), 343.

56 All translations, unless stated, come from Edith Grossman's translation *Sor Juana Inés de la Cruz: Selected Works* (New York: W. W. Norton & Company).
57 Molina, "True Lies," 368.
58 Electa Arenal, "Where Woman Is Creator of the Wor(1)d," in *Feminist Perspectives on Sor Juana Inés de la Cruz,* ed. Stephanie Merrim (Detroit: Wayne State University Press, 1991), 135.
59 Sor Juana Inés de la Cruz, *Obras completas de Sor Juana*, 335.
60 Arenal, "Where Woman Is Creator of the Wor(1)d," 135.
61 Arenal explains that Kircher himself offers illustrations of both Mexican and Egyptian pyramids in the book Sor Juana used as a reference (135). (I believe Arenal is referring here to *Oedipus Aegyptiacus*.)
62 Sor Juana Inés de la Cruz, *Obras completas de Sor Juana*, 342.
63 Alessandra Luiselli, "*Primero Sueño*: Heresy and Knowledge," in *The Routledge Research Companion to the Works of Sor Juana Inés de la Cruz,* ed. Emilie L. Bergmann and Stacey Schlau (Abingdon: Routledge, 2017), 183.
64 Sor Juana Inés de la Cruz, *Obras completas de Sor Juana*, 69.
65 Although speaking of twenty-first-century literature, Amy J. Elias and Christian Moraru's theorizing of planetarity can be applied, in a longue durée fashion, to Sor Juana's work: "planetarization and its outcome, planetarity, trace a three-layered process whereby (1) the earth qua material planet becomes visible to theory and its abstractions as the non- negotiable ecological ground for human and nonhuman life; (2) individuals and societies of the earth as cosmo-polis heed an imperative to 'worlding,' that is, the creation of an ethical, 'diversal,' and relational ensemble so as to guarantee the survival of all species; and (3) the phenomenal earth seeps into our conceptual elaborations and ways of seeing the world, thus refounding our interpretative categories, our aesthetics, and our cultural lives." *The Planetary Turn: Relationality and Geoaesthetics in the Twenty-First Century* (Evanston: Northwestern University Press, 2015), xxiii.
66 Walter Mignolo, "Delinking the Rhetoric of Modernity, the Logic of Coloniality and the Grammar of De-Coloniality," in *Globalization and the Decolonial Option,* ed. Walter D Mignolo and Arturo Escobar (Abingdon: Routledge, 2010), 363 n. 69.
67 Wai Chee Dimock, *Through Other Continents: American Literature across Deep Time* (Princeton: Princeton University Press, 2009), 4.
68 The Anthropocene is an unofficial geological time marker that attempts to chart the impact of human life on the natural world. See also Carolyn Fornoff's chapter in this volume.
69 On the philosophical principles undermining the politics of mining in the Hispanic empire see, for example, Orlando Bentancor's *The Matter of Empire: Metaphysics and Mining in Colonial Peru* (Pittsburgh: Pittsburgh University Press), 2017.
70 Sor Juana Inés de la Cruz, *Obras completas de Sor Juana*, 102. Translation mine.
71 Ibid., 335.
72 Ibid.
73 Ibid., 337.
74 Ibid., 342.
75 Ibid.
76 Dodds Pennock and Powers, "Globalizing Cosmologies," 95.
77 Dimock, *Through Other Continents*, 23.

3

World-Making in the New Spain of the Eighteenth Century

Karen Stolley

In order to explore "world-making" in eighteenth-century New Spain, I take as my point of departure Franco Moretti's much-debated observation that "world literature is not an object, it's a problem" whose elucidation requires a new critical methodology in order to make sense of the ever-expanding number of languages and texts included under its umbrella.[1] Moretti would later propose a division of world literature into two categories ("one that precedes the eighteenth century—and one that follows it"), leaving unanswered the question of where the eighteenth-century "en español" might fit in Moretti's world literature system.[2] "World-making" refers to the ways that cultural texts represent the world or, better said, a world—and make it intelligible for others.[3] In this context we will explore how world literature theory illuminates aspects of the literary production of eighteenth-century New Spain, but we will also consider how the literary production of eighteenth-century New Spain permits us to see world literature not in a narrow sense as an object or, as Moretti suggests, as a problem, but rather as an inclusive conversation among an expanded community of writers and readers.

Eighteenth-century Mexican writings and the viceregal, imperial, and transatlantic networks in which they circulated provide an opportunity to engage with, challenge, and expand current theoretical formulations and debates about world literature. These texts represent a range of genres and literary kinds and reflect spirited debates about American nature and its much-disputed relationship with Europe, the place of indigenous civilizations in narratives of stadial history and enlightened cosmopolitanism, and the role of translation in the creation and circulation of knowledge emerging from encyclopedic transnational humanism. They provide a compelling example of the role of historical and cultural variables in determining how we define and read world literature, particularly literature produced during a time of transition from empire to nation and from coloniality to modernity, and in a place that has not traditionally been named on the map of world literature, neither when Goethe first proposed the idea of *Weltliteratur* nor in many subsequent theorizations and anthologies. The hybridity of eighteenth-century Mexican literature, informed not only by European notions of print-based literacy but also by indigenous oral and pictographic traditions, further suggests that we re-imagine the European

Enlightenment link between reason, civilization, and writing that is at the heart of the Republic of Letters.[4] Thus, my essay will consider how to write eighteenth-century New Spain into the eighteenth-century Republic of Letters that foregrounds the notion of world literature, and into world literature itself.

Ignacio Sánchez Prado and other contributors to this volume make compelling arguments about why Mexico and, more broadly, Latin America have played a minor role in discussions of world literature until relatively recently.[5] My interest is focused more narrowly on a particular omission within that larger omission—the tendency to dismiss the eighteenth century in discussions of Spanish American literary history as well as the tendency to ignore eighteenth-century Spanish America in discussions of the global eighteenth century. Eighteenth-century New Spain has played an often-overlooked role in the particular world-making of what is now called the global Enlightenment, expanding and challenging its theoretical dimensions through praxis and lived experience.[6]

The transition to the Bourbon dynasty at the beginning of the eighteenth century led to a reordering of the imperial functions of expansion and preservation, with an increasing focus on free trade and administrative centralization.[7] These functions were mapped onto viceregal centers and peripheries in a far-flung and diverse Hispanic empire, of which New Spain was an important center. Eighteenth-century New Spain faced a particular set of complex realities on the ground: the governance of imperial subjects who included *criollos* (American-born Spaniards), indigenous peoples, African-descendants, mestizos, mulatos, and Spaniards; efforts to put in place enlightened reforms of the imperial political economy; scientific and philosophical debates about the nature of the New World. These issues do not always align with the imperial ideologies and practices of England and France, and this has led to a scholarly blind spot in discussions of the eighteenth-century Hispanic world and the global Enlightenment. For example, Spanish America barely makes an appearance in Dorinda Outram's classic study, even in the context of extensive discussions of cross-cultural contact, political economy, and the problem of slavery.[8]

Christopher Prendergast has observed that going global implies "time mapped onto space, history onto geography."[9] In order to take eighteenth-century New Spain as a global vantage point, we need to understand the place of Mexico's "ciudad letrada" in the Republic of Letters, a global community of intellectuals, scholars, philosophers, and scientists in Europe and the Americas that in many ways anticipated the world literature community.[10] This self-proclaimed community was at the same intimate and distanced, functioning in private and in public, and producing texts that circulated in a market of ideas that predates the publishing industry assumed in most discussions of world literature today.[11] Indeed Goethe's thinking about *Weltliteratur* was rooted in the understanding of humanist universalism as an extension of the classical, as was the Enlightenment.

As Theo D'haen has observed of these eighteenth-century members of the Republic of Letters, "What they corresponded about, more importantly, were 'letters' in the sense of any writing about any kind of 'knowledge,' stretching from poetry to politics, from astronomy to astrology."[12] The hybridity of eighteenth-century

Mexican letters reflects a similarly wide range of knowledge production that includes historiography, scientific accounts, encyclopedic entries, translations, and editions, reflecting the emerging importance of print-based literacy studied by Benedict Anderson.[13] Mapping this Republic of Letters is the subject of an ambitious project sponsored by Stanford University's Digital Humanities Center.[14] The goal is to visualize eighteenth-century intellectual networks by mapping epistolarity through the movement of mail. This study has only fairly recently been expanded to move beyond Europe and Anglophone North America to include epistolary interlocutors in Spain and Spanish territories in the Americas, despite the fact that Spanish America contributed to the circulation of enlightened thinking in the eighteenth century in important ways.

The imperial subjects who made their home in eighteenth-century New Spain were indigenous persons, castas, *criollos*, afro-descendants, and Spaniards whose identity emerged from the dynamic relationship between colonial structures and lived experiences.[15] This dynamic challenges philosophical and demographic categories of the enlightened Republic of Letters as these subjects cross boundaries and rework entangled colonial hierarchies through their everyday engagement of social and administrative relationships, formally and informally. Even the much-vaunted rivalry between *criollos* and peninsular Spaniards, or *gachupines*, is now understood as sometimes real, sometimes rhetorical, frequently negotiable. The imperial subjects of New Spain embody the idea of a lived rather than a theorized Enlightenment, an Enlightenment that was geographically expansive, involving the circulation of people, commodities, and ideas far beyond the continental confines that traditionally served to define it.[16]

Jesuits play an important role that defies easy categorization, first as a part of a global community deeply rooted in local projects related to evangelization and education that are reflected in their reports and public and private correspondence and, later, after their 1767 expulsion, as a global community in exile.[17] Once exiled, and having lost access to firsthand experience of the land and its indigenous inhabitants as well as many of their personal papers, the Jesuits produced natural histories fueled by nostalgia, continuing to engage energetically in the so-called "dispute of the New World." As Ivonne del Valle has observed, "These newer texts no longer centered on advancing Christianity and its accompanying civilization, but rather on creating a space for New Spain in the international world of letters and knowledge—a New Spain that was not necessarily connected to old Spain."[18] Guillermo Wilde explains further:

> In the eighteenth century, especially, the order published collections of letters and administrative documents in formats destined for a broad public; relating the experiences from Jesuits from diverse European provinces in missions overseas, these texts were widely embraced by European readers. In this manner, the Jesuit press acquired a leading role in the emergence of a "world consciousness" that contributed to the monumentalization of the order in the expansion of the Catholic world. (211)[19]

As I have suggested previously, *criollo* patriotism emerges as an imperative to "write back" to European armchair philosophers—Louis Leclerc Buffon, *Histoire naturellle* (1747); Corneille De Pauw, *Recherches philosophiques sur les Americains* (1768); Guillaume-Thomas Raynal, *Histoire philosophique des . . . deus Indes* (1770, 1774, 1781); and William Robertson, *History of America* (1777)—who had penned critiques of indigenous civilizations, Spanish Conquest, and the state of nature in the New World.[20] D.A. Brading writes, "For the Spanish Americans, still subject to the Bourbon dynasty, the Enlightenment's attack proved all the more hurtful, since its combination of climatic determinism and historical scepticisim wounded their patriotic tradition at every point" (*First America* 447). Zealously safeguarding their reputation in the Republic of Letters, *criollos* in New Spain produced natural histories as well as institutional histories, and contributed to the "belated flowering" of interest in the Virgin of Guadalupe described by Jacques Lafaye in *Quetzalcóatl and Guadalupe* (86).[21] Their *criollo* patriotism informs the celebratory vindication of indigenous culture prior to the arrival of the Spaniards that has come to be known as neo-Aztecism, and it leads to the creation of various avenues for the circulation of knowledge such as *Bibliothecas*, periodicals, editions, and translations—all of which contribute to a global Republic of Letters and which I will discuss in the pages that follow.[22]

Perhaps the most important representative of neo-Aztecism is Francisco Javier Clavijero (1731–87). Clavijero wrote the *Historia Antigua de México* during his exile in Bologna and translated it into Italian for publication there in 1780–1.[23] The *Historia* is divided into ten books, with a lengthy prologue that includes a catalogue of those who have written about Mexican history; the final two books consist of nine "dissertations" which Clavijero considered to be the heart of the work and which represent a systematic refutation of De Pauw's claims about Amerindians. Although the author in presenting his work calls it "una historia de México escrita por un mexicano" [a history of Mexico written by a Mexican], his intended audience is both local and global. The lengthy dissertations, he explains, "son necesarias para disuadir a los incautos lectores de los errores en que han incurrido muchos autores modernos que, sin suficientes conocimientos, han escrito sobre la tierra, los animales, y los hombres de la América" [are necessary to dissuade incautious readers from the errors incurred by many modern authors who, without sufficient knowledge, have written about the land, the animals, and the people of America].[24] Clavijero claimed to have based his work on his knowledge of Nahuatl and familiarity with indigenous sources, product of the more than three decades he spent living in Mexico, although the originality of his interpretations has been questioned.

On the other hand, Antonio de León y Gama (1735–1802), who offered a systematic explanation of the Mexican calendar and Aztec chronology in his *Descripción histórica y cronológica de las dos piedras* (1792), has proven to be remarkably accurate.[25] He too learned classical Nahuatl and reviewed the writings of sixteenth-century indigenous scholars for clues to the glyphs of the two pre-Hispanic monoliths that were uncovered in 1790 as the main plaza of Mexico City was being cleared in preparation for renovations, a statue of the goddess Coatlicue and the Sun Stone, a great disk carved with calendrical markings. For his research León y Gama relied heavily on the collections of sources that had been gathered by Fernando de Alva Ixtlilxochitl, Carlos de Sigüenza y Góngora, Lorenzo Boturini Benaduci, and others, carrying on, as David Brading argues, "a tradition of inquiry into the native past of Mexico which had been initiated by the Franciscans, assisted by their Indian collaborators at the College of Santa Cruz Tlatelolco, continued by native and mestizo annalists of the late sixteenth century, and thereafter transitted by the line of *criollo* patriots that started with Ixtlilxochitl and Sigüenza y Góngora."[26]

Historians such as John Leddy Phelan have argued that the neo-Aztecism project to integrate *criollo* culture with pre-Hispanic antiquity would later provide a foundation for Mexican political independence: "The outstanding feature of Clavijero's text is his contribution to the development of neo-Aztecism. He brought out for the first time its anti-Spanish implications, and he related the cult of Aztec antiquity to the social problems of contemporary Indians."[27] But Phelan is imposing a retrospective teleological interpretation and overstating *criollo* interest in the often miserable circumstances of their indigenous contemporaries in eighteenth-century New Spain. This may explain why Clavijero's central role in neo-Aztecism has obscured his other writings, notably the *Storia della California* (1786), which chronicles Jesuit missionary activity along the Western frontier in what is now Baja California and can be read as both institutional history and ethnography.[28] The obvious contrast between the magnificence of Aztec civilization and the abject misery of the people of Baja California, as portrayed by Clavijero, points to the ambiguities of neo-Aztecism and *criollo* positioning vis-à-vis the indigenous other. And in recent years the consensus that eighteenth-century *criollo* patriotism included a wholesale rejection of imperial loyalties and anticipated nineteenth-century independence movements has become more nuanced.[29]

Sánchez Prado, discussing the paradoxes of the Hispanist/nationalist foundations of Miguel León-Portilla's project to invent the pre-Columbian past, notes "an ideological appropriation: the legitimization of classical humanism as a form of understanding the Pre-Columbian heritage as a 'culture' in the same sense of other Western cultures" (44).[30] His assessment bears a striking resemblance to what might be said about the eighteenth-century neo-Aztecism practiced by Clavijero and León y Gama, their attempt to substitute the colonial conquest with a pre-Hispanic past that links directly to the eighteenth century. In assessing the significance of eighteenth-century neo-Aztecism we must recognize that it is only possible to approximate the pre-Hispanic world and the encounter through layers of transcription, transliteration, and translation; in that necessary, but imperfect, process we must let go of any aspirational or imagined authenticity.[31]

Writing back also took the form of natural histories that highlighted first-person experience of the land, its flora and fauna, and also familiarity with the knowledge of its indigenous inhabitants. Here, too, Jesuits were important interlocutors, as indigenous culture was observed, appropriated, and transmitted by *criollos* to what Antony Higgins has called the *criollo* archive in a process that involved both received European textual authority and pragmatic experimentation informed by autochthonous practices, but always with the goal of legitimizing American-born whites in New Spain.[32] As Ivonne del Valle points out, "The Jesuits' writings might be understood as an effort to bridge this gap between a history that was not their own, since it belonged to the Indians, and their aspirations to assume a leadership role in the production of knowledge about the places in which they lived and worked."[33] Jesuit writings regarding their encounters with Amerindian knowledge of local climate and geography, agriculture, and mining in the larger context of the Spanish Bourbon empire and debates about nature in the Americas position them squarely in eighteenth-century world literature, particularly in the context of debates about Wallerstein's world-systems theory, the place of the nation, and the "self/other polarity of western metropolitan discourse."[34]

Rafael Landívar's *Rusticatio Mexicana* reflects enlightened ideas about how humans (*criollos*, Indigenous Americans, and Europeans) interacted with and transformed their natural environment.[35] Born in Guatemala and schooled by the Jesuits in Mexico, the author resettled in Bologna after the 1767 expulsion of the Jesuits from all Spanish territories. There, fueled by nostalgia and the nascent *criollo* patriotism which drives other writers of whom I speak in this essay, Landívar composed the *Rusticatio Mexicana*, a poetic treatise in the Georgic tradition on the geography, flora and fauna, mining, and agriculture of the author's homeland. Written in hexameter verse in Latin (the lingua franca for Jesuits and the medium used for many educational and ecclesiastical documents in Spain and Spanish America at the time) the *Rusticatio* was published in 1781, again in a slightly expanded version in 1782, and shortly thereafter translated into Spanish (there is an excellent English translation by Andrew Laird, which includes extensive introductory materials and notes).[36] Like Virgil, Landívar celebrates a life connected to the land, and his description of a New World economy organized around agriculture—cochineal dye, sugar cane, cattle-raising—and mining becomes a narrative of enlightened *criollo* agency in which the poet emphasizes the central place of labor in colonial society, invoking the value of indigenous knowledge and traditions as well as eighteenth-century debates about physiocracy and mercantilism while insisting on the modes of knowledge that enable *criollos* to intervene upon and assert authority over parts of their environment.

At the same time Landívar acknowledges that there are moments—like the violent eruption of the Jorullo volcano in 1759—when American nature resists all human efforts to control or tame it, when the natural environment imposes its own terrible ecological pedagogy. The opening lines of Book II assault the reader with a vision of "ungovernable fury [that] has belched forth balls of fire and rocks from its bursting furnaces as if it were planning the world's final doom, arousing in the people cold chills of fear."[37] This is followed by a fleeting allusion to "those who at times are pleased to watch and study with keen eye scenes of horror, observing them from a distance."[38] The mention of these discerning, but distant, observers who study nature with a keen eye without ever venturing forth in the geographical territory under investigation may be read as a response to European armchair travelers such as Raynal, DePauw, and Buffon who found much to criticize in the Americas without ever having been there.

But the Jorullo eruption is not the only natural disaster depicted in Book II, which concludes with a description of yet another terrifying earthquake that shook the city of Bologna as the author was composing the *Rusticatio*. In both cases, it proves impossible to merely "study with keen eye scenes of horror, observing them from a distance," as the brute force of Nature's power is felt in Europe as well as in the Americas. Ecological restoration after the Jorullo earthquake is manifest via Nature's slow, but steady, hand, while in Bologna recovery is the result of the convergence of religion and culture. The Jesuit focus on both nature and culture reflects dynamic exchanges between *criollos* and indigenous inhabitants as cohabiters and co-cultivators of the land, even as *criollos* embrace a notion of spiritual and material progress for which they consider themselves to be the principal agents. Landívar's pairing of the two earthquakes—Jorullo and Bologna—serves as a cautionary reminder to his readers of the degree to which natural disasters and human responses are linked in a global ecosystem that transcends an Old World/New World binary.

Furthermore, the *Rusticatio Mexicana* exemplifies Yolanda Martínez-San Miguel's concept of "minor discourse" in that it challenges the binaries of major literatures/minor literatures, colonizer/colonized that have been central to discussions of world literature.[39] Martínez-San Miguel echoes Rolena Adorno and other scholars of the Spanish American colonial period on "the need to study voices that could be simultaneously marginal and central, subaltern and hegemonic."[40] The fact that the Jesuits are both marginal and central to the late colonial project in New Spain, first as missionaries on the imperial periphery and after their expulsion as exiles, is reflected in works like the *Rusticatio Mexicana*. We must also underscore the limitations of the modern concept of nation to account for early modern and colonial geographical and political categories. Landívar's *Rusticatio Mexicana*, as John Beverley has observed, is neither colonial nor proto-national and covers a geographic territory that corresponds to what is now Guatemala and Mexico.[41]

As I have argued elsewhere, the Americas were often the laboratory where enlightened ideas about nature, human agency, governance, and empire were employed, contested, and negotiated on the ground, and New Spain provides numerous examples of the scientific, moral, social, political, and cultural implications of this negotiation.

Scientific expeditions sponsored by the Spanish Crown during this period involved collaborative teams from all across Europe and resulted in copious amounts of information, reports, and specimens that circulated widely. As Daniela Bleichmar has demonstrated, botanical illustrations are an undervalued aspect of this exercise in knowledge production; she argues that "the visual culture of natural history was global both in deed and ideology."[42] Her observation reminds us of the potential for including visual culture in our discussions of world literature.[43]

Finally, to conclude this discussion of natural history and scientific travelers, I must add a brief aside about Alexander von Humboldt (1769–1859), whose towering stature as the quintessential scientific traveler in Spanish America guarantees his writings a place in the world literature canon. Humboldt's fascination with Mexican codices and the Calendar Stone (which he had observed thanks to the helpful intervention of León y Gama) is reflected in his *Essay politique sur le royaume de la Nouvelle-Espagne* (1807–11), which also includes a critique of Spanish conquistadors and missionaries, discussions of silver mining technologies, and predictions regarding New Spain's role in the future of global commerce. What is often overlooked is the essay's reliance at every point on not only the author's personal observations but evidence generously provided to him by *criollo* patriots in New Spain, who functioned as testimonial informants for Humboldt's gestor.[44]

Eighteenth-century New Spain was the site of diverse manifestations of cultural activity related to the organization and dissemination of knowledge that are consistent with those of the global Republic of Letters and also reflect an awareness of the sited nature of knowledge production. Juan José de Eguiara y Eguren (1696–1763) conceived of his *Biblioteca Mexicana* as an ambitious bio-bibliographical project: a catalogue composed in Latin of all Mexican authors, a list of more than a thousand names based on a capacious definition of "Mexican" that included all those born in New Spain— Indians, Spaniards, and castas—as well as those he considered Mexican by virtue of residence. Eguiara's goal was to repudiate the stinging critique of *criollo* intellectual capacity and the quality of Mexico's colleges and universities made by Manuel Martí (1663–1737) in his 1756 *Epístolas*. The first volume of the *Biblioteca Mexicana*, consisting of a series of prologues (or "Anteloquia") and entries corresponding to the letters A, B, and C, did not appear until 1755. Not surprisingly, the *Biblioteca* was unfinished at the time of Eguiara's death, although the volumes corresponding to the letters D through J existed in manuscript form.[45]

Eguiara imagined his *Biblioteca Mexicana* as a physical space, a collection of books, and a catalogue—all meant to circulate and explicate knowledge in eighteenth-century New Spain rather than encrypt it (in the Foucauldian sense of "archive").[46] Higgins has characterized Eguiara's attempt to create an encyclopedic moment of origin for a Mexican intellectual and literary tradition "as a cipher for *criollo* subjectivity and authority in an era of widening schisms within the colonial order."[47] He sees Eguiara, perhaps not without irony, as "a forerunner of modern Mexican nationalism, one step in a seamless narrative of identity that can be traced back to pre-Hispanic times."[48]

Newspapers and gazettes have not traditionally been considered under the rubric of world literature, although in the eighteenth-century transatlantic Hispanic world periodical publications functioned as "cultural commodities . . . engaged in some of the most ambitious projects of educating their citizens by focusing on key ideas of the Enlightenment including the ideas of progress, education, utility, and the well-being or pursuit of happiness" (Meléndez, "Transnational Exchanges," 116).[49] José Ignacio Bartolache (1772–3) published the *Mercurio Volante*, sometimes considered America's first medical journal, and also wrote an essay on the Virgin of Guadalupe.[50] José Antonio Alzate y Ramírez (1737–99) published four different periodicals, including the *Gazeta de literatura de México*, the longest-running and most important across whose pages Alzate carried on a vigorous exchange with his contemporary León y Gama about the correct interpretation of Mexican antiquities.[51] The issues of the *Gazeta* reflected an understanding of "literature" in the broadest terms as knowledge of any kind (reminiscent of D'haen's characterization of the members of the Republic of Letters). Those who contributed articles and letters were writing for an emerging "imagined community" interested in pre-Hispanic culture, commerce, mining, hydraulics, and a range of issues related to women as well (who are, regrettably, underrepresented in the canonical literature of the time).

Reviewing the work of eighteenth-century writers in New Spain, one is struck by the reach of their global aspirations and the intensity of their local grounding even as we acknowledge what John Beverley has called "the perennial problem in both Hispanism and Latin-Americanism of the anomalous character of the eighteenth century."[52] We can identify why the texts discussed here might profitably be included in the world literature conversation. But how can eighteenth-century New Spain help us rethink world literature?

One answer is that it compels us to first rethink world history by redefining the modernity that is traditionally constitutive of world literature, by accepting the possibilities of a continuum between that modernity and what came before. For Enrique Dussel the myth of modernity is a discovery of America that is subsumed in European history but is not recognized as constitutive of modernity itself, leading to the erasure of Latin America in world history.[53] Expanding the map and timeline of world literature to include eighteenth-century New Spain is one way "to write Iberian imperialism into world systems theories by focusing on the specific links, nodes, agents, and processes that produced the conditions for globalization."[54]

The textual production of eighteenth-century New Spain offers expanded opportunities for considering cross-cultural encounters in practice as well as in theory, for understanding the representation of cross-cultural encounters as the way enlightened cosmopolitanism functioned on the ground in order to at the same time acknowledge difference and affirm a common, universalizing humanity.[55] As Michael Palencia-Roth asks, "What is the history of humanity if not the history of cross-cultural encounters?"[56] Or we might note that Prendergast quotes Carlos Fuentes's idea that "reading, writing, teaching, learning, are all activities aimed at introducing civilizations to each other," intrigued by the formulation yet finding it problematic because of the unequal terms that are inevitably involved in such introductions.[57]

Eighteenth-century New Spain also provides evidence of a particular manifestation of linguistic world-making, given that it was a moment when indigenous languages coexisted with modern and classical European languages, reminding us that the invention of Spanish as a "national language" in Europe and the Americas has a long and complicated history. This coexistence was a kind of *convivencia*, not without tensions, ambivalences, and hierarchies that were continually negotiated and renegotiated. Emily Apter objects to the way that world literature has been rendered apolitical or politicized for the wrong reasons: "In returning to a Goethean humanist project, it restitutes the model of the translator as cultural universalizer, evangelizer of transcultural understanding" (197); however, this assessment does not account for the complexities of language ideologies in eighteenth-century New Spain.[58]

I close by turning to the idea of "lo mexicano," central to the purpose of this collection of essays on Mexican literature as world literature, to ask to what degree is it relevant in a discussion of the eighteenth century in New Spain. Is the eighteenth century the moment when "lo mexicano" becomes important under the guise of *criollo* patriotism, even if the birth of the nation-state of Mexico lies in an unforeseen future? Clavijero looks to Mexican antiquity as a vindication and defense against European slights. Eguiara uses the term "Mexican" ("Mexicanus") to designate a territory larger than just Mexico City, to invoke at the same time an urban intellectual history and something more expansive.[59] Landívar, as we have seen, also used the term capaciously in a way that does not align with the current nation-states of Mexico and Guatemala. The multiple ways in which "Mexican" identity was claimed and deployed in eighteenth-century New Spain anticipate the complexities of identity formulations to come.[60] Indeed, the writers and writings of eighteenth-century New Spain anticipate many of the "paradigms and problems of *Weltliteratur*— global translation, linguistic imperialism, transnational humanism, nationalism and modernity."[61] It is past time to bring them in from the periphery to engage fully in our world literature conversation.

Notes

1. Franco Moretti, "Conjectures on World Literature," in *Debating World Literature*, ed. Christopher Prendergast (London: Verso, 2004), 149. For an overview of "World literature as system," see Theo D'haen, *The Routledge Concise History of World Literature* (New York: Routledge, 2012), 96–116.
2. Franco Moretti, "Evolution, World-System, *Weltliteratur*," in *The Princeton Sourcebook in Comparative Literature*, ed. David Damrosch, Natalie Melas, and Mbongiseni Btheluzi (Princeton: Princeton University Press, 2009), 407; qtd. by D'haen in *The Routledge Concise History*, 110.
3. Sara Castro-Klarén refers to Inca Garcilaso's world-making as "an attempt to produce a book that could encompass and translate the intelligibility of the Andean world to present and future readers all over the world." "Introduction" in *Inca Garcilaso & Contemporary World-Making*, ed. Sara Castro-Klarén and Christian Fernández (Pittsburgh: University of Pittsburgh Press, 2016), 4. See also D'haen's discussion of Djelal Kadir's notion of the "worlding" of work and critic (*The Routledge Concise History*, 41).
4. Prendergast, "The World Republic of Letters," in *Debating World Literature*, ed. Christopher Prendergast (London: Verso, 2004), 4.
5. This question is addressed in the important collection of essays edited by Gesine Müller and Mariano Siskind, *World Literature, Cosmopolitanism, Globality: Beyond, Against, Post, Otherwise* (Berlin: De Gruyter, 2019), which focuses on Latin America to discuss the blind spots of a globally oriented Humanities.
6. For a recent overview that incorporates earlier scholarship and includes useful bibliography on this question, see Elizabeth Franklin Lewis, Mónica Bolufer Peruga, and Catherine M. Jaffe, eds., *The Routledge Companion to the Hispanic Enlightenment* (London and New York: Routledge, 2020). As the editors of this volume argue, even recent work on "Other," national, or peripheral Enlightenments has tended to overlook Spain and Spanish America.
7. The Spanish Habsburg dynasty came to a close in 1700 with the death of Charles II, who left no heirs. Philip of Anjou was proclaimed Philip V of Spain, and Bourbon ascendancy was confirmed by the War of Spanish Succession (1701–14). Historians generally make a distinction between the first half of the eighteenth century and the second, when the Bourbon reform agenda took root and accelerated the rate

of change. For the purposes of this essay, I will consider the full expanse of the eighteenth century as an evolving political culture.

8. Dorinda Outram, *The Enlightenment,* 3d ed. (1995; Cambridge and New York: Cambridge University Press, 2013). See also Mariselle Meléndez and Karen Stolley, "Introduction: Enlightenments in Spanish America," *Colonial Latin American Review* 24, no. 1 (2015): 1–16.

9. Prendergast, "The World Republic of Letters," 1. See also Charles W. Withers, *Placing the Enlightenment: Thinking Geographically about the Age of Reason* (Chicago: University of Chicago Press, 2007).

10. D'haen defines the Republic of Letters as "the communities of intellectuals, writers, and philosophers that during especially the seventeenth and eighteenth centuries kept in touch with one another, across Europe, by the exchange of, precisely, letters" (*Routledge Concise History,* 7).

11. Prendergast discusses the difference between the seventeenth- and eighteenth-century Republic of Letters, based on a "cooperative community of knowledge" through private correspondence, and "the more commercially based conditions that permit the international flows Goethe has in mind" ("The World Republic of Letters," 11, n. 4).

12. D'haen, *Routledge Concise History of World Literature,* 7.

13. Efraín Kristal questions the privileging of the novel in world literature, given that poetry and essay are genres which predominate in Spanish American cultural production; see "Considering Coldly . . . A Response to Franco Moretti." *New Left Review* 15 (May–June 2002): 61–74; qtd. D'haen, *The Routledge Concise History,* 112. For a discussion of novelistic production in eighteenth-century Mexico, see Nancy Vogeley, "La novela," in *Historia de la literatura Mexicana,* Vol. 3, ed. Nancy Vogeley and Manuel Ramos Medina (Mexico City: Siglo XXI, 2011), 222–42.

14. http://republicofletters.stanford.edu/casestudies/spanishempire.html

15. See Andrew B. Fisher and Matthew D. O'Hara, "Introduction: Racial Identities and Their Interpreters in Colonial Latin America," in *Imperial Subjects: Race and Identity in Colonial Latin America* (Durham: Duke University Press, 2009), 1–37. Rolena Adorno has a similar understanding of the term: "I posit 'identity' as consisting of many varieties of appropriating actions carried out by individuals or communities, all of whom exercise agency in subscribing to, rejecting, creating, and modifying identities either individual or collective. My point is that identities are mobile, multiple and sequential or simultaneous, even within a single subject" ("Artifact, Artifice, and Identity: Nativist Writing and Scholarship on Colonial Latin America and Their Legacies," in *To Be Indio in Colonial Spanish America,* ed. Mónica Díaz (Albuquerque: University of New Mexico Press, 2017), 35. These scholars of colonial Spanish America are speaking of the sixteenth and seventeenth centuries, but their observations hold for the eighteenth century as well.

16. The writings we will examine in what follows support Jesús Astigarraga's observation in *The Spanish Enlightenment Revisited* that "the Spanish Enlightenment was essentially pragmatic, utilitarian and applied" (Oxford: The Voltaire Foundation, 2015), 9.

17. The bibliography on the Jesuits is extensive. See the seminal studies on Jesuits in New Spain by Juan Luis Maneiro and Manuel Fabri, *Vidas de mexicanos ilustres del siglo XVIII* (México: Universidad Nacional Autónoma de México, 1951) and Bernabe Navarro, *Cultura Mexicana moderna en el siglo XVIII*

(México: Universidad Nacional Autónoma de México, 1964). See also *Escritura, imaginación política y la Compañia de Jesús en América Latina [siglos XVI–XVII]*, ed. Alexandre Coello de la Rosa and Teodoro Hampe Martínez (Barcelona: Bellaterra, 2011); *Jesuit Accounts of the Colonial Americas: Intercultural Transfers, Intellectual Disputes, and Textualities*, ed. Marc André Bernier, Clorinda Donato, and Hans-Jürgen Lüsebrink (Toronto: University of Toronto Press/UCLA Center for Seventeenth- and Eighteenth-Century Studies and the William Andrews Clark Memorial Library, 2014); María Cristina Torales Pacheco, "Los jesuitas novohispanos, la modernidad y el espacio público ilustrado," in *Los jesuitas y la modernidad en Iberoamérica 1549–1773* (Lima: Fondo Editorial de la Pontificia Universidad Católica del Peru/Universidad del Pacífico/Instituto Francés de Estudios Andinos, 2007), 158–71. Ivonne del Valle has written extensively on the Jesuits; see *Escribiendo desde los márgenes: Colonialismo y jesuitas en el siglo XVIII* (Mexico City: Siglo XXI, 2009) and "Jesuit Enlightenment: Interventions in Christianity and Intellectualism," in *A History of Mexican Literature*, ed. Ignacio Sánchez Prado, Anna M. Nogar, and José Ramón Ruisánchez Serra (New York: Cambridge University Press, 2016), 81–96.

18 Ibid., 87.

19 "Jesuits and Indigenous Subjects in the Global Culture of Letters: Production, Circulation, and Adaptation of Missionary Texts in the Seventeenth and Eighteenth Centuries," in *Iberian Empires and the Roots of Globalization*, ed. Ivonne del Valle, Anna More, and Rachel Sarah O'Toole (Nashville: Vanderbilt University Press), 207–32.

20 *Criollo* patriotism is the focus of D.A. Brading's *The First America: The Spanish Monarchy, Creole Patriots, and the Liberal State 1492–1867* (Cambridge and New York: Cambridge University Press, 1991). See Antonello Gerbi, *The Dispute of the New World: The History of a Polemic, 1750–1900*, trans. Jeremy Moyle (1955; Pittsburgh: University of Pittsburgh Press, 2010). Jorge Cañizares-Esguerra explores debates about the historiographical reliability of indigenous codices and Spanish chronicles in *How to Write the History of the New World: Historiographies, Epistemologies, and Identities in the Eighteenth-Century Atlantic World* (Stanford: Stanford University Press, 2001).

21 Jacques Lafaye, *Quetzalcóatl y Guadalupe: La formación de la conciencia nacional en México* (Mexico City: Fondo de Cultura Económica, 1999). Francisco Javier Alegre (1729–88) wrote *Historia de la Provincia de la Compañía de Jesús de Nueva España* as both an institutional history and an account of the Jesuit expulsion in 1767 (3 vols., ed. Carlos María Bustamante, Mexico City: J.M. Lara, 1841–3). See Karen Stolley, "The eighteenth century: narrative forms, scholarship, and learning," in *The Cambridge History of Latin American Literature: Vol. 1 Discovery to Modernism*, ed. Roberto González Echevarría and Enrique Pupo-Walker, 3 vols. (New York and Cambridge: Cambridge University Press, 1996), I: 336–74; see also Stolley, "East from Eden: Domesticating Exile in Jesuit Accounts of Their 1767 Expulsion from Spanish America," in *Jesuit Accounts of the Colonial Americas*, 243–63. Alegre also writes about the Virgin of Guadalupe.

22 See Francisco Javier Clavijero, *Historia de la literatura Mexicana*, Vol. 3, ed. Nancy Vogeley and Manuel Ramos Medina (México: Siglo XXI, 2011).

23 The publication history is complicated and reflects the global reach of the history: Francisco Javier Clavijero, *Storia antica del Messico*, 4 vols. (Cesena: Gregorio Biasini,

1780–1781); *The History of Mexico*, 3 vols. Transl from the original Italian by Charles Cullen (London: G.G.J. and J. Robertson, 1787); *Historia antigua de Mégico*, 2 vols. Transl. from the Italian by José Joaquín de Mora (London, R. Ackermann, 1826). There are numerous re-editions of this Spanish translation based on the Italian edition: 1844, 1868, 1883, 1917, 1944. Mariano Cuevas published his edition of the *Historia antigua de México* based on the original Spanish manuscript (Mexico City: Porrúa, 1987).

24 *Historia antigua*, Libro X, 422.
25 The second and complete edition was published in Mexico City (Imprenta del Ciudadano Alejandro Valdés, 1832).
26 Brading, *The First America*, 463. See also Jorge Cañizares-Esguerra, "La historiografía nueva," in *Historia de la literatura Mexicana*, 3: 399–413.
27 "Neo-Aztecism in the Eighteenth Century and the Genesis of Mexican Nationalism," in *Culture in History. Essays in Honor of Paul Radin,* ed. Stanley Diamond (New York: Octagon, 1981), 763. See also Brading, *First America*, 450–62.
28 Clavijero died in 1787, soon after completing the *Storia della California*. A Spanish translation was published in 1852; a second Spanish translation, *Historia de la Antigua o Baja California*, appeared almost a century later (Mexico City: Imprenta del Museo Nacional de Arqueología, Historia y Etnografía, 1933).
29 See Stuart M. McMahan, "The *Bibliotheca Mexicana* Controversy and *Criollo* Patriotism in Early Modern Mexico," *Hispanic American Historical Review* 98, no. 1 (2018): 1–41.
30 Ignacio M. Sánchez Prado, "The Pre-Columbian Past as a Project: Miguel León Portilla and Hispanism," in *Ideologies of Hispanism*, ed. Mabel Moraña (Nashville: Vanderbilt University Press, 2005), 40–61.
31 Ibid., 45–6.
32 Anthony Higgins, *Constructing the Criollo Archive: Subjects of Knowledge in the* Bibliotheca Mexicana *and the* Rusticatio Mexicana (West Lafayette: Purdue University Press, 2000), 9. Higgins clarifies that his investigation of the writings of Jesuit *letrados* Rafael Landívar and Juan José de Eguiara y Eguren aims to "track how the mechanisms of *criollo* knowledge and subjectivity unfold in relation to the process of the emergence of sociocultural spaces and practices that articulate a markedly contradictory form of modernity" (8–9). See also *El saber de los jesuitas, historias naturales y el Nuevo Mundo,* ed. Luis Millones Figueroa and Domingo Ledezma (Frankfurt and Madrid: Vervuert/Iberoamericana, 2005).
33 del Valle, "Jesuit Enlightenment," 88.
34 Prendergast, "Introduction," in *Debating World Literature*, ix. Prendergast is referring here to Timothy Reiss's "Mapping identities: Literature, Nationalism, Colonialism" in the same collection (110–47) in which Reiss proposes a vision of cultural difference that "concerns learning to listen, precisely, to differences; with trying to understand cultures in their own terms as wholes, rather than ingesting them as 'our' other; with knowing that diverse cultural processes *do* exist, binding people in different relations and different understandings of being" (111).
35 The existence of accessible translations from the Latin into Spanish and English, and the *Rusticatio*'s thematic divisions, make this lengthy epic poem surprisingly accessible to students; here I am thinking of the pedagogical possibilities of teaching eighteenth-century Mexican literature as world literature discussed by David Damrosch, "Introduction: All the World in the Time" (1–11) and "Major Cultures

and Minor Literatures" (193–204), in *Teaching World Literature*, ed. David Damrosch (New York: Modern Language Association of America, 2009). For the Spanish translation, see Rafael Landívar, *Rusticatio Mexicana*, ed. and Spanish trans. Faustino Chamorro González (San José: Associación Libro Libre, 1987).

36 Andrew Laird, *The Epic of America: An Introduction to Rafael Landívar and the Rusticatio Mexicana* (London: Duckworth, 2006). See also Andrew Laird, "Patriotism and the rise of Latin in eighteenth-century new Spain: Disputes of the New World and the Jesuit constructions of a Mexican legacy," in *The Role of Latin in the Early Modern World: Latin, Linguistic Identity and Nationalism 1350–1800* (Aarhus and Copenhagen: Forum for Renaissance Studies, 2012), 163–93. Laird discusses at length the importance of Mexican neo-Latin humanism as a site of interdisciplinary inquiry beyond the legacies of Greece and Rome, despite "the consistent omission of Latin America from histories of the classical tradition" (*The Epic of America*, 5), and he provides background on the "golden age of Mexican Latin" in the 1700s. Laird's translation is a valuable resource for non-Hispanist scholars in eighteenth-century Mexican neoclassical humanism, expanding the canon for eighteenth-century studies, Latin literary and cultural studies, and world literature. For a discussion of Landívar's *Criollo* patriotism, see Luis Ramos, "The Art of Patriotic Epistemology: Mapping New Spain in Rafael Landívar's *Rusticatio Mexicana*," *Dieciocho* 39, no. 2 (Fall 2016): 275–89.

37 Laird, *The Epic of America*, 133.

38 Ibid.

39 "Colonial and minority discourses share a major characteristic that could be useful in producing a reading that is sensitive to these contradictory impulses of coloniality described as in-betweenness, ambiguity, or ambivalence" (Yolanda Martínez-San Miguel, *From Lack to Excess: "Minor" Readings of Latin American Colonial Discourse* [Lewisburg: Bucknell University Press, 2008], 32). Reading Ignacio Sánchez Prado's reflections on Rulfo's indigenist narrative as an invisible contribution to world literature in "La literatura mundial como praxis: apuntes hacia una metodología de lo concreto" (Müller and Siskind, *World Literature*, 62–75), I am struck by the intriguing possibility of putting Rulfo and Landívar in dialogue.

40 San Miguel, *From Lack to Excess*, 31.

41 John Beverley, "Afterword," in *Inca Garcilaso & Contemporary World-Making*, 359.

42 Daniela Bleichmar, *Visible Empire: Botanical Expeditions and Visual Culture in the Hispanic Enlightenment* (Chicago: University of Chicago Press, 2012), 8.

43 We might consider the casta paintings produced in eighteenth-century New Spain as another aspect of visual culture that has entered a global conversation. See Magali M. Carrera, *Imagining Identity in New Spain: Race, Lineage, and the Colonial Body in Portraiture and Casta Paintings* (Austin: University of Texas Press, 2003); Carrera, "The Visual Culture of New Spain: An Introductory Lesson." *Dieciocho* 30, no. 1 (Spring 2007) issue devoted to Teaching the Eighteenth Century/Enseñar el XVIII, 55–64. See also Ilona Katzew, *Casta Painting: Images of Race in Eighteenth-Century Mexico* (New Haven: Yale University Press, 2004).

44 See Brading, *First America*, 515–34; Mary Louise Pratt, *Imperil Eyes: Travel Writing and Transculturation*, 2nd ed. (1992; New York: Routledge, 2008), 109–40. Andrea Wulf's biography of Humboldt, *The Invention of Nature: Alexander von Humboldt's*

New World (New York: Alfred A. Knopf, 2016), has received glowing praise. For an incisive critique of the way in which Wulf sees Humboldt as a representative of world literature in ways that efface the agency of thinkers and writers in Spanish America, see Cañizares-Esguerra, Jorge. "Replay: The Problem with Andrea Wulf's Biography of Humboldt," in *Time to Eat the Dogs*, https://podcasts.apple.com/ca/podcast/replay-the-problem-with-andrea-wulfs-biography-of-humboldt/id1315347103?i=1000451025269

45 See Stolley, "Narrative Forms," 367–8. See *Biblioteca Mexicana*. Facsimile ed. Prologue and Spanish translation Benjamín Fernández Valenzuela, 5 vols. (Mexico City: UNAM, 1986–1990); *Prólogos a la 'Biblioteca Mexicana,'* Bilingual ed. and Spanish trans. Agustín Millares Carlo (Mexico City: Fondo de Cultura Económica, 1944).

46 See Jonathan Earl Carlyon, *Andrés González de Barcia and the Creation of the Colonial Spanish American Library* (Toronto: University of Toronto Press, 2005), 8–9. Carlyon explores González de Barcia's tireless efforts to expand the Spanish bibliography related to the New World by publishing new editions of sixteenth- and seventeenth-century historiography.

47 Higgins, *Constructing the Criollo Archive* 23.

48 Ibid., 25. See also Stuart McManus, "The *Bibliotheca Mexicana* Controversy and *Criollo* Patriotism in Early Modern Mexico," *Hispanic American Historical Review* 98, no. 1 (2018): 1–41. McManus argues that *criollo* identity in eighteenth-century New Spain was "entirely compatible with a strong loyalty to the Hispanic Monarchy, a larger pan-Hispanic caste identity, and a sense of membership in the Catholic Republic of Letters" (1).

49 Mariselle Meléndez, "Women in the Print Culture of New Spain," *History of Mexican Literature*, 97–112. See also Meléndez, "Spanish American Enlightenments: Local Epistemologies and Transnational Exchanges in Eighteenth-Century Newspapers," *Dieciocho* Anejo 4 (Spring 2009): 115–34.

50 Stolley, "Narrative Forms," 344–5.

51 See Chapter 5, "Whose Enlightenment Was It Anyway?," in *How to Write the History*, ed. Cañizares-Esguerra, 266–300.

52 359, "Afterword," in *Inca Garcilaso and Contemporary World-Making*, ed. Castro-Klarén and Fernández, 355–67). Beverley, drawing on Antonio Benítez Rojo's notion of "bifurcated desire," argues that *criollo* patriotism is marked by "a desire that seeks to found its authority on an appeal to the local and the indigenous or native, and at the same time to transpose in a utilitarian fashion for the purpose of hegemony or nation-building the European forms of cultural and administrative modernity" (356).

53 Dussel's counter hypothesis is that "Latin America, since 1492, is a constitutive moment of modernity, and Spain and Portugal are part of its originary moment ... the alterity, essential to modernity.... This interpretation will permit a new definition, a new world vision of modernity, which will uncover not only its emancipatory concept, but also the victimizing and destructive myth of a Europeanism based on Eurocentrism and the developmentalist fallacy.... I affirm the reason of the Other as a step toward a transmodern *worldhood*" (*The Invention of the Americas: Eclipse of "the Other" and the Myth of Modernity* (New York: Continuum, 1995), 26).

54 Enrique Dussel, "Introduction: Iberian Empires and a Theory of Early Modern Globalization," in *Iberian Empires and the Roots of Globalization*, ed. Ivonne del Valle, Anna More, and Rachel Sarah O'Toole (Nashville: Vanderbilt University Press, 2019), 9. Higgins proposes that we see the eighteenth-century *criollo* archive as an organically grounded intellectual and experiential alternative rather than merely a preexisting condition for nineteenth-century independence, a moment that is no longer entirely colonial but is not yet national.

55 The excellent essays included in *World Literature, Cosmopolitanism, Globality: Beyond, Against, Post, Otherwise*, ed. Gesine Müller and Mariano Siskind (Berlin and Boston: De Gruyter, 2019), consider the contemporary cosmopolitan experience. Alejandra Uslenghi finds it "unsettling in its confrontation of difference, requiring introspection and negotiation" in terms that would also apply to its eighteenth-century manifestation (196, "The Contemporary Cosmopolitan Condition: Borders and World Literature," in *World Literature, Cosmopolitanism*, 193–204).

56 "Pioneering Cross-Cultural Studies and World Literature at Illinois," in *Teaching World Literature*, 149–50).

57 Prendergast, "The World Republic of Letters," 3.

58 Unfortunately, the first three volumes of the exhaustively researched *Historia de la literatura Mexicana* (México: Siglo XXI, 2010) have had limited circulation in the English-speaking world, leading to a need that *A History of Mexican Literature*, ed. Ignacio M. Sánchez Prado, Anna M. Nogar, and José Ramón Ruisánchez Serra (Cambridge: Cambridge University Press, 2016), attempts to address.

59 McManus, "The *Bibliotheca Mexicana* Controversy," 3.

60 In an important essay, "Mapping Identities: Literature, Nationalism, Colonialism" (*Debating World Literature*, 110–47), Timothy Reiss explores the binaries that inevitably emerge from discussions of cultural difference defined as opposition between a metropolitan self and an "other." Reiss argues that many scholars of world literature "posit cultural antagonisms taking the form of oppressor and oppressed, of colonizer and colonized . . . Such conflictual separations, such neat boxes of explanation, correspond neither to the reality of cultural meetings nor to the complexity of their creation" (112).

61 Prendergast, *Debating World Literature*, ix.

4

On (Re)productive Worlds

Transpacific Materiality and Mexican World Literature

Laura Torres-Rodríguez

In the past few years my research has addressed Mexican literature from a global perspective. Specifically, it has stressed the importance of the Pacific Ocean in the making of Mexican and larger Latin American histories and literatures. This critical approach has allowed me to think against the grain of a literary tradition that has customarily been studied, like institutionalized "world literature" itself, from a transatlantic perspective, due in large part to the colonial history that ties it to European cultural legacies. Cognizant of the increasing importance and visibility of the transpacific circuit in "world literature" theories, and the escalating economic influence of East Asia over Latin America, this chapter aims at a diachronic understanding of these new developments by analyzing Mexican literature's significant and long-standing involvement with Pacific global configurations. Nevertheless, from within the hegemonic models of comparison that have determined the "world literature" canon, an East Asia-Mexico connection seems illegible. My main purpose, then, is to argue that the transpacific aspect of Mexican literature allows us to locate Mexico more strongly within recent debates about "world literature," especially those articulated from a polycentric conception of literary modernity. In the same vein, I want to argue that Mexican literature represents a forgotten precedent of US literature about the Pacific. As Wai Chee Dimock has argued, "American literature emerges with a much longer history than one might think."[1] Therefore, as she does with Persian, Hindu, and Chinese literary traditions, I would like to thread "the long durations" of Mexican colonial literature "into the short chronology of the United States" in order to reflect on how its most proximate relative has become the most disavowed.[2]

Although I will be concentrating on literary texts from the first colonial modernity, I would like to start this chapter by addressing the present moment with an example from the visual arts. This allows me to underscore the capacity of the fictional episteme to evoke the historicity and materiality of transregional relationships that have been previously perceived as dissonant, irrelevant, or accidental. Specifically, the example I will discuss allows me to reflect on how transpacific imagination proposes an aesthetic form that concretizes the subterranean economies and ecologies that are still to be made apparent in the hegemonic geopolitical models that inform institutionalized theories of "world literature."

In the summer of 2019, I was able to visit a retrospective exhibition of the Argentine-Israeli artist Mika Rottenberg at the New Museum in New York City. There, a video installation titled *Cosmic Generator* (2017) especially caught my attention. Its thematic axis, to my surprise, consisted of cinematographically exploring a system of fictional tunnels that facilitate a strange commerce between the Chinatown of Mexicali, a border city in Baja California, Mexico, and a plastic goods market in Yiwu, China. Rottenberg's aesthetic, which has already been characterized by the artist herself as "social surrealism,"[3] usually explores the (mainly women's and migrant) labor that actively, but invisibly, connects different geographies, the interstices (factories, sweatshops, offices, stores, restaurants) that assemble the globalized world. *Cosmic Generator* thus starts with a Chinese restaurant in Mexicali where a waitress, in uncovering a food tray, reveals a mysterious tunnel at its center. The camera travels through the tunnel only to reemerge at the Yiwu market. From then on, the tunnels seem to crop up in the most unexpected places, and are all guarded by a series of female characters: a food cart vendor, a sleepy employee, and so on. The montage, which combines documentary aesthetics with animation, increasingly collapses the degrees of distance between Mexico and China.[4] I was especially struck by how the China-Mexico relationship, to which I have dedicated a great part of my research, is here shown as a subterranean link whose ties remain invisible: the hasty circulation through the regions of commodities that saturate popular markets, food and tastes, and the women's work that is their binding force. The haptic effects, the sounds, the color palate in the film are all marked by a register that Naomi Polonsky calls "dystopian kitsch," and which emulates the textures of ASMR videos and wholesale commodities.[5]

In this piece, it is as if the Mexico-China relationship required fiction in order to be thought. But despite its surrealist character, the piece captures in a futuristic way a long-standing transpacific history. The border city of Mexicali was, and still is, one of the most important Chinese migration centers in Mexico. Its Chinatown, la Chinesca, is known for a series of subterranean basements that the Chinese-Mexicans who owned stores and storage houses would use to take shelter from the heat of the desert. According to popular belief, though, there were also tunnels connecting Mexicali with the city of Calexico, and they were used for transporting contraband during Prohibition, allowing Chinese migrants to cross the border clandestinely, since Chinese people were the first to be declared "undocumented immigrants" by US authorities.[6] In this sense, the history of militarization of the US-Mexico border is closely linked to the history of Chinese migration to the Americas. The exploration of the Mexicali-Calexico axis in Rottenberg's video installation points to a contemporary visibilization of the forgotten transpacific connection within the historical configuration of US-Mexico borderlands. Rottenberg's work wields a hallucinated memory that serves as a context for the recent transpacific turn in Mexico and Latin America's informal and formal economies, and which is due in part to the growing importance of China as the main commercial partner of the region. Hence, the attention to the Mexican Pacific region in Rottenberg's piece offers the possibility of a comprehensive understanding of the Americas' common history, thereby bypassing the national and linguistic divisions that inform "world literary canons."

With respect to this chapter, which aims to reflect on the difficulties that comparative hegemonic models have in capturing the transpacific Mexican relation, Rottenberg's work configures a theoretical axis to think the aesthetic and economic relations between Mexico and China, and to depict it within an imaginary framework that we may call "reproductive." The transpacific connection is narrated from the point of view of the wholesale commerce of commodities that saturate popular markets like Tepito, and which nourish the informal-popular economies. Many of these commodities come from Yiwu, China, and are transported, sold, and handled by Chinese immigrant women.[7] In general terms, the transpacific relation is thus narrated through the "feminization" of work processes that make possible the production of communication technology, in both Mexico and different localities in South and East Asia.[8] When I talk about "reproductive aesthetics," then, I am alluding to an understanding of the term that mobilizes feminist problematizations of the classical Marxist distinction between productive and reproductive labor. So-called reproductive labor is that which, although essential to the survival and production of wealth, is constantly devalued or rendered invisible. The emphasis that Rottenberg places on the problem of reproduction in order to explore the Mexico-China connection, although treated in a fictional form, allows me to comment on the critical limitations and difficulties that scholars of Asia-Latin America studies run into when they try to insert themselves into academic fields such as comparative literature, or in Anglophone debates that revolve around "world literature." Latin American literature, because it has been associated with the domain of imitation and the reproduction of metropolitan forms, has been historically affected by a devalued status in the canon of "world literature."[9] By the same token, when I started my research, every literary reference to East or South Asia in Latin American literature was considered in Latin American studies of "cheap" or "eccentric" aesthetic value because it was mainly conceptualized as an imitation, a reproduction of Orientalist European literary trends. Hence, critics in Asia-Latin American literary studies seem to be obligated to doubly justify their interventions due to the Eurocentrism of existing comparative frameworks. In response to this situation, I had to problematize both the productive/reproductive divide in the study of literary forms within "world literature" and Latin American literature, and the relationship between global precursors and reproducers.

However, I am also interested in another aspect of the reproductive angle proposed by Rottenberg: as her work suggests, the Mexico-Asia relationship has been invisibilized or disavowed—like reproductive labor and the processes of primitive accumulation—by the type of transpacific materialities—ecologies, raw materials, manufactured goods—that have historically linked Mexico and Asia since the first colonial globalization. In the case of Rottenberg's work, this is expressed by the devalued commodities that fuel the popular economy. And yet, the economy and ecology that opens up globalized transpacific commerce is the extraction of silver. From 1571 to 1815, colonial Mexico became the main source of silver in the world. This was also a time when China was its main importer, and Acapulco the most important American port for the trade with Asia.¹⁰

In light of these facts, my research on the transpacific aspect of Mexican literature, although concentrated on the twentieth century, had to delve into lineages of literary production dating back to the colonial period in order to flesh out the historicity of the Mexican intellectual and cultural orientation toward East and South Asia. As I argued in my book *Orientaciones transpacíficas: la modernidad mexicana y el espectro de Asia* [Transpacific Orientations: Mexican Modernity and the Specter of Asia], Mexico is the missing link in the history of imperial successions in the Pacific.¹¹ During the Spanish empire, the Viceroyalty of New Spain (colonial Mexico) became, because of the Manila Galleons route, the very center of the Seville-Veracruz-Acapulco-Manila route, a commercial infrastructure that directly linked Asia with the Americas through the circulation of commodities and people in both directions. In consequence, as historian Katharine Bjork explains, during a large part of the colonial period, the Philippines were conceived by Mexican *criollos*—American-born white descendants of Spanish colonists—as a territory subordinated not to Seville, but to the Viceroyalty of New Spain.¹² Nevertheless, after Mexican independence from the Spanish empire, the Mexican ambition of inheriting the colony's lucrative transpacific commerce was prematurely interrupted. Instead, the United States inherited the Iberian transpacific infrastructure previously centered in colonial Mexico: in 1898 the United States annexed the Philippines, and San Francisco—a Mexican territory until 1848—displaced Acapulco as the main port in the Americas for commercial exchange with Asia. Despite the loss of this direct commerce, in my book I argue that the transpacific connection remains fundamental for understanding Mexican literature as a worlding endeavor, and for thinking the ways in which Mexican cultural modernity was articulated not only on the basis of the European model but also through a consideration of East and South Asian modernities. In a certain way, the very sense of the world in Mexican literature is given by an opening toward the Pacific, since the colonial transpacific silver route was what allowed Mexican *criollo* writers to locate themselves at the very center of the world, as the linking territory between the Atlantic and the Pacific.¹³

Scholars in "world literature" have recently begun analyzing the importance of transpacific commerce and extractive economies in the constitution of modern literary forms. For example, in her remarkable study *The Age of Silver: The Rise of the Novel East and West* (2017), Ning Ma proposes the Sino-Spanish silver commerce (via the Acapulco-Manila route) as the material basis for establishing an " 'Anthropocenic' materialist perspective" in the study of the realist novel's simultaneous emergence in China, Japan, Spain, and England.¹⁴ In the corpus of texts selected and analyzed by Ma—the Chinese anonymous novel *The Plum in the Golden Vase* (c. 1580s or 1590s), Miguel de Cervantes's *Don Quixote* (1605, 1615), Ihara Saikaku's *Life of an Amorous Man* (1682), and Daniel Defoe's *Robinson Crusoe* (1719)—the English novel appears as "a belated response "to its Sino-Spanish precursors.¹⁵ Ma's purpose is not only to disorganize the received Eurocentric models of literary history but also to show the forgotten centrality of the East Asian world-system during global early modernity.

From a study of the "horizontal continuities" between these texts, *The Age of Silver* succeeds in "pluralizing the trajectories" of the modern novel.[16]

From the perspective of this chapter, however, I was surprised by the absence of Mexican colonial literature from Ma's corpus, which is bounded by the geographies attached to the circulation of colonial silver. As I previously discussed, colonial Mexico constituted itself as the center of the global silver route; that is, as the territorial and administrative link that allowed for the reproduction of this world-system, given that silver was extracted mainly from colonial Mexico and the Americas. In this sense, the canon of "world literature" mirrors the silver economy's international division of labor: the role of the Viceroyalty of New Spain as a "manufacturer" and producer of complex literary worlds during the silver age is imperceptible or illegible; this responds to its classification *in advance* as a colonial provider of raw materials, a *reproducer*, instead of a producer of the globalized world. However, the absence of Mexican literature in world literature scholarship is not exclusive to Ma's book, and the critical labor that she does of linking diverse literary traditions in this magnificent study is already monumental. Therefore, my interest is not, by any means, to further burden scholars who are already doing the most remarkable comparative work. On the contrary, I want to argue that *The Age of Silver* constructs a theoretical framework that could dialogue with debates around the rise of the novel in colonial Mexico, in light of the fact that Mexico occupied a central place in the commodities chains that articulated the literary age of silver that Ma associates with the emergence of the novel. As Héctor Hoyos states in a recent essay on the relationship between global supply chains and contemporary literature, "what I am attempting to do here is deploy the resources of world literature to fill the vacuum of storytelling in supply chains that, in turn, make world literature even possible."[17] This perspective could help us render legible Mexican literature's forgotten labor in linking Asia, the Americas, and Europe.

On the other hand, Mexican literature has also been particularly absent from critical literary studies dedicated to the transpacific aspect of American literature. For instance, in one of the chapters of *Emergent Worlds: Alternative States in Nineteenth-Century American Culture*, Edward Sugden purports to study US literature related to the Pacific from 1810 to 1848. This period entails significant political changes in the Pacific, ranging from the independence of Latin American countries to the signing of the Treaty of Guadalupe Hidalgo, which incorporated the California coast, until then part of Mexico, into the United States. Sugden argues that literature from this period represents an oceanic geography in transition, capable of articulating alternative literary worlds to the nationalist and imperialist accounts of the Pacific that dominate the rest of the American nineteenth century: "We must look instead, then, for the sort of fissures, discontinuities, contingencies, and chronologies that might be embedded in such moments and that work, contrary to the logic of the inevitable emergence of a glorious nation, to reveal alternative visions for the organization of history and community that might otherwise have been rendered invisible."[18] Sugden thus proposes a "Pacific literary archive" of a multilingual and transnational nature. However, despite the fact that he recognizes the importance of Mexico in this moment of political indeterminacy in the Pacific, he claims that he has not "been able to find any Mexican or Chilean reckonings of the Pacific World."[19] This lack of Mexican and Chilean archives is particularly striking if one considers that José Joaquín Fernández de Lizardi's *El periquillo sarniento* [*The Mangy Parrot: The Life of Periquillo Sarniento Written by Himself for His Children*] (1816, 1831), considered the first novel of independent Mexico (and Latin America), devotes several chapters to a transpacific journey.[20] The book, moreover, is not difficult to find even for an Anglophone public, since it is considered a canonical text in the literary history of Latin America, and its first English translation dates back to 1942. Furthermore, even before the publication of *The Mangy Parrot*, Carlos de Sigüenza y Góngora's *Infortunios de Alonso Ramírez* [The Misfortunes of Alonso Ramírez: The True Adventures of a Spanish American with 17th-Century Pirates] (1690), considered by many critics as the first novel written in colonial Spanish America, also narrates the story of a transpacific journey. Therefore, these two examples point to the importance of the silver trade in the literary genealogies that constituted the emergence of the novel in a Mexican context.

In *Emergent Worlds*, Sugden also identifies a series of literary tropes associated with the representation of the Pacific as a geography in transition: for example, the figure of what he calls "the queer immigrant," or the persistence of a subgenre that he identifies as a "Pacific Elegy," in authors such as Herman Melville, James Fenimore Cooper, and Washington Irving.[21] Interestingly, these tropes he associates with the world of a Pacific in transition find their precedent in a long-standing colonial literary tradition. By neglecting this historical precedent, one risks reproducing the very discourses on American exceptionalism that one seeks to dissipate.

I am therefore interested in inquiring about the difficulties that ensue from the confrontation between a text of early Mexican modernity and the literary corpuses that *The Age of Silver* and *Emergent Worlds* propose. Specifically, in this chapter I will analyze how the text *The Misfortunes of Alonso Ramírez* (1690) functions within these critical narratives. *The Misfortunes* can be conveniently located within the periodization proposed by Ma; it was published almost simultaneously with Saikaku's novel (1682) and precedes the publication of Defoe's *Robinson Crusoe* (1719) and *The Further Adventures of Robinson Crusoe* (1719). The exclusion of this text from Anglophone debates around "world literature" is due in part to its limited circulation in translation, or what Ignacio Sánchez Prado calls the problem of "uneven distribution" of Mexican literature in general.[22] However, the most determining factor of this generalized exclusion responds to the privilege that studies on world literature, even the one mentioned earlier, tend to give to the novel as the marker of modernity in literature par excellence.[23] This certainly disqualifies the hybridity that characterizes colonial textualities and renders them invisible beforehand from the study of "world literature" in early modernity.

For this reason, the first difficulty we encounter when attempting to place *The Misfortunes* within debates on the global emergence of the novel, as proposed by Ma, is that the text's genre has been the object of a sophisticated debate within Latin American colonial studies. In a nutshell, *The Misfortunes* narrates the circumstances behind the voyage of Alonso Ramírez, a low commoner *criollo* subject, from his native island of Puerto Rico to the Philippines. Due to a series of events that include the capture of the character and his crew by an English pirate ship, the voyage turns into a trip around the world and concludes with a disenchanted return to his native Caribbean and to Mexico City. Although critics have long considered the book the "first Latin American novel,"[24] the truth is that its parameters of reception and production place it, rather, within the colonial nonfiction genre of the *relación*.[25] Nevertheless, in no way does this formal indeterminacy detract from its modern literary character. As Martínez-San Miguel has noted, the final objective of the text was to serve as entertainment for the court, so "this transposition from the official register of the *relación* (relatio) in the sixteenth century to the fictional nature of a *relato* (relatus) marks the foundation of literature as a modern institution in which political representation takes an alternative (symbolic) route as the Spanish empire faces the early crisis of its overseas aspirations in the seventeenth century."[26] Moreover, the complexity of its classification also stems from the fact that the text claims a double authorship. It presents itself as the veridical testimony of Ramírez, but the official author is one of the most important *criollo* intellectuals and baroque authors of the Mexican colonial period: Carlos de Sigüenza y Góngora (1645–1700), cosmographer and professor of mathematics of the Mexican Academy. The novel is thus written in the first person, that of Ramírez (a trait that ties it to travel writing and to the picaresque novel), but is addressed, like the *relación* and the *crónica de Indias*, to the Viceroy of New Spain. Thus, a large part of the criticism about the novel has delved into the complexities of this *criollo* double authorship, which makes reading the text's political agendas complicated, since there is a power hierarchy between both subjects that constantly creates tension in the narrative's becoming. As Mabel Moraña has argued, the complex use of the first person in the narrative configures a "critical I," which coincides with the literary structuralization of a *criollo* discourse understood as a position of "viceroyal marginality."[27] Ramírez's voice is ambiguous and at times contradictory with the account of ideal serfdom to the Spanish empire that the paratexts of the text explicitly try to make. This tensed-up narrative framework is certainly common to the *crónica de Indias*. However, it is worth wondering if the hybridity at play in this text is not precisely the condition of possibility of the novel in a Spanish colonial context, since there was an explicit prohibition to read, print, or publish novels in colonial America as of 1531. Therefore, my intention is not to defend a first-order *belonging* of *The Misfortunes* to the genre of novel, insofar as this genre has been defined by metropolitan "technologies of recognition."[28] Rather, following Jacque Derrida's ideas in "The Law of Genre," I prefer to envision it as a kind of *participation* in the global set of texts that appear during the same period, and which are connected by the silver route. I understand the demarcations between the aforementioned genres not as closures but as folds, as continuities toward a generic and extratextual exterior.[29]

In this sense, I follow Dimock's and Ma's criteria when they propose a model of literary comparison that is alternative to the diffusionist formats of the "tree" or the "wave" used by critics such as Franco Moretti, and which wagers on the redefinition of literary genres based on degrees of affinity and shared contexts.[30] Under this comparative methodology, *The Misfortunes* participates in an innovative way in the demarcation criteria of the novel genre proposed by Ma, which stems from her rereading of critics such as Georg Lukács, Fredric Jameson, and Mikhail Bakhtin. In *The Age of Silver*, Ma defines the selection criteria for her novels in the following way:

> The cases we have further suggest that the representation weight assumed by these characters of lower social tiers functions to enact *dramas of mobility*. Their biographies are thus allegories of a collective process of deconstitution and reconstitution, a process wherein the individual is no longer a fixed component within a transcendentally ordained identity system, but a transmutable part within the secular domain of horizontal exchange. In this light, the texts in question all engage with the spiritually hollowing yet politically equalizing forces of money and commerce, or what we can otherwise name *the national problem of materiality*. The novelistic modernity at the center of my comparative inquiry then connotes a *nationally symbolic realist mode*, which emerged at both ends of the Eurasian continent during the Age of Silver in response to a historical condition of "transcendental homelessness."[31]

Due to its colonial context, then, *The Misfortunes* dramatizes these characteristics in a particularly complex form. The text recounts the biography of Alonso Ramírez, a *criollo* colonial subject native to the island of Puerto Rico, illegitimate son (as is typical of picaresque novels) of Andalusian ship's carpenter Lucas de Villanueva and Ana Ramírez. It is Ramírez's condition as a peripheral subject that "enacts the dramas of mobility" in the text. The book narrates Ramírez's attempts to escape the manual labor of ship's carpenter forced on him by his father and birthplace: "My father was a ship's carpenter and imposed on me, when my age permitted it, the same employment."[32] As José Buscaglia-Salgado argues, "There could be no doubt that the protection and defense of the imperial frontier was Ramírez's birthright, his burdensome duty as a child of the treasure fleets and as a native of the place we might call . . . San Juan de la Frontera [Saint John of the Border]."[33] Ramírez's characterization as a "child of the treasure fleets" (*la flota*) allows us to place the text in a particularly privileged way within the geographies, infrastructures, materialities, and subjectivities created by the silver trade, what Ma calls "the national problem of materiality." Being a child of the *flota* entailed being charged by birth with materially (re)producing the convoy system used to protect the ships transporting commodities between the Pacific, the Americas, and Spain, in other words the infrastructure that linked the commodity chains of the silver trade.

As Martínez-San Miguel analyzes, the Caribbean islands were considered during this time a mainly *Mexican archipelago*, charged with the military defense of the Viceroyalty of New Spain, and completely dependent on the Viceroyal treasure, the so-called Mexican *situado*, which periodically arrived by boat.[34] In Ramírez's account, the discourse of ideal serfdom that underpins the Spanish empire's structures of privilege was already undermined by a language that emulated the economic discourses associated by Ma with "the forces of money and commerce or what we can otherwise name *the national problem of materiality*."[35] Ramírez describes the material difficulties of fulfilling his duties as an island subject in a language that suggests that the material bankruptcy of the island makes it harder to "repay the moral debt" that is imposed on him as an islander:

> Native islanders *repay the debt* which these merits impose with a sense of due honor and loyalty, despite the alterations of time. For *the riches* it [Puerto Rico/ Rich Port]was named after have vanished; the veins of gold that could be found through the island are no longer mined for lack of the original natives to work them; tempestuous hurricanes razed the chocolate trees which came in due time to supplant gold as a means of trafficking in life's necessities; and thus, in the case of islanders born in recent years, *yesterday's riches have become today's penury*.[36]

In this sense, if *Robinson Crusoe*, a novel which is almost contemporary with *The Misfortunes*, presents the geography of the Caribbean island as a literary chronotope without history, as an isolated geography where the *homo economicus* can recreate *ex nihilo* a capitalist fantasy, the archipelagic perspective of *The Misfortunes*, on the contrary, presents an integrated archipelagic reality conditioned beforehand by the financial and material instability of the global extractive economies. The island seems subjected to financial, military, and environmental conditions that are out of its control; it is the historical place marked by debt, poverty, and environmental disaster. To be sure, both texts share this economic substrate. However, we can say that if *Robinson Crusoe* represents the fantasy of capitalism as a purely productive and self-generative model, *The Misfortunes* instead presents an archipelagic perspective on island labor and on the reproduction of capitalism at a global level. Thus, any similarity to contemporary reality in Puerto Rico is not a coincidence. This is precisely what I was referring to when I argued that the history of US imperialist interventions in the Atlantic and the Pacific gains intelligibility when studied from the perspective of Mexican colonial history.

The passage just quoted explains the reason why the narrator decides to migrate to Mexico: "I determined to steal myself from my own land to seek more convenience in foreign ones."[37] Ramírez employs a language associated with stealing and contraband to justify abandoning his island's military enclave, and therefore, not repaying the colonial debt. After various unsuccessful attempts in Puebla, Mexico City, and Oaxaca to escape manual labor and to gain social mobility, the narrator resigns himself to a second major migration: "I despaired of ever turning myself into a person of consequence, and finding that in the tribunal of my conscience I had not only accused but condemned myself for being useless, my determination became to receive the sentence meted out to delinquents in Mexico, namely, exile in the Philippine Islands."[38] This time, the narrator presents his desire for social mobility as a kind of self-punishment. As Anna More analyzes, Ramírez's "self-exile" to the Philippines reflects "the abandonment of both the picaresque frame and the Atlantic geography that dominates most texts of the Spanish Empire."[39] For the purposes of this chapter, it is important to note that entry into the transpacific circuit is what marks the creolization of Mexican novelesque narrative.

In this sense, we can say that the "nationally symbolic realist mode" of which Ma speaks in relation to the emergence of the novel, associated with the historical condition of "transcendental homelessness" proposed by Lukács, appears precisely at the moment in the narrative where Ramírez's character embarks on the Manila galleons.[40] This is because Ramírez's discourse takes the law into his own hands by applying to himself a means of punishment traditionally used against poor white *criollos* for urban vagrancy during the Viceroyalty. As More argues:

> In substituting the vassal for the sovereign, the narrative reads this distance as a crisis rather than a break: the *criollo* commoner, becoming both executioner and executed, preserves the law by internalizing it in the "tribunal of my own conscience." Thus, as the patrimonial system that linked the two sides of the Atlantic breaks down, sovereignty itself becomes the province of the individual.[41]

In this particular case, the transpacific silver route serves as the historical condition of possibility for the process of subjective individuation by the narrative voice from the Spanish imperial system of patrimonialism. As argued before, the narrative opening toward the Pacific inaugurates in literature a sense of subjectivity vis-à-vis a world.

In the Philippines, the narrator moves from ship's carpenter to independent merchant. Just as in *The Mangy Parrot* (1816), the transpacific voyage of the Mexican *criollo* coincides with his social and economic mobility, which demonstrates the central role that the Pacific plays in New Spanish *criollos*' dreams of political and economic autonomy. The narrator describes the Pacific islands in the following way:

> There is much abundance in those islands, and you can especially enjoy those offered by the city of Manila. Whatever you desire for sustenance and raiment is easily available there for a moderate price. . . . Through this occupation, I not only trafficked in profitable commerce which promised great returns in the future but also saw many cities and ports in the East Indies on my several voyages. . . . I visited Batavia, a most famous city. . . . The concourse of Malay, Macassar, Sianes [sic], Bugises, Chinese, Armenian, French, English, Danish, Portuguese, and Castilian ships are innumerable. Any European manufacture may be found in this emporium as well as those which Asia sends back in exchange. . . . I might say to sum up that the entire World is encompassed in this city.[42]

This passage contrasts with the "poor ports" of the Caribbean-Atlantic system from which the character hails. As Martínez-San Miguel has noted in her analysis of the novel, in "the routes traveled by Ramírez and reimagined by Sigüenza y Góngora, the Atlantic network had a secondary and almost dependent place *vis-à-vis* the Asia-America-Europe connection that is portrayed as the new mercantile center of the universe."[43] In this sense, *The Misfortunes* resembles *The Further Adventures of Robinson Crusoe* (1719), the sequel to *Robinson Crusoe*, which takes place in East Asia, and where, as Ma claims, Defoe expresses his worry about the lack of British economic centrality during the first colonial modernity.[44] By shifting the action toward Asia, *The Misfortunes* also contradicts hegemonic accounts that place Europe at the center of the world-system. The presence of European ships in these islands shows not only a Pacific in transition where various imperial systems coexist in competition but also the desire of these European powers to gain access to the center of the world-system, represented here by the archipelagos that surround the Chinese empire.

As the narrative unfolds, Ramírez's life takes a drastic turn when an English pirate ship in Cavite captures the frigate he was captaining. The account then concentrates on narrating the horrors committed by the English "barbarians" in the different Pacific islands or the Indian Ocean, as well as the humiliations and episodes of physical and psychological torture suffered by Ramírez, together with his crew, for a period of two years.[45] On this vessel, Ramírez circumnavigates the world, until the pirates reach the Cape of New Hope and the Brazilian coasts. After various negotiations, Ramírez convinces the pirates to free his remaining crew and himself in a frigate loaded with munitions close to the Lesser Antilles. Martínez-San Miguel argues that this tortuous path, which allows him to return to the Caribbean, and which entailed capture, slavery, disorientation, and suspicion, makes it possible for Ramírez to negatively "recover" his identity as a Spanish subject and colonial vassal: "Once he recovers his freedom, Ramírez becomes a quite defective leader of his failing expedition, since he is unable to recognize the regions of the Caribbean he abandoned when he was thirteen years old."[46] In his native Caribbean, Ramírez finds a hostile territory, stalked by other European powers. His mixed-race crew refuses to replenish the ship in French- and English-occupied Caribbean islands, for fear of being enslaved due to the color of their skin: "My companions, however, were greatly opposed to my reasoning . . . addressing themselves to the color of their skin and the fact that they were not Spaniards, argued that they would be made slaves upon the instant and pledged it would pain them less to be sent headlong into the ocean by my hands than to place themselves into those of foreigners and endure their mistreatment."[47] Thus, the return to the Caribbean marks the closing or impoverishment of the world as a habitable space, or the impossibility of the world itself under imperialism.

Based on the foregoing, we can identify *The Misfortunes* as a form of narrating the transpacific world during full imperial succession, with what Sugden calls the subgenre of "the Pacific Elegy," and which he locates in the works of Cooper and Melville during the nineteenth century: "a set of texts that memorialized and lamented the passing of the transitional Pacific world with the coming of an increasingly ossified world-system and its corollary in that ocean, the US-inflected nation-state."[48] Even if *The Misfortunes* predates the American incursion into the region by at least a century, the brief, but nostalgic, evocation of Ramírez's five years spent as a free merchant in the Pacific, before his captivity, contrasts with the oppression felt by the character in his native archipelago, a sea "ossified" by a sustained imperial occupation.

In *Through Other Continents*, Dimock proposes literary culture as "the lexical form" of "global civil society," this last notion understood as "a sphere of life that is both smaller and larger than the territorial regime: it is subnational in one sense, transnational in another. This duality of scale means that its sphere of action is on either side of the state apparatus."[49] "World literature" would thus allow us to think the articulation between different civil formations on larger or smaller scales as dictated by the different historical forms of sovereignty. In this sense, the study of colonial literature is essential to the constitution of the different literary modernities, especially those united by the silver route. *The Misfortunes* explores precisely the civilian networks and types of subjectivities that were hierarchically articulated in the border zones of different imperial formations in the Atlantic and the Pacific.

For example, through his narrative, Sigüenza y Góngora describes Ramírez's crew in language that reproduces the caste system of the Spanish empire:

> Here are the names of those from the original twenty-five in my Company who were freed at this place . . . Juan de Casas, a Spaniard born in Puebla de los Angeles New Spain, Juan Pinto and Marcos de la Cruz, the former a Pangasinan Indian and the latter a Pampanpango Indian [Philippine Islanders]; Francisco de la Cruz and Antonio Gonzalez, *sangleyes* [Chinese immigrants on Luzon]; Juan Diaz, a Malabar Indian; and Pedro, a black boy from Mozambique who was my slave.[50]

The text casts Ramírez's character, the white *criollo* captain, as a paternal figure for the rest of the crew, most of whom come from the Asian and African borders of the Spanish empire. The vulnerability of these bodies on dry land points to the representation of their community of place as only viable in the transitional geography of the ocean. None of these subjects has a place where they can disembark and exist outside of slavery or colonial serfdom. However, especially for Pedro, even the frigate is not a space free of colonial hierarchization and enslavement. Thus, the frigate on the high seas functions as a literary chronotope that captures in a particularly dramatic way the historical condition of "transcendental homelessness" that Ma invokes. As Buscaglia-Salgado notes, "Alonso Ramírez was captain of a motley crew that was representative of the vast geography of the *flota*. His ship was manned by men whom Washington Irving . . . would have seen as a collection of mongrels and vile rabble."[51] The Irving reference is interesting because he is also one of the authors Sugden studies in *Emergent Worlds*. Sugden identifies this type of sea character, belonging to a multiracial and multilingual labor force, as one of the most habitual figures of American literature about the Pacific from 1810 to 1845: the character of the "queer immigrant." Hence, these characters "who came from local tribal island communities," and who were characterized by "the desire of perpetual movement" and of inhabiting oceanic imperial blind spots, find important precedents in texts such as *The Misfortunes*.[52]

Therefore, we can say that the utopian connotations that concepts such as "global civil society" and "transcendental homelessness" entail, even after being stripped of Eurocentric origins, as Dimock and Ma do, are partially undone when confronted by colonial textualities. The study of the emergence of the novel-form in a colonial context shows that coloniality is not the prehistory of the modern novel, but rather its most disavowed contemporary. The literary contribution of *The Misfortunes* is precisely that of speculating on new forms of citizenship and subjective positionalities in the context of early global capitalism. Bearing in mind the double perspective of the text, that of the elite and the common *criollo* subject, More, for one, argues that Sigüenza y Góngora theorizes through his emplotment of Ramírez's story "new forms of recognition tied to citizenship" at the moment when social hierarchies in the Atlantic imperial system are being loosened due to the impact of the exchange economies associated with the East-West global market. According to More, for Sigüenza y Góngora, "these subjects [the Creole commoners] could nonetheless be incorporated into a nascent polity composed of more horizontal social relations."[53] Following this reading, Sigüenza y Góngora's *criollo* project would consist of proposing "an autonomous form of Creole citizenship" charged with protecting and reinforcing the hierarchy of values of the Spanish imperial system and its territorial unity based on virtue and the white racial lineage in light of the new economic and political context.[54]

Nevertheless, Buscaglia-Salgado and Martínez-San Miguel advance a different reading; one which draws alternative political subtexts from the analysis of Sigüenza y Góngora's narration. For instance, they analyze the use of the ellipsis, and Ramírez's reticence and silences, to argue that *The Misfortunes* delves into spheres of life that escape civilian or citizen modes of subjectivation typical of colonialism, imperialism, and (proto-)nationalism. What's more, Martínez-San Miguel sees the text as a failed epic: "I focus on the constitution of Ramírez as an anti-hero and a possible pirate to question the hegemony of the Spanish order in the articulation of the Caribbean and the Philippines as archipelagic heterotopias for the Spanish empire."[55] These two divergent readings (More and Martínez-San Miguel) decidedly allow me to place the text within the corpus of novels organized by Ma in *The Age of Silver*: "Their biographies are thus allegories of a collective process of deconstitution and reconstitution, a process wherein the individual is no longer a fixed component within a transcendentally ordained identity system, but a transmutable part within the secular domain of horizontal exchange."[56]

By inserting a text such as *The Misfortunes* into the debate on the global emergence of the novel, in this chapter I have aimed to reconsider the valuation systems that render invisible or that marginalize the study of Mexican literature as world literature. *The Misfortunes*' experimentation with different forms of citizenship and subjective disidentification in the context of a world geography in transition allows us to emphasize the colonial genesis of the discursive grammars that configured the so-called global civil society. *The Misfortunes* stages the reproductive economies, materialities, and subjectivities that linked the Eurasian world-systems during early modernity. For this reason, the text makes visible the role of colonial Mexico in what Lisa Lowe has called "the political economy" between continents in the rise of liberal modernity: "I use the concept of intimacy as a heuristic, and a means to observe the historical division of world processes into those that develop modern liberal subjects and modern spheres of social life, and those processes that are forgotten, cast as failed or irrelevant because they do not produce 'value' legible within the modern classification."[57] Although Lowe is not referring to the study of "world literature" when she speaks of these "modern classification systems," her idea allows us to problematize self-generative and monoglossic notions like the ones *Robinson Crusoe* puts into play concerning the emergence of liberalism, "global civil society," and the novel as its preferred literary analogue.

Notes

1. Wai Chee Dimock, *Through Other Continents: American Literature across Deep Time* (Princeton: Princeton University Press, 2009), 4.
2. Ibid., 3.
3. Mika Rottenberg, "Mika Rottenberg Interview: Social Surrealism," interview by Christian Lund, *Louisiana Channel*, September 5, 2017, video, https://www.youtube.com/watch?v=V_eKV76E2K8.
4. Margot Norton, "Not-So-Easy Pieces," in *Mika Rottenberg Easypieces*, ed. Margot Norton (New York: New Museum, 2019), 16.
5. Naomi Polonsky, "Surreal Glimpses of the Absurd Labor of Global Capitalism," *Hyperallergic*, October 17, 2018, https://hyperallergic.com/465694/mika-rottenberg-goldsmiths-centre for-contemporary-arts/.
6. Robert Chao Romero, *The Chinese in Mexico, 1882–1940* (Tucson: University of Arizona Press, 2010), 31. For an analysis on how contemporary Mexican literature reflects this history, see Laura J. Torres-Rodríguez, "'Esto es un Western': el giro norte mexicano hacia el Pacífico en la literatura mexicana contemporánea," *Revista de Crítica Literaria Latinoamericana* 44, no. 87 (2018): 89–111.
7. Ximena Alba Villareal and Felipe Rubio, "New Patterns of Chinese Migration to the Americas: Mexico City and Lima," in *New Migration Patterns in the Americas: Challenges for the 21st Century*, ed. Andreas E. Feldmann, Xóchitl Bada, and Stephanie Schütze (New York: Palgrave Macmillan, 2018), 276.
8. In my book, I analyze the references to Asia in diverse literary and artistic border practices linked to the presence of Japanese and Korean *maquiladoras* on the US-Mexico border. Due to the structural similarities between the Economic Special Zones in East Asia and the *maquila* industry in Mexico, these references reflect on the processes of "feminization" of labor that make the production of technology possible. Laura J. Torres-Rodríguez, *Orientaciones transpacíficas: la modernidad mexicana y el espectro de Asia* (Chapel Hill: North Carolina Studies in the Romance Languages and Literatures, 2019), 213.
9. Ignacio Sánchez Prado, *Strategic Occidentalism: On Mexican Fiction, The Neoliberal Book Market, and the Question of World Literature* (Evanston: Northwestern University Press, 2018), 8.
10. Jason Oliver Chang, "Four Centuries of Imperial Succession in the *Comprador* Pacific," *Pacific Historical Review* 86, no. 2 (2017): 198.
11. Torres-Rodríguez, *Orientaciones transpacíficas*, 19.
12. Katharine Bjork, "The Link That Kept the Philippines Spanish: Mexican Merchant Interests and the Manila Trade, 1571–1815," *Journal of World History* 9, no. 1 (1998): 50.
13. Barbara Fuchs and Yolanda Martínez-San Miguel, "'La grandeza mexicana' de Balbuena y el imaginario de una 'metrópolis colonial,'" *Revista Iberoamericana* 75, no. 228 (2009): 677.
14. Ma, *The Age of Silver: The Rise of the Novel East and West* (Oxford: Oxford University Press, 2017), 6.
15. Ibid., 13.
16. Ibid., 6.
17. Héctor Hoyos, "Global Supply Chain Literature Vs. Extractivism," in *Re-mapping World Literature: Writing, Book Markets and Epistemologies between Latin America*

and the Global South, ed. Gesine Muller, Jorge Locane, and Benjamin Loy (Berlin: De Gruyter, 2018), 40.
18 Edward Sugden, *Emergent Worlds: Alternative States in Nineteenth-Century American Literature* (New York: New York University Press, 2018), 38–9.
19 Ibid., 45.
20 For an analysis of *The Mangy Parrot* from a transpacific perspective see Koichi Hagimoto, "A Transpacific Voyage: The Representation of Asia in José Joaquín Fernández de Lizardi's *El periquillo sarniento*," *Hispania* 95, no. 3 (2012): 389–99. For a reading of the text from the perspective of the silver trade, see Laura Torres-Rodríguez, "Into the 'Oriental' Zone: Edward Said and Mexican Literature," in *Mexican Literature in Theory*, ed. Ignacio Sánchez Prado (London: Bloomsbury Publishing, 2018).
21 Sugden, *Emergent Worlds*, 31.
22 Sánchez Prado, *Strategic Occidentalism*, 15.
23 Ignacio Sánchez Prado, "Writing the Necropolitical: Notes around the Idea of Mexican Anti-World Literature," in *World Literature and Dissent*, ed. Lorna Burns and Katie Muth (London: Routledge, 2019), chap. 8, Kindle.
24 Aníbal Gonzalez, "*Infortunios de Alonso Ramírez*: picaresca e historia," *Hispanic Review* 51, no. 2 (1983): 189–204.
25 In general terms, the *relación* consisted of a report made to a judge or court as part of a juridical process. It also included texts drafted by the *letrados* in charge of preparing cases with the help of autobiographical documents. They would normally be written in the form of sworn statements made before a notary and would be obtained following a special request by the Viceroy. Julio López-Arias, "El género en *Los infortunios de Alonso Ramírez*," *Hispanic Journal* 15, no. 1 (1994): 193.
26 Yolanda Martínez-San Miguel, *From Lack to Excess: "Minor" Readings of Latin American Colonial Discourse* (Lewisburg: Bucknell University Press, 2010), 152.
27 Mabel Moraña, "Máscara autobiográfica y conciencia criolla en *Infortunios de Alonso Ramírez*," *Dispositio* 15, no. 4 (1990): 112.
28 Shu-Mei Shih, "Global Literature and the Technologies of Recognition," *PMLA* 119, no. 1 (2004): 17.
29 Jacques Derrida, "The Law of Genre," trans. Avital Ronell, *Critical Inquiry* 7, no. 1 (1980): 55–81.
30 Ma, *The Age of Silver*, 39.
31 Ibid., 44.
32 Carlos Sigüenza y Góngora, *The Misfortunes of Alonso Ramírez: The True Adventures of a Spanish American with 17th-Century Pirates*, trans. Fabio López Lázaro (Austin: University of Texas Press, 2011), 107.
33 José F. Buscaglia-Salgado, *Undoing Empire: Race and Nation in the Mulatto Caribbean*, (Minneapolis: University of Minnesota Press, 2003), 142.
34 Yolanda Martínez-San Miguel, "Colonial and Mexican Archipelagoes: Reimagining Colonial Caribbean Studies," in *Archipelagic American Studies*, ed. Brian Russell Roberts and Michelle Ann Stephens (Durham: Duke University Press, 2017), 157.
35 Ma, *The Age of Silver*, 44.
36 Sigüenza y Góngora, *The Misfortunes*, 107 (emphasis added).
37 Ibid.
38 Ibid., 110.

39 Anna More, *Baroque Sovereignty: Carlos Sigüenza y Góngora and the Creole Archive of Colonial Mexico*, (Philadelphia: University of Pennsylvania Press, 2013), 220.
40 Ma, *The Age of Silver*, 44.
41 More, *Baroque Sovereignty*, 220.
42 Sigüenza y Góngora, *The Misfortunes*, 112–13.
43 Martínez-San Miguel, *From Lack to Excess*, 162.
44 Ma, *The Age of Silver*, 43.
45 It is important to emphasize that the episodes of torture will not be narrated in Chapter 3 with the rest of the events of Ramírez and his crew's captivity. Rather, they will be told retrospectively in Chapter 4, after his liberation. Since it has already been well studied by other critics of the text, I will not concern myself with this ellipsis and disruption of the linear development of the story, which adds a psychological element to the construction of the narrative voice.
46 Martínez-San Miguel, *From Lack to Excess*, 156.
47 Sigüenza y Góngora, *The Misfortunes*, 133.
48 Sugden, *Emergent Worlds*, 72.
49 Dimock, *Through Other Continents*, 8.
50 Sigüenza y Góngora, *The Misfortunes*, 126.
51 Buscaglia-Salgado, *Undoing Empire*, 163.
52 Sugden, *Emergent Worlds*, 66.
53 More, *Baroque Sovereignty*, 205.
54 Ibid., 207.
55 Martínez-San Miguel, *Coloniality of Diasporas: Rethinking Intra-Colonial Migrations in a Pan-Caribbean Context* (New York: Palgrave Macmillan, 2014), 24.
56 Ma, *The Silver Age*, 44.
57 Lisa Lowe, *The Intimacies of Four Continents* (Durham: Duke University Press, 2015), 18.

5

World-Making in Nineteenth-Century Mexico

Shelley Garrigan

This chapter offers an exploration of how the founding phases of Mexican national literature and cultural institutions developed in dialogue with world contexts. Because of the coincidence of Mexican independence, political consolidation, and the entrance into Occidental markets, the nineteenth century offers a ripe vantage point from which to assess the evidence of an acute awareness of the inceptions of global culture during the phases of institutionalization of the core bases of Mexican national patrimony. From its origins, literary tradition was wedded to institutional growth in Mexico. During the second half of the century, several foundational cultural organizations arose that marked the intersection of national political consolidation and modernization in Mexico. Institutions such as the *Academia de Letrán* (1833–9) and the *Biblioteca Nacional* (1884) were bolsters for the social imperatives of progress and order that describe the national political and cultural climate of the late nineteenth century and also precursors to globalization in the constitution of an institutionalized social capital that put Mexico in dialogue with Western economic and cultural currents. Through the lenses of institutionalized cultural contexts, with a focus on the various ways in which Western letters intersected with the Mexican public arena, this chapter traces the ways in which the founding phases of modern Mexican literature involved a parallel and strategic configuration of cosmopolitan Others.

A core consideration here is the recognition that the well-examined processes of national development that occurred in nineteenth-century Mexico did so in conjunction with the fashioning of a series of images of the cosmopolitan "world," or the hegemonic system of values in which social, economic, and cultural status both influenced and in turn were affected by the discourses, infrastructures, and articulations of the nation. In the case of Mexico, the multiple dialogues with Western political, economic, and cultural models have been approached in terms of both the rejection of the colonial past and the Spanish literary and cultural legacy on the one hand, and the active seeking of modern and progressive trends represented by the West (with emphasis on France) on the other. While there is critical consensus in approaching the "national" and the "cosmopolitan" as standing in theoretical and practical tension with one another, this perspective risks overlooking the important ways in which national cultural edification occurred in dialogue with the *internal* production of versions and visions of the cosmopolitan world. What follows, then, is an exploration of the simultaneous, mutual, and contiguous nature of national cultural consolidation and "world" consciousness in this particular context. In this investigation, I explore two of the key representative cultural institutions that span different decades within the nineteenth century and offer unique vantage points through which this process can be traced: the *Academia de Letrán* and the *Biblioteca Nacional*.

The *Academia de Letrán*

Founded by brothers José María and Juan Nepomuceno Lacunza as well as Manuel Tossiat Ferrer and Guillermo Prieto, the *Academia de Letrán* (1836–8) enters history not only as one of the key birthplaces of modern Mexican literature but also as a democratic and collaborative space in which writers of different ages, social classes, and political creeds gathered to discuss, debate, and create a common literature capable of representing and reflecting the circumstances of an independent and identity-hungry Mexico. Recognized since the nineteenth century in Mexican intellectual circles as the first "effort to reflect on Mexican literature and its public function," the *Academia de Letrán* offers a curious viewpoint to examine the intricate bonds between the configuration of the national and the "world."[1] Brought into the arena of recent critical discussions due to the work of scholars such as Marco Antonio Campos and Víctor Barrera Enderle,[2] the *Academia* provides an important venue from which to consider the foundational connections that bind the art of self-definition to the reception of Western cultural products.

While much investigation has been dedicated to the Mexicanization of letters and the publications through which they gained cultural legitimacy during the nineteenth century,[3] the strong presence of the Western literary tradition during this process presents more of a methodological challenge. While studies focusing on late-century *modernismo* and its contiguous cultural expressions have modeled innovative ways to complicate and invert the apparent contradictions between national and cosmopolitan letters,[4] the task becomes more challenging as the critical lens shifts closer toward the earlier part of the century, when the independent nation was fairly new and its cultural expressions still tentative. As a result, critical engagement may dismiss the presence of Western letters as distractions from the question of what was happening nationally, or deal with the Western literary tradition as an influence,[5] or read national and foreign or "cosmopolitan" letters as standing in opposition to one another.[6] While acknowledging the legitimacy of these approaches, it is possible to pursue a more nuanced reading of the dialogues between self and Other that impacted national cultural consolidation, and to explore how Mexican writers consumed the works of Western authors during the decades following independence in full awareness of what was at stake.

The overlap between the decades following Mexican independence and the translation, publication, and circulation of the literary works among nations considered to be of "high" cultural, economic, and political status has opened some promising lines of inquiry. In *Inéditos del siglo XIX*,[7] Lilia Vieyra Sánchez offers a thorough exploration of the circulation and critical reception of writers Víctor Hugo (1802–85), Jules Verne (1850–1905) and Adolfo Llanos y Álcaraz (1840–1904) in Mexican print culture based on the interactions of editors, newspapers, magazines, and readers during the second half of the nineteenth century. Along similar lines, the Mexican-French collaborative project that produced Lise Andries and Laura Suárez de la Torre's *Impressions du Mexique et de France: Impresiones de México y de Francia* offers a transcultural, transnational, and bilingual perspective on nineteenth-century periodical publications and specifies, among many other relevant points, the ways in which cultural "borrowings" from France responded to internal political tensions in Mexico:

> The borrowings from France and the European continent could only occur in the measure in which they responded to specific needs linked, for example, to the political situation of the country; in this way, the reception of Renan in Mexico or the decision, on the part of Mexican newspapers, to publish French or Spanish serial novels seems to be linked to the fight of influences between liberals and conservatives.[8]

While this point regarding liberal and conservative visions (and productions) of the world offers an important opportunity for expanding the present discussion, important here is the observation of agency on the receiving end of cosmopolitan consumption: in nineteenth-century Mexico, the world shows up by invitation and in ways that reflect and propel specifically national concerns.

Casting a broader lens, Andrea Pagni has written several illuminating articles that address the translation and dissemination of European literature in nineteenth-century Latin America and its role in the creation and evolution of the Spanish language and a series of national cultural identities that were distinct from both that of Spain and the colonial era.[9] Although they focus on different positions with respect to the influx of Western cultural products in Mexico and the rest of the Latin America, then, together these investigations approach transnational cultural currents in ways that shift the critical lens toward the specific political and material circumstances under which the world actually *happened* in Mexico and Latin America during the post-independence era.

In their descriptions of the *Academia de Letrán*, both Víctor Barrera Enderle and Marco Antonio Campos reference the importance of foreign literary canons. In his contribution to *A History of Mexican Literature*, Enderle writes about the controversial arrival of the God-denying Ignacio Ramírez, who "encouraged his peers to read Víctor Hugo and Alexandre Dumas" while mapping out a scientific and universal approach to literature with a "spatial dimension" that must not be "limited to local phenomena."[10] Along a similar vein, Campos points out the *Academia* writers' efforts to distance themselves from Spanish lettered culture and their tendency to look to French, Italian, and English models as fodder for their literary explorations. He also identifies several factors that contribute to this phenomenon, including the scarce circulation of Mexican (and/or Latin American) literature at the time, the fact that consumption was limited to those historical and contemporary books which could be found in Spanish translation, and the recent colonial legacy that could not be shed overnight.[11]

Reaching beyond the question of influence and not yet pushing into the era of "cosmopolitan desires" that Mariano Suskind identifies in fin de siglo Latin American literary culture,[12] further examination of the connection between the national and the international in the formative phases of modern Mexican letters reveals a pattern of consumption that highlights the interdependence of self-construction and the role of Western publications. How and where do cosmopolitanism and nationalism coincide, without ruling either of them out? Although the *Academia de Letrán* serves as the primary focus for this section, due to its foundational role, the lines of inquiry opened here are applicable to several other key foundational literary institutions of nineteenth-century Mexico, including the three phases of the *Liceo Hidalgo*, the *Veladas literarias* of 1867–8, the *Liceo Mexicano* and its product,[13] the renowned literary nineteenth-century literary newspaper *El Renacimiento*, directed by the author/politician, mentor, and fierce advocate for national letters Ignacio Altamirano (1834–93), whose frequent, profound, and comprehensive treatment of Western authors and letters appear throughout the newspaper and again in volume II of his complete works.[14]

While respecting the individual contributions of each and in addition to their protagonism in the foundation and development of Mexican letters, one point of convergence for these institutions is the fact that their contributing authors consistently read, translated, analyzed, and published commentary on the Western literary tradition, even as the availability and frequency of treatment of Mexican authors and literary works increased over time. This binding of Western cultural *consumption* and national *production*, in turn, produces a rhetorical reformulation of time in which the full actualization of Mexican letters is framed as both inevitable—given the rapid rate of maturation that ensued once political stability allowed for it—and suspended or projected into the indefinite future. Product cedes center stage to process, and in the absence of a fully formed canon, Mexican writers published not only new and exploratory writing but also, in various ways, models of Western cultural consumption. In the section dedicated to the *Academia de Letrán* in Guillermo Prieto's canonical *Memorias de mis tiempos* (1906), the first reference to European letters appears in the form of a set of gaudy prints of *Atala* (Chateaubriand, 1801) and *William Tell* (popularized by Schiller's 1803–4 dramatical rendition) that decorate the stained walls of the degraded venues surrounding the *Colegio de Letrán,* along with a mishmash of other items that together paint the picture of an unlikely setting for a meeting of great minds:

> Un santo con su lamparilla ardiendo; el brasero á la puerta, la cama escondida, [. . .] tales eran aquellos antros de degradación.
>
> [A saint with his burning oil lamp, the brazier at the door, the bed hidden, [. . .] such were those cheap places of degradation].[15]

Similarly, and with a touch of humor, Prieto describes the impaired state of the "pestilent," smokey kitchen of the *Colegio de Letrán* as one which "sólo imaginada habría producido un ataque nervioso a Brillat de Savary" [even if only imagined would have given Brillat de Savary a nervous breakdown], a French lawyer and politician who became well known as a culinary expert and critic.[16]

These anecdotal references to a European cultural repertoire set the stage not only for illustrating the challenging conditions under which the first sustained discussions about Mexican letters were openly conceived and debated but also showing a glimpse of the outer fringes of European cultural consumption. The mentioned posters of *Atala* and *William Tell* point to the frequent circulation of translated versions of new European literature within the newly independent Latin America; in fact, the Spanish translation of *Atala*—which has been attributed to both Simón Rodríguez (Venezuela) and Fray Servando Teresa de Mier (Mexico)—appeared during the same year of its publication in 1801.[17] The enduring importance of this particular work in nineteenth-century Mexico, with its tragic Romantic and colonial plotline involving the condemned love of a young, Euro-American Christian woman for a Native American man, also surfaces in the form of Mexican artist Luis Monroy's 1871 painterly rendition—*Últimos momentos de Atala* (Last moments of Atala)—now a part of the permanent collection of the *Museo Nacional de Arte*.

Two of the main organs of diffusion for the *Academia de Letrán*—*El recreo de familias* (1837–8) and *El año nuevo* (1837–40), which were founded and/or directed by Academia member Ignacio Rodríguez Galván (1816–42)—contain frequent treatises of European (including Spanish) authors. Fascinated with Romantic literary trends, both contain multiple detailed explorations, close readings, biographies and/or translations of poetry, literary excerpts, and analyses of authors including Bretón de los Herreros (1796-1893), Lamartine (1790-1869),[18] Nicasio Gallego (1757-1853), and Victor Hugo (1802-85). The translations that were published included both literary works and criticism, as illustrated by a lengthy piece titled "Hugo," penned by French writer and theater critic Jules Janin (1804-74) for the *Diccionaire de la Conversation et la Lecture*[19] and then translated for *Recreo* by Mexican archaeologist Isidoro Rafael Gondra.[20] Gondra (1788-1861), in turn, who founded *El Mosaico Mexicano* in 1836 and published and translated frequently for the annals of the *Museo de Arqueología, Historia y Etnografía*, was a regular collaborator and editor for members of the *Academia de Letrán*, and his contributions included assistance in the translations of literature from German and English into Spanish. The point here is that the frequent appearance and depth of treatment of Western authors in these periodicals suggests that modern Mexican letters are linked at the foundational level to a concerted effort to publicize a specifically national mode of consumption for cosmopolitan literature.

In light of these views, the translation and publication of European novels, plays, poems, author biographies, and literary commentary in this particular context can be understood as a form of rhetorical proprietorship.[21] In other words, within the processes of self-edification that describe Mexican lettered culture at this time juncture, it is not so much the *original*, but rather the translated, adapted *version*, that bears the weight of cultural influence and clears the path for national self-actualization. In this context, translation itself doubles over into a type of literary act: Pablo Mora, in his introductory comments for the republication of an illuminating article titled "Sobre la imitación" (On Imitation) (1838) by José Ramón Pacheco, affirms that translation within the *Academia de Letrán* was a frequent activity, an essential component of the learning process of its members and the source of a considerable portion of what wound up in publication.[22]

Pacheco's article, which Mora suspects is product of a discussion that had likely taken place in the *Academia de Letrán*, is revealing in the distinction between translation-as-copy and translation-as-imitation. While the former offers no contribution to the original on the part of the translator, the latter, argues Pacheco, allows the translator to make corrections, embellish, and improve the original in a way that has its own irreducible originality and critical merit. In fact, many "originals" are indeed copies themselves, as the lauded literary geniuses of Golden-Age Spain, were themselves imitators: Garcilaso de la Vega and Fray Luis de León imitated Virgil and Horace respectively; more recently, Mexican writer Fernando Calderón y Beltrán had composed "El soldado de la libertad" (1838) in imitation of José de Espronceda, who himself had done a "beautiful" imitation of Lord Byron.[23] New writing as already an imitation reframes the question of the "anxiety of influence" in terms of its own form of originality.[24] Widening the argument to include industry, Pacheco challenges readers to extend their appreciation beyond the few great authors and inventors and onto the many who have embellished their works:

> Los descubridores de la pólvora, de la imprenta, y del vapor, son tan raros en el mundo, como los compositores de la Odisea, del Paraíso Perdido, de los Infiernos. Mas ¿cuándo no han aprovechado, por mejor decir, cuándo no han cambiado la condición del género humano, las infinitas mejoras y aplicaciones de aquellos inventos?
>
> [The discoverers of gunpowder, of the printing press, and of steam are so rare in the world, as are the composers of the Odyssey, of Paradise Lost, of the Inferno. But when have they not benefitted, or better said, when have the infinite improvements and applications to these inventions not changed the human condition?].[25]

Not only do the few Western literary greats merit critical recognition and consideration but also the many who—through imitation—create, improve, and reshape the original masterpiece into a novel product.[26] Worth considering here is not only Pacheco's democratizing gesture in appealing to the unrecognized contributions of the "infinite" many whose labors manage to improve upon greatness but also an unlikely tie to current critical queries. While the complexities of translation and the multiple, bidirectional forces that it brings into play has been the subject of much critical reflection, it is interesting to place Pacheco's apology for imitation alongside Emily Apter's concept of "untranslatability," which she describes as a linguistic form of creative failure that points to the inabilities of translation (and other global movements) to gloss over the irreducibly local, national, contextual, political, social, and linguistic differences that inform a text.[27] While Pacheco clearly believed in the exercise of translation-as-copy, it is within the very notion of linguistic *failure* in the exercise of "imitation" that he locates the exercise of creativity and originality.

It is important to consider the question of how "cosmopolitan" cultural consumption operates in this context: it is an act of appropriation, the product of which—the translation, the imitation—earns critical merit not only through its creative improvements to the original but also as incubator and catalyst for future national cultural productions. The point here is not to suggest that Western literature should be understood as a Mexican production, but rather that the frequency and depth with which Western letters were strategically translated, republished, circulated, and discussed within this particular context of nineteenth-century cultural consolidation allowed them to *function*, at times, as such.

In what follows of Prieto's detailed descriptions of various members of the *Academia de Letrán*, the physical and intellectual profiles of some of its key members (Juan Lacunza, Quintana Roo, and Ignacio Ramírez) are interspersed with references to classical Greek and Roman as well as historical, recent, and contemporary European authors and literary works. Whether referencing Lacunza's ability to discourse on Spanish literature using the literary styles of Golden-age authors Fernando de Herrera (1534–97) or Fray Luis de León (1527–91), or the variety of authors discussed during meetings (including Horace, Virgil, Goethe, Schiller, Ossian [James Macpherson] and Byron, and several others), Prieto weaves a scenario in which the creation process is revealed as inextricably linked to the translation, circulation, and consumption of foreign letters and at times direct correspondence with the European cultural elite.[28]

The display and performance of knowledge and its relation to originality surfaces in Prieto's text in contradictory ways. At times, in-depth knowledge of European literary works serves as a type of credential to represent the intellectual capacities of Academy members, such as in his descriptions of Ramírez:

sabía de memoria los griegos y latinos; Voltaire y los enciclopedistas le eran familiares, especialmente D'Alambert, á quien profesaba veneración.

[He knew the Greeks and Latins by memory; Voltaire and the encyclopedists were familiar to him, especially D'Alambert, for whom he professed veneration].[29]

Another example can be found in his praise of Quintana Roo, who through correspondence had won the admiration of European intellectuals such as Blanco White (1775–1841) and Benjamin Constant (1767–1830).[30] At others, however, foreign authors serve as points of comparison that allow the raw talent of Mexican writers to shine, such as Joaquín Navarro (1820–51), who managed to rival his European counterparts despite his own lack of critical consideration of them:

Era un talento práctico, como ahora se diría, muy capaz de honrar la escuela de Spencer o Mill, sin que tales genios le hubiesen pasado por las mentes.

[He was a practical talent, as one would say now, very capable of honoring the school of Spencer or Mill, without such geniuses ever having occurred to him].[31]

While it is undeniable that the numerous comparisons and homages to Western authors that appear across the spectrum of nineteenth-century Mexican cultural productions seem to reinforce the most obvious of social hierarchies—a problem that was publicly debated even at the time—it is also important to nuance this view by considering the semantic framing through which different "brands" of foreign authors were introduced and discussed. Of course, there was a difference between authors who would be considered "cosmopolitan" and those from Spain, and this is an important distinction that routes through the conflicting liberal and conservative visions of Mexican cultural consolidation that recur throughout the nineteenth century. Interestingly, however, both what were considered "Western" and "Spanish" influences were handled rhetorically in similar ways when it came to conjugating them with national interests. One debate, published in *El recreo de las familias* in 1838, is particularly indicative of an effort to link the publication of non-Mexican letters to Mexican national interests. Originating as an editorial comment first published in *El voto nacional* and directed to the editors of *El recreo de las familias,* the writer expresses dismay at the newspaper's insistent featuring of Spanish authors to the detriment of important Mexican writers from the colonial past, especially considering that the editors of *El recreo* insist on their desire to nationalize the newspaper. In response, while there were various practical reasons put forth by the editors of *El recreo de las familias* for not including Mexican colonial authors, the question of why they featured Spanish writers in particular is framed as a simultaneous homage to the peninsular "father"—a common conservative paradigm—and a challenge for current Mexican writers to match and eventually supersede:

> y porque sólo estudiando sus obras pueden los megicanos llegar á competir con esas celebridades que hoy deben envidiar, pero que dentro de pocos años, gracias al talento natural que distingue á los habitantes de esta parte del globo, mirarán como émulos, y nada más [. . .]
>
> [and because only by studying their works can Mexicans compete with those celebrities whom today they should envy, but whom within a few years, due to the natural talent that distinguishes the inhabitants of this part of the world, they will view only as competitors].[32]

Mexican superiority is not always positioned as a goal for the distant future; in Prieto's *Memorias*, Europe is referenced as a cultural barometer against which Mexican progress could already at times measure superior, such as the progressive thinking of the Constitution of Chipalcingo (1814), which laid out ideas that Prieto claims had only barely taken root following the French Revolution in Europe.[33] Curiously, even blatant humility takes on an air of cultural pride, as Prieto both humbly acknowledges the lack of "geniuses of first order" in the *Academia* and praises the immense efforts made to democratize ideas and lay the foundations for future Mexican literature:

> Es cierto que no pueden citarse genios de primer orden como Shakespeare, Calderón, Cervantes, Byron, Goethe y otros astros de primera magnitud, de otras naciones. Pero mucho fué que por la primera vez, de un modo científico y concienzudo se abrieran discusiones, se expusieran doctrinas y se fijaran principios, ó ignorados completamente, ó como sepultados en las librerías de algunos sabios

[It is true that you cannot cite geniuses of a first order like Shakespeare, Calderón, Cervantes, Byron, Goethe and other stars of first magnitude of other nations. But it is considerable that for the first time, in a scientific and conscious way, discussions were opened, doctrines were presented and principles were established that had either been completely ignored or buried in the libraries of a few sages].[34]

With this reading of the *Academia de Letrán*, the marked tendency to summarize, list, and create inventories of world letters demonstrates a specific kind of rhetorical mastery: proof that the writer knows what and how to read while demonstrating profound levels of critical understanding, an essential criteria during the hyperconscious processes of creating Mexican letters. There is open acknowledgment that Mexican letters are in their infancy, and that they have not yet reached the levels of greatness of the European masters whom they quote. Yet the act of citing itself is also an exercise of power: it is an expression of discernment and competence, a benchmark in the rapid process of maturation taking place in Mexican literature that is unparalleled in the Western world. Witness, for example, the mission statement that appears at the beginning of the first issue of *El recreo de las familias*:

Mégico, movido por un poderoso impulso, vuela rápidamente en seguimiento de las naciones civilizadas, y con pasos agigantados vemos caminar nuestra regeneración social. [. . .] Únicamente de esta manera podremos desmentir algún día, llenos de placer y de orgullo, á esas naciones que nos deprimen sin conocernos; que olvidando los dias de su infancia, sólo se acuerda de su actual poder, y que debian avergonzarse al contemplar lo que fueron en las circunstancias en que nosotros nos hallamos.

[Mexico, moved by a powerful impulse, *flies rapidly in pursuit of the civilized nations, and with gigantic steps, we see our social regeneration walking.* [. . .] Only in this way will we be able to refute, full of pleasure and pride, those nations that push us back without knowing us; which forgetting the days of their infancy, only remember their current power, and should be ashamed upon contemplating what they were in the circumstances in which we find ourselves].[35]

In the early stages of modern Mexican letters, the strategic use of rhetorical framing creates a unique space for writers to publish the act of reading in such a way that both acknowledges and demonstrates mastery over Western cultural capital. At the same time—and this is an essential point—there was a conscious effort to provide guidelines for the rapid cosmopolitan cultural consumption that coincided with the creation of modern Mexican literature. In this way, the introduction of Western letters into nascent Mexican cultural institutions is not reducible to an expression of influence or the result of pragmatic obstacles based on what was available to read; it is also a performance of cultural competence that combines the voices of cosmopolitan literary "masters"—as focalizations within the literary story being told—with the voice of the emergent national writers through whose works Western cultural products were presented and disseminated to national consumers. At the same time, in these public acts of consumption, there was an implicit acknowledgment that original national literature is inherently and at the same time both specific—wedded to the particular contexts of Mexico—and connected to the world. By continuously citing, analyzing, translating, and "imitating" Western letters while bringing argumentative emphasis to the rate of cultural acceleration that this entailed, the Mexican scholars of the *Academia de Letrán* constructed a rhetorical incubator for national letters in the form of a nineteenth-century "worldly" vocabulary that forged a space for them to dialogue, to practice—and to create.

La Biblioteca Nacional

Published the same year of its official public opening in 1884, the detailed description of the complete event of the inauguration of the *Biblioteca Nacional* of Mexico reveals a strategy through which this key cultural institution was scripted into the public domain. More than a decade prior to then-President Benito Juárez's 1867 decree announcing the creation of the National Library and designating the Ex-Convent of Saint Augustine as its dwelling, Mexican newspaper snippets such as the following from *El siglo XIX* (1853)—referring to the status, collections, and visitor statistics of the Western world's major libraries—speak not only to the vast symbolic capital that the library represented but also to its public standing as a serialized phenomenon, as I have argued previously with respect to nineteenth-century Mexican patrimonial institutions:

> Del Daily News, periódico inglés, tomamos el siguiente notable artículo: "Las principales bibliotecas públicas de Europa deben considerarse, con respecto a su grandeza, por el órden siguiente:"
>
> [From the Daily News, English newspaper, we take the following noteworthy article: "The principal main public libraries of Europe should be considered, in terms of their greatness, in the following order:"].[36]

Following is a list of twenty-three European libraries placed in order of the number of volumes catalogued in each, with the first five located in Paris (the National Library; 824,000 volumes), Munich (The Imperial Library; 600,000 volumes), Saint Petersburg (the Imperial Library; 446,000), London (the British Museum; 435,000), and Copenhagen (The Royal Library; 412,000 volumes).

As is well known, a feverish collection of statistics and comparative documentation that crossed the boundaries of several cultural and scientific domains ensued as the century progressed. Cultural foundations such as the *Biblioteca Nacional* materialized the efforts to develop a cultural institutional infrastructure that could bridge national circumstances with cosmopolitan status—a balance that would prove, at times, difficult to reconcile, as reflected in this excerpt from *Universal: diario de la mañana* in 1890:

> 43,125 lectores concurrieron a la biblioteca pública de la Escuela Nacional Preparatoria durante el año de 1880, ó sean [sic] casi la mitad de los que concurrieron en el mismo año a la Biblioteca Nacional de París. ¿Cómo puede explicarse eso de un modo satisfactorio?

[43,125 readers came to the public library of the National Preparatory School in the year 1880, or almost half of those who went the same year to the National Library of Paris. How can this be explained in a satisfactory way?].[37]

A close reading of the inauguration of the *Biblioteca Nacional* in 1884, which includes several passages written by then-director José María Vigil,[38] suggests that the relationship between Mexican cultural institutions and Western knowledge far exceeds that of comparison and contrast, however, and indeed suggests—in such a way that parallels Arjun Appadurai's claims about the commodity—the ability of national institutions to "move in and outside" of inter/national status.[39] This is not so unusual, and indeed occurs across the boundaries from so-called Western cultural "centers" to "peripheries" in the nineteenth century, which world literature scholars including David Damrosch (undoubtedly due in part to the oft-cited concept of *Weltliteratur*) and, from the Latin American perspective, Guillermina de Ferrari have identified as the era in which the mutual definition and shaping of national and cosmopolitan arenas reached a particular kind of urgency.[40] Turning back to Vigil's text, there is a distinct series of transitions—a slippage between national and international (or cosmopolitan) domains that occurs, first, in the physical descriptions of the library itself. For example, while the front door of the Library was accented on either side with the busts of the deceased President and liberal hero Benito Juárez and the ex-Minister of Justice D. Antonio Martínez de Castro—both were instrumental in the original decree that established the institution—occupying the nave of the building were sixteen statues of a variety of figures of "worldly" status, ranging from Valmiki and Confucius to Alexander Von Humboldt, who together represented a distilled version of the Western "universal" canons of knowledge. This kind of broad representation of world knowledge was necessary, maintained director José María Vigil:

> Considerando desde luego que una biblioteca del carácter de la Nacional es un establecimiento eminentemente cosmopolita, puesto que en él hallan cabida todas las obras que la inteligencia ha producido en todos los tiempos, pueblos y civilizaciones, [. . .]
>
> [Considering of course that a library of the National character is an eminently cosmopolitan establishment, since in it are to be found all of the works that intelligence has produced in all times, places and civilizations].[41]

Echoing this example, the cosmopolitan emphasis is echoed in several ways and from different perspectives in Vigil's text. For one, he offers a lengthy account of the first recorded libraries in human history, ranging from that of King Osimandías of Egypt 4,000 years prior to the invention of paper and later the printing press, in which he seamlessly weaves ancient Mexican history and the destruction of the codices that ensued during pre-Colombian regime changes together with similar feats of destruction that characterized world political and ideological shifts.[42] Following is an explanation of the logic of classification that Vigil used to organize the collection of the *Biblioteca*, which he had adapted from that of a P. Namur, librarian at the University of Liin (Belgium) in 1834.[43] Finally, there is the range of the collection itself, as the 1891 catalogue of the Library's Philology and Fine Arts collection (8th division) boasts a vast international scope, ranging from antique to modern Greek, Italian, Dutch, Spanish, Portuguese, French, German, Swiss, English, and American authors, as well as Latin American and Caribbean.[44]

Taken together, then, there are several levels of material and rhetorical reinforcement suggesting not only that the National Library is indeed a cosmopolitan institution—the newest link in a chain that reaches across the Atlantic and bridges national and transnational fields of knowledge—but also one that has the distinct feature of maturing rapidly. With its "world" spatial orientation presented in the form of historical summary, Vigil's inauguration speech introduces the Mexican library in the temporal mode—as a formal embodiment of a type of velocity capable of accounting and compensating for uneven spatial distributions of power. The *Biblioteca Mexicana* is cosmopolitan in the sense that its founders frame it—both physically and rhetorically—as fluent in world *time*.

Equally insistent, however, is the Library's fundamentally *national* status. At times, this appears in the form of a list of similar Mexican institutions, comparable in cultural significance to that of the National Library, which were also recently inaugurated and made effective use of colonial buildings, such as the National Preparatory School (1867), the Secondary School for Ladies (1867), or the Conservatory of Music (1866) (among several others listed), or in the central framing of the list of national politicians and cultural leaders who attended the inaugural event in the explanatory text, which included the President of the Republic himself (at the time Manuel Gutiérrez). At other moments, the links to Mexican national culture occur within the structure of the inauguration ceremony itself, such as when Vigil points reader attention to the musical interludes of the program, which, he affirms, testify to the magnificent gains made in that arena of national cultural production, or to Guillermo Prieto's laudatory odes that were read by the poet himself, or to the aforementioned statues and sculptures adorning the building, all done by Mexican artists, and the modifications made to the convent building that were realized by Mexican architects.[45] Finally, also similar to the rhetoric of not-yet-there that characterized Prieto's description of the *Academia de Letrán*, there are the repeated references to the future building of the collection, and to the goal of creating of an institution truly worthy of Mexican culture.

The simultaneity of the national and yet cosmopolitan orientation of the Library provides an opportunity to contribute to dialogues around center-periphery negotiations that frame current discussions on world literature. In Ignacio Sánchez Prado's thorough summary of world literature theory as an introduction to *América Latina en la literatura mundial* (2006), of particular interest for this investigation are his observations regarding the proposals of Alfonso Reyes, for whom the inherent internationalism of Latin America position grant it automatic agency with respect to world cultural currents, and that it is within deeper investigations of the specific material and historical circumstances under which Latin American subjectivities have been constituted that the gaps and deficits in world literature theory can begin to be addressed.[46] Prior to the immense contributions of scholars such as Ángel

Rama, Fernández Retamar, Benítez Rojo, Reyes, and Borges, whose work, as Sánchez Prado points out, paved the way for current reformulations of world literature, it is important to note that this question of how to cast conceptualizations of the West in such a way that positions Latin American subjectivities as "givens" was already in place in the nineteenth century.[47] Indeed, the founding stages of Mexican letters and their corresponding institutions reflect a key awareness of the power mechanisms in play with respect to Western cultural models, as well as a variety of rhetorical and material strategies to both mobilize their positions and re-map the boundaries of center and margin from both outside and within that network.

There is, in Vigil's text, a reformulated or alternative genealogy in play that seamlessly inserts the Mexican National Library into a timeline of "universal" cultural infrastructure. On the other hand, there is evidence that the Library functions, at the conceptual level, as a kind of shifting hyperlink that exhibits the capacity to alternate between Mexico and the "world" as the spatial, political, and cultural destination. In other words, the textual description of the Library's inauguration is written from a doubled perspective—one that acknowledges Mexico as a point of enunciation for both national and cosmopolitan orientations. There is a national celebration in play, but one that emerges while simultaneously demonstrating a thorough and informed mastery over perspectives generated from other Centers. This is not to say that there is a lack of humility, as indicated by the tireless admission of a lack of "giants" produced on the home front with respect to world literary and artistic canons, which spans across the discourses of both institutions investigated here. There was a hyperconsciousness, indeed quite performative at times, regarding Mexico's peripheral status on the Western world stage. One of the key ways in which this hierarchy was both acknowledged and undermined, however, was through the rhetorical mobilization of that margin. Vigil's text frames the library as a point of departure in which the logic of Mexican national cultural institutions could take on a decidedly national and/or a cosmopolitan scope. This doubling of positions occurred both physically—through the circulation of material productions and the participation in international institutions and events, for example—and rhetorically, through careful narrative focalizations that rewrote Mexico's position from one of a former colonial subject to that of a rapidly developing world member with the distinct advantage of stepping over time into an accelerated maturation process. From the world perspective, the center may not rest *in* Mexico, Vigil's text seems to suggest, but Mexico could display its capacity to know how to *happen* there.

Conclusion

With this investigation, I interpret the phenomenon of Western culture as deployed and practiced in Mexico as a type of rhetorical and material production that was inextricably linked to national self-fashioning during the critical era of the nineteenth century. Pushing beyond the conclusion that the Mexican cultural elite fashioned a repertoire of institutions, publications, and federally sanctioned cultural governing bodies while negotiating with cosmopolitan cultural trends, I argue here that the versions of cosmopolitanism that circulated in Mexico at this time juncture—in a series of multifaceted and often contradictory interactions—achieve a particular kind of persuasive force in Mexico mainly as by-products *of* Mexican national cultural consolidation and construction. As demonstrated in this investigation, there are distinct rhetorical and material efforts among Mexican intellectuals to display and perform the ability to read Occidental models, which complicate presumptions of Eurocentric influence precisely by drawing attention to the ways in which these models were purposefully constructed and then publicly disseminated and consumed. This point of view entails not simply a reversal in perspective from margin to center or from effect to cause, but rather the proposal that world cultural influence itself in this nineteenth-century context was, among other things, also a hyperconscious rhetorical construction that Mexican *letrados* selected and deployed within the cultural bases that laid the foundations for Mexican letters and institutionalized culture.

Considerable attention has been given to Mexican nation building, its coincidence with modernization, and the inevitable dialogues with Eurocentric cultural models. There is an important point to consider within this arena of investigation, which reveals itself in close readings of the painstaking and complex negotiations between home-grown perspectives and cosmopolitan letters, figures, and cultural institutions that surfaced regularly in the newspapers, institutional annals, and commemorative speeches that circulated throughout nineteenth-century Mexico: there were systematic efforts to showcase and publicize a process of negotiation in which circuits of world influence were not so much imposed from outside as willfully selected (or rejected), imported, translated, and disseminated. In conjunction with the processes of national political consolidation, infrastructural development, and cultural institutionalization that characterize this time period, then, Mexican *letrados* produced the consumption of the cosmopolitan world, and strategically used that process as a bolster against which to define and test the parameters of national letters.

Notes

1 Víctor Barrera Enderle, "The Emergence of the Mexican Literary Field (1833–1869)," in *A Cambridge History of Mexican Literature*, ed. Ignacio M. Sánchez Prado, Anna M. Nogar, and José Ramón Ruisánchez Serra (New York: Cambridge University Press, 2016), 161.
2 See Marco Antonio Campos, *La Academia de Letrán*, 1st ed., Colección de Bolsillo (México: Universidad Nacional Autónoma De México Instituto De Investigaciones Filológicas, Centro De Estudios Literarios, 2004), 23. For earlier studies, see Ángel Luis Fernández Muñoz, *José María Lacunza: estudio y recopilación: los muchachos de Letrán* (México, DF: Factoría, 1997), and also Alicia Perales Ojeda's *Las asociaciones literarias mexicanas*, 2nd ed., Rev. y Aum, ed. Al Siglo XIX, Ida y Regreso (México: Universidad Nacional Autónoma De México, Coordinación de Humanidades, Programa Editorial, Instituto De Investigaciones Filológicas, 2000).

3 See "Part II: The Nineteenth Century" to consult the investigations of Amy E. Wright, Víctor Barrera Enderle, Shelley Garrigan, Juan Pablo Dabove, José Ramón Ruisánchez Serr, and Adela Pineda Blanco," in *A Cambridge History of Mexican Literature*, ed. Ignacio M. Sánchez Prado, Anna M. Nogar, and José Ramón Ruisánchez Serra (New York: Cambridge University Press, 2016), 141–229.
4 See, for example, Adela Eugenia Pineda Franco, *Geopolíticas de la cultura finisecular en Buenos Aires, París y México: las revistas literarias y el modernismo*, Serie Nuevo Siglo (Pittsburgh: Instituto Internacional de Literatura Iberoamericana, Universidad de Pittsburgh, 2006).
5 See Wolfgang Vogt, "Influencias extranjeras en la literatura mexicana anterior a la revolución de 1910," *Relaciones: Estudios de Historia y Sociedad* 42, primavera 1990, vol. XI. https://www.colmich.edu.mx/relaciones25/index.php/numeros-anteriores/9-numero/129-relaciones-42-primavera-1990-vol-xi
6 See María Rita Plancarte Martínez, "La novela mexicana: entre lo nacional y lo cosmopolita: gestación de las líneas en debate," *ConNotas: Revista de Crítica y Teorías Literarias II*, no. 3 (2004): 171–92.
7 Lilia Vieyra Sánchez, *Inéditos del siglo XIX: escritores, traductores, periodistas, editores y empresas editoriales* (México: Gobierno del Estado de México, 2015).
8 Lise Andriès and Laura Suárez de la Torre, *Impressions du Mexique et de France: Imprimés et Transferts Culturels au Xixe Siècle= Impresiones de México y de Francia: edición y transferencias culturales en el siglo xix*, Horizons Américains (Paris: Maison des Sciences de L'homme, 2009), 33.
9 Andrea Pagni, "Hacia una historia de la traducción en América Latina," *Iberoamericana* 14, no. 56 (2014): 205–24. See also Andrea Pagni, "Los intelectuales-escritores y la importación cultural en Argentina y México entre mediados de los años treinta y fines de los cuarenta. Una aproximación," in *La historia intelectual como historia literaria*, ed. Friedhelm Schmidt-Welle (México: El Colegio de México, Cátedra Guillermo y Alejandro von Humboldt, 2014), 129–46.
10 Marco Antonio Campos, "La Academia de Letrán," *Literatura Mexicana: Revista Semestral de Centro de Estudios Literarios* 8, no. 2 (1997): 161–2. https://revistas-filologicas.unam.mx/literatura-mexicana/index.php/lm/article/viewFile/288/288
11 Ibid., 569–96.
12 Mariano Siskind, *Cosmopolitan Desires: Global Modernity and World Literature in Latin America*, Flashpoints (Evanston: Northwestern University Press, 2014), 14.
13 For an excellent summary of this institutional network, see Miguel Ángel Castro, "El Liceo Mexicano," *Revista de la Universidad de México* 500 (September 1992): 37–40. https://www.revistadelauniversidad.mx/articles/ff7dfa37-e09d-4c03-a80a-fbc1ed6aa639/el-liceo-mexicano
14 See, for example, his writings on English writer Charles Dickens (1812–70), Italian novelist Alejandro Manzoni (1785–1873), the literary value of Jorge Isaac's *María* versus Chateaubriand's *Atala*, and on "American studies" in Ignacio Manuel Altamirano, *Obras completas XIV: escritos de literatura y arte*, ed. José Luis Martínez (México: Consejo Nacional para la Cultura y las Artes), 9–74.
15 Guillermo Prieto, *Memorias de mis tiempos*, ed. Nicolás León (Paris: Vda. De C. Bouret, 1906), 158. http://www.cervantesvirtual.com/obra-visor/memorias-de-mis-tiempos-tomo-i-1828-a-1840--0/html/00b08888-82b2-11df-acc7-002185ce6064.htm
16 Ibid., 159.

17 Ignacio Soldevila-Durante, "Las primeras traducciones castellanas de la *Atala* de Chateaubriand," *Bulletin Hispanique*, tome 108, no. 2 (2006): 421–58. https://doi.org/10.3406/hispa.2006.5262
    https://www.persee.fr/doc/hispa_0007-4640_2006_num_108_2_5262
18 See, for example, Lamartine, *"Pensamiento de los muertos,"* trans. Francisco M.S. de Tagle, ded. Quintana Roo, in *Recreo de las familias* (Mexico: Hemeroteca Nacional digital de México, 1838), 17–18. http://www.hndm.unam.mx/consulta/publicacion/visualizar/558a32ba7d1ed64f1689f622?intPagina=213&tipo=pagina&palabras=V%C3%ADctor_Hugo&anio=1838&mes=01&dia=01&butIr=Ir
19 Belin-Mandar, *Diccionaire de la Conversation*, t. XXXII (1833): 197. https://www.persee.fr/doc/caief_0571-5865_1983_num_35_1_2409
20 *Recreo de las familias* (Mexico: Hemeroteca Nacional Digital de México, 1838), 203–213. http://www.hndm.unam.mx/consulta/publicacion/visualizar/558a32ba7d1ed64f1689f622?intPagina=213&tipo=pagina&palabras=V%C3%ADctor_Hugo&anio=1838&mes=01&dia=01&butIr=Ir
21 See, for example, "Estado actual de la literatura en Europa," originally published in France in 1837 and then translated by I. R. Gondra and republished in *El recreo de las familias* (Mexico: Hemeroteca Nacional digital de México, 1838), 334–8.
22 José Ramón Pacheco, "Sobre la imitación," in Pablo Mora, "Reflexiones sobre la imitación y la traducción en la academia mexicana del siglo XIX: un texto de José Ramón Pacheco," *Acta Poética* 25, no. 1 (2004): 167–81.
23 Ibid., 179, 181.
24 The fact that imitation was also a pressing concern at the time is reflected, from a medical standpoint, in an article titled "Fiebre imitatoria" by doctor and less-known Academia member Manuel Andrade y Pastor (1809–1848), published in *El recreo de las familias*, 19–24. http://www.hndm.unam.mx/consulta/publicacion/visualizar/558a32ba7d1ed64f1689f56f?intPagina=24&tipo=pagina&palabras=Lamartine&anio=1838&mes=01&dia=01
25 Pacheco, "Sobre la imitación," 180.
26 In his article ("Sobre la imitación," 177), Pacheco includes an anecdote about his translation of George Lillo's play *The London Merchant, or the History of* George Barnwell (1731), which the public applauded without the knowledge that he had "taken away various of its beautiful elements due to my incapacity to present it to them as they are originally found"/"pero el público que la aplaudió, no sabía que la privé de varias bellezas del original por la incapacidad en que me hallé de presentárselas como en él se hallaban."
27 Emily Apter, *Against World Literature: On the Politics of Untranslatability* (London: Verso, 2013).
28 Prieto, *Memorias de mis tiempos*, 166. http://www.cervantesvirtual.com/obra-visor/memorias-de-mis-tiempos-tomo-i-1828-a-1840--0/html/00b08888-82b2-11df-acc7-002185ce6064.htm
29 Ibid., 190–2.
30 Ibid., 170–1.
31 Ibid., 168.
32 *El recreo de las familias*, 242–3. http://www.hndm.unam.mx/consulta/publicacion/visualizar/558a32ba7d1ed64f1689f55b?intPagina=4&tipo=pagina&palabras=naciones_civilizadas&anio=1838&mes=01&dia=01

33 Prieto, *Memorias de mis tiempos*, 172. http://www.cervantesvirtual.com/obra-visor/memorias-de-mis-tiempos-tomo-i-1828-a-1840--0/html/00b08888-82b2-11df-acc7-002185ce6064.htm
34 Ibid., 214.
35 *El recreo de las familias*, 4. http://www.hndm.unam.mx/consulta/publicacion/visualizar/558a32ba7d1ed64f1689f55b?intPagina=4&tipo=pagina&palabras=naciones_civilizadas&anio=1838&mes=01&dia=01
36 *El siglo diez y nueve*, March 29, 1853, 2. http://www.hndm.unam.mx/consulta/publicacion/visualizar/558a3dfb7d1ed64f1715e2ee?intPagina=2&tipo=pagina&anio=1853&mes=03&dia=29
37 *El universal diario de la mañana/diario politico de la mañana*, February 2, 1890, 3. http://www.hndm.unam.mx/consulta/resultados/visualizar/558a36b97d1ed64f16cccb33?resultado=1&tipo=pagina&intPagina=3&palabras=Biblioteca_Nacional_de_Paris
38 Vigil also served as President of the Academia Mexicana de la Lengua from 1894 until his death.
39 Arjun Appadurai, *The Social Life of Things: Commodities in Cultural Perspective* (Cambridge: Cambridge University Press, 1986).
40 See David Damrosch, *What Is World Literature?* Translation/transnation (Princeton: Princeton University Press, 2003). See also Guillermina de Ferrari, "Utopías críticas: la literatura mundial según América Latina," *1616: Anuario de literatura comparada* 2 (2012): 15–32. For an excellent and succinct explanation of the evolution of the concept of *Weltliteratur* from August Ludwig von Schlözer (1773) to Goethe's first public use of the term (1827), see Marko Juvan, "Introduction to World Literatures from the Nineteenth to the Twenty-First Century," *CLC Web: Comparative Literature and Culture* 15, no. 5 (2013). https://doi.org/10.7771/1481-4374.2333
41 Biblioteca Nacional de México, José María Vigil, Joaquin Blengio, and Gustavo E Campa, *Inauguracion De La Biblioteca Nacional De México: abril 2 de 1884* (México: Impr. De I. Paz, 1884), 12. http://cdigital.dgb.uanl.mx/la/1080020327/1080020327.PDF
42 Ibid., "Informe del director," iv–xx.
43 Very little information is available on P. Namur. The information I found was in Wallace Koehler, *Ethics and Values in Librarianship: A History* (Lanham: Rowman & Littlefield, 2015), 209.
44 Biblioteca Nacional de México, *Catálogos de la Biblioteca Nacional de México*, ed. José María Vigil (México: Oficina Tip. De La Secretaria De Fomento, 1891), *Indice* n.p.
45 Ibid., VI–XVIII.
46 Ignacio M. Sánchez Prado, *América Latina en la "literatura mundial,"* Serie Biblioteca de América (Pittsburgh: Instituto Internacional de Literatura Iberoamericana, Universidad de Pittsburgh, 2006).
47 Ibid., 30–5.

6

Rethinking Mexican Modernismo and World Literature

Adela Pineda Franco

In order to revisit Mexican modernismo within a world literature criticism framework, a few considerations on the meaning of modernismo in the Spanish American context are in order. Most critical approaches to modernismo (albeit their many conceptual differences) have been enmeshed in the paradigm of Latin Americanism, which took center stage in the field of literature for great part of the twentieth century since Rubén Darío coined the term modernismo under conditions of self-imposed exile. Darío's modernismo (and to great extent that of José Martí) was the ground for the development of a Latin Americanist perspective of literary, cosmopolitan modernity in the last decades of the nineteenth century. Such perspective was initially articulated in large metropolitan centers, like Buenos Aires, Paris, and New York, by writers, whose places of origin (Nicaragua and Cuba) were fragile or inexistent nation-states and, for that reason, direct targets of imperialism. Such conditions had little to do with Mexican literature under the Porfiriato. Furthermore, even relatively recent transatlantic approaches on modernismo still conceptualize this phenomenon in terms of its constitutive Spanish American decolonizing condition.[1] Hence, due to its semantic and conceptual associations with twentieth-century Spanish American imaginaries of the world, the term modernismo, albeit its ubiquity and polysemy, might lead to overgeneralizations regarding the conceptualization of Mexican literature as national-world literature at the turn of the twentieth century.

Furthermore, there is the risk of applying value judgments derived from current prerogatives in world literature criticism and thus frame modernismo within an evolutionary view of literary history. Despite its myriad approaches, world literature cannot be disconnected from the globalization of culture during the neoliberal age, and from specific epistemological shifts in academia, particularly in the United States. The outburst of progressive pluralism within the humanities not only diversify literary criticism beyond the formalist concern with deciphering literature's literariness but also gave way to privileging ethics over literary self-referentiality. Hence, some recent approaches in world literature criticism have adopted valuation criteria derived from the liberal quest of inclusion and diversity; and a few others from paradigms pertaining to postcolonial studies. The assessment of the capacity of literatures from the Global

South to disrupt the discursive legacies of colonialism is central to these approaches, which reject the idea, initially attributed to Pascale Casanova, that critical recognition for modern literature comes from standards set by Paris, the Greenwich Meridian of modernity.[2] Globalization has also problematized the role of academic criticism in a volatile post-Bourdieuan scenario, where literature's symbolic capital fluctuates according to shifting conditions within transnational markets of cultural production. Literary success depends less on academic recognition than on the dynamics of market fragmentation and industry conglomeration.[3] Furthermore, the question of literary *meaning* is bound to the post-literary ethos of our epoch, and to literature's connectedness with other media, a sign of the decline of print culture within the field of aesthetic production.

In this context, there is nothing more outdated than the ontology of the literary as the purified territory of art for art's sake. The question then is, how do we approach the literary practices of modernistas from such a perspective, if modernistas were endowed with the task of inaugurating the domain of literature precisely as literariness, that is, as the domain that granted literature's authority in terms of the specificity of style? Furthermore, if world literature criticism aims to diversify "the world" of world literature, how do we avoid the triumphalist temptation of condemning modernistas as old-fashioned elitists not only for their longing for aesthetic form, but also for their emulation of European paradigms of modernity? A common assumption in literary historiography is modernistas' outspoken exaltation of Paris as the Western metropole determining the prestige of literary works worldwide, and their appropriation of European literature as a strategy to place themselves at odds with their own cultural milieu, which they envisioned as backward. Mariano Siskind's approach to modernismo as world literature is based on this last premise. Siskind equates modernistas' Europeanized cosmopolitanism with a desire of the world, which he characterizes as a signifier of exterior universality, a blank screen onto which these writers projected their modern hopes as well as their frustrations with Latin America's sociocultural stagnation.[4] Siskind's argument has encountered a few reservations regarding the prevalence of Eurocentric criteria in his own approach.[5]

More relevant in the study of modernismo than the suspicion of this movement's ingrained Eurocentrism is the predicament of bringing a fresh perspective to the field without relegating the contributions of Latin American criticism that preceded the paradigm of world literature to an obscure corner.[6] From previous studies on modernismo that have interpreted the syncretic style of specific modernistas as heretical reformulations of French literature in order to deprovincialize the Hispanic norm of the literary, it is hard to qualify modernismo as merely Eurocentric. Robert Stam rightly demonstrates that Eurocentrism does not refer to Europe but to the persistence of colonialist intellectual orientations embedded in premises that imagine Europe (and Neo-Europes, like the United States) as universally normative.[7] The many syncretic styles modernistas forged within the transnational circuits of journalism revealed more complex, historically grounded engagements with European metropoles. In the newspapers, these writers left traces of their own historicity, delving into their self-creative processes in order to transform the symptoms of time-space compression, inaugurated by the capitalist world-system, into a critique of modernization.[8] Furthermore, if world literature criticism should ground its arguments considering the "specific cultural locations and material practices" at work behind literary writing,[9] then one should acknowledge the work of previous critics who tackled such conditions within the transnational contexts in which modernistas proclaimed artistic isolation and Europeanized cosmopolitanism. By considering the production and circulation of modernista texts, written by specific authors in Latin America, but also in Europe and the United States, their desire of the world comes into light not so much as a signifier of abstract universalism to cope with Latin American cultural stagnation, but as dissimilar discursive strategies in order to navigate the uneasy worldliness of the fin de siècle.

Ericka Beckman has developed a convincing argument on the relationship between modernismo's aesthetic pursuits and commodity fetishism, examining the confluence of literature and finance during Latin America's export age, which has problematized the view of art for art's sake as the evidence of literary autonomy.[10] Yet, a reading of modernista aesthetic in terms of the sublime fantasies of capitalism does not necessarily invalidate a parallel understanding of literary form as the result of displacement and exile, which was the case of José Martí, who conveyed, precisely through the question of style, not only capitalism's voluptuousness, but also the unsettling feelings of social fragmentation. Hence, not one, but several, diverse scenarios came to define the relationship of modernista writers with their own Latin American countries and with the world at large, allowing some of them to exert a literary critique of European colonialism during its twilight and of US interventionism at the dawn of its twentieth-century hegemony. Hence, a retroactive reconstruction of the "world" envisioned by modernistas in terms of a critique of the center-periphery paradigm might fall short in acknowledging the structural dynamism of some of these writers' position-takings within a transnational field of literary production.

Now, returning to the central topic of this chapter, even though many fin de siècle Mexican writers partook of the structural dynamism that came to define modernismo as a transnational Spanish American phenomenon, the relationship between literature and the nation-state gives the Mexican variant a peculiar character. Mexican modernistas could not disentangle their cosmopolitanism from the set of private and public institutions, which, despite their diversity and inherent contradictions, were instrumental to consolidate the ruling ideology of the Porfiriato. In Mexico, the press, which was the paradigmatic forum of modernista literature, was not only centralized but also subsidized by the state. The cultural infrastructure of the Porfiriato did enable the incorporation of literature to a developing bourgeois market of cultural production; furthermore, this infrastructure also offered young Mexican writers, many of them provincial émigrés to the capital, the opportunity to partake of the structures of feeling that came to define Spanish American modernismo as a Bolivarian brotherhood of aesthetes. However, as a national practice, literature remained ancillary to the consolidation of the state, which based its success on Mexico's parallel advancement to that of Western civilization. Europeanized cosmopolitanism was inherent to this state's national ideology, and the cult of style, a vehicle to instantiate its legitimacy.

Nowhere is this fact more palpable than in the lush representations of cosmopolitan nationalism that the Porfirian "wizards of progress" displayed at world fairs during the last decade of the nineteenth century. These "wizards" were representative of the Porfirian professional and intellectual class, including financiers and historians, but also artists and writers, such as Amado Nervo.[11]

Modernista journals, such as *Revista Azul* (1894–6) *Revista Moderna* (1898– 1911), and *El Mundo Ilustrado* (1894–1914), were also showcases of Porfirian cosmopolitanism and of the Western idea of progress. They provided their readers, mostly men and women of the urban and lettered elites,[12] a miscellaneous assortment of literary works by national but also Latin American and European writers. In other words, they offered a comprehensive picture of the actuality of "world" literature. Even if a few modernista journals identified with the creed of decadence as art's spirited protest against the positivist creed of the era, the majority embraced a liberal editorial policy under the guiding principle of eclecticism. In this sense, they promoted the encounters of literary form and Porfirian cosmopolitanism, including its Orientalist leanings.

In order to illustrate this convergence, let us remember José Juan Tablada's role as both an introspective Orientalist poet and a globetrotter journalist, special envoy to Japan for *Revista Moderna* during the period 1900–1. Tablada's poems of Japanese inspiration, and his translations of Japanese utas and Japonist European poetry, conveyed an image of the journal as the modernista interior that secluded the poet from the exterior.[13] Conversely, his travel chronicles, allegedly written from Japan during the same period, were explicit endorsements of the propaganda machinery of Porfirian cosmopolitanism: vistas of the Far East brought home by a worldly connoisseur.[14] Tablada's selection of Orientalist motifs was not only the evidence of his uniqueness as a decadent Mexican aesthete; it also revealed the journal's editorial strategy to provide its readers a suitable idea of modernity and the world, which was also distinctively Porfirian.

Laura Torres-Rodríguez argues that Tablada's Orientalism during the Porfiriato responds not necessarily to a derivative Eurocentric view of progress but to the growing interest on Japan as an alternative case of modernization for Mexico. Mexico's diplomatic and commercial opening to Japan during the Porfiriato attests to the emergence of a transpacific circuit within the context of a multipolar, global capitalism. Torres-Rodríguez recalls the editorial publicity around Tablada's trip to Japan in *Revista Moderna* that promoted Japan not only as the place where art and industry meet, but also as an Oriental aesthetic that had managed to influence Europe.[15] Although I agree with Torres-Rodríguez's overall premise, the relative autonomy from European models of literary modernity in *Revista Moderna* is hard to sustain. In the case of Tablada, I have previously written about the ways in which Tablada modeled his trip to Japan based on the routes and motifs of Pierre Loti, the French Orientalist writer that preceded his steps in Japan.[16]

Beyond the relative degree of autonomy from European mediation that Tablada's Orientalist writings might exhibit, the complicities between his vision of cosmopolitanism and that of Porfirian nationalism are indisputable. When the Mexican

Revolution disrupted the Porfirian Pax, Tablada's Orientalism not only revealed itself as the literary interior against the unexpected violence of a revolution; it also unveiled his leanings toward Japanese imperialism and the militaristic fantasies of the Porfiriato.[17] Ironically, it was Tablada, one of the most reactionary writers of the Porfiriato in the political sense, who bridged the aesthetic distance between modernismo and the avant-gardes. It was precisely during the period of revolutionary violence and early post-revolutionary state-formation that Tablada became not only a key mediator of Mexican art in the international arena, but also a sophisticated cosmopolitan writer, responsible for introducing the Japanese haiku and the avant-gardist aesthetics of visual poetry to the Mexican scene.[18] Manuel Gutiérrez Silva considers that Tablada's writings on art and literature, written in Paris and New York for newspapers such as *The New York Times*, *International Studio*, *Parnassus*, and *The Arts*, were fundamental in consolidating his role as a transnational intellectual who crafted a critical cosmopolitanism in post-revolutionary Mexico.[19] Whether Tablada's critical cosmopolitanism after the fall of the Porfiriato should be regarded as the result of his political disaffection with the post-revolutionary state, or whether such cosmopolitanism owed much to the transnational infrastructure of that very state, which created the necessary conditions for artists of all creeds to join the efforts of reconstructing the nation, diversifying and expanding the possibilities of culture during the 1920s, is a question beyond the scope of this chapter.

Certainly, the armed phase of the Mexican Revolution came to disclose the chauvinistic side of modernistas' cosmopolitan creed and not their "void" vis-à-vis Porfirian modernization. The appearance of the industrial press and the generalized use of photographic images in Mexican newspapers at the dusk of the Porfirian regime not only provided the context for future literary experimentation. Modern journalism also encouraged the confluence of modernista poetry (a belated form of romantic expression) with bourgeois forms of entertainment and with Porfirian political ideology. Since 1903, *Revista Moderna* was already predisposing its readers to a visual economy, in which the poetic interior of modernismo and the public face of Porfirian leisure culture converged. The journal's newsroom became a metaphor of such comingling; it was described as a closed space favoring lyrical introspection but also as a showcase of the commodity effect, with its Oriental carpets, its finely sculpted lubricious fauns, and its stately drapery.[20] By 1907, the photographic illustrations accompanying poems by writers such as Luis G. Urbina in *El Mundo Ilustrado* contributed to discredit the visionary and introspective function of such type of poetry by turning contemplation into itemized exhibition. Furthermore, the format and textual arrangement of the magazine page also determined the experience of literary readership. Alongside photographs documenting Porfirian leisure culture, modernista poetry distracted attention away from news related to growing political unrest.[21] With the outbreak of the revolution, the transnational significance of Mexican modernismo revealed itself in its faithful servitude toward the decaying regime of Porfirio Díaz. A case in point is Amado Nervo's chronicle, published in the Paris-based journal *Mundial Magazine*, in May 1911, in which he extolls Mexico's mighty economic and political infrastructure and takes pride in its courteous Indigenous people for their proclivity to adopt Western civilization. At the same time, he celebrates the alleged absence of peoples of African descent in the country, whom he belittles with racist overtones.[22] Nervo's Porfirian eulogy is accompanied by several photographic images of the Taft-Díaz meeting in El Paso-Juárez (the first US presidential visit to Mexico) and followed by a political statement by Mexico's Minister of Foreign Affairs Francisco León de la Barra, guaranteeing Porfirian peace in the wake of alarming press coverage around the world on the impending revolution.[23] In this chronicle, Nervo also resorts to poetry by quoting himself, in order to fan the flames of the political crisis and turn uncertainty into an anthem to the Mexican landscape to be consumed by worldly and affluent readers in Paris and beyond.

Up to this point, my argument suggests that the affiliation of Mexican modernista writers to European forms of cosmopolitanism cannot be taken as a stance of literary autonomy vis-à-vis Porfirian national politics. This argument is based on an understanding of literature as a formation that becomes socially meaningful only in connection to the material conditions of its production, circulation, and consumption. From this perspective, I have argued that modernismo is closely linked to the role of the press, a field permeated by contradictions yet unified by a policy of conciliation, which was the basis of the ruling ideology of the Porfiriato. However, it is also possible to problematize this approach through a diachronic lens, by looking into the ways specific Mexican modernista writers became points of reference for future literary polemics on the conception of a cosmopolitan national literature. A paradigmatic case is that of Jorge Cuesta, who, in 1928, published a controversial anthology in which he put forward a selection of Mexican poetry based on a self-indulgent and anti-utilitarian view of literature, disassociating it from any form of homogenizing school or ideology.[24] Certainly, such criteria echoed the creed of art for art's sake fervently espoused by modernistas three decades earlier. In the 1890s, Manuel Gutiérrez Nájera, the alleged founder of Mexican modernismo, had waived the flag of art for art's sake as his strategy to portray *Revista Azul*, the supplement of the Porfirian newspaper *El Partido Liberal*, as an independent literary forum. The need to dissociate literature from any sort of political principle and the celebration of literary crossbreeding in order to overcome the colonial heritage of Spain as well as the nationalist tendencies of writers like Juan de Dios Peza, were among Gutiérrez Nájera's mission statements.[25] Ironically, Cuesta left not only Juan de Dios Peza, but also Gutiérrez Nájera, out of his anthology. Alternatively, he included Manuel José Othón, Salvador Díaz Mirón, Luis G. Urbina, Amado Nervo, Efrén Rebolledo, José Juan Tablada, Enrique González Martínez, and Ramón López Velarde, all of them associated with the eclectic modernismo, and its immediate sequels. Cuesta's literary purism (an inquiry into the abstraction of poetic form) does not justify his selection, since the formal quality of the anthologized poems is not necessarily even.[26] The argument that Cuesta wanted to subvert the canonical edifice of modernismo by anthologizing its marginal "poets maudits" is also hard to sustain.[27] Urbina, Tablada, and Nervo, whom Cuesta included in his anthology, were all central players of Porfirian cultural politics, even more so than Gutiérrez Nájera, who died at a young age. On the other hand, Cuesta's poetic genealogy did constitute a strategic move to develop a personal and thus arbitrary canon. In *Strategic Occidentalism*, Sánchez Prado associates the construction of personal canons with tactical self-fashioning exercises in order to counteract the homogenizing demands of the neoliberal market. Such strategy goes back to modern times and is verifiable in Spanish American modernismo with Rubén Darío, who loudly rejected the edifice of Hispanic literary tradition by heretically engaging with dissimilar figures of European literature.[28] If Darío's imperative was to resist the homogenizing demands of the Spanish literary institution at the turn of the twentieth century, Cuesta's personal canon aimed to consolidate a space for the young generation of writers outside of Mexico's post-revolutionary nationalist ideology, which, from the 1920s onwards, began to internationalize the rural Indigenous as the cradle of Mexican national belonging. Conversely, literary purism in Cuesta (and the group Contemporáneos) might constitute an indicator of this group's effort to retain the last strakes of the auratic-aesthetic in the midst of its destruction by the commodification of literature during the roaring twenties. This might also be another reason why Cuesta decided to exclude Gutiérrez Nájera from his anthology, although this explanation is not deprived of irony.

As a cosmopolitan writer in the Porfirian sense of the word, Gutiérrez Nájera was not interested in Mexico's countryside or its indigenous *pueblos*. Therefore, his idea of the nation could not be more distant from the one associated with the clichés of post-revolutionary nationalism. Yet, despite their Parisian flavor, his chronicles and poems were idiosyncratically Mexican to the extent that they helped create a mythology of the Mexican urban experience. Furthermore, against the grain of his outspoken purist view of literature, Gutiérrez Nájera developed a "democratic" literary style. In Mexican newspapers, he extended the scope of literary readership through his crafty emulation of models of perception derived from optical technology, but also from the conversational exchanges associated with coffeehouse culture. His idiosyncratic humor and the wit of his performative narrators, whose distinctive voices invaded the silent space of lonely readers with a wink of malice, exposed the one-dimensional happiness of the Mexican Belle Époque. In his poems, such a style came to discredit, albeit unintentionally, the solemnity of poetic revelation, turning it into pre-cinematic kitsch. Yet, in his prose writings, it fostered an acute sense of that "shared intimacy of everyday life" that characterizes the chronicle, a modern hybrid genre par excellence.[29] Hence, Cuesta, who, like Valéry, understood poetry negatively by refusing commodification, excluded Gutiérrez Nájera from his anthology probably for the same reasons that would impel Salvador Novo (another affiliate of Contemporáneos) to re-edit a selection of his prose writings in the 1940s: the confluence of literature and popular entertainment, a prime characteristic of his distinctive cosmopolitan style, one that still speaks to the contemporary reader. Only for this reason, I would argue against Cuesta that Gutiérrez Nájera well deserves more recognition as a uniquely worldly writer of his time. From Gutiérrez Nájera's case, it is clear then that neither the complicities between literature and national politics, nor selective processes of alternative canon formation, can be taken as decisive factors in evaluating the scope of Mexican modernismo in its entirety.

As a case of literary historiography, Cuesta's anthology also brings to light the absence of women writers not only from the canon of Mexican modernismo but also from Cuesta's own genealogy of modern Mexican poetry in the 1920s.[30] Despite fundamental contributions on the part of critics, who have rescued female literary voices from oblivion through archival research and investigated the role of women in the exchanges between literature and society, particularly the development of a female readership for modernista literature, the historiography of women modernista writers remains scarce.[31] The turn to the subject and the body in the 1990s gave way to gender-related approaches to modernismo, particularly in reference to modernistas' self-proclaimed feminization of literary discourse, understood by these male writers themselves as a retreat from the virile positivist age into inward aesthetic pursuits. Modernistas' appropriation of the European decadent subject (and this subject's narcissistic conception of romantic love, which made communion with the opposite sex a fleeting impossibility) has also been interpreted, by critics like Sylvia Molloy, Oscar Montero, and Robert McKee, among others, as a sign of a latent homoerotic aesthetics.[32] Indeed, the fin de siècle was a period of disarray in gender relations as women burst into the public sphere reclaiming their civil rights, particularly in countries like England and France. An ecumenical moment in history, the fin de siècle also shucked off the conventions of Victorian respectability in Mexican literature to a certain degree. During its first years, *Revista Moderna* cultivated a taste for the bizarre. Some of the contributions by the journal's founders, including Julio Ruelas's illustrations, exhibited a "queer" aesthetic avant-la-lèttre. As a symptom of the waning of power/knowledge relations centered on enlightened reason, modernismo signaled a shift in literary practice with the advent of multiple processes of subjectivation that included the destabilization of gender categories. With its disruptive elements of masochistic and narcissistic pleasure, Amado Nervo's short novels *El bachiller* (1896) and *El domador de almas* (1904) are conducive to such a reading of modernismo. Indeed, Nervo's decadent literary heroes seemed to be incompatible with the virile imaginary of a positivistic order, yet as a public and celebrated intellectual during the Porfiriato, Nervo himself was anything but marginal.

Furthermore, excessive retroactive theorizing on conceptual models of later date might obscure the fact that the public face of Mexican literature at the turn of the twentieth century was eminently masculine and, in the case of modernistas, even misogynist.[33] In the age of globalization, Mexican women writers have become key participants of the dynamics of literary production within the market of world literature in English translation. This was not the case during the fin de siècle, when the category of the "Mexican female writer" was not conducive to the development of a strong literary market for women writers domestically and transnationally. Despite endorsing economic modernization, the Porfirian intellectual elite, Catholics and positivists alike, sought to stabilize the social order by resisting the incorporation of women to the public sphere.[34] This patriarchal establishment interpellated women in controlled ways.[35] Hence, even if modernista writers exhibited a less rigid conception of gender relations through their self-proclaimed "feminine spirit," there were very few women writers ascribed to their own literary circles and journals.

On the other hand, despite the fact that the dominant climate of opinion was still anchored in the promotion of traditional values that confined women to the domain of private life, women were indeed becoming productive agents in certain cultural institutions, notably education. A case in point is Laura Méndez de Cuenca, whose trajectory is indicative of the structural changes that came to diversify the role of lettered intellectuals in the Mexican public sphere, adding another layer of complexity to the loss of certainties that characterized the modern experience. Méndez de Cuenca, whose life and poetry produced and reproduced the romantic fictions of Mexican modernismo, was indeed a prolific multifaceted writer and journalist; one of the architects of Mexico's public school system; and a Porfirian public intellectual, who held important commissions in the United States and Europe.[36] On the other hand, her case is also illustrative of the contradictions inherent in a conservative-liberal order that celebrated laissez-faire and individual's natural rights while enforcing social restrictions and centralized state power.[37] Her work resulting from her stays abroad, particularly in San Francisco, St. Louis, and Berlin, evidenced her cosmopolitan role as an intermediary between the idea of Western progress (particularly in the realm of education) and Mexico's modernization. From this lens, Méndez de Cuenca's agency does not seem too distant from that of the modernizing patricians, who made recourse to the "import journey" as the discursive vehicle to assert their own intellectual authority as translators of Western modernity for their Latin American audiences.[38] Yet, Méndez de Cuenca's understanding of American and European versions of modernization carried with it the destabilization of gender divisions defining the private and public spheres, precisely because of her own unsettled authority as a Mexican female intellectual. It is from the standpoint of this conflictive authority that she could adopt and adapt European feminist perspectives to the Mexican context, advocating for women's incorporation to the public sphere while defending the family as the indisputable basis of society, and of woman's central role within it:

> Instead of Americanizing the Mexican woman, emancipating her entirely, I am for instructing her liberally, enabling her to work for her bread, for when single, badly married or widowed, she needs to earn it for herself and for her children. I don't believe we should yank her out of the home, as has happened here, since she is neither happy in the midst of so much liberty, nor feels gratitude toward the man who has awarded it to her, but rather deep hatred, if not contempt.[39]

Whether Méndez de Cuenca's middle-ground views on the role of women in the public/private spheres reflected the mechanisms of ideological subjection during the Porfiriato (the effects of Porfirian ideology on individual subjectivity), or whether such views reflected her own experiential response to the fragmentation of social bonds and the intense rationalization of the public sphere under advanced capitalism in the United States and Europe, remains an open question.

I conclude this chapter with a brief inquiry into the impact of technology and new media on modernista literature at the turn of the century in order to further explore the world envisioned by modernista writers. With this approach, I propose expanding world literature's epistemological assumptions of literature and the world, particularly with regard to literature's engagements with other media.[40] Although technological progress in nineteenth-century Mexico was dependency-based (characterized by a massive importation of new technologies combined with an absence of specialized knowledge),[41] the technological adventure captivated the imagination of Mexicans, whose perception of world events was shaped by press reports transmitted by telegraph at unprecedented speeds from large metropolitan capitals, such as Paris and New York.[42] Modernista writers, transatlantic readers of this press, produced themselves the kind of literature that allowed the century's technological imagination to take hold in the minds of Mexicans. By providing a few examples on the impact of optical media and technology on literature, I hope to illustrate that modernista writers made recourse to European literature in this context, not necessarily (or exclusively) to emulate European literary modernity, but to gloss their own experience with a technological era. Within the background of time-space compression brought about by technological acceleration, let us examine one of the first chronicles on the arrival of the cinematograph published in the newspaper *El Universal* on August 23, 1896. Unsurprisingly, it came from the pen of a writer associated with modernismo, Luis G. Urbina.[43] A brief discussion of this text would provide a framework to further discuss the "world" envisioned by Mexican writers at the turn of the twentieth century.

Urbina structures "El cinematógrafo" as an allegorical narrative. Its protagonist is Fantasia, a personification of the poetic muse transformed into a virtual traveler. Without going anywhere, she travels through multiple viewscapes of a world without borders. Through Fantasia's virtual travels, the author-narrator's "cosmopolitan desires" become mediatized; they no longer pertain to the landscape of literature but are now arrayed before audiences thanks to optical inventions. Indeed, in this chronicle Urbina foreshadowed the era of industrial cinema that was to hardwire cosmopolitan dreams into the means of production, interconnecting audiences around the world much more massively than literature. On the other hand, Urbina makes recourse to "La Lunette de Hans Schnaps" (1858) by Émile Erckmann and Alexandre Chatrian,[44] as a mediating mechanism to convey his own experiential encounter with cinema: a frontal clash with the future, and the end of the literary as the vehicle of visionary voyages.

In the French story, an eccentric inventor, Hans Schnapps, has developed a spyglass that materializes the hidden desires of the unconscious and, more importantly, enhances the faculty of reasoning by accelerating conscious cognition. The syntactic and semantic procedures of language become obsolete in the face of photographic immediacy—the basis of Schnaps's invention—which yields instant knowledge of the complex. For this reason, Schnapps aims to use his newly designed spyglass to reorient and instruct the masses by providing them with an instantaneous and sensorial knowledge of ideas, metaphysics, and even poetry. Ironically, by making the acquisition of knowledge more efficient and democratic, Schnaps puts his own existential purpose as a creator at risk. In the end, he decides not to share his invention with anyone. Facing the cinematograph, Urbina's narrator imagines Fantasia wearing Schnaps's spyglass. Through her experience, the narrator realizes that the entities projected cinematographically did not only take on movement and life, but also lost all concern for artistic creation. Indeed, with its "fractions of a second" (Benjamin's words), cinema blew up, in the absorbed retina of mass audiences, not only the incarcerating world of preindustrial space-time with its virtual journeys at hitherto undreamed-of speeds.[45]

It also ruined the role of the demiurge-creator, whether inventor or poet. By attending the Mexican premiere of the cinematograph in 1896, Urbina foresaw the disappearance of his persona as a visionary poet, a persona he would try to refashion anachronistically in illustrated magazines like *El Mundo Ilustrado* at the dawn of the revolution.

In the same year that Urbina published "El cinematógrafo," Amado Nervo released "El periódico-teléfono," a chronicle on the acceleration of journalism, in which the narrator envisions a future newspaper made of electrical characters that appear on a plate for the reader to view.[46] The multiplication of audiovisual processes referenced in Nervo's chronicle conveys an implicit anxiety about an uncertain future in which seeing and living would become indistinguishable: the instantaneous ubiquity that would come to characterize writing in the virtual era. Fifteen years earlier, Manuel Gutiérrez Nájera had extended Nervo's conjectures about the future virtuality of journalism to all human activities in a futuristic text through a reflection on electricity. In "Joshua Electricman y sus máquinas" (Joshua Electricman and His Machines)[47] the narrator describes the extravagant inventions of a scientist, whose office appears as a power plant that harnesses the principle of the telegraph to connect itself to the globe. Electricman has managed to dissolve time and disintegrate space, thanks to the instantaneous speed with which his inventions store, process, and transmit information around the world. Electricman is characterized as a man-machine: he is autonomous because technology has allowed him to overcome the limitations of human perception; he is an automaton because he is subject to a production regime whose insatiable velocity exceeds him. He prays while swinging on a trapeze, and enjoys poetry by moving "wire number 1,027," which activates a machine named "poetogeno." Clearly, Gutiérrez Nájera' chronicle forecasts not only the poet's replacement by machines but also the cinematic construction and deconstruction of the world in the "flash of an eye."[48]

Despite its political loyalties to the chauvinistic cosmopolitanism that characterized the Porfirian regime, Mexican modernista literature at the turn of the century was decisively worldly by exposing, albeit inadvertently, the illusory notion of order and progress (the Porfirian motto), insofar as it exposed a continual anxiety about the function (aesthetic, social, political) of literature in the face of mechanical reproducibility. Telecommunication and optical inventions like cinema put the notion of literary writing as a mimesis of exterior reality to test. Moreover, they suspended the idea of literature as a vehicle of worldly visions and universal transcendence, which was indeed the central ideology behind modernismo. In the world we inhabit today, the awareness of the limitations of our psychic perception of a constantly shifting technologized environment is probably the most significant aspect we could retrieve from Mexican modernistas' cosmopolitan, albeit skeptical, dreams.

Notes

1   Alejandro Mejías-López, *The Inverted Conquest: The Myth of Modernity and the Transatlantic Onset of Modernism* (Nashville: Vanderbilt University Press, 2010).

2. Pascale Casanova, *The World Republic of Letters* (Cambridge, MA: Harvard University Press, 2007). In *What Is a World?: On Postcolonial Literature As World Literature* (Durham: Duke University Press, 2016), Pheng Cheah characterizes world literature as an ethico-political practice counteracting Eurocentric models of time.
3. Raphael Dalleo, *Bourdieu and Postcolonial Studies* (Liverpool: Liverpool University Press, 2016), 95.
4. Mariano Siskind, *Cosmopolitan Desires: Global Modernity and World Literature in Latin America* (Evanston: Northwestern University Press, 2014), 3, 8.
5. Oswaldo Zavala, "The Repolitization of the Latin American Shore: Roberto Bolaño and the Dispersion of World Literature," in *Roberto Bolaño as World Literature*, eds. Nicholas Birns and J. D. Castro (London: Bloomsbury, 2017), 93. Ignacio Sánchez Prado, *Strategic Occidentalism: On Mexican Fiction, the Neoliberal Book Market, and the Question of World Literature* (Evanston: Northwestern University Press, 2018), 191.
6. In the introduction of *América Latina en la "literatura mundial,"* ed. Ignacio Sánchez Prado (Pittsburgh: Instituto Internacional de Literatura Iberoamericana, 2006), Sánchez Prado argues that a fundamental barrier in expanding world literature's theoretical sources is the limited access to Latin American thinkers in English translation. This is the case of many fundamental works on modernismo published during the 1980s, such as Ángel Rama, *Las máscaras democráiticas del modernismo* (Montevideo: Fundación Ángel Rama, 1985) and Rafael Gutiérrez Girardot, *Modernismo: Supuestos Históricos y Culturales* (Mexico City: Fondo de Cultura Económica, 1988).
7. Robert Stam, *World Literature, Transnational Cinema, and Global Media: Towards a Transartistic Commons* (London and New York: Routledge, 2019), 7.
8. Works by Ángel Rama, Julio Ramos, Aníbal González Pérez, Graciela Montaldo, and Susana Rotker are fundamental in the study of modernismo and journalism. A recent approach is Andrew Reynolds, *The Spanish American Crónica Modernista, Temporality and Material Culture: Modernismo's Unstoppable Presses* (Plymouth: Bucknell University Press, 2012).
9. Sánchez Prado, *Strategic Occidentalism*, 15.
10. Ericka Beckman, *Capital Fictions: The Literature of Latin America's Export Age* (Minneapolis: University of Minnesota Press, 2013).
11. Mauricio Tenorio Trillo, *Mexico at the World's Fairs: Crafting a Modern Nation* (Berkeley: University of California Press, 1996), 63.
12. Readership was limited due to socioeconomic reasons. While the price of a regular newspaper fluctuated between 3 and 12 cents per month, *Revista Moderna*'s monthly subscription was 50 cents. Elisa Speckman, "La prensa, los periodistas y los lectores (Ciudad de México, 1903–1911)," *Revista Moderna de México (1903–1911) II. Contexto*, ed. Belem Clark de Lara and Fernando Curiel Defossée (Mexico City: Universidad Nacional Autónoma de México, 2002), 107–42.
13. *Revista Moderna. Arte y Ciencia (1898–1903),* dir. Jesús E. Valenzuela, facsimile edition, 6 vols. (Mexico City: Universidad Nacional Autónoma de México, 1987). "Musa japonica," (September 15, 1900): 276–77; "La venus china," (February 1, 1901): 54; translations of Japanese utas (October 1, 1900): 298; translation of the legend "La mujer de Tjuang-Tsé," (December 15, 1901): 378–80.

14 See issues corresponding to: July 1, 1900: 200–3; September 1, 1900: 257–61; September 15, 1900: 282–3; October 1, 1900: 290–3; October 15, 1900: 312–15; November 1, 1900: 333–6; November 15, 1900: 342–44; December 1, 1900: 257–9; December 15, 1900: 370–3; January 15, 1901: 27–9; February 1, 1901: 45–8; March 15, 1901: 90–1.
15 Laura Torres-Rodríguez, *Orientaciones transpacíficas: La modernidad mexicana y el espectro de Asia* (Chapel Hill: University of North Carolina Press, 2019), 52–64.
16 Adela Pineda Franco, *Geopolíticas de la cultura finisecular en Buenos Aires, París y México: las revistas literarias y el modernismo* (Pittsburgh: Instituto Internacional de Literatura Iberoamericana, 2006), 108–10 and "Japan in the Mind's Eye of Two Mexican Travelers (1874, 1900)," *Journal of Iberian and Latin American Studies* 12, nos. 2–3 (2006): 159–72.
17 Torres-Rodríguez, *Orientaciones transpacíficas*, 65–6.
18 Ibid., 67–73 and Manuel Gutiérrez Silva, "Aesthetic Rivalries in Avant-Garde Mexico: Art Writing and the Field of Cultural Production," *Pierre Bourdieu in Hispanic Literature and Culture*, ed. Ignacio Sánchez Prado (New York: Palgrave Macmillan, 2018), 87–129.
19 Ibid., 107.
20 Rubén M. Campos, *El bar. La vida literaria en México en 1900* (Mexico City: Universidad Nacional Autónoma de México, 1996), 113.
21 To give a specific example, the coverage of a major labor strike in Río Blanco and its violent repression in *El Mundo Ilustrado* (January 13, 1907) went unnoticed due to the superabundance of photographic illustrations featuring the leisure culture of Porfirian high society as well as those accompanying Urbina's long poem "El poema del lago."
22 Amado Nervo, "México. Los últimos sucesos," *Mundial Magazine* (May, 1911): 7–10. Nervo's celebration of the "Indian race" for its sculptural bronze-like beauty takes place outside the precipitous motion of the revolutionary present.
23 Francisco Leon de la Barra, "La situación actual de México," *Mundial Magazine* (May, 1911): 12.
24 Cuesta Jorge, ed., *Antología de la poesía mexicana moderna* (Mexico City: Contemporáneos, 1928).
25 *Revista Azul, 1895–1896*, ed. Manuel Gutiérrez Nájera and Carlos Díaz Dufóo, facsimile edition, 5 vols. (Mexico City: Universidad Nacional Autónoma de México, 1988). "Al pie de la escalera," (May 6, 1894): 1–2; "El bautismo de la Revista Azul," (June 17, 1894): 97, and "El cruzamiento en literatura" (September 9, 1894): 289–92.
26 Cuesta's modern understanding of poetic language would explain the inclusion of Salvador Díaz Mirón, whose poetry exhibits the tense cohabitation of formal perfection and abrupt rhythmical variation, or that of López Velarde, which entails a defamiliarization of Mexican provincial life through an appropriation of decadent poetic motifs. Yet this argument does not work in the case of Icaza or Urbina.
27 Ignacio Sánchez Prado argues that Cuesta interpreted the anthologized modernista writers beyond the canon of their time. *Naciones intelectuales: las fundaciones de la modernidad literaria mexicana, 1917–1959* (West Lafayette: Purdue University Press, 2009), 91.
28 Rubén Darío, "Palabras liminares," *Prosas profanas*. 1896 (México City: Librería de la Viuda de Charles Bouret, 1925).

29 I am borrowing the expression from Viviane Mahieux's book *Urban Chroniclers in Modern Latin America: The Shared Intimacy of Everyday Life* (Austin: University of Texas Press, 2014).
30 Cuesta did not include a single woman in his anthology.
31 Two representative examples of this line of research are: José María Martínez, *Amado Nervo y las lectoras del Modernismo* (Madrid: Editorial Verbum, 2015) and Ana Rosa Domenella and Nora Pasternac, eds., *Las voces olvidadas: antología crítica de narradoras mexicanas nacidas en el siglo XIX* (Mexico City: El Colegio de México, 1991).
32 Sylvia Molloy compiled her well-known articles written between 1990 and 2001 in: *Poses de fin de siglo: desbordes del género en la modernidad* (Buenos Aires: Eterna Cadencia, 2012). Oscar Montero, 1993. *Erotismo y representación en Julián del Casal* (Leiden: Almenara, 2019). For the case of fin de siècle Mexico and particularly Amado Nervo, see Robert McKee Irwin, *Mexican Masculinities* (Minneapolis: University of Minnesota, 2003), 50–115.
33 Modernismo's misogyny is associated with the movement's decadent aesthetic leanings, and a desire to shock bourgeois respectability through an aggressive comingling of aesthetic form and sexual perversion. *Revista Moderna*'s founding members made women the target of their obsessive self-fashioning as members of a solipsistic decadent brotherhood. Ciro B. Ceballos' depiction of Ruelas reads: "... él cree como yo, que la hembra es inmuda dañina y amarga como la hiel" ("...he believes, as I do, that females are filthy, harmful, and bitter like bile"), *Revista Moderna* 1, no. 4 (September 15, 1899): 56.
34 As late as 1911, Horacio Barreda attempted to justify the domestic role of women by making recourse to a determinist explanation of female nature. He wrote in *Revista Positiva*: "La mujer será feliz, cuando se encuentre colocada en un medio social que no le exija una actividad incompatible y en desacuerdo con su constitución orgánica" (In order to achieve happiness, woman needs an adequate social environment to perform activities that do not contradict her biological nature). Lourdes Alvarado, *El siglo XIX ante el feminismo. Una interpretación positivista* (Mexico City: Universidad Nacional Autónoma de México, 1991), 5.
35 The symbol of that type of femininity was Díaz's wife, Carmen Romero Rubio de Díaz, often represented, even by modernistas, as the nation's mother due to her Christian goodness and charitable actions. Manuel Gutiérrez Nájera, "Carmen Romero Rubio de Díaz," *Revista Azul* 1, no. 11 (July 15, 1894): 162; Carlos Díaz Dufóo, "Azul Pálido," *Revista Azul* 1, no. 11 (July 15, 1894): 176.
36 Mílada Bazant de Saldaña, *Laura Méndez de Cuenca: Mexican Feminist, 1853–1928* (Tucson: University of Arizona Press, 2018).
37 On the politics of reconciliation and the crafting of a liberal myth during the Porfiriato see Charles Hale, *The Transformation of Liberalism in Late Nineteenth-Century Mexico* (Princeton: Princeton University Press, 1989).
38 On the "import journey" in Domingo Faustino Sarmiento and its critique in José Martí, see Julio Ramos, *Divergent Modernities: Culture and Politics in Nineteenth-Century Latin America* (Durham: Duke University Press, 2001), 104–5.
39 Bazant de Saldaña, *Laura Méndez de Cuenca*, 114.
40 Robert Stam proposes a transdisciplinary approach to the study of literature in the age of new media. He criticizes the term world literature as "a certificate of

quality, premised on the gatekeeping role of cosmopolitan experts, ... who are thus equipped to discern the difference between long-lasting masterpieces and pop-cultural ephemera." *World Literature, Transnational Cinema, and Global Media*, 22.

41 Edward Beatty, *Technology and the Search for Progress in Modern Mexico* (Berkeley: University of California Press, 2015).
42 David Harvey, *Paris, Capital of Modernity* (New York; London: Routledge, 2006), 271.
43 "El cinematógrafo," *Los exaltados: antología de escritos sobre cine en periódicos y revistas de la ciudad de México, 1896–1929*, ed. Ángel Miquel (Guadalajara: Universidad de Guadalajara, Centro de Investigación y Enseñanza Cinematográfica, 1992), 32–7.
44 Émile Erckmann and Alexandre Chatrian, "La lunette de Hans Schnaps. Conte fantastique," *Revue française*, IV, XV (1858): 289–96.
45 Walter Benjamin, "The Work of Art in the Age of Its Technological Reproducibility," in *The Work of Art in the Age of Its Technological Reproducibility, and Other Writings on Media*, eds. Michael W. Jennings, Brigid Doherty, and Thomas Y. Levin (London: The Belknap Press of Harvard University Press, 2008), 19–55.
46 Amado Nervo, "El periódico-teléfono," in *Cuentos y crónicas de Amado Nervo* (Mexico City: Universidad Nacional Autónoma de México, 1993), 128–9.
47 Manuel Gutiérrez Nájera, "Joshua Electricman y sus máquinas," in *Obras X. Historia y ciencia. Artículos y ensayos (1879–1894)*, vol. X, ed. Ana Laura Zavala Díaz (Mexico City: Universidad Nacional Autónoma de México, 2009), 331–3. It was originally published under the pseudonym M. Can in *El Cronista de México* (October 1, 1881).
48 Paul Virilio, *Negative Horizon* (New York; London: Continuum, 2007), 132.

7

World-Making in the Twentieth Century
The Rise of Mexican World Literary Institutions

Ignacio M. Sánchez Prado

In his 1940 text "Apollo, or About Literature," Mexican humanist Alfonso Reyes challenges the idea of national literature as a useful framework. A committed universalist who spent his long career as a writer, critic, and diplomat advocating for what he called the "universal citizenship" of Mexico and Latin America, Reyes believed that "outside of limited sociological applications that are used as testimony for non-literary purposes, national literatures in and of themselves do not explain anything." Reyes further affirmed that national literature was "a recent notion" that was becoming muddled due to the "global development of communications."[1] This is quite the statement when one considers the outsized role Reyes played in the formation of Mexican literary institutions in the mid-century, at a time when cultural nationalism was key to the general project of governance and the state in the country.[2] Yet, Reyes's foundational role in Mexican cultural institutions was rendered possible by the fact that his thinking was firmly rooted at the fluid intersection of three cultural geographies: Mexico, where he was an agent of the diplomatic body and the cultural state, and a key point of reference during the first fifty or so years of the Revolutionary era; Latin America (or América, as he termed it), where he was, in the words of Robert T. Conn, " the spokesperson for an antifascist liberal *americanista intelligentsia*" concerned with both the strengthening of the region's culture and the affirmation of the region as a site for universalism;[3] and the world, both in the Classicist bent of his thinking and in his careful attention to the developments of Western culture in his time.

Reyes is a key figure for the aims of this chapter. The Mexican Revolution played a significant role in turning Mexico into a site of world literature in many significant ways. I will privilege in this chapter the formation of the cultural institutions and practices that permit the emergence of what I call a "Mexican world literature." By this I do not mean the works of Mexican literature that circulate outside of Mexico, but rather the idea of world literature that implicitly underlies both literary writing and the engagement of Mexico in the world. As an exhaustive account of this would require a book of its own, I will set aside on the issues addressed by other chapters in this collection: the avant-garde, the legacies of *modernismo*, the role of UNESCO, the figures of Octavio Paz, Juan Rulfo, and Carlos Fuentes. Complementing those themes, I am more interested in discussing twentieth-century Mexico as a site of world literature and as a country that develops a unique infrastructure to read, translate, circulate, and export works of literature.

Indeed, one of the fundamental features of Mexican culture, perhaps the most stunning, is that post-revolutionary culture enabled the simultaneous rise of the most intense and influential cultural nationalism in Latin America, as well as one of its most sophisticatedly cosmopolitan cultural fields. While literature aligned to cultural nationalism most certainly existed, it never reached the prominence that it found in other forms of art. There are, at least in my opinion, no works of literature in the first half of the twentieth century that match the cultural resonance of nationalist culture in muralism and other visual arts, classical and popular music, crafts or cinema. As has been widely studied, the literary field in Mexico was formed as a direct result of the tension between nationalism and cosmopolitanism, as manifested particularly in two polemics, in 1925 and 1932, focused in general terms on whether there should be a national literature at the service of the revolutionary process or the affirmation of literature as such.[4] The assertion of the relative autonomy of the literary field, to use Bourdieusian terminology, was fundamentally based on the resistance of nationalist imperatives and the assertion of the right of the Mexican writer to write without the constraints of the state.[5] Even towering works explicitly seeking to account for Mexicanness in form and content—works of world resonance like Octavio Paz's *The Labyrinth of Solitude* (1950) and Carlos Fuentes's *Where the Air Is Clear* (1950)—were shaped primarily by cosmopolitan strains, and in dialogue with world modernisms and versions of the avant-garde.[6]

From the perspective of Anglophone literary studies, the idea of a Mexican world literature may seem odd, particularly because theories of world literature, in the rare cases when they focus on Mexican writers, often read them as purveyors of resistance through cultural specificity. This is the case of Pascale Casanova, who focuses on Fuentes and Paz as writers coming from a country "at a relatively great distance from the center" and fundamentally invested on providing "a foundation for Mexican national identity" and the restoration of "continuity" with the pre-Columbian past, notwithstanding the fact that they were writers widely read at the global level with works in translation that address issues beyond their discussions of Mexicanness.[7] In his cameo in the book, Alfonso Reyes is barely named as a critic of Latin American literature's ancillary commitment to the political, in an argument that problematically claims, following an equally problematic argument on Fuentes, that until the Boom Latin American writers were tied to "pure political functionalism."[8] Even in terms of Casanova's widely panned Francocentrism, she noticeably misses the fact that Reyes had many substantive connections with French literature over decades.[9]

Yet, this kind of authenticity claims of Mexican literature *qua* peripheral tradition take many forms across the spectrum of world literature theories. The Warwick Research Collective, whose work I find productive in many ways, nonetheless frames Rulfo as part of the "invention of a Mexican gothic irrealism couched in a fragmentary structure drawing on indigenous Amerindian mythology and orality," as part of the "transition from the emulation of received forms" to the creation of ones that purportedly reflect local society "more adequately."[10] This perspective, which serves as conclusion for a chapter on peripheral realism as a cultural form in alignment to radical politics, is sustained in a fairly outdated understanding of Rulfo that ignores the fact that, per his own admission, his primary sources were not Amerindian texts, but Northern European rural writers like Selma Lagerlöf and Knut Hamsun.[11] From a different front, David Damrosch devotes a chapter of his *What Is World Literature?* to the discovery and expansion of Aztec and Maya manuscripts over time, a worthy pursuit other weakened by his conclusion. Damrosch seeks to debunk "the traditional consensus that native Mexican culture ended almost overnight upon the arrival of the Spanish," something that no one serious, other than the author of the *Britannica* entry he cites, has believed since at least the 1950s.[12] Within Damrosch's own framework it would have been worth studying the figure of Ángel María Garibay, one of the key editors and translators of pre-Columbian literature, a humanist priest deeply versed in European philological traditions, who was also instrumental in the publication of Classical Greek and Middle Eastern literary works in Spanish.[13]

I do not intend here to be critical of these specific theories, particularly since I have laid out my case against these reductions of Mexican and Latin American literature elsewhere.[14] Rather, my point is that the errors and imprecisions in these accounts stem from the way in which the focus on international circulation often erases the complexity of world literary engagements in societies branded as peripheral. This is acutely true in a country like Mexico, the largest country in one of the largest linguistic circuits in the world. Alexander Beecroft is correct when he characterizes Spanish as a "regional world-language" that does not quite cover the planet in the way English does, but that nonetheless "constitutes worlds" and exists in a sort of in-between space between their participation in Eurocentric logics of world literature, while being capable of functioning within themselves in polycentric and autonomous ways.[15] Within a system like that, Mexican literature in the twentieth century provides a unique case study for the formation of world literature not as a literature for export in world markets, but as an effect of complex institutions with multicentric attachments to national, regional, and world literary systems. Methodologically, I would contend that world-making in twentieth-century Mexico can be read only if one considers the institutional infrastructure that renders it possible. This is crucial to overcome the flat essentialism that generally places a literature like Mexico's as a site of enunciation of authenticity and specificity. Instead, literary production in Mexico (and in pretty much any other system branded as "semiperipheral" or even "peripheral" to world literature) becomes and creates world literature through the material workings of editorial and cultural ventures, and the work of actors such as writers, translators, and editors acting upon a conception of world literature as such.

Reyes was such a key figure in these pursuits, because he sought the theorization of the problem of world literature while he played a significant role in the formation of cultural institutions. It is worth noting that Reyes wrote "Apollo" and many of his major works in literary theory right at the moment when President Lázaro Cárdenas summoned him to direct La Casa de España, an institution originally conceived to host intellectual exiles fleeing Spain, to later become El Colegio de México, Mexico's foremost social science and humanities research institution. As his biographer Javier Garciadiego documents, he also played a key role in the foundation of El Colegio Nacional—an institution to house the top practitioners of all disciplines of knowledge, modeled after the Collège de France—and in the development of Fondo de Cultura Económica, which grew to become the largest and most respected academic and intellectual press in Latin America.[16]

In "Apollo," Reyes follows the rejection of national literature as a category discussed earlier with a ponderation of the methodologies that could adequately reflect the literary beyond "the nationalist magnet." Although the term "universal literature" was very much in vogue, Reyes makes a distinction. For him, universal literature named "a theoretical catalog of all existing literary manifestations, that is, a utopian image," whereas world literature constitutes "the only way to capture literary thought. It can be seen as an inventory of works and facts that still affect our civilization; they are still alive in our minds, and having transcended all else, they continue to have a function."[17] Reyes revises here Albert Guérard's *Preface to World Literature*, published the very same year. While Reyes and Guerard agree on the limits of comparative literature as excessively bound to the idea of influence, the latter understands world literature merely as the aggregate of works appreciated in common by mankind as opposed to the totality of works—a definition that Damrosch has essentially actualized without in-depth reference to Guerard's *Preface*.[18] In any case, Reyes recognizes that the idea of world literature entails "notions of anthology, sociology, and democracy, all founded on the dominant customs of a society."[19] Reyes was a devoted reader of Goethe, to the point that his lifetime writings on Goethe's life and ideas occupy the last volume of Reyes's complete works, comprising four books (organized posthumously by his editor) and over 400 pages.[20] It is thus unsurprising that the idea of world literature played a significant role in his thinking while he was deeply involved in the large-scale reconfiguration of literary and cultural institutions in this period.

Understanding world literature as the works that circulate universally would make no sense to someone like Reyes because the cosmopolitan circulation of literature is a given to him. Reyes instead navigated in an interesting paradox, advocating for literariness as an autonomous feature and for literature as an anti-dogmatic form of thinking (something that Horacio Legrás has studied in terms of its post-Kantian and Romanticist filiations), while at the same time spending significant energy on pedagogical efforts aimed not only at the formation of literary institution but at the writing of manuals aimed at the teaching of the classics and of literary theory.[21] In this, Reyes is at the core of editorial and critical efforts that, building on the work done across various publications in the first three decades of the revolutionary period, would set the stage of the institutions of Mexican world literature. One of the salient features of the period is the way in which translation, particularly at the Fondo de Cultura Económica, brought into Mexico a wide array of works very much engaged in various forms of classicism and universalism in the 1940s and 1950s.

The main thrust of the literary institutions of mid-century Mexico was the democratization of world literature and world culture, by making it accessible to the reading class that had begun to multiply due to the educational reforms of the post-revolutionary period. An example of this is at Fondo de Cultura Económica is the series Breviarios, conceived by Fondo editor Arnaldo Orfila Reynal as a low-cost, high print-run collection that would bring the disciplines of knowledge from academia to the home of Mexicans.[22] The very first book of the collection was Reyes's 1948 translation of C. M. Bowra's *Ancient Greek Literature* (1933), which he later followed with a 1949 translation of Gilbert Murray's *Euripides and His Age* (1913).[23] This was nothing but the beginning of a steady flow of works from European and American philology and criticism that would be fostered by Reyes and his contemporaries. Werner Jaeger's *Paideia* was a long-term undertaking that began with Joaquín Xirau's translation of the first two books, published in German between 1933 and 1935, in 1942, to which book III and IV were added in Wencelao Roces's translation of the unpublished German manuscripts in 1944 and 1945, until the publication of a consolidated volume in 1957.[24] In fact, the third and fourth books appeared in Spanish, and in the simultaneous English translation by Gilbert Highet in the United States, after Jaeger moved to the United States, before they were published in German. Amid all of this, Reyes and Jaeger wrote to each other consistently, and read each other's works between 1942 and 1958, connected in part by their dialogue on Greek culture.[25]

One could add here Highet's own *The Classical Tradition* (1949), translated in 1954 by Antonio Alatorre. Per their own notes in the book, Highet and Alatorre worked closely on the translation to the point in which the Spanish edition corrects elements of the original and includes addenda by Alatorre (not all authorized by Highet) related to the Iberian tradition.[26] There were other significant projects beyond this circle of classicists. Alatorre and Margit Frenk also translated Erns Robert Curtius's *European Literature and the Latin Middle Ages* (1948) in 1955.[27] And, very significantly, Erich Auerbach's *Mimesis* (1942) appeared in Fondo de Cultura in 1950, to become a very widely read book in the Mexican literary world. Many of these books appeared in another series, Lengua y Estudios Literarios, which would over time publish a very influential roster of Western literary critics (Mario Praz, Paul Veyne, George Steiner, Roman Jakobson, Albert Béguin, and many others) alongside many major figures of Mexican and Latin American criticism (Octavio Paz, Tomás Segovia, Irlemar Chiampi, among others). All of the major books mentioned in these two paragraphs remain in print and the series continue to run to this day.

The legibility of such erudite critical canon results in part from decades of construction of editorial and translational networks of world literature that trace back to *modernismo*.[28] Even as the dawn of *modernismo* and the last stages of the military stage of the Revolution unfolded between 1915 and 1920, young thinkers and writers, in a growing number of short-lived magazines like *Gladios, San-Ev-Ank*, or *La Nave*, would set the stage for the booming of new cultural institutions that would arise in the 1920s, alongside Mexico's full entrance into the avant-garde.[29] A very important first instance of editorial work is Colección Cvltvra, an editorial venture created by Julio Torri and Agustín Loera y Chávez, which published eighty-seven titles of Mexican and world literature between 1916 and 1923 in a hybrid model of subscription and circulation in national and international bookstores through the postal service, going around both the armed conflict in Mexico and the First World War in Europe. As Freija I. Cervantes and Pedro Valero have studied, Cvltvra translated authors like Jules Renard, Gabrielle D'Annunzio, Rabindranath Tagore, and Marcel Schwob, as well as anthologies of Belgian poetry and of poets killed in the First World War.[30] Cvltvra is an early, but paradigmatic, example of the ways in which literary collections in Mexico would shape through idiosyncratic choices framed both within and outside mainstream circuits of literary circulation. I have used the term "strategic occidentalism" to describe the ways in which idiosyncrasy, choice, and strategic engagement produce literary circulation in Mexico and other Global South literatures.[31]

In this particular case, the alignment of national classics alongside Latin American and world authors helps understand the coexistence between nationalist and cosmopolitan culture as a feature of post-revolutionary literature. This model would continue to unfold in other ventures. An example is *La novela quincenal*, by the México Moderno press, which published biweekly serial renditions of authors that range from Maxim Gorki and Robert Louis Stevenson to the science fiction writer Bernhard Kellerman or the historical novels of Prosper Merimée. It also developed anthologies of various genres, from short stories from around the world, to detective fiction, to children's literature.[32] These are the infrastructures that in the 1920s and 1930s would fuel the cosmopolitan bents of the avant-garde and would set the material conditions for the development of a literary culture *tout court* in Mexico.[33]

To understand the hold that world literature would have in Mexico, it is important to remember the significant paradox between the high illiteracy rate (80 percent at the outset of the 1920s) and the outsized role of culture in the process of post-revolutionary modernization. The formation in 1921 of the Secretaría de Educación Pública (SEP) as a direct result of the constitutional duty of the state to provide education, consecrated in Article 3 of the 1917 Constitution, triggered both large-scale educational campaigns aimed at the expansion of educational institutions and literacy, and the use of state infrastructure to reach the masses rendered visible by the Revolution through coordinated efforts that ranged from the aggressive promotion of the visual arts, to the harnessing of mass media, to the appropriation of crafts and popular productions.[34] Within this framework, the role of world literature in this period is tied to the apparent contradiction between a mass state project carried by an intellectual class committed to use the arts and culture as a way to shape "the order of the world," as Legrás puts it, and the idea—positivistic in nature and tracing back of the nineteenth century—of the civilizational importance of Western culture as a tool to bring indigenous and *mestizo* Mexicans into the fold of the nation.[35]

The development of a world literary culture in a country with high rates of illiteracy nonetheless carried a democratizing bent that was defined by, and exceeded in some cases, the paternalistic agenda of civilizing the population. Scholars often emphasize the role of national culture as an instrument of assimilation of indigenous and peasant populations to modernity.[36] Yet, the idea of public art and mass distribution of the classics carried a populist and democratic strain in its refusal to accept the idea that only elites could access the best works of human culture. As Engracia Loyo recounts, José Vasconcelos, the minister of culture in the early 1920s and a founding figure of both educational and cultural policy, defined a patriotic duty comprising the translation of works of world literature into Spanish, their publication in accessible editions unburdened from hermetic annotation, and their distribution in schools, libraries, and low-cost retail spaces.[37] Even though the literacy campaigns were still many years away from their major successes, Vasconcelos fostered an extensive and wide-ranging print culture out of the Ministry of Education, which included books aimed at readers of all ages, and to different audiences. As Garciadiego notes, Vasconcelos understood well the different forms of reading as a social praxis, and the need to foster reading not only as an educational and professional pursuit but also as a formative and recreational one.[38]

The collections created under Vasconcelos provide in themselves a fascinating case study on the ways world literature was envisioned as an object of both pedagogy and democratization. An example is the two-volume anthology *Lecturas clásicas para niños* (1924), an anthology of world literary texts distributed in mass scale at either a lower price or free.[39] The framework of this is an idea, still prevalent in Mexico, that it is the duty of the state to edit, publish, and provide free textbooks to all students, in order to make sure that culture becomes accessible to the vast majority of the people. *Lecturas clásicas para niños* was one such endeavor. The selection is far wider than one can imagine. The first volume begins in the "Orient" and compiles texts from the Veddas, the Kata Upanishad, the Ramayana, The Legend of Buddha, as well as the Panchatantra, selections from the work of Tagore, *The Arabian Nights*, and some Japanese legends. It later moves to Greece, excerpting some myths, fragments of the *Iliad* and the *Odyssey*. It closes with a selection of Hebrew texts from the Old and the New Testament. Volume Two opens with classic works from Medieval Spain and excerpts from *Don Quixote*. It continues with medieval works from France, followed by Parsifal, Goethe's *Hermann and Dorothea* and other German texts, a text on St. Francis for Italy, selections of Shakespeare and an aggregate of European children stories, such as *Sleeping Beauty* and *The Ugly Duckling*. It closes with an extensive historical selection of Latin American texts by period, from pre-Columbian legends, to texts from the Conquest and the Colonial period, concluding with writings by and on independence leaders like Hidalgo, San Martín, and Sucre.

There is an evident concept of world literature here, in which the classics are the representation of what is considered to be the highest achievements of ancient and early modern literature, to which the history of Latin American literature is added as equal. It is notable, though, that the project does not engage with the notion of teaching any modern or contemporary literature. This idea is replicated in a different scale with a series of books known as the Clásicos Verdes, in reference to their green covers, an ambitious attempt to publish the great works of world literature in mass editions published between 1921 and 1924. In the various accounts of this project it is unclear how many copies were published, but we do know that thirteen titles were released in seventeen volumes.[40] They include the *Odyssey* and the *Iliad*, the tragedies of Aeschylus and Euripides, Plato's *Dialogues*, Plutarch's *Parallel Lives*, Dante's *Divine Comedy*, and, more puzzlingly, the Gospels and a selection of Plotinus' *Enneads*, a text that raised great controversy due to the contradiction between its esotericism and the populist mission of the series. There are various details to note here that exceed the purposes of this essay, most notably the fact that these books imagined a mass reading public that was yet to come: they were addressed to a reading public in construction, yet nonexistent. But the fact is that these concepts of the classic left an imprint in the institutions of world literature in Mexico, and set the stage for many ventures of world-making in the twentieth century. In fact, the Clásicos Verdes were recently republished in a facsimile edition, and some of them are freely available online in the website of the National Commission of Free Textbooks.

By the mid-1940s, it was clear that the intellectual class in Mexico had found in the idea of the public classics and of the wide distribution of world literature a significant project. It is not only the fact that cosmopolitanism was regarded to be an important complement, or even a resistance, to cultural nationalism. It is also that the articulation of mass educational projects with mass media provided invaluable opportunities to expand and democratize world literature. A telling case study is the significant number of Mexican films of the time based on world literary texts. One can invoke here the 1942 adaptation of *The Count of Montecristo*, directed by Roberto Gavaldón and Chano Urueta, two key figures of the Golden Age of Mexican cinema, with the acclaimed actor Arturo de Córdova in the title role. Paul Féval's novel *The Hunchback* became a 1943 film by Jaime Salvador, starring one of the biggest couples in Mexican cinema history: Jorge Negrete and Gloria Marín. Even comedians took a stab at this. Cantinflas, the most widely known Mexican comedian in history, starred in satirical adaptations of *Romeo and Juliet* and *The Three Musketeers* in the 1940s, and played Passepartout opposite David Niven's Phileas Fogg in the 1956 Hollywood adaptation of Jules Verne's *Around the World in Eighty Days*, which won the Oscar for Best Picture. The other great film comedian in Mexico, Tin Tan, starred in many of these adaptations over decades, from *Simbad el mareado* (a parody of Sindbad the Sailor, renamed "the seasick") in the early 1940s to *Tintansón Crusoe* in 1965. Combined with the steady flow of adaptations from Hollywood and various European industries that filled Mexican screens from the 1940s forward, and in parallel of the efforts of introduction of world literature through both collections of classics and the education system, Mexicans of all social strata had access to world literary texts regardless of whether they were book readers or not. It should not be surprising that Mexico produced a truly cosmopolitan literature in the twentieth century.

These kinds of classical collections have a long, continued history. The Sepan Cuantos collection in Porrúa, launched in 1959 and reputedly named by Reyes, boasts over 700 titles, from ancient to contemporary literature, from around the world. In some cases, collections like Cien del Mundo, created by the National Council for the Culture and the Arts (precursor of the Ministry of Culture) in the 1990s, not only published classic works but feature anthologies with topics such as post-Kafkian Austrian literature or 18th-century Portuguese arcadian poetry. This kind of cosmopolitanism fostered the work of translators like the great novelist and writer Sergio Pitol, who published over fifty translations of Eastern European, British, and Italian literature in his life. World literature in Mexico is a cultural practice inherent to the literary field, and a core project of many forms of elite and popular understandings of the right to literature. In this vein, the long-standing infrastructure of Mexican literature's world-making in the twentieth century was established and remains very much alive today.

Notes

1. Alfonso Reyes, *Anthology*, ed. José Luis Martínez, trans. Dick Gerdes (Mexico: Fondo de Cultura Económica/ Fundación para las Letras Mexicanas, 2000), 393.
2. On the foundational role of cultural nationalism in post-revolutionary Mexico, see Rick López, *Crafting Mexico: Intellectuals, Artisans and the State after the Revolution* (Durham: Duke University Press, 2010).
3. Robert T. Conn, *The Politics of Philology: Alfonso Reyes and the Invention of the Latin American Literary Tradition* (Lewisburg: Bucknell University Press, 2002).
4. On these polemics, see, respectively, Víctor Díaz Arciniega, *Querella por la cultura "revolucionaria" (1925)* (Mexico: Fondo de Cultura Económica, 1989) and Guillermo Sheridan, *Mexico en 1932. La polémica nacionalista* (Mexico: Fondo de Cultura Económica, 1999).
5. For a very detailed Bourdieusian account of this process of autonomy, see Pedro Ángel Palou, *La casa del silencio. Aproximación en tres tiempos a Contemporáneos* (Zamora: El Colegio de Michoacán, 1997). I have an account of this process, which underlies this essay, in Ignacio M. Sánchez Prado, *Naciones intelectuales. Las fundaciones de la modernidad literaria mexicana (1917–1959)* (West Lafayette: Purdue University Press, 2009).
6. See Octavio Paz, *The Labyrinth of Solitude, Life and Thought in Mexico*, trans. Lysander Kemp (New York: Grove, 1962). Carlos Fuentes, *Where the Air Is Clear: A Novel*, trans. Sam Hileman (New York: Farrar, Straus and Giroux, 1982).
7. Pascale Casanova, *The World Republic of Letters*, trans. M. B. Debevoise (Cambridge, MA: Harvard University Press, 2004).
8. Ibid., 325.
9. Paulette Patout, *Alfonso Reyes et la France* (Paris: Klincksieck, 1978).
10. Warwick Research Collective, *Combined and Uneven Development: Towards a Theory of World-Literature* (Liverpool: Liverpool University Press, 2015), 80.
11. Ángel Rama has a well-known discussion of Rulfo as a transcultural writer at the crossroads of modernism, European rural realism, and regional (but not "Amerindian") oral registers in *Writing across Cultures: Narrative Transculturation in Latin America*, trans. Daniel Frye (Durham: Duke University Press), 65–77: I have written on Rulfo's idea of the global novel in Ignacio M. Sánchez Prado, "La literatura mundial como praxis. Apuntes hacia una metodología de lo concreto," in *World Literature, Cosmopolitanism, Globality: Beyond, Against, Post, Otherwise*, ed. Gesine Müller and Mariano Siskind (Berlin: De Gruyter, 2019), 62–75.
12. David Damrosch, *What Is World Literature?* (Princeton: Princeton University Press, 2003), 78–109.
13. On Garibay, see Rafael Mondragón, *Un arte radical de la lectura. Constelaciones de la filología latinoamericana* (Mexico: Universidad Nacional Autónoma de México, 2019), 163–96.
14. See Ignacio M. Sánchez Prado, *Strategic Occidentalism: On Mexican Fiction, the Neoliberal Book Market and the Question of World Literature* (Evanston: Northwestern University Press, 2018) and Ignacio M. Sánchez Prado, ed., *América Latina en la "literatura mundial"* (Pittsburgh: Instituto Internacional de Literatura Iberoamericana, 2006).

15 Alexander Beecroft, *An Ecology of World Literature: From Antiquity to the Present Day* (London: Verso, 2015), 267–70.
16 Javier Garciadiego, *Alfonso Reyes* (Mexico: Planeta DeAgostini, 2002), 107–32. I have written about this perido in Sánchez Prado, *Naciones intelectuales*, 147–66.
17 Reyes, *Anthology*, 394.
18 Albert Guerard, *Preface to World Literature* (New York: Henry Holt & Co., 1940), 16. See also Damrosch, *What Is World Literature?*
19 Reyes, *Anthology*, 394.
20 Alfonso Reyes, *Obras completas de Alfonso Reyes XXVI. Vida de Goethe. Rumbo a Goethe. Trayectoria de Goethe. Escolio Goethianos. Teoría de la sanción* (Mexico: Fondo de Cultura Económica, 1993).
21 See Horacio Legrás, *Culture and Revolution: Violence, Memory and the Making of Modern Mexico* (Austin: University of Texas Press, 2017), 65–77.
22 For a history of Breviarios, see Víctor Díaz Arciniega, *Historia de la casa. Fondo de Cultura Económica (1934–1996)* (Mexico: Fondo de Cultura Económica, 1996), 113–15.
23 C. M. Bowra, *Historia de la literatura griega*, trans. Alfonso Reyes (Mexico: Fondo de Cultura Económica, 1948); Gilbert Murray, *Eurípides y su época*, trans. Alfonso Reyes (Mexico: Fondo de Cultura Económica, 1949).
24 Werner Jaeger, *Paideia. Los ideales de la cultura griega*, trans. Joaquín Xirau and Wenceslao Roces (Mexico: Fondo de Cultura Económica, 1957).
25 Alfonso Reyes and Werner Jaeger, *Un amigo en tierras lejanas. Correspondencia (1942–1958)*, ed. Sergio Ugalde Quintana (Mexico: El Colegio de México, 2009).
26 Gilbert Highet, *The Classical Tradition*, 2 vols., trans. Antonio Alatorre (Mexico: Fondo de Cultura Económica, 1954).
27 Ernst Robert Curtius, *Literatura Europea y Edad Media Latina*, 2 vols., ed. Antonio Alatorre and Margit Frenk (Mexico: Fondo de Cultura Económica, 1955).
28 On *modernista* cultural cosmopolitanism and literary culture, see Adela Pineda Franco, *Geopolíticas de la cultura finisecular en Buenos Aires, París y México. Las revistas literarias y el modernismo* (Pittsburgh: Instituto Internacional de Literatura Iberoamericana, 2006).
29 On this period, see Alfonso García Morales and Rosa García Gutiérrez, *México 1915–1920. Una literatura en encrucijada* (Sevilla: Renacimiento, 2020).
30 Freija Cervantes y Pedro Valero, *La colección Cvltvra y los fundamentos de la edición mexicana moderna 1916–1923* (Mexico: Juan Pablos Editor, 2016).
31 See Sánchez Prado, *Strategic Occidentalism*.
32 Some titles can be found in the facsimiles of *Mexico Moderno I. 1920–1923* (Mexico: Fondo de Cultura Económica, 1979). A short study can be found in Yanna Hadatty Mora, "La Novela Semanal," *Enciclopedia de La Literatura Mexicana*, September 26, 2018, web.
33 An in-depth collective discussion of the rise of literary institutions in Mexico between 1900 and 1950 can be found in Yanna Hadatty Mora, Norma Lojero Vega, and Rafael Mondragón Velázquez, *Historia de las literaturas en México. Siglos XX y XXI vol. 1. LA revolución intelectual de la Revolución Mexicana (1900–1946)* (Mexico: UNAM, 2019).
34 On educational campaigns, see Mary Kay Vaughan, *Cultural Politics in Revolution: Teachers, Peasants and Schools in Mexico, 1930* (Tucson: University of Arizona Press, 1997). On the cultural campaigns stemming from SEP, see López, *Crafting Mexico*.

35 Legrás, *Culture and Revolution* 9.
36 A good summary of this period in these terms can be found in William H. Beezley, "Creating a Revolutionary Culture. Vasconcelos, Indians, Anthropologists and Calendar Girls," in *A Companion to Mexican History and Culture* (Oxford: Wiley-Blackwell, 2011).
37 Engracia Loyo, "La lectura en México 1920–1940," in *Historia de la lectura en México* (México: El Colegio de México, 1998), 262–3. The mass importance and many dimensions of Vasconcelos's editorial work are too complex and wide to discuss here. On the editorial end, see also Javier Garciadiego, *Autores, editoriales, instituciones y libros. Estudios de historia intelectual* (Mexico: El Colegio de México, 2015), 121–58. A very extensive view of Vasconcelos as Minister of Education can be found in Claude Fell's *José Vasconcelos. Los años del águila, 1920–1925. Educación, cultura e iberoamericanismo en el México posrevolucionario* (México: El Colegio de México, 1989).
38 Garciadiego, *Autores*, 139–41.
39 *Lecturas clásicas para niños* (Mexico: SEP, 1924). The book is available for free download in the website of Mexico's National Commission for Free Textbooks: www.libros.conaliteg.gob.mx. For a discussion of the inception of this project, see Fell, *Los años del águila*, 494–7.
40 The information I use here, and the extensive history of the Clásicos verdes, can be found in Fell, *Los años del águila*, 484–92 and Yasmín Liliana Cortés Bandala, "Domar al caballo que conquistó Troya. Los clásicos verdes de José Vasconcelos rumbo a su primer centenario," in *De la piedra al pixel. Reflexiones en torno a las edades del libro*, ed. Marina Garone Garvier, Isabel Galina Russell, and Laurette Godinas (México: Universidad Autónoma de México, 2016), 697–726.

From Post-Revolutionary Cosmopolitanisms to Pre-Bolaño Infrarealism
Mexican Avant-Garde Literatures in/as World Literature

Sara Potter

In the aftermath of the Mexican Revolution, *Estridentista* founder Manuel Maples Arce proposed the following in his 1921 manifesto: "Cosmopoliticémonos. Ya no es posible tenerse en capítulos convencionales de arte nacional" [We must cosmopolitanize ourselves. It is no longer possible to have conventional chapters of national art].[1] Maples Arce's proposition stands in sharp contrast with a long-standing critical tendency to describe the *Estridentistas* as a nationalist literary and political movement and as an inferior counterpart to the cosmopolitan and (purportedly) apolitical *Contemporáneos* writers. On the contrary, despite the famously antagonistic relationship between the two avant-garde groups, both movements exhibited, drew from, and contributed to what Mariano Siskind has described as *deseo de mundo* or world-desire, synthesizing a variety of historical and literary influences that are consumed and articulated from a particular space in time to address their own historically and politically specific realities. This chapter will examine the ripple effects of and between the *Estridentistas*' and the *Contemporáneos*' cultural production during the aftermath of the Mexican Revolution (1910–20), including their connections and contributions to the current world literature status of authors such as Roberto Bolaño and Valeria Luiselli.

My analytic focus is on three points of interaction between Mexican avant-garde literatures and world literature: first, the ways in which Mexican avant-gardes' competing notions of cosmopolitanism work between the national and the international, the particular, and the universal in the aftermath of the Mexican Revolution. I read their negotiations of the national and the cosmopolitan as a continuation and evolution of the "split body" of modernism that Mariano Siskind discusses in *Cosmopolitan Desires* in which "the desire to be part of the universality of cultural modernity (as *modernistas* conceived it) coexisted in a productive and unresolved tension with the particular goal of producing differential identity."[2] Both avant-gardes took shape in the midst of intense polemics on how to unify the country, principally through the establishment of "genuine" nationalism and a national literature. These fierce debates emerged as

Mexico was thrust into an intense but uneven, process of modernization while also recovering from the trauma and fragmentation of ten years of armed conflict.[3]

Second, I look at the use of avant-garde impulses and influences and technology to decenter cultural production from Europe and the United States and to push back at center-vs.-periphery frameworks of reading and writing. While Mexican avant-gardes certainly drew from various aspects of European movements, Mexican and other Latin American avant-gardes had no illusions about discovering what Rosenberg calls "the repressed soul of the universal human" in non-Western cultures as the Europeans did.[4] Rather, as Vicky Unruh argues, identity was built and sought through "a New World of disorderly collections" as a part of overcoming ideas of national or continental identity rooted in a particular landscape or notion of original nature.[5] The focus on machine aesthetic and technology is another common avant-garde element used and represented by the *Estridentistas* and the *Contemporáneos* (albeit with varying degrees of enthusiasm and/or ambivalence) as both groups explored the capacity of technology to isolate or to connect various subjects on a local and global scale.

Lastly, I will explore some of the ways in which the Mexican avant-gardes troubled and complicated the notion of literary legacy and trace the groundwork that both groups laid that would prove influential to future generations of writers who are more widely recognized as "world literature" authors. If the *Estridentistas*' and the *Contemporáneos*' measure of success and cultural impact were considered only in terms of current readership, books in print, or number of translations (primarily into English), this framework would diminish and erase the larger ripple effects of both groups that reached beyond their published work. While close readings of individual texts are certainly valuable, as Vicky Unruh and Hector Hoyos have observed, I agree with Unruh's suggestion to go beyond collections of particular texts and "to approach vanguardism as a form of activity rather than as an assemblage of individually outstanding texts."[6] This approach allows for a richer and more holistic view of the two movements in Mexico, as well as the discourses that emerged between creative and critical texts and projects: ongoing debates in local newspapers, theatrical performances, radio presentations, and the members' work as artists, activists, and politicians, all of which would lay the groundwork for future world literature authors from or associated with Mexico.

"Attending the Spectacle of Ourselves": The Emergence of the Mexican Avant-Gardes

Estridentismo was formed out of Manuel Maples Arce's impatience with the stagnant literary and cultural atmosphere in Mexico. He refused to look up to or imitate the masters of previous eras, declaring, "En este instante asistimos al espectáculo de nosotros mismos" [In this instant, we attend the spectacle of ourselves].[7] By plastering his audacious manifesto, *Actual No. 1*, all over Mexico City and by publishing his work in various national and international periodicals, Maples Arce drew in writers and artists such as Árqueles Vela, Luis Quintanilla (Kyn Taniya), and Germán List Arzubide, and would soon attract admirers and collaborators within and beyond Mexico, including Tina Modotti, Edward Weston, Diego Rivera, Nahui Olin/Carmen Mondragón, Pablo Neruda, Miguel Angel Asturias, Jorge Luis Borges, and John Dos Passos.[8] Maples Arce's *Estridentismo* (an invented word in Spanish) contains various elements: auditory and textual noise, the performative and the oral nature of the texts (many were written to be read out loud in public gatherings), the celebration of technology and speed, and the concept of *actualismo* or presentism, which insisted on focusing not on the past or the future but on the present moment.

Estridentismo was one of the first Latin American avant-gardes, coming into being just after Vicente Huidobro's *creacionismo* [creationism] in Chile (which Maples Arce considered exemplary in theory and uninspiring in practice), and alongside Argentine *ultraísmo* [ultraism] and Brazilian *antropofagia* [anthropophagy].[9] The *Estridentistas* frequently addressed political and social concerns in their manifestos and other writings, as in Maples Arce's 1924 poem *Urbe* [Metropolis], which he dedicated "a los obreros de México" [to the workers of Mexico] as "Los pulmones de Rusia / soplan hacia nosotros / el viento de la revolución social" [The great lungs of Russia / breathe toward us / the wind of social revolution].[10] It is no surprise that they were, as Germán List Arzubide would later defiantly proclaim, "los *punks* de nuestra época" [the punks of our era] due to their brash and confrontational interactions with the Mexican literary and political establishment.[11]

While the *Contemporáneos* emerged a bit later as a group (or non-group), both avant-garde movements took shape during what Rubén Gallo calls 'the other Mexican Revolution': that is, amid the sudden onslaught of cultural transformations that took place due to the new media and technology that landed in Mexico City after 1920.[12] Many of the *Contemporáneos* began to publish poetry, narrative, and essays in the late 1910s and early 1920s, though they did not coalesce into anything that might be considered a group or generation until the mid- to late 1920s. They did undertake aesthetic projects together, such as the Teatro Ulíses [Ulysses Theater], and the literary journals *Ulíses* (1927–8) and *Contemporáneos* (1928–31). Nearly all of them attended the prestigious Escuela Nacional Preparatoria [National Preparatory School] in Mexico City, even though, like the *Estridentistas*, many came from the countryside: Jorge Cuesta (Córdoba, Veracruz), José Gorostiza (Grijalva, Tabasco), Gilberto Owen (Rosario, Sinaloa), Carlos Pellicer (Villahermosa, Tabasco), and Rodolfo Usigli (San Juan de Letrán, Puebla), while Salvador Novo, Antonieta Rivas Mercado, Jaime Torres Bodet, and Xavier Villaurrutia hailed from Mexico City. The *Contemporáneos* did not share the *Estridentistas*' enthusiasm for revolution, but neither did they retreat from conflict; Xavier Villaurrutia notes in a letter in 1934 that it was a group formed "por diferencias más que por semejanzas" [more through their differences than their similarities],[13] and they were active participants in the series of nationalist polemics that rocked Mexico in the years following the Revolution.

While the *Contemporáneos* were criticized for being an apolitical, cosmopolitan group interested only in aesthetics, Octavio Paz proposes that the group's posture is a reaction to "ciertas experiencias de la vida mexicana" [certain experiences of

Mexican life], most particularly the Revolution.[14] The group was never as politically or aesthetically distanced as they pretended to be; indeed, I read their supposedly apolitical stance as a deliberately provocative gesture in a political and cultural environment in which the literary and cultural formation of *lo mexicano* and corresponding associations of masculinity in nationality and in literature had taken on a new and overwhelming importance. Given that many of the *Contemporáneos* were gay or bisexual (as opposed to the aggressively heterosexual *Estridentistas*), their refusal to engage in prescribed performances of masculinity and their cosmopolitan approach to literature and to art were subversive responses to idealized notions of the national subject and national literature. Indeed, despite their celebrated status according to Mexican intellectuals like Carlos Monsiváis and Octavio Paz, Hugo Verani reminds us that the *Contemporáneos'* work was harshly criticized in Mexico at the time of its publication, even as it was warmly received by an international audience.[15]

Dueling Cosmopolitanisms: Inhabiting the Particular and the Universal

While there was little love lost between the *Estridentistas* and the *Contemporáneos*, it would be inaccurate to say the two groups had nothing in common, or that there was no overlap in their political, cultural, and theoretical positions. The *Estridentistas* assumed an über-masculine and nationalistic stance but also defined themselves as cosmopolitan; the *Contemporáneos*, meanwhile, expressed their Mexicanness by omission; that is, by *not* forcing their texts into nationalist contortions. As Xavier Villaurrutia puts it,

> Qué importa que alguien pida que pongamos etiquetas de Made in Mexico a nuestras obras, si nosotros sabemos que nuestras obras serán mexicanas a pesar de que nuestra voluntad no se lo proponga, o, más bien, gracias a que no se lo propone.
>
> [What does it matter if someone asks us to put Made in Mexico labels on our works, if we know that our works will be Mexican in spite of the fact that we do not propose to make them so, or rather, because we do not propose to make them so].[16]

In a period that was consumed with debates over who and what Mexico and Mexicans should be after the Revolution, both groups explored and interrogated various perspectives from which to approach these questions of identity on a national and international scale.

While the *Estridentista* call for cosmopolitanization in its first manifesto may appear to be at odds with the group's nationalist platform, it is worth noting—as César Domínguez argues in his work on world literature and cosmopolitanism—that the concepts of cosmopolitanism and nationalism need not be mutually opposed.

Indeed, to do so overlooks Latin American theories of analysis, such as Uruguayan theorist Ángel Rama's construct of narrative transculturation.[17] Likewise, it would be inaccurate to assume that the *Contemporáneos*' more explicitly cosmopolitan texts do not also address issues particular to Mexican concerns. As such, I will be exploring the ways in which the two groups' constructions of cosmopolitanism overlap and differ, as well as the elements of cosmopolitan literature that are most explicitly and intimately linked to world literature.

These negotiations of the cosmopolitan/universal and national/particular are not unique to the Mexican avant-gardes; rather, they are continuations and evolutions of the sorts of negotiations that were an essential element of Latin American *modernismo* (roughly 1880-1920). Mariano Siskind observes that as Latin American writers like Rubén Darío, José Martí, and Manuel Gutiérrez Nájera approached the end of the nineteenth century, they felt their duty was to create what Sylvia Molloy calls a "rhetoric of foundation" that would serve to establish modern culture in a place where none existed (or, rather, where they did not perceive any to exist). Even as Darío, Martí, and other *modernistas* sought to modernize and to define Latin America, they also articulated "a universalist discourse on the literatures of the world that is in blatant contradiction to their own particularistic goals."[18] Nevertheless, Siskind insists, "*modernismo*'s world literary discourse does not invoke foreign literatures to signify 'otherness' but rather views foreign works and authors, in classical cosmopolitan fashion, as distant relatives and kindred spirits whose names signify the presence of a world that includes Latin America."[19] Rather than imitating foreign literatures, then, these authors dialogued with them in a declaration of equality and of Latin America's place in the world, and made strategic use of their self-proclaimed cosmopolitan subject position "as a way of responding to specific modernizing demands that a particularistic, nationalist or regionalist discourse of cultural difference would not satisfy."[20] To create a new Mexican literature in keeping with the *Estridentistas*' vision for the country, the members of the group used a very similar strategy, particularly in their manifestos, creating an international collage of ideas, ideals, and tactics to propose alternative and dynamic ways of operating as modern Mexican subjects.

The *Contemporáneos*, meanwhile, sought to create literature that would create a universal subjectivity untethered from hegemonic ideals of Mexicanness. Jorge Cuesta, for example, argued that fixations on nationalism are not Mexican at all, but rather rooted in Eurocentric discourses that do not speak to Mexico's ongoing debate regarding national literature. As Ignacio Sánchez Prado observes in *Naciones intelectuales* [Intellectual Nations], "Cuesta plantea que . . . el culto al color local y la vuelta a lo mexicano no son más de maneras de adscribirse a un debate europeo que nada tiene que ver con el problema de la literatura nacional" [Cuesta proposes that . . . the cult of local color and the turn toward Mexicanness are nothing more than ways of ascribing to a European debate that has nothing to do with the issue of national literature].[21] Xavier Villaurrutia had a similar stance, arguing that their works were Mexican in spite of or perhaps even because of the group's refusal to place the kinds of "Made in Mexico" stamps on their work that Cuesta critiques. Indeed, texts such as Gilberto Owen's *Novela como nube* [*Novel Like a Cloud*] and Xavier Villaurrutia's

Dama de corazones [*Queen of Hearts*] are clear responses to post-revolutionary concerns that work against the explicitly nationalist *novelas de la revolución* and notions of Mexicanness as proposed by intellectuals such as philosopher and Secretary of Education José Vasconcelos.[22] The idealized Mexican citizen at the time was a virile, masculine mestizo figure, and the *Contemporáneos*' representations of effeminate men who were more concerned with foreign literature and high culture than workers' rights and agrarian reform served as deliberately provocative responses to limited and limiting constructs of national literature and identity.

While cosmopolitan literature and world literature are not always synonymous, I find it productive to draw upon César Domínguez's reading of Sheldon Pollack's definition of cosmopolitanism to explain how the two forms of literature overlap. For Pollack, cosmopolitan literature is "literary communication that . . . *thinks of itself as unbounded, unobstructed, unlocated.*"[23] Seen in this light, Domínguez asserts that cosmopolitan literatures are indeed also world literatures; the primary difference is on the "emphasis on the cultural process itself."[24] Both *Estridentista* and *Contemporáneos* literatures and cultural production assert themselves as cosmopolitan through their negation of various boundaries. The *Estridentistas* insist on the importance of breaking free from previous standards of Mexican literature and poetry as part of their aesthetic and political program, alternating between nationalist and universal perspectives in order to establish Mexico as a modern nation and to declare its presence on a global scale. Meanwhile, the *Contemporáneos* refuse to be bound to a singular definition of Mexico or Mexicanness, using foreign literature and influences to work beyond European constructions of national literature. Both groups' navigations of the national and the universal require careful attention to the historical context in which their texts and activities took place, as well as to the cultural processes that shaped their work and perspectives. For Maples Arce, part of the process and possibilities of cosmopolitism are located in influences drawn from other avant-garde movements, as well as the equalizing potential of technologies of communication, construction, and transportation that had only recently arrived in Mexico. During this period of cultural interrogation and transformation, the *Estridentistas* and other "technological revolutionaries" (to use Rubén Gallo's term) "rejected the nationalist obsession . . . in favor of a cosmopolitan avant-gardism that put them in dialogue with like-minded innovators in Moscow and New York, Paris and São Paulo."[25] This use of technology and dialogues with foreign avant-gardes to decenter cultural production from Europe and the United States and to disrupt center/periphery frameworks of reading and writing are the focus of the next section of this chapter.

Creating Collages and Destroying Centers with Avant-Garde Influences

In, immediately after Manuel Maples Arce urged his audience to become cosmopolitan as a necessary alternative to conventional approaches to national art, he explained that technology was a vital component of the process of cosmopolitanization: "Las noticias se expenden por telégrafo; sobre los rasca-cielos . . . El medio se transforma y su influencia lo modifica todo" [The news are distributed by telegram; over the skyscrapers . . . The medium is transformed and its influence changes everything].[26] As Tatiana Flores points out, Maples Arce believed that "new technologies made possible 'the psychological unity of the century,' " and that "because of the rapid spread of information brought about by the radio, the telegraph, and the airplane, it was possible to stay abreast of current developments from anywhere in the world, and therefore old frameworks of center and periphery no longer applied."[27] Maples Arce's perspective on technology as a great equalizer had some significant failings, as it ignored the uneven arrival of modernization to Mexico and purported to eliminate and render unnecessary all considerations of race and class. Nevertheless, new technologies of communication and transportation did allow for greater and more immediate participation in a wide range of intellectual networks that, for Maples Arce, placed him on equal footing with his contemporaries and predecessors in other parts of the world.[28]

The presence of machines and other technology in Mexico was not new—dictator Porfirio Díaz (1877–80, 1884–1911) was a renowned technophile—but the difference lies in what Rubén Gallo describes as "the sudden interest that writers and artists expressed in technological artifacts" in the aftermath of the Revolution.[29] These new technologies offered new perceptions of reality and possibilities of representation, as well as the potential to reach a broader audience and to reduce the communication and information lapses between large urban centers and small rural towns. Due to high levels of illiteracy in post-revolutionary Mexico, radio broadcasts proved highly effective in reaching a wider audience than print media; as such, "it was not newspapers but radio that allowed citizens to identify with the new state that emerged from the revolution."[30]

Enthusiasm for technology is a well-known element of estridentismo in Maples Arce's manifestos and poems as well as Kyn Taniya's poetic production on developments from radios to typewriters to concrete, though the collected works of *Estridentista* writers exhibit a more nuanced and ambivalent relationship with the technologies that accompany modernization (as, for example, in Árqueles Vela's short novel *La Señorita Etc.* [*Miss Etc.*] [1922]). While the *Contemporáneos* did not explicitly share the *Estridentistas*' machinist aesthetic, the (non-)group also engaged with technology in significant ways in their written works and other creative projects. Their perspectives varied widely, from Xavier Villaurutia's tortured experience of modernity in his 1926 poem "Fonógrafos" [Phonographs] to Salvador Novo's irreverent and amusing descriptions of the chaos of modern urban life in his narrative and essays.[31] Both groups, however, were actively involved in using and representing new technologies and their impacts on daily life, particularly regarding their work on and about the wireless radio after the first station was launched in Mexico City by the literary magazine *El Universal Ilustrado* in 1923.

While representation and use of new technologies could not entirely break down the boundaries between the city and the countryside or between Mexico and the world beyond, both avant-garde movements, particularly estridentismo, drew upon an assemblage of strategies and characteristics of foreign avant-garde movements to further decenter European cultural production and articulate the mosaic of experiences in and beyond the capital in the post-revolutionary nation. Both movements were formed in Mexico City, and both produced pointed observations on the startling contrasts of race, culture, origin, and socioeconomic status that intensified with the rapid modernization of the capital, but the *Estridentistas* also made significant efforts to spread their movement beyond the metropolis to Puebla, Zacatecas, and, most famously, Xalapa, where they also occupied political positions during the final two years of the movement's official activity.

The influence of Italian and Russian futurisms on the group is particularly evident in the group's early work: along with Maples Arce's references to Marinetti and Mayakovsky in the first *Estridentista* manifesto, Odile Cisneros observes that his poetry collections *Andamios interiores: Poemas Radiográficas* [*Interior Scaffolding: Radiographic Poems*, 1922] and the previously mentioned *Urbe* [*Metropolis*, 1924] "employ Futurist vocabularies to construct a vision of the city peculiarly divorced from the realities of post-Revolutionary Mexico."[32] If we read *Andamios interiores* and *Urbe* as extensions of Maples Arce's manifestos, however, the gap between vision and reality makes sense, as both poems contain the performative and utopic impulses that are innate characteristics of the manifesto as a genre. Here, I follow Martin Puchner's work on early-twentieth-century manifestos in *Poetry of the Revolution* in which he argues that it is not the job of manifestos to be descriptive. Instead, it is more productive to read these texts as "a means to an end, as a genre that uniquely represents and produces the fantasies, hopes, aspirations, and shortcomings of modernity."[33] As was discussed in the previous section, the *Estridentistas* and the *Contemporáneos* shared the *modernista* conviction that their role was to establish a modern (or modernized) culture through literature where none previously existed. The aggression and anti-establishment energy of Italian and Russian futurisms propelled the *Estridentistas'* vision of how to pull Mexico out of its literary stagnation, but it is French cubism that provided the group with the tools to represent the simultaneous mosaics of Mexican post-revolutionary experience.

In her analysis of futurism and cubism in Mexican and Brazilian avant-garde movements, Odile Cisneros observes that "Cubist poetry and painting share the concept of 'simultaneism,' roughly synonymous with ... the juxtaposition of difference phrases or images, and the view of the work of art as autonomous."[34] Furthermore, as Peter Nicholls argues, the poetry of French Cubists such as Guillaume Apollinaire is comparable to the Cubist paintings of Pablo Picasso and Georges Braque in that they share "a refusal to make the work a transparent window on the world. The artistic material—paint, lines, words—assumes a new kind of self-sufficiency, and we are not invited to look beyond the work for something to explain or legitimate it."[35] These aspects of cubism—the multiple and simultaneous representations of perspective, demanding that the reader engage with the work, and its refusal to live in the shadows of other artists or artistic movements—appear in much of the *Estridentistas'* writing and art, and, to a certain extent, to the *Contemporáneos'* cultural production as well, though their connections to other avant-garde movements are rarely, if ever, explicitly stated. While the language and strategies of futurism appear in Maples Arce's manifestos and poems like *Urbe*, the underlying themes and images represent a city and a country in a state of intense and uneven transition, a dizzying collage of perspectives that is grounded in the movement's *actualista* or presentist philosophy. The use of Cubist simultaneity in the movement creates space for texts as disparate as Maples Arce's *Urbe*, Árqueles Vela's ambivalent and anxious interactions with city life in *La Señorita Etc.*, and Xavier Icaza's dizzying marriage of costumbrist literature, sociopolitical critique, and surrealism in *Panchito Chapopote*. As different as they are, these texts do not reflect Marinetti's or Mayakovsky's futurist inclinations so much as they oscillate between celebrating the possibilities of the post-revolutionary present moment and expressing serious reservations about what might go wrong. Together and separately, the corpus of *Estridentista* texts carry out what the Warwick Research Collective (WReC) describe as an "'accordionizing' or 'telescoping' function of combined and uneven development as a form of time travel within the same space."[36] By representing the simultaneous and disparate experiences of modernization, the *Estridentistas* create multifaceted and challenging representations of the parts of the capital and the country in which modernization processes had arrived only partially or not at all, as well as the demand that the reader engage with this sort of "time travel within the same space" between harsh social realities and calls to action toward utopic visions for the future. While the *Contemporáneos'* texts were less explicitly engaged with avant-garde strategies, texts such as Gilberto Owen's *Novela como nube* [*Novel Like a Cloud*] and Xavier Villaurutia's *Dama de corazones* [*Queen of Hearts*] can also be read as narratives that mix elements of cubism and surrealism to carry out similar journeys of time travel in the same (psychological, urban, or national) space, albeit with a greater focus on the internal reaction of the narrative subject to the experience of fast-changing and uneven development. These visions, strategies, and responses to current sociopolitical realities would carry forward with ripple effects of influence into other disciplines as well as to more officially canonical writers and cultural production throughout the rest of the twentieth century and up to the present day, which will be the focus of the final section of this chapter.

Complicating Notions of Literary Legacy and the Path(s) to World Literature Status

In his 1957 essay collection *Las peras del olmo* [*The Pears of the Elm*], Octavio Paz offered a backhanded defense of estridentismo and its legacy. The critical response to the *Estridentistas*, he said, had been unjustly harsh to a movement that represented "una saludable y necesaria explosión de rebeldía" [a healthy and necessary outburst of rebelliousness].[37] Apparently not content with the suggestion that the *Estridentismo* had been little more than a group of defiant teenagers going through a rebellious phase, Paz continued, "Lástima que durara tan poco. Lástima, también, que no haya tenido herederos" [Too bad it didn't last very long. Too bad it has not produced any heirs either].[38] Some forty years later, Daniel Balderston would come to a similar, albeit less sympathetic, conclusion: "For all their noise about procreative sexuality, the *Estridentistas* have no progeny among contemporary poets."[39] While Balderston is justified in his critique of the homophobia that figured heavily into post-revolutionary polemics in general and *Estridentista* texts in particular, neither he nor Paz was able to recognize the full extent of the *Estridentistas*' cultural and literary impact in the years after the movement had officially ended. However, the work of scholars like Clemencia Corte Velasco, Evodio Escalante, Esther Hernández Palacio, Silvia Pappe, and Elissa Rashkin offer compelling refutations of this long-existing tendency to deny the impact or legacy of the *Estridentistas*. This final section will examine the impact of the activities of the *Estridentistas* and *Contemporáneos*, as well as the ways in which these groups have laid the groundwork for future canonical and world literature writers.

Regarding both groups, but particularly in the case of the *Estridentistas*, their poetry is not widely read, nor is it readily available to many would-be consumers for various social, linguistic, and economic reasons that are too complicated to expand on here.[40] That is not to say, however, that their written production had no impact on future generations. Delia Ungureanu's reading of critic Marcel Raymond's assessment of the surrealist movement offers some useful parallels for considering the Mexican avant-gardes as well. In a 1933 article, Raymond says, "It is true that [surrealist] poetry has few readers, and that it sometimes discourages the readers."[41] (This occasional discouragement is something to which I can attest in my experiences in reading and teaching texts like *Estridentista* Kyn Taniya's *Radio: Wireless Poem in Thirteen Messages* or *Contemporáneo* José Gorostiza's *Death without End*.) Nevertheless, Raymond does not dismiss the possibility of the movement's future impact; it "registers . . . changes in the atmosphere, it makes the gesture that others will imitate and develop."[42] Following Raymond's reading, Ungureanu argues that surrealist poetry and cultural production "survived as a mode of thinking, as an attitude towards life, and as a way to represent the world in works that belong to writers who became canonical in their turn."[43] While none of the Mexican avant-gardes ruled Mexico City as surrealism did Paris, Ungureanu's point about the possibility of future impact is well taken and applicable to the avant-gardist ripple effects in post-revolutionary Mexico. Also, as with the surrealist program, the Mexican avant-gardes' impact extended well beyond poetry to other mediums and modes of expression. Vicky Unruh's work on Latin American avant-garde movements recognizes this tendency as well, as she posits that "Latin America's early twentieth-century avant-gardes may best be understood . . . as a multifaceted cultural activity, manifested in a variety of creative endeavors and events" rather than a discrete corpus of canonical texts or authors.[44] Reading the *Estridentistas* or the *Contemporáneos* as strictly poetic movements or reducing their legacy to one kind of textual output drastically underestimates and even erases their intellectual, social, and artistic contributions; to do so also unjustly minimizes the multidisciplinary nature of their projects and the assortment of genres and mediums (*crónica*, essay, manifesto, narrative, poetry, painting, theater, spoken radio discourses) that formed a larger constellation of activity and influence.

Another important element of the ongoing survival and aesthetic contributions of the Mexican avant-gardes lies in the very discursive and decentering work mentioned in the previous section, as these strategies create modes of thinking that, in turn, create platforms for more canonical writers in the future who are presently accepted as "world literature" authors. The *Estridentistas*' influence expanded beyond literature to inspire social, artistic, and political groups after their official dissolution in 1927. Roughly half a century later, the members' continued presence in academic and literary circles drew the attention of the *infrarrealistas* [infrarealists], an avant-garde poetry group formed in Mexico City in the late 1970s that included a young Roberto Bolaño among its members. My use of "pre-Bolaño" in the title refers to Bolaño as a world literature phenomenon rather than the author himself, before his 1998 novel, *Los detectives salvajes* [*The Savage Detectives*], would catapult him to world literature status in Spanish and, posthumously, in English, with Natasha Wimmer's 2007 translation. Significantly, the novel does not only include *Estridentista* writers as characters, but the movement's influence on the novel is evident to the point that it has been described by Mexican scholar Evodio Escalante as "the last Estridentista novel."[45] The relationship between Bolaño and the *Estridentistas* turned out to be mutually beneficial: Bolaño's interviews with the three surviving *Estridentistas* in 1976 (Germán List Arzubide, Manuel Maples Arce, and Árqueles Vela) brought renewed attention to the *Estridentista* movement that had inspired the infrarrealistas' anti-establishment activities and aesthetic, while also providing the inspiration for the backbone of the plot of *The Savage Detectives*. The exchanges between Bolaño, the infrarrealistas, and the *Estridentistas* were just one example of numerous interactions between estridentismo, *Estridentista* artists, and other poets and movements in various parts of Mexico, from Baja California to Chiapas.[46]

The *Contemporáneos*' influence, meanwhile, can be seen from the Mid-Century Generation in the 1950s and 1960s to the Crack Generation of the mid-1990s and, most recently, in the work of Valeria Luiselli. The *Contemporáneos* never issued a manifesto, but the group's members frequently articulated their views on literature, art, culture, and politics in essays, newspaper articles, radio presentations, and epistolary exchanges. While this makes the assemblage of a coherent position difficult to ascertain at first glance, certain commonalities emerge: an intense devotion to critical rigor, a knowledge of literature that ran wide and deep, across centuries and continents; the confidence with which they integrated Spanish-language literature and literature from other continents into their work as part of their own canon, and a cosmopolitan approach to literature. The Mid-Century Generation, like the *Contemporáneos*, never wrote a manifesto as such. Nevertheless, the writers of this generation, which included Octavio Paz, Juan José Arreola, Inés Arredondo, Juan Vicente Melo, Juan García Ponce, and Sergio Pitol, shared an "afán cosmopolita" [cosmopolitan zeal] that linked them to the *Contemporáneos* even as, like their predecessors, that very cosmopolitan inclination resulted in resistance and criticism from other members of the Mexican intelligentsia.[47] For Pitol and his generation as well as for the *Contemporáneos* who preceded them, cosmopolitanism was, as Ignacio Sánchez Prado reminds us, "a way to resist the national imperatives of the culture fostered by the postrevolutionary regime."[48] That said, both generations sought to avoid strict oppositions of nationalism versus cosmopolitanism in which one was the antithesis of the other. "Rather," Sánchez Prado proposes, "[Pitol's cosmopolitanism] exists as a repository of cultural ideas and freedoms that resist diverse forms of political repression and power."[49] The definition of the type of cosmopolitism exhibited by Sergio Pitol hews closely to Jorge Cuesta's critique of the limits of post-revolutionary expectations of nationalist literature.

This cosmopolitan impulse that expands the possibilities of the national rather than serving as an antithesis of it is also apparent in the Crack Generation. In their 1996 manifesto, jointly written by members Ricardo Chávez Castañeda, Ignacio Padilla, Pedro Ángel Palou, Eloy Urroz, and Jorge Volpi, the writers declare the importance of producing totalizing and challenging literature that requires serious engagement on the part of the reader. According to Eloy Urroz, the best way to reach and fully access the narrative of the Crack Generation is "persiguiendo . . . esa genealogía que desde los Contemporáneos (o un poco antes) ha forjado la cultura nacional cuando ha querido correr verdaderos riesgos formales y estéticos" [by following . . . this genealogy that, from the time of the Contemporáneos (or a bit before that) has forged national culture when it attempts to take genuine formal and aesthetic risks].[50] While the Crack Generation was not able to interact with the *Contemporáneos* as directly as Roberto Bolaño did with the *Estridentistas*, the *Contemporáneos* form part of the Crack's literary production as well as their influences: Pedro Ángel Palou's 1992 novel *La alcoba de un mundo* [*In the Bedroom of a World*] works from Xavier Villaurrutia's poems, narrative, essays, and correspondence to imagine the internal workings, perspective, and voice of the poet. In the same year, Jorge Volpi's *A pesar del oscuro silencio* [*In Spite of the Dark Silence*, translated in 2010 by Olivia Maciel] features a narrator named Jorge, who goes on an obsessive quest to understand the life of *Contemporáneo* Jorge Cuesta. This ripple effect of influence extends backward to the *Contemporáneos* as well: while little of Cuesta's work has been translated into other languages (the exception being a 2003 French translation of his 1942 poem "Canto a un dios mineral" [Song to a Mineral God]), Volpi's extensive use of Cuesta's writing in his own novel required Maciel to engage with Cuesta's work and language as well in the process of translating the novel, bringing at least part of Cuesta's work into the public eye in English for the first time.

In a similar vein, Valeria Luiselli's debut novel *Los ingrávidos* [*Faces in the Crowd*, 2011; translated in 2014 by Christina MacSweeney] weaves Gilberto Owen, another *Contemporáneo* poet whose work has been little translated, into her novel as a character and as one of the narrators. The book's perspective shifts between that of a young mother, writer, and translator who thinks she sees the ghost of Gilberto Owen on the subway while she lobbies her boss to commission a translation of some of his lost poems, and Gilberto Owen himself during his time in Philadelphia and New York with Spanish poet Federico García Lorca, reflecting on the city and on the young woman he thinks he sees through the windows of the subway cars. While it has been argued that Luiselli is largely riding Roberto Bolaño's coattails into world literature status, I am more convinced by Ignacio Sánchez Prado's assertion that Luiselli's literary production is deeply embedded in "an ecosystem of Mexican literature" that significantly precedes Bolaño's emergence as a world literature author. Sánchez Prado's sketch of this ecosystem, which includes direct connections to the Mid-Century Generation (specifically Pitol) and the *Contemporáneos* as well as possible associations with the Crack Generation, traces the ripple effects of avant-garde confrontations with modernism and modernization to the phenomenon of Luiselli as a world literature author, though he also rightly includes Mexican women writers of the 1950s and 1960s as well as the "feminine boom" in Mexican letters in the 1990s as elements of the ecosystem that would nurture Luiselli's own emergence in the early twenty-first century.[51]

Conclusion

In his 2006 book *Poetry of the Revolution*, Martin Puchner reads avant-garde movements as manifestations of radical modernism and modernization rather than niche or marginalized forms of cultural production. He refers to avant-garde movements in Italy, Russia, and Latin America as proof that "the most radical forms of modernism occurred . . . in places where the forces of modernization confronted violently older forms of production and social organization," producing avant-garde groups who intended to change the world by participating in the economics, politics, and literatures of that world.[52] The emergence of the Mexican avant-gardes is an excellent example of this sort of violent confrontation, as the *Estridentistas* and the *Contemporáneos* emerged during the fears, fragmentations, and possibilities of the immediate post-revolutionary period. Puchner goes on to describe modernization not as a single process but rather as a series of different waves, "each bringing with it new avant-gardes."[53] This proposed reading of modernization is useful in two ways: first, it allows for broader and more inclusive conceptions of avant-garde activity and its ramifications in ways that go beyond the frequently marginalized representations and limitations of the historical avant-garde. Second, Puchner's imagery of waves of modernization accompanied by new avant-gardes speaks more fully to the dynamic connections and interactions between the two phenomena while also drawing attention to the importance of reading the specific historical, political, and cultural conditions that produce and are produced by these waves.

From the aftermath of the Mexican Revolution to the present, each of the groups and authors following the historical avant-gardes in the 1920s and 1930s participated in their own "violent confrontations" with older forms of production and social organization on a national and global scale in a way that interrogates limited and limiting definitions of national identity and literature and that creates meaningful, horizontal platforms from which to engage in the global market of ideas. Each produced literatures and cultural activities that occupied the unstable, but productive, ground between constructions of national and universal literatures without placing them in opposition to one another, creating rich networks of impact and influence as they did so.

Notes

1. Manuel Maples Arce, "Actual No. 1." in *El estridentismo: México 1921–1927*, ed. Luis Mario Schneider (Mexico City: Universidad Nacional Autónoma, 1985), 46. Unless otherwise indicated, all translations from Spanish to English are mine.
2. Mariano Siskind, *Cosmopolitan Desires: Global Modernity and World Literature in Latin America* (Evanston: Northwestern University Press, 2014), 106–7.
3. Guillermo Sheridan, *México en 1932: La polémica nacionalista* (Mexico City: Fondo de Cultura Económica, 1999), 25–37. See also the first part of Ignacio Sánchez Prado's *Naciones intelectuales: Las fundaciones de la modernidad literaria mexicana (1917–1959)* (West Lafayette: Purdue University Press, 2009), covering 1917–1939.
4. Fernando J. Rosenberg, *The Avant-Garde and Geopolitics in Latin America* (Pittsburgh: University of Pittsburgh Press, 2006), 2.
5. Vicky Unruh, *Latin American Vanguards: The Art of Contentious Encounters* (Berkeley: University of California Press, 1994), 164.
6. Ibid., 8.
7. Maples Arce, "Actual No. 1," 42.
8. Elissa J. Rashkin, *The Stridentist Movement in Mexico: The Avant-Garde and Cultural Change in the 1920s* (Lanham: Lexington Books, 2009), 61–77.
9. Among the excellent and comprehensive sources on Latin American avant-gardes are Jorge Schwartz's *Las vanguardias latinoamericanas* [*Latin American Avant-Gardes*] (1991, 2002), Vicky Unruh's *Latin American Vanguards*, Hugo Verani's *Narrativa vanguardista hispanoaméricana* [*Avant-garde Hispanic American Narrative*], (1996), and the five-volume *Vanguardia latinoamericana: Historia, crítica y documentos* [*Latin American Avant-Garde: History, Criticism, and Documents*], published between 2000 and 2015.
10. Maples Arce, "Urbe: Super-poema bolchevique en 5 cantos," in *El estridentismo: México 1921–1927*, ed. Luis Mario Schneider (Mexico City: Universidad Nacional Autónoma de México, 1985), 191. Trans. John Dos Passos, 1929, republished by Rubén Gallo in "John Dos Passos in Mexico," *Modernism/modernity* 14, no. 2 (2007): 329–45.
11. Germán List Arzubide, *Revista Generación* 1 no. 3 (1995): n.p.
12. Rubén Gallo, *Mexican Modernity: The Avant-Garde and the Technological Revolution* (Cambridge, MA: The MIT Press, 2005), 1.
13. Xavier Villaurrutia, "Carta a un joven [1934]," in *Los "Contemporáneos" por sí mismos*, ed. Miguel Capistrán (*Revista de la Universidad de México* 6 [February 1967], xii).
14. Octavio Paz, *Xavier Villaurrutia en persona y en obra* (Mexico City: Fondo de Cultura Económica, 1978), 22.
15. Hugo J. Verani, *Las vanguardias literarias en Hispanoamérica (Manifiestos, proclamas y otros escritos)* (Rome: Bulzoni, 1986), 13.
16. Gregorio Ortega, "Conversación en un escritorio con Xavier Villaurrutia," in *México en 1932: La polémica nacionalista*, ed. Guillermo Sheridan (Mexico City: Fondo de Cultura Económica, 1999), 158.
17. César Domínguez, "World Literature and Cosmopolitanism," in *The Routledge Companion to World Literature*, ed. Theo D'haen, David Damrosch, and Djelal Kadir (New York: Routledge, 2012), 243.
18. Siskind, *Cosmopolitan Desires*, 107.

19 Ibid., 105.
20 Ibid., 107.
21 Sánchez Prado, *Naciones intelectuales*, 102.
22 Evodio Escalante offers an excellent overview of the Contemporáneos' responses to the Mexican Revolution and the subsequent polemics regarding national identity and literature in "Espectralidad y eficacia de la Revolución en *Dama de corazones* de Xavier Villaurrutia," *Signos Literarios* 5 (2007): 97–107.
23 Sheldon Pollock, "Cosmopolitan and Vernacular in History," in *Cosmopolitanism*, ed. Carol A. Breckenridge et al. (Durham: Duke University Press, 2002), 22. Italics mine.
24 Domínguez, "World Literature and Cosmopolitanism," 247.
25 Gallo, *Mexican Modernity*, 2.
26 Maples Arce, "Actual No. 1," 45.
27 Tatiana Flores, "Starting from Mexico: Estridentismo as an Avant-Garde Model," *World Art* 4 no. 1 (2014): 50, 53.
28 Ibid., 53.
29 Ibid., 4.
30 Ibid., 125–6.
31 Sara Potter, "Nocturnos vacíos y silencios fructíferos: El sonido y el espacio en la poesía de Xavier Villaurrutia," *Confluencia* 27, no. 2 (2012): 141; Gallo, *Mexican Modernity*, 5.
32 Odile Cisneros, "Futurism and Cubism in the Early Poetics of Mexican *Estridentismo* and Brazilian *Modernismo*," *International Yearbook of Futurism Studies* 7 (2017): 211.
33 Martin Puchner, *Poetry of the Revolution: Marx, Manifestos, and the Avant-Gardes* (Princeton: Princeton University Press, 2006), 7.
34 Cisneros, "Futurism and Cubism in the Early Poetics of Mexican *Estridentismo* and Brazilian *Modernismo*," 211.
35 Peter Nicholls, *Modernisms: A Literary Guide* (New York: Palgrave Macmillan, 2009), 115.
36 Warwick Research Collective, *Combined and Uneven Development: Towards a New Theory of World-Literature* (Liverpool: Liverpool University Press, 2015), 17.
37 Octavio Paz, *Las peras del olmo* (Mexico City: Imprenta Universitaria, 1957), 57.
38 Ibid.
39 Daniel Balderston, "Poetry, Revolution, Homophobia: Polemics from the Mexican Revolution," in *Hispanisms and Homosexualities*, ed. Sylvia Molloy and Robert McKee Irwin (Durham: Duke University Press), 75.
40 Elissa J. Rashkin and Carla Zurián offer an excellent overview of the *Estridentista* legacy and an in-depth examination of the issues of availability of *Estridentista* texts and other creative projects in "The Estridentista Movement in Mexico: A Poetics of the Ephemeral," *International Yearbook of Futurism Studies* 7 (2017): 309–33.
41 Cited in Delia Ungureanu, *From Paris to Tlön: Surrealism as World Literature* (New York: Bloomsbury, 2017), 14.
42 Cited in Ibid., 14.
43 Ibid., 14.
44 Unruh, *Latin American Vanguards*, 2.
45 Evodio Escalante in discussion with the author, June 2010.
46 Rashkin, *The Stridentist Movement in Mexico*, 236.

47 Armando Pereira, "La generación del medio siglo: un momento de transición en la cultura mexicana," *Literatura Mexicana* 6, no. 1 (1995): 207.
48 Ignacio M. Sánchez Prado, *Strategic Occidentalisms: On Mexican Fiction, the Neoliberal Book Market, and the Question of World Literature* (Evanston: Northwestern University Press, 2018), 59.
49 Ibid., 59.
50 Eloy Urroz, "II. Genealogía del Crack," *Manifiesto Crack* in *Lateral. Revista de Cultura* 70 (October 2000): unpaginated.
51 Sánchez Prado, *Strategic Occidentalisms*, 13.
52 Puchner, *Poetry of the Revolution*, 5.
53 Ibid., 5–6.

9

Beyond the Literary Field
Octavio Paz in World Literature

Manuel Gutiérrez Silva

In 1990, when Octavio Paz was awarded the Nobel Prize in literature, his future biographer, Christopher Dominguez Michael, telephoned to congratulate him. After exchanging cordial greetings, Dominguez Michael had a brief, though revealing, conversation with Paz:

> I obviously asked him if he was happy. [Paz] said, "yes, of course," but went on to say that other events in his recent life had made him happier. I thought he might be referring to the fall of the Berlin Wall or the [symposium] *The Experience of Liberty*, all of which were still fresh in recent memory, but he wasn't. Instead, he told me that *The Privileges of Sight* had filled him to the brim with joy.[1]

Upon winning the literary fields' most coveted prize, which ensures worldwide recognition, Paz confessed that an art exhibit that he organized a few months earlier had made him *happier*. It would be easy to dismiss this exchange as an episode of modest deflection by a poet of Paz's stature. Yet, the anecdote provides a useful point of entry for discussing the role that cultural and political institutions outside of the immediate literary field had in facilitating Paz's entrance into world literature.

Ever the polymath, Paz's candid reply suggests he may have understood better than most the important role his incursions into other fields had in bolstering his international reputation. Though scholars in world literature theory have tried to account for how exactly a poet from a "semi-peripheral" country intruded in an unprecedented way on the North American, European, and South-Asian literary fields, they have yet to thoroughly consider the significant impact Paz's position in Mexico's foreign service and his critical campaigns in the emerging international art world had in securing this worldwide prestige. Paz's poetry (*Sun Stone, A Tree Within*) and essays on national and international politics (*The Labyrinth of Solitude, Itinerary, In Search of the Present*), modern art (*Marcel Duchamp or The Castle of Purity*), and world literature (*Children of the Mire*) bear the marks of these two institutions. If the literary critic Evodio Escalante is correct in warning readers that the one thing that cannot be done with Paz's writing is to circumscribe it into "the narrow confines of literature," it follows that trying to account for Paz's international prominence cannot rely on simply describing how he successfully navigated the literary field's rules, habits, institutions, and consecrating mechanisms.[2]

First-wave world literature theory, mainly work by Pascale Casanova and David Damrosch, may illuminate certain aspects about how Paz reached an international audience. However, Paz's worldwide recognition challenges the way scholars have understood the autonomy of literary institutions (Casanova) and reach of translations (Damrosch).[3] More recent world literature scholarship by Sarah Brouillette and Delia Ungureanu questions previous formulations of how world literature is instituted. Their respective insights invite *pacean* scholarship to reconsider the role extra-literary institutions played in creating figures of Paz's stature. For example, in *UNESCO and The Fate of the Literary*, Brouillette describes how social policy and "the political economy" of the book industry exert unique pressure on authors, subsequently shaping world literature.[4] While Casanova believed "world literary space" was "stateless," Brouillette shows how political institutions have been responsible for defining world literature. For her part, in *From Paris to Tlön: Surrealism as World Literature*, Ungureanu describes how for surrealist poets, translation was ineffective for promoting their work to wider audiences. Though Damrosch famously proposed that "literature thrives in translation," Ungureanu argues that surrealist poets were forced to find avenues outside of poetry to reach an international readership.[5] Building on Brouillette's and Ungureanu's insights, I will map the political and cultural institutions that contributed to promoting Paz's celebrity on an international scale.

Paz's presence in the global cultural field is insufficiently accounted for if we focus solely on how he adopted the rules that govern the autonomy of the literary field or on the success of the translations of his work or even on the "gatekeepers" who published them.[6] Unlike many of the novelists associated with the Latin American literary Boom of the 1960s that joined large publishing firms and acquired renown literary agents in New York, Barcelona, Frankfurt, and Paris, Paz never had a traditional literary agent or publicist.[7] More perplexing, his international prestige was not predicated on having access to large publishing firms such as Penguin, Gallimard, Suhrkamp Verlang, or Seix Barral—admittance to these often came after Paz had already achieved a modicum of international renown. In other words, Paz did not ride the Boom's editorial tide. As a poet and essayist, Paz made his presence felt in a different way. He carried the concerns he had explored in his literary work to other fields, specifically the visual arts and politics, forums where his ideas often had a more immediate impact.

Paz in Casanova's *World Republic of Letters*

In *World Republic of Letters*, Casanova proposes that Paz entered world literature by aligning himself with literary Paris, the capital of what she describes as "world literary space." She quotes, in the following order, from Paz's *In Light of India* (1997), *In Search of the Present: Nobel Lecture, 1990* (1990), and *The Labyrinth of Solitude* (1950), to chart the way Paz "discovered" Paris, viewed the city as a "gateway to the present," and felt like an "intruder" who snuck into modernity "through the West's back door."[8] These citations help Casanova illustrate her central theoretical premise: "world literary space" is an international market of symbolic goods and unevenly distributed power dynamics. Drawing on Pierre Bourdieu's "field" theory, Casanova expands the concept of a "field" to spatially envision "a world republic of letters."[9] In her map, Paris is the physical and spiritual site where literature's mechanisms for granting worldwide prestige are located. Moreover, this literary capital functions autonomously and is structured by its own unique temporality, rules, and logic:

> This improbable combination of qualities lastingly established Paris, both in France and throughout the world, as the capital of a republic having neither borders nor boundaries, a universal homeland exempt from all professions of patriotism, a kingdom of literature set up in opposition to the ordinary laws of states, a transnational realm whose sole imperatives are those of art and literature: the universal republic of letters.[10]

The aim of Casanova's cartography is to expose how the "kingdom of literature" is unjustly controlled by institutions found in developed countries and to point out that authors from "peripheral" sites may, over time, accumulate the sufficient cultural capital to be granted entrance. Following this logic, Casanova suggests that Paz gained international recognition by adopting the appropriate rules of the Parisian literary field, and by adjusting his literary practice to the legitimation apparatus that structures the "world republic of letters."

Though Casanova's description of how Paz may have entered world literature relies on his genuine enthusiasm for Paris, she overlooks the political and cultural institutions that sponsored his writing, and the bureaucratic and intellectual networks that promoted his prestige. Moreover, Casanova's insistence that "world literary space" is "stateless" and rises "above political laws" disregards Paz's historical relationship to the Mexican state and to the international political left, subjects I will discuss later.[11] Nowhere in Casanova's account does she mention the Mexican Foreign Service that for over thirty years sponsored Paz's writing.

Notwithstanding Casanova's omission, Mexico's Foreign Service sustained Paz's early literary career and shaped his writing. In his most autobiographical essay, *Itinerary*, Paz acknowledges this debt:

> I do not disown the years I spent in the Mexican diplomatic service, on the contrary I recall them with gratitude. Apart from the fact that, *grosso modo*, I was nearly always in agreement with our foreign policy, I could travel, know countries, and cities, deal with people of diverse trades, languages, races, capacities, and, in the end, I could write.[12]

Upon a closer reading, in *Itinerary*, and the aforementioned *In Search of the Present*— the very essay Casanova uses to illustrate her theory about literary autonomy—it is difficult to distinguish the language of an elder statesman from the lyrical ruminations of a poet. Both essays close with operatic reports on the state of the Mexican nation and the world that could readily be found in the diplomatic dispatches Paz penned when he worked for the Mexican embassy in France (1946–51) or India (1952, 1962–8). Sketching his poetic and political evolution, in these essays Paz deplores environmental degradation, ideological extremism, rampant nationalism, international inequality, free-market instability, and irrational consumerism, all while defending democratic ideals and institutions.[13] For Paz, the poet-diplomat, literature was never a "stateless" affair.

If Paz's autobiographical writing blends his poetic voice with the concerns of a career diplomat, it is futile to separate Paz's work as a state functionary from his writerly interests. In a study of Paz's first diplomatic post in France (1946–51), historian Froylán Enciso details how Paz's literary persona "benefitted" from the "public relations" campaigns he carried out for the Mexican state. Reading through Paz's foreign service dossier, Enciso documents how as a cultural attaché Paz dedicated his time "away from the office," and practiced an "open cultural diplomacy" that put him in contact with a broad international network of state bureaucrats, writers, artists, and philosophers.[14] Mixing official work with personal interest, Paz's extra-office activities enabled his collaboration with a variety of cultural and political institutions.[15] Furthermore, while Paz promoted Mexico's diplomatic agenda abroad, including its literature and art, he publicized his own writing and ideas on these matters. Indeed, as we will see herein, Paz's promotion of Mexican culture internationally mirrored his critical interests. After reviewing Paz's work for the embassy, we can only conclude, as Enciso does, that "Octavio Paz's service as a *de facto* cultural attaché—obviously—produced consequences and results in more than one direction."[16]

During Paz's last year (1950–1) working for the Mexican embassy in France, he published his career-defining *The Labyrinth of Solitude* (1950) and penned three key-works that, to different degrees, would bolster his international reputation. While it would take almost a decade for the now-canonical *Labyrinth* to be translated to other languages, Paz's three incursions into different fields brought him immediate international attention. Interestingly, these three works developed and extended ideas that Paz had explored in *Labyrinth* and formed part of Paz's broad effort to promote modern Mexican culture globally and to undo political and aesthetic platitudes that he believed had mired its progress. The first effort in this three-pronged campaign, *Anthologie de la poésie mexicaine* (1952) / *An Anthology of Mexican Poetry* (1958), was a problematic, and much later, a pioneering work of world literature. It introduced Paz to an elite group of French and English readers.[17] The second, an essay titled "Tamayo in Mexican Painting" (1951), would shake Mexican art historiography and reshape the way international viewers understood modern Mexican painting.[18] The third, a dossier in the famed Argentinian literary magazine *Sur*, titled "David Rousset and Soviet Concentration Camps" (1951), would signal Paz's rupture with the Latin American left and connect him to a growing worldwide coterie of disenchanted Marxists.[19] The fallout from Paz's campaign would cost him his position at the Mexican embassy. A detailed discussion of these three efforts lays beyond the scope of this essay, yet a brief comparison between their different receptions is useful for illustrating the role institutions outside of, or adjacent to, the literary field played in bolstering Paz's international prestige.

An Anthology of Mexican Poetry and the Closed Doors of the Parisian Literary Field

Paz's first effort to reshape international perceptions of Mexican literature was his *Anthologie/An Anthology*, which he began working on at the end of 1950. The collection was commissioned by the United Nations Educational, Scientific, and Cultural Organization (UNESCO) and the Mexican embassy in Paris. Both institutions proposed the volume as part of the UNESCO's first major literary program, The Collection of Representative Works, which translated "representative works" for English and French readers, the official languages of the UNESCO.[20] According to the program's charter, the aim was to disseminate "the great works of all nations" and to promote "the mutual knowledge of peoples." Ultimately, the UNESCO hoped international cultural exchange would contribute to the maintenance of "world peace and security."[21] Following these values, *Anthologie/An Anthology* was a project of cultural diplomacy intended to forge transatlantic political and artistic alliances.

In hindsight, the significance of the English-language edition of *Anthologie* as a pioneering work of world literature has been assured by the virtue of being the product of a unique collaboration between two future Nobel Prize winners: Octavio Paz selected the poets and poems, while Samuel Beckett translated them.[22] However, when it was published (many years after Paz prepared it), critics did not consider it a success. George G. Wing believed the book was "marred" by defects and that Becket's translations were "uninspired."[23] Boyd Carter also noted that Becket was incapable of maintaining the "form, musicality, verbal delicacy" and "imagery, of their original poetic incarnation," and chided the UNESCO for not including the originals alongside the English translations for North American readers: "their omission [. . .] will merely reinforce the argument that we are a nation of provincials."[24] Oddly, Carter concluded that the collection was saved by Cecil Maurice Bowra's (vice-chancellor of the University of Oxford) "preface" for the English translation: "Bowra helps compensate for the shortcomings of this anthology."

Paz too was unconvinced by the anthology's literary merits and doubted the potential impact the collection could have in introducing international readers to modern Mexican poetry. According to Patricia Novillo-Corvalán, Paz "condemned the cultural politics of UNESCO's translation program."[25] Mainly, he was frustrated by the UNESCO's public-spirited aims, yet contradictory execution. The editors demanded that Paz include "classic" works of Mexican poetry and exclude lesser-known, important "living" Mexican poets, including Paz, with one exception: Alfonso Reyes. Paz was also "furious" that UNESCO commissioned prominent European authors to promote *Anthologie/An Anthology*: Paul Claudel, member of the Académie Française, was asked to write a preface for the French edition and the aforementioned Bowra was asked to write a preface for the English edition.²⁶ Paz adamantly opposed the notion that a European imprimatur was necessary to validate an anthology of Mexican poetry.²⁷ Novillo-Corvalán concludes that the UNESCO located the anthology's significance "not so much in the poems themselves" or in Paz; rather, for them, *Anthologie/An Anthology*'s value lay in the "participation of European intellectuals."²⁸ With Bowra's and Claudel's names prominently displayed on its respective covers, *Anthologie/An Anthology* was presented as the achievement of a European institution.

Paz's campaign to promote the living poets he considered most representative of modern Mexican literature was thwarted and absorbed by the UNESCO's and the Mexican embassy's diplomatic agenda. According to Brouillette, The Collection was part of a newly secured global polity:

> [For UNESCO] security was tied inexorably to modernization, and being modern meant living in a liberal capitalist society and, ideally, participating actively and equally as workers and consumers, in the globalizing market economy. It is hardly surprising that white experts played dominant roles in the early years of The Collection of Representative Works—that it turned out to be largely an incorporative cannon. The world's various literatures were absorbed into English and French, which were thereby solidified in their roles as the languages of expert adjudication of the merit of literary works from any region.²⁹

Brouillette's insight into the institutional drives propelling the UNESCO's program contextualizes the editorial interventions that Paz was forced to accept. The mandate to only translate "classic" Mexican poetry was framed by the UNESCO's desire to offer readers a "non-decadent and precapitalist holism" that "evinced the respectful interest of the imperial 'partner' in the underdeveloped."³⁰ In essence, the UNESCO constructed an exoticized catalogue of the world's literatures. Within this framework, Paz functioned as a mere cultural laborer who compiled information for the capital to consume. Though it is strange to think of Paz, the later world-renown intellectual, in this light, during the year (1950/1) he published the now widely recognized *Labyrinth*, his anthology served as a stand-in for the "knowledge" of "other" peoples. Under the UNESCO's vision, the *Anthologie/An Anthology* looked backward to Mexico's literary past and treated it as a trophy to the developed world's power to consume the planet's cultural wealth.

Two conclusions may be drawn from this episode. First, *Anthologie/An Anthology* was a product of the UNESCO's political aims and the Mexican embassy's interest to meet them. Consequently, the collection did not confirm the declaration that Paz had made in *Labyrinth*, that Mexicans, and thereby, Mexican poets, were "contemporaries of all humanity."³¹ Rather, *Anthologie/An Anthology* was the outcome of the parochial political economy that shaped postwar world literature. Second, though Paz followed the Parisian literary field's rules, these did not guarantee access to the "kingdom of literature" as Casanova proposed. In fact, the obstacles that Paz encountered while preparing the collection suggest that the adoption of editorial policies and aesthetic norms did little to ensure Paz's international reputation or that of the poets he tried to promote. Forced to accept the UNESCO's editorial interventions, Paz threatened to abandon the project, and to pull his prologue and notes from the anthology if his work was not properly recognized.[32] After reaching an acceptable compromise (his name would also appear on the book's cover), Paz would always describe his experience editing *Anthologie/An Anthology* as "frustrating," and, according to Gustavo Guerrero, he will always suspect his disagreements with the UNESCO and with his superiors at the embassy contributed to his ouster from his position.[33] Under these restrictive conditions, Paz had to find a "back door" into the world republic of letters. Propitiously, Paz's cultural campaigns breeched the narrow confines of the literary field. Though the world republic of letters remained elusive, Paz pushed his effort to undo platitudes about Mexican culture to other forums.

The Tamayo Affair: A "Back Door"

If Paz's attempt to introduce modern Mexican poets to world literature was forestalled, his essay "Rufino Tamayo in Mexican Painting" had a decisive impact on the international art world. Working for the Mexican embassy, Paz campaigned for Rufino Tamayo's first solo-show in Paris, which opened in November of 1950, at the *Galerie des Beaux-Arts*. As part of this effort, Paz's article introduced readers to Tamayo's paintings and located their place in modern art. A detailed reading of Paz's essay lays beyond the scope of this chapter. However, a brief discussion of it is necessary because, unlike *Anthologie/An Anthology*, "Rufino Tamayo in Mexican Painting" marked a watershed moment. It broke with the art historiography of the period, reconfigured the way modern Mexican art was understood, and placed Paz at the center of a debate about Mexican visual culture that would immediately magnify his international visibility.

Paz's campaign to introduce national and international viewers to Tamayo's work challenged the then-conventional thesis that Mexican art was a product of the Mexican Revolution.[34] Most controversially, Paz argued that Mexican Muralism, specifically the work of Diego Rivera, David Alfaro Siqueiros, and José Clemente Orozco, was by no means "revolutionary." Instead, their work presented an institutional and political contradiction: "One cannot be both an official artist of the regime and a revolutionary artist without introducing confusion and equivocation."[35] For Paz, this paradox was the outcome of two larger, yet interrelated, problems that he had already described in *Labyrinth*.[36] First, that the Mexican Revolution was unable to articulate "a vision of the world." And, second, that Mexican intellectuals were incapable of reconciling Mexican artistic and literary traditions, with a "demand for Universality."[37] In the absence of a clear philosophy that could bridge this impasse, the muralists "turned their eyes to Marxism," and covered Mexico's walls with an imaginary that was removed from Mexico's reality. In short, Paz believed Muralism's Marxist worldview was a "cascara" [shell], or a "mask," to borrow a similar formulation from *Labyrinth*, that perpetuated "inauthenticity."[38]

The purpose of Paz's critical survey of Mexican Muralism was to introduce a group of painters, later known as *La ruptura*, that he believed broke with the aesthetic and political rhetoric espoused by post-Revolutionary Mexican artists. In Paz's account, Tamayo's work represented a "rupture" that was "driven by a desire to find a new aesthetic universality" that did not "appeal to an 'ideology.' "[39] In a search for original forms, Paz believed artists like Tamayo were able to reconcile disparate Mexican artistic traditions with modern currents, while demonstrating a formalist "will to purity." More importantly, for Paz, by eschewing political dogma, Tamayo and *La ruptura* displayed an intellectual "independence" that distinguished their work from the Muralists. As Mexican Muralism lost its luster, and Parisian painting floundered in the aftermath of the Second World War, Paz imbued Tamayo's work with a moral, aesthetic, and political authority that he believed had the potential to define a new international artistic language.

Whether Paz's genuine interest in or assessment of Tamayo as a torchbearer of modern art was accurate, or remains relevant today, is beside the point. The essay's reception illustrates how Paz's incursions into the visual arts produced the immediate results that had eluded him in his efforts to introduce Mexican poets to international readers. For example, in Mexico Paz's salvo was met with acrimony by artists, critics, and politicians alike. The art critic and leftist activist Antonio Rodriguez defended the muralists and skewered Paz for carrying out a "campaign" to disparage their art and reprimanded him for valuing Tamayo's "non-ideological" paintings.[40] Again, a complete history of the debate Paz sparked is impossible. However, it is important to note that Paz's essay rankled the Mexican art establishment and had an impact on his diplomatic career. In a letter to Alfonso Reyes written a year after the essay's publication, Paz described how the embassy terminated his position in Paris and moved him to India because he had pushed for Tamayo's inclusion in another art exhibit, *Art Mexicain du précolumbien à nos jours*.[41]

If in Mexico Paz was chastised for his effort to promote Tamayo, internationally he found himself at the center of a critical reassessment regarding the future of Mexican and European painting. According to the curator Cuauhtémoc Medina, Paz's essay reconfigured the artistic field: "[he] established the place that Rufino Tamayo would acquire in the second half of the Twentieth Century as the visible figurehead of post-mural Mexican art."[42] Medina goes further and notes that Paz's effort was more than just an attempt to place Tamayo at the center of Mexican art: "Paz's importance does not rest in pointing out for his contemporaries a rupture in muralism's hegemony. Rather, it rests in being the origin of a new visual hegemony."[43] Medina does not overstate the impact of Paz's intervention: Paz was essentially proposing Mexico City as the new capital of modern painting. The article's significance was immediately recognized and was reprinted throughout the decade, culminating in a special trilingual edition (Spanish, English and French), *Rufino Tamayo*.[44] His unorthodox views on Mexican art were echoed by American and European intellectuals, including André Bretón and Jean Cassou.[45] Yet, unlike *Anthologie/An Anthology*, which required the imprimatur of international "experts" to reach a worldwide audience, Paz's essay was his own and it established him as a leading commentator on Mexican art.[46]

The timing of Paz's essay on Tamayo could not have been better suited for jumpstarting Paz's reputation among a broader international public. Its publication coincided in Mexico with an explosion in private and public art galleries. In 1951, the year the essay appeared, only 14 galleries existed in the nation's capital.[47] But a decade later, in 1960, when Paz wrote a follow-up essay on Tamayo, there were 27.[48] By 1968, when Paz wrote a third essay about Tamayo, there were 35.[49] And by 1970, when Paz published an English translation of *Marcel Duchamp or The Castle of Purity* (which I will discuss herein), his first monograph dedicated to an artist, there were 37.[50] Finally, in 1973, when Paz published a second and expanded edition of this book, retitled *Marcel Duchamp: Appearance Stripped Bare*, there were fifty-two art galleries in Mexico City alone.[51]

The exponential growth in private and public galleries was the result of President Miguel Alemán's (1946–52) policies for infrastructural and financial development that sparked a period of relative economic prosperity.[52] Mexico's economic modernization had two significant consequences relevant for this discussion. First, it shifted Mexico's political discourse from a rhetoric grounded in revolutionary nationalism, to one of "progress" characterized by foreign investment and capital accumulation.[53] Second, these material transformations fostered the emergence of a small urban middle class that would consume popular and highbrow visual culture in unprecedented ways. Coupled with the arrival of mass media—including new technologies of reproduction, transmission, and reception—these changes fomented a reconsideration of the nationalist visual imaginary that since 1921 had characterized post-revolutionary Mexican culture, but that by 1950 appeared anachronistic. Amid these material, institutional, and symbolic transformations, the task of reassigning a new value to artistic images and reconceptualizing what *Art* was and why it remained relevant fell on writers like Paz, who began distinguishing for elite viewers between post-revolutionary Mexican art and mid-century international modernism.

Paz's art writing would also benefit in exposure from the emergence of an international art market that began compelling Mexican art dealers to export national art on an unprecedented scale. In 1971 when Paz founded *Plural*, an important cultural magazine that would include extensive art criticism, Mexico imported annually 5,833 art objects and exported 20,744 art pieces for an estimated total value of 5,747,248 pesos. By 1976, when Paz left the magazine, Mexico imported approximately 20,454 art works and exported 663,774 for an estimated total value 31 million pesos.[54] It is not surprising, then, that in the context of an expanding art market, all of Paz's collections of essays published between 1950 and 1976 included extensive essays on Mexican and European art.[55] The centrality of this practice to Paz's larger reputation has lead his biographer to quip: "If Paz had never been a poet, or political essayist, or literary critic, and had only written about art, he would still be a notable writer in that field, in Spanish and even in other languages."[56]

In the 1980s, as readers began to drift from Paz's modernist poetry and ever-increasing conservative politics, the 200 hours he spent on Mexico's television network *Televisa* discussing culture and modern art kept him visible among audiences.[57] These programs were also translated into English and French, further exposing Paz to international viewers. The culmination of this art writing, and television programing, came in 1990, when the massive exhibit titled *The Privileges of Sight* was inaugurated at *Televisa*'s Cultural Center for Contemporary Art and to which Paz referred to with such fondness in the quote that opens this article.[58] The first of its kind, this retrospective of Western art followed Paz's nearly 1,000 pages of art writing and included an unprecedented 350 works of national and international art, some of which had never been seen in Mexico. By some estimates, in the first two weeks alone 40,000 people visited the exhibition and spawned a small museological industry that would repeat similar exhibits.[59] For example, in June 2009, a decade after Paz's death, the Museum of National Art in Mexico City inaugurated another exhibit titled *Materia y sentido: El arte mexicano en la mirada de Octavio Paz*.[60] The show grouped 319 Mexican paintings, sculptures, and codices that populate Paz's poetry and essays. Again, in the fall of 2014, 200,000 people visited another exhibit based on Paz's art writing, this time titled *En esto ver aquello: Octavio Paz y el arte*.[61] It is the most visited art exhibit in Mexico's recent history. Finally, Paz's art writing has also been used internationally to curate massive art exhibits. One relevant example: on the morning that Paz won the Nobel Prize, he was in New York City to inaugurate *Mexico: Thirty Centuries of Splendor* (1990) at the Metropolitan Museum of Art.[62] This monumental exhibit, which according to *The New York Times* was "one of the largest and most ambitious exhibitions ever mounted by the museum," was the result of a collaboration between Paz and Emilio Azcárraga, the owner of the media conglomerate *Televisa*.[63] To further underscore the diplomatic and institutional significance of this exhibit, Mexican president Carlos Salinas de Gortari attended its opening.

In the public imagination at large, it is this image of Paz, the erudite poet in touch with the visual arts, so well promoted by museums, galleries, and media outlets, which contributed to propelling Paz's international prestige. Additionally, writing about art for journals, magazines, and museum catalogues, publications that move through different transnational institutions from the literary field provided much needed monetary and promotional support.[64] It is no wonder then that in 1990, when his biographer called to congratulate him for winning the Nobel Prize, Paz described the happiness that the opening of *The Privileges of Sight* had brought him: the exhibit was the conclusion of a decades-long campaign that Paz began waging in 1950–1, and which kept him present in the public eye. In fact, opening in April of the year Paz would win the Nobel Prize, this exhibit—which was a collaboration with many international art museums, foundations, and private collections—may have contributed in more than one way to the Swedish Academy's attention.

Escaping and Embracing the Left: The Rousset Affair and *The Experience of Liberty*

In the surprising conversation that Dominguez Michael recalled about the morning Paz was awarded the Nobel Prize, he was stunned that Paz had not mentioned the political events of the day. At the very least, he expected Paz to discuss the fall of the Berlin Wall and/or the international symposium *The Experience of Liberty* that Paz had convened, "still fresh in recent memory."[65] Dominguez Michael's astonishment is understandable for two reasons. First, since 1950–1, Paz had waged a forceful campaign to denounce Marxist-Leninist regimes and to remind the international left of its error for supporting Soviet communism.[66] Second, Paz's political evolution from leftist sympathizer to liberal stalwart had imbued his literary persona with the moral and political credibility that made him a sought-after intellectual by international cultural and academic institutions, including the Nobel Committee, looking to undo Cold War political orthodoxy.

Yet, despite Paz's political evolution and decades-long criticism of the international left, Paz's connection to world literature was facilitated by the intellectual networks of twentieth-century Marxism. In *Itinerary* Paz details how his generation was the first in Mexico to "live world history as its own" and to embrace "the international communist movement."[67] Surprisingly, even late in life, Paz linked his early "enthusiasm" for leftist politics to his interest in world literature: "Another distinctive trait of our generation: the influence of modern Spanish literature." In Paz's words, Marxism, coupled with Spanish literature, introduced him to a "universalism" that was "embodied in the communist movement."[68] Despite his political transformation, for Paz world literature and radical politics remained intimately linked: "I found no contradiction between poetry and revolution: they were two facets of the same movement, two wings of the same passion. This belief would link me later to the surrealists."[69] Paz's understanding of world literature was rooted in leftist politics and the combination of the two informed his embrace of surrealism, a point I will return to. Paradoxically, Paz's forceful critique of Soviet communism, which began between 1950 and 1951, drew him closer to Marxism and to world literature.

As is well known, Paz's disillusionment with Marxism lead him toward liberalism, yet the early links that he made between international communism and world literature remained a constant personal and professional resource. Traversing continents as a representative of the Mexican government, Paz befriended and collaborated with an extensive network of disenchanted leftist writers and unorthodox Marxists. These included the Russian revolutionary writer Victor Serge, the French novelist and member of the Workers Party Jean Malaquais, the Catalan anarchist José Bosch Fonserré, and Paz's lifelong friend, the Greek Marxist philosopher Kostas Papaïoannou.[70] According to Dominguez Michael, this coterie of "anti-totalitarian teachers" shaped Paz's own political views, and alerted him to the dangers of unchallenged ideology.[71]

Paz's earliest critique of Marxism and the first publication that linked him to this tradition of disenchantment came in early 1951 when he published a then-controversial dossier titled "David Rousset and the Soviet Concentration Camps" in the Argentine literary magazine *Sur*.[72] Along with an extensive explanatory note that Paz later described as his first "public break" with the Latin American left, he compiled and translated a series of firsthand accounts by Rousset, a survivor of Nazi camps, regarding his experience in Soviet concentration camps.[73] A year earlier, in *Figaro Litteraire*, Rousset had published several dispatches describing the arbitrary crimes for which Russian citizens had been imprisoned and sketched the gruesome conditions under which they lived. Most condemning, Rousset concluded that the structure of the prison camp was the actual core of Soviet communism and argued that his exposé was intended to encourage fellow leftist dissidents to create an international commission to investigate the camps.⁷⁴

Working for the Mexican embassy in France, Paz witnessed the backlash that Rousset's call generated on the left. In *Les Lettres Françaises* or *Les Temps Moderns*, many intellectuals, including Jean-Paul Sartre, Maurice Merleau-Ponty, and Louis Aragon, denounced Rousset "as falling into the anti-Soviet trap."⁷⁵ However, Paz sided with Rousset, and in his introduction to the dossier speculated that the camps may well have served an economic purpose that exposed the Soviet Union's hierarchical social structure. Though Paz's break with socialism was years away, through this dossier he began to publicly express skepticism about the Soviet Union, an unpopular position among Marxists. Again, the details of the Rousset Affair lay beyond the scope of this essay. However, with the dossier Paz courted controversy and challenged political orthodoxy. Quickly, he found himself isolated from European, Mexican, and Latin American leftists, and once again at the center of an international debate, this time regarding the left's crimes.

Emboldened by his detractors, Paz continued to seek out dissenters like Rousset and expanded his network of anti-totalitarian thinkers. He connected with the historian and former member of the communist-party-turned-virulent-anti-communist François Furet; with the Greek philosopher Cornelius Castoriadis; with Erich Fromm, a member of the Frankfurt school; and other disenchanted Marxists. Most of these intellectuals would collaborate in Paz's cultural magazines *Plural* (1971–6) and *Vuelta* (1976–98), thereby raising Paz's profile as an internationally renown editor. Through this network Paz became associated with a tradition of Cold War disillusionment that would increasingly shape cultural policies and institutions in the West and former Eastern Bloc countries.

According to Paz, the distinguishing mark that bonded him to this growing coterie of disenchanted leftists was a spiritual rift that led many twentieth-century intellectuals to feeling unmoored: "We were truly divided souls in a divided world. Some of us eventually transformed that psychic wound into intellectual and moral independence."⁷⁶ Among these "independent" thinkers Paz experienced a renewed sense of political purpose and principled solidarity. In 1990 thirty-six of these "divided souls" from around the world—including the Polish-American poet and Nobel Prize winner Czeslaw Milosz, the Mexican Marxist thinker Adolfo Sánchez Vázquez, the American literary critic and prominent member of the Democratic Socialists of America Irving Howe, the Hungarian Marxist political thinker Ágnes Heller, the former Marxist and now liberal French philosopher Jean-Francois Revel, the Cuban revolutionary dissident Carlos Franqui, and others—were convened by Paz to participate in *The Experience of Liberty*, a televised symposium held in Mexico City, and to which Dominguez Michael referred in the opening quote of this article.⁷⁷ Sponsored by *Televisa* and other private entities, the purpose of the gathering was to consider the future of international politics in light of the fall of the Berlin Wall and the collapse of the Soviet Union. The event, which according to *pacean* scholar Maarten Van Delden demonstrated "a bit of gloating [by Paz] over the defeat of [Paz's] ideological enemies," was the culmination of the campaign against Marxist-Leninist regimes that Paz began waging decades earlier with his dossier about Rousset.[78] Finally, as if to highlight the cohesiveness between Paz's political ideology and aesthetic values, above the perfectly designed rostrum on which the symposium took place hung a large painting by Rufino Tamayo.[79]

The Experience of Liberty's international makeup, which was held in late August, a month or so before the Nobel Prize was announced, certainly contributed to the Swedish Academy's attention. If disenchanted Marxists provided Paz with an alternative to leftist orthodoxy, as we will see in the final section, writing about surrealist art and chastising the Mexican state through a surrealist poem tinged with Marxist rhetoric would further connect Paz to world literature.

Surrealism, Marcel Duchamp, 1968, and World Literature

Damrosch has proposed that translation is paramount for entering world literature, yet Paz's major works were translated long after their first appearance in Spanish and often only after Paz had already become an internationally recognizable figure, either for his political stances or for his art writing. For example, as mentioned earlier, the first translations of *El laberinto de la soledad* (1950) appeared a decade or two after its first publication: French (1959), English (1961), Italian (1961), German (1970), and Portuguese (1976).[80] Paz's poetry faced a greater time lag. Thirty years after his first poems were printed in Spanish, a collection of *Selected Poems* (1963) appeared in English.[81] Though six of Paz's poems had been translated into English before and included as an appendix in Muriel Rukeyser's *The Green Wave* (1948), this collection did not circulate widely.[82] In fact, it has never been reissued. Furthermore, when Paz's poetry appeared in the United States or Britain, it did so in minor publishing firms like New Directions and university presses, or in limited-run poetry magazines such as the London-based *Horizon* (1939–50). In either case, few copies were sold among specialized readers. True, throughout the 1950s Paz's books were readily mentioned and reviewed in academic journals, including *Revista Hispánica Moderna*, *Books Abroad*, *Hispania*, and *The Hispanic American Historical Review*. However, these early commentaries were frequently minor references in "books received," "book notices," or passing inclusion in general "panoramas" of "Spanish American Literature" by Latin American, Spanish, and American Hispanists in academia.[83] Similarly, though a few of Paz's poems were translated into French in the 1950s, including a collection of surrealist-inspired prose poems ¿*Aguila o sol?* (1950) [*Aigle ou Souleil?*, 1957], these early translations were scarce and appeared in surrealist publications such as the journals *Almanaque surréaliste du démi-siècle*, *La Nef* and *Le Surrealisme, Même*, all of which circulated in limited numbers among surrealist writers and artists.[84] In other words, translation did not ensure Paz access into world literature.

In France, the delay in translations and the limited circulation of Paz's poems was not unique, especially when we consider that his first translators into French were associates of the Surrealist movement. In *From Paris to Tlön*, Ungureanu argues that Damrosch's definition of world literature does not adequately describe how surrealism became world literature.[85] According to Ungureanu, translations of surrealism's most important poetry experienced "a relative failure" and points to a revealing paradox: the poetry that made surrealism famous "was little read outside of surrealist circles" even after it was translated.[86] Following Ungureanu's insight, though Paz's early translations undeniably earned him the recognition of fellow international surrealists, a broader readership would have to come from a different field, one that reached beyond the limited circles of surrealist poetry.

Given that surrealist poetry was incapable of garnering a wide readership and lacked the institutional sponsorship that would allow it to break from the confines of its immediate cliques, Ungureanu argues that surrealist poetry came to the attention of a wider audience only by transferring surrealist strategies to other cultural fields. Here, my thesis about Paz's incursions into other fields aligns with Ungureanu's. According to her, poetic surrealism experienced a two-stage transformation: it gradually moved "into visual art and then into the novel."[87] In other words, surrealist poetry did not become world literature by mere textual translation but rather by the adoption of its central practices to other disciplines. The mélange of surrealist techniques and attitudes, including *defamiliarization*, collage, collaborative practices, dream-imagery, and eroticism, was adopted by cultural producers across several continents, and throughout a variety of fields, including the visual arts, film, politics, anthropology, fashion, and cuisine.[88] As these practices were embraced by different disciplines, surrealism piqued the interest of a wider audience.

Ungureanu's insight is especially useful for understanding how exactly Paz, a poet and cultural critic, managed to garner international attention beyond the confines of surrealist circles. Though in the 1950s Paz wrote surrealist poems that shook the Mexican literary establishment, cementing him as a leading poet, internationally his belated surrealist poems and broad defense of the movement's aesthetics had less of an impact. Yet, true to his surrealist sympathies, Paz adopted surrealist strategies to his writing about visual culture. In fact, Paz's first public connection to surrealism came in 1951, when he wrote a pamphlet titled "The Poet Buñuel" and with it waged a campaign at the Cannes' International Film Festival to defend the surrealist filmmaker Luis Buñuel from the Mexican government's attempt to censor *Los olvidados* (1950).[89] Paz's international recognition would occur, as it did for other surrealists, not by the translation of his poetry alone but by branching out to other fields.

The book that confirmed Paz as an international art writer was the monograph he dedicated to Marcel Duchamp, *Marcel Duchamp o el castillo de la pureza*.[90] The study was part of an experimental and collaborative artist's book that meticulously reproduced Duchamp's *Boîte-en-valise* (1941), which compiled notes by Duchamp and authorized miniature reproductions of his works. Intrigued by Paz's project, Duchamp collaborated with Paz on the Spanish translation of his notes and also helped the Mexican artist Vicente Rojo recreate miniature reproductions of his art works to include alongside Paz's essay. The international interest in Paz's monograph was immediate; before it appeared in Spanish, it was published in French.[91] It was also translated into English and, as mentioned earlier, was revised, expanded, and reissued twice only a few years after its appearance.[92] Since then, it has been translated into Dutch, German, Hungarian, Italian, Portuguese, and Japanese.[93] The book's appearance in Japanese illustrates how writing about different fields exposed Paz to new audiences. One revealing example, the Japanese artist Katayama Toshihiro came across Paz not by his poetry, but by his art writing:

> I wasn't too familiar with Paz's work, except that I knew him as someone who had helped introduce Marcel Duchamp [to Japan], and that he had written a lot of poetry. However, his poems weren't translated into Japanese at the time and they were too difficult for me to read in English.[94]

As occurred in other languages, Paz's book on Duchamp was translated into Japanese (1990), several years before his poetry (1997).

In addition to exposing Paz to new audiences, the critical importance of Paz's *Marcel Duchamp* was threefold. First, it was the earliest monograph written in Spanish about Duchamp, a feat that introduced Mexican and Latin American artists to the avant-gardist's work. Second, as an art-object, Paz's and Rojo's collaboration inaugurated a decade-long trend in the creation of artist's books in Mexico.[95] Third, it exhibited Paz's ability to engage the Western artistic canon as his own, often providing heterodox readings of it. For example, writing from Delhi where Paz was serving as ambassador, Paz *defamiliarized* Duchamp's work as an avant-gardist and placed the iconoclast into a lineage of religious and secular artistic practices that included Hindi imagery, Mayan myths, and symbolist poetry. If Duchamp was known for *defamiliarizing* ordinary objects, Paz displaced Duchamp from the history of Western avant-garde art and inserted him into a global visual history that included Eastern and Western representational practices.

As is the case with Paz's essay about Tamayo, whether his interpretation of Duchamp was or remains valid is beside the point. The essay exposed Paz to a different field. In fact, Duchamp himself contributed to Paz's international reputation as an art writer: he included Paz's essay in the catalogue for his very first retrospective at the Philadelphia Museum of Art.[96] The inclusion in this historic exhibit introduced Paz to new publishing channels, including the Philadelphia Museum of Art and the French Editions d'Art Albert Skira, a publisher dedicated to specialized artist's books. Duchamp's endorsement helped turn Paz into a sought-after author of catalogue and introductory essays for international exhibits, further exposing him to the art world's institutions. The monograph's surrealist art writing, which blended literary criticism and art history, would also garner the attention of the Charles Elliot Norton Lecture Series at Harvard University, a colloquium specifically dedicated to "the study of the history of the fine arts as connected with literature."[97]

Paz's Charles Elliot Norton lectures, published as *Children of the Mire*, continued his practice of *defamiliarizing* artists, in this case poets. In his survey, modern poetry was spread across borders and languages and not confined to a specific "kingdom" (Casanova), tradition, or historical progression. Instead, as Paz had argued about

Tamayo and Duchamp, modern European, Latin American, and North American poets belonged to a lineage of "rupture," or "a tradition against itself."[98] Citing the art historian Harold Rosenberg, Paz believed that modern art was "the offspring of the age of criticism" and similarly, what made poets modern was their negation of the past. While Paz's *Anthology* was thwarted from introducing modern Mexican poets to international audiences, through this logic of "rupture" Paz now affirmed that Mexican and Latin American poets were indeed contemporaries of world poetry.

If Paz's book about Duchamp secured his international reputation as an art writer, the year it appeared in Spanish proved fateful for Paz's diplomatic career. On October 2, 1968, (coincidently, the same day that Duchamp died), the Mexican military massacred students at Tlatelolco. Upon hearing the news, Paz resigned from his ambassadorship in protest, and drew the attention of the international press. The following day he penned one of his most important poems, "Mexico: The XIX Olympiad," and sent it to the International Reunion of Poets that was then convening in Mexico City as part of the 1968 Olympics.[99] The poem, dedicated to the American art critic Dore Ashton and to the Russian-born artist Adja Yunkers, was a blistering condemnation of the Mexican state's actions. In surrealist fashion, the poet, rendered speechless by the atrocity, contemplates the limpid whiteness of the sheet of paper before him, until finally bursting with a quote from Karl Marx: "Shame is anger turned against oneself: if a whole country feels shame it is a lion crouched ready to leap."[100] Paz's blunt verses expressing disgust at the Mexican state's violence were immediately translated into English and published in the *New York Review of Books*. It was the first time Paz appeared in the celebrated journal. From then on his books would be reviewed in it, thus joining the visible international circle of liberal intellectuals, political dissidents, and poets that regularly populated the magazine's pages. Yet, as in the Rousset Affair, it was Paz's political stance, here expressed in a surrealist poem with Marxist language, which garnered international attention and granted him access to the premier literary English-language magazine of the 1960s.

My aim with this interpretation of Paz's surprising quote was twofold. First, to explore the concrete three-pronged campaign through which Paz gained international acclaim during an important year in his literary career: 1950–1. Second, to draw attention to a methodological oversight in world literature studies. There remains an unexamined assumption that the literary field on its own, with its rules, institutions, and prizes, is effective in generating global recognition, even for less visible genres than the novel, such as poetry and the essay. As I have demonstrated, Paz's presence on the international stage was in part affirmed by his campaigns in the international art world, and by his service to the Mexican state. Though it is undeniable that *The Labyrinth of Solitude* and his late-surrealist poetry drew the attention of specialized readers, these publications on their own, or in translation, could not secure the worldwide recognition Paz enjoyed. It is incumbent on scholars in Mexican and world literature studies to begin a more thorough interrogation of how Paz's writing was materially sustained and promoted by many public and private, cultural, and political institutions, and, later, even media conglomerates. An assessment of the exact roles they played in promoting Paz as an intellectual, and public figure, may revise romantic descriptions that posit Paz's "spiritual leadership" or disinterested "vocation" as responsible for his prominence.[101] Moreover, this analysis could bring into sharper relief the cultural campaigns that Paz waged in order to, as he described, "open doors onto the field" in the Mexican context, while asserting himself on the international stage. Finally, it will make visible the varied interpersonal networks, publishing channels, and platforms that Paz navigated. A comprehensive understanding of authorship from a world literature perspective must include the complex promotional mechanisms that poets like Paz used and, which in the past, have been insufficiently accounted for by previous theoretical formulations about how world literature is instituted that rest largely on theories of literary autonomy and/or the reach of translations. Excavating the international cultural and political institutions that sponsored Paz's writing and linking these to his actual prose and poetry may shed further light on Mexico's mid-century cultural infrastructure and illuminate neglected aspects of world literatures' canonizing apparatus. In and of itself, the literary field is incapable of creating a worldwide celebrity of Paz's stature.

Notes

1. Christopher Domínguez Michael, *Octavio Paz en su siglo* [Octavio Paz in his Century] (México: Aguilar, 2014), 488–9. All translations are mine unless otherwise indicated.
2. Evodio Escalante, *Las sendas perdidas de Octavio Paz* [Octavio Paz's Lost Pathways] (México: Universidad Autónoma Metropolitana, 2013), 57.
3. Pascale Casanova, *The World Republic of Letters*, trans. M. B. Debevoise (Cambridge, MA: Harvard University Press, 2004). David Damrosch, *What Is World Literature?* (Princeton: Princeton University Press, 2003).
4. Sarah Brouillette, *UNESCO and the Fate of the Literary* (Stanford: Stanford University Press, 2019).
5. Delia Ungureanu, *From Paris to Tlön: Surrealism as World Literature* (New York: Bloomsbury, 2018).
6. William Marlin, *Gatekeepers: The Emergence of World Literature & The 1960s* (New York: Oxford University Press, 2016).
7. Dominguez Michael, *Octavio Paz*, 533.
8. Cited in Casanova, *World Republic*, 28, 43, 82.
9. Pierre Bourdieu, *The Field of Cultural Production* (New York: Columbia University Press, 1993), 29.
10. Casanova, *World Republic*, 29.
11. Ibid.
12. Octavio Paz, *Itinerary*, trans. Jason Wilson (Harcourt: New York, 2000), 76.
13. Paz, *In Search of the Present*, trans. Anthony Stanton (New York: HBJ, 1990), 23–4, 31. *Itinerary*, 76–98.
14. Froylán Enciso, *Andar fronteras: El servicio diplomático de Octavio Paz en Francia (1946-1951)* [Walking Along Borders: Octavio Paz's Diplomatic Service in France] (México: Siglo XXI, 2008), 325–6.
15. Ibid., 325.
16. Ibid., 325–6.

17 Octavio Paz, ed., *Anthologie de la poésie mexicaine*, trans. Guy Levis (Paris: Editions Nagel, 1952) and Octavio Paz, ed., *An Anthology of Mexican Poetry*, trans. Samuel Beckett (Bloomington: Indiana University Press, 1958).
18 Octavio Paz, "Tamayo en la pintura mexicana," in *Las peras del olmo* [The Elm's Pears] (México: Imprenta Universitaria, 1957), 244–64.
19 Octavio Paz, "David Rousset y los campos de concentración soviéticos," *Sur. Revista Mensual* 197 (1951): 48–76.
20 Brouillette, *UNESCO*, 21–53.
21 Ibid., 21. And, for a detailed history of the role the Mexican embassy played in establishing the UNESCO's charter see the next chapter in this volume, Gustavo Guerrero, "Brief History of an Anthology of Mexican Poetry".
22 Patricia Novillo-Corvalán, *Modernism and Latin America: Translation Networks of Literary Exchange* (New York: Routledge, 2018), 192.
23 George G. Wing, "Review: *An Anthology of Mexican Poetry*," *Books Abroad* 33, no. 4 (1959): 465.
24 Boyd Carter, "Mexican Poetry in English Translation," review of *An Anthology of Mexican Poetry*, by Samuel Becket, Octavio Paz, and C. M. Bowra, *Prairie Schooner* (Winter 1960).
25 Novillo-Corvalán, *Modernism and Latin America*, 192.
26 Ibid., 195.
27 Octavio Paz and Eliot Weinberger, "Beckett/Paz," *Fulcum: An Annual of Poetry and Aesthetics* 6 (2007): 617.
28 Novillo-Corvalán, *Modernism and Latin America*, 199.
29 Brouillette, *UNESCO*, 34.
30 Ibid.
31 Octavio Paz, *The Labyrinth of Solitude* (New York: Grove Press, 1985), 195.
32 Enciso, *Andar fronteras*, 128.
33 Paz and Weinberger, "Beckett/Paz," 617, and Gustavo Guerrero, "Brief History," in this volume.
34 Paz, "Tamayo en la pintura mexicana," 244.
35 Ibid., 247.
36 Paz, *Labyrinth*, 358.
37 Paz, "Tamayo en la pintura mexicana," 247.
38 Ibid.
39 Ibid., 252.
40 Antonio Rodriguez, "¡Tamayo no es el mejor pintor!" [Tamayo is not the best painter!] *Impacto* 104 (June 1951): 48–50.
41 "¿Tienen algo contra mi en Relaciones? Le aseguro que soy un buen empleado. Me echaron de París cuando lo de la Exposición—acaso mi presencia hería ciertas vanidades—. Y desde entonces no me dan tiempo ni de respirar. Ni siquiera aprovechan mis servicios. En París pude ayudarles en Exposición. Acaso les hubiera ahorrado ciertas cosas penosas. (¿Han llegado allá las opiniones sobre la pintura mexicana? No las comparto, pero me parece saludable empezar a deshacer equívocos. Los tabús, en arte, me irritan)." Anthony Stanton, ed., *Correspondencia: Alfonso Reyes/Octavio Paz (1939–1959)* [Correspondence: Alfonso Reyes/Octavio Paz] (México: FCE, 1999), 189.
42 Cuauhtémoc Medina, "La oscilación entre el mito y la crítica. Octavio Paz entre Duchamp y Tamayo," [The Oscillation Between Criticism and Myth. Octavio Paz

between Duchamp and Tamayo] in *Materia y sentido: El arte mexicano en la mirada de Octavio Paz* [Material and meaning: Mexican Art in Octavio Paz's Gaze] (México: INBA, 2009), 275–304.
43 Ibid.
44 Octavio Paz, *Rufino Tamayo*, trans. Sita Garst (México: UNAM, 1959).
45 André Breton and Jean Cassou, *Rufino Tamayo* (Bruxelles: Palais des Beaux-Arts, 1951).
46 Marta Traba, *Dos décadas vulnerables en las artes plásticas latinoamericanas, 1950-1970* [Two Vulnerable Decades in Latin American Art] (México: Siglo XXI, 2005), 83.
47 All figures in this section come from Christine Frérot, *El mercado del arte en México 1950-1976* (México: INBA, 1990), 165–85.
48 Octavio Paz, "From Criticism to Offering," in Octavio Paz, *Essays on Mexican Art*, trans. Helen Lane (New York: Harcourt, 1993), 205–15.
49 Octavio Paz, "Transfigurations," in Ibid., 216–38.
50 Octavio Paz, *Marcel Duchamp or The Castle of Purity*, trans. Donald Garner (London: Cape Goliard, 1970).
51 Octavio Paz, *Apariencia desnuda: la obra de Marcel Duchamp* (México: Era, 1973).
52 Gilbert M. Joseph and Jürgen Buchenau, *Mexico's Once and Future Revolution* (Durham: Duke University Press, 2013), 141–66.
53 Ibid., 141.
54 Christine Frérot, *El mercado*, 187–8.
55 A similar study could be carried out regarding the increase in Paz's poems dedicated to artists and art works.
56 Dominguez Michael, *Octavio Paz*, 489.
57 Héctor Tajonar, *México en la obra de Octavio Paz* [Mexico in Octavio Paz's Work] (México: Televisa, 1984).
58 Octavio Paz, *Los privilegios de la vista* (México: Centro Cultural de Arte Contemporáneo, 1990).
59 Torcuato Tena Benjumea, "Los privilegios de la vista," *ABC*, April 13/14 (1990): 47.
60 Octavio Paz, *Materia y sentido: El arte mexicano en la mirada de Octavio Paz* (México: Océano, 2009).
61 Octavio Paz, *En esto ver aquello: Octavio Paz y el Arte* (México: Conaculta, 2014).
62 Octavio Paz, ed., *Mexico: Thirty Centuries of Splendor* (New York: MET, 1990).
63 Dullea, Georgia, "At the Met, 30 Centuries of Mexican Art," *The New York Times*, October 2, 1990, B5.
64 "Moved by admiration, curiosity, indignation, complicity, surprise, I wrote: to comment on an exhibition or to introduce a friend to the public, at the request of a museum or on commission from a magazine to make a few extra *centavos*." Paz, *Essays on Mexican Art*, 22.
65 Dominguez Michael, *Octavio Paz*, 488–9.
66 Maarten Van Delden, *Reality in Movement: Octavio Paz as Essayist and Public Intellectual* (Nashville: Vanderbilt, 2020), 207.
67 Paz, *Itinerary*, 34.
68 Ibid.
69 Ibid., 33.
70 Ibid., 51.
71 Dominguez Michael, *Octavio Paz*, 104.
72 Paz, "David Rousset y los campos de concentración Soviéticos," 51.

73 Paz, *Itinerary*, 68.
74 Maarten Van Delden and Yvon Grenier, *Gunshots at the Fiesta: Literature and Politics in Latin America* (Tennessee: Vanderbilt University Press, 2009), 115–36. And, Klaus Meyer-Minnemann, "Octavio Paz, David Rousset y el universo de los campos de concentración," *Literatura Mexicana* 13, no. 1 (2002): 149–72.
75 Paz, *Itinerary*, 66.
76 Ibid., 68.
77 Octavio Paz and Enrique Krauze, *La experiencia de la libertad* (México: Vuelta, 1991).
78 Van Delden, *Reality in Movement*, 207.
79 Enrique Krauze, "La experiencia de la libertad," *Letras Libres*, September 7, 2020.
80 Hugo J. Verani, *Octavio Paz: Bibliografía Crítica (1931–2013)* (México: El Colegio Nacional, 2014).
81 Octavio Paz, *Selected Poems*, trans. Muriel Rukseyer (Bloomington: Indiana University Press, 1963).
82 Muriel Rukseyer, *The Green Wave* (New York: Doubleday, 1948).
83 "Book Notices," *The Hispanic American Historical Review* 39, no. 2 (May 1959): 297–364.
84 Octavio Paz, *¿Águila o sol?* (México: Tezontle, 1951), *Aigle ou Souleil?*, trans. Jean-Clarence Lambert (París: Falaize, 1957).
85 Ungureanu, *From Paris to Tlön*, 13.
86 Ibid.
87 Ibid.
88 Melanie Nicholson, *Surrealism in Latin American Literature: Searching for Breton's Ghost* (New York: Palgrave, 2013).
89 Octavio Paz, "Buñuel the Poet," in *On Poets and Others*, trans. Michael Schmidt (New York: Arcade, 1986), 152.
90 Octavio Paz, *Marcel Duchamp o el castillo de la pureza* (México: Era, 1968).
91 Octavio Paz, *Marcel Duchamp, ou le Chateau de la pureté*, trans. Monique Fong-Wust (Genève: Claude Givaudan, 1967).
92 Paz, *Marcel Duchamp or The Castle of Purity*, 1970.
93 Verani, *Octavio Paz*.
94 Jordan Smith, "Octavio Paz and Collaborativity: Notations/Rotations with Katayama Toshihiro," *Tokyo Poetry Journal* 7 (2018): 75–86.
95 Cuauhtémoc Medina, "Systems (Beyond So-Called 'Mexican Geometrism')," in *The Age of Discrepancies: Art and Visual Culture in Mexico 1968–1997* (México: UNAM, 2006), 128.
96 Anne d'Harnoncourt and Kynaston McShine, eds., *Marcel Duchamp* (New York: Museum of Modern Art, 1973).
97 Donald Preziosi, *Rethinking Art History: Meditations on a Coy Science* (New Haven: Yale University Press, 1989), 9.
98 Paz, *Children of the Mire* (Cambridge, MA: Harvard University Pres, 1974), 9.
99 Octavio Paz, "The Shame of the Olympics," trans. Mark Strand, *The New York Review of Books* (November 1968).
100 Cited in Guillermo Sheridan, "De nuevo, la limpidez," *Letras Libres*, October 29, 2014.
101 Dominguez Michael, *Octavio Paz*, 411. And, Ángel Gilberto Adame, *El misterio de la vocación* [The Mystery of a Vocation] (México: Aguilar, 2015).

10

Brief History of an Anthology of Mexican Poetry

Gustavo Guerrero

In a letter sent to Alfonso Reyes from Paris on June 1950, Octavio Paz informs him about his reservations regarding an anthology of Mexican poetry recently commissioned to him and that was going to be published in French and English: "With the exception of some names, I do not have full faith in the book. I do not think it can capture the interest of a foreign readership. In any case, it will only appear many years from now— depending on the UNESCO and the [Secretary of] Public Education bureaucracy."[1] Today, after half a century, we know that he was not incorrect in his complaint neither about the selection he was obliged to produce, nor about the book's improbable reception in Francophone and Anglophone countries. Paz had already edited other anthologies, had dealt with the problems posed by poetry translation, and by then knew well the reading horizons of Parisian, European, and North American intellectual circles. But one has to acknowledge that he was wrong, in part, about the publication's timeline, since, though the English version will only appear in 1958, the French one is published in Paris just a couple of years later, in 1952. Indeed, *Anthologie de la poésie mexicaine* is printed and distributed in November of that year by the French-Swiss publisher Nagel as the brand-new second volume of the Iberoamerican Series of the UNESCO Collection of Representative Works.[2] This may explain Paz's misperception: the young anthologist did not at the moment appreciate the importance of the program in which his work would be inscribed, neither the determined voluntarism of the different agents implied in the development of a collection that soon would count with more than a hundred titles translated into and from languages as varied as Arabic, Italian and Farsi.[3]

Although it has not received a lot of attention until now, Paz's anthology is not a minor book. Besides being one of the first attempts to present in French and English a systematic view of Mexico's poetry, the volume condenses the history of a key moment of Mexico's participation in the debates on world literature, as this notion was conceived during the European postwar period. Let's remember that at that time UNESCO and its Collection of Representative Works, which aspired to grow into a vast international library, emerged as one of the primordial scenarios of an intense geopolitical, diplomatic, and literary discussion in which the Mexican delegates intervene as invitees to what should have been a fraternal meeting of the world of letters but that in reality becomes the theater of a conflict between hegemonic centers and subaltern peripheries, old empires and young nations, Western and non-Western literatures. Product of this dispute between antagonistic forces, the Mexican anthology, more than any of the other volumes published in the collection during a decade, gives us an idea of the literary and political ambition that animates UNESCO's cosmopolitan project and its principal agents. At the same time, and throughout its genesis and development, the making of the volume externalizes the internal contradictions that distort and tear the project apart from its very beginnings. Both aspects are so intimately connected that it is difficult to analytically separate them and clearly present them in an interpretation. Nevertheless, it is possible to elaborate a narrative that recontextualizes the book within UNESCO's institutional history and makes visible the continuity of the tensions that run through its editorial project and that take place in the text of the anthology, since even before it was published.

UNESCO, Mexico, and World Literature

At the end of the Second World War, according to recent works by Susanne Klengel and Céline Giton, Europe witnesses a renaissance of liberal humanism and cosmopolitanism in response to the disasters of war and the geopolitical and ideological polarized climate that dominated the 1930s.[4] To put the cultivation of letters at the foundation of the reconstruction projects and as the consensual basis of the new societies was an essential part of the attempt to return to the origins of European civilization and to the values of the Enlightenment. In fact, for many intellectuals, the war was a betrayal of those principles, as if, all of a sudden, the space of experience, in Reinhardt Koselleck's sense, had been incapable of determining the horizon of expectations and would have opened the doors of history to the unpredictable and the ineffable. Klengel summarizes the postwar situation in Europe as follows:

> The political and cultural figures of the time energetically asked for and promoted a new and reinvigorated universal Humanism to confront the destructions of the war and the Jewish genocide that was starting to enter the world conscience. The concept of Humanism, shared by Communists, Existentialists and Catholics with differing meanings, functioned as common denominator and consensus builder.[5]

As the ideological branch of the United Nations in its search for a new world order that guarantees peace, the UNESCO could not but appropriate and interiorize this very old and very recent horizon of expectations, transforming it in one of its sources of legitimation and in one of the main goals of its activities. Indeed, only a few months after its foundation in 1945, the UNESCO implemented three programs that clearly echoed the attempt to give new luster to the blazons of humanisms and liberal cosmopolitanism. The first one is the exploratory seminars on languages and literatures organized in Sèvres, France, in the summer of 1947. As a way of assessing how the teaching of world literature could foster understanding among peoples, these sessions brought together representatives from thirty-one countries from Europe, Africa, America, and Asia with the objective of drafting a list of works that could serve as a reading material for young people between fourteen and nineteen years old.[6] The second program was the reactivation of *Index Translationum*, a gigantic bibliographic repertoire that aspired to trace all the translations made in the world and that was (and is) a sort of frozen image of the constant circulation of texts and languages that ideally defines world literature. Created under the auspices of the International Institute for Intellectual Cooperation in 1932 and brought to a halt by the war, this ambitious project resumed under UNESCO and continues its bibliographic reviews until now, although it can only be consulted today in digital form through a database and a user interface available on the organization's web portal.[7] Finally, and unsurprisingly, the third program is a large collection of translated international literary works that should have served to strengthen ties between the nations of the world and whose official presentation took place during UNESCO's Second General Meeting in Mexico City, in December 1947.

Not by coincidence the conference takes place in the Mexican capital and the program for the collection is presented there. As Nuria Sanz and Carlos Tejada have shown, it is practically impossible to narrate the first years of UNESCO without considering the key role played by Mexico.[8] By the end of the war, backed by an antifascist record and surrounded by the aura of having been the land of asylum for European refugees, the North American country not simply participates in the preliminary meeting in London in 1945, but is represented by an important delegation chaired by the acting Minister of Education, Jaime Torres Bodet, and which included such intellectuals as José Gorostiza, Director of Political Affairs of the Mexican Foreign Ministry, and the philosopher Samuel Ramos, Dean of UNAM's Faculty of Philosophy and Letters. Mexico is the first Latin American country to ratify the organization's charter, the world's first to institute a Permanent Delegation to the UNESCO, and that, during those seminal years, imposes by its sheer weight Spanish as official language alongside English and French.[9] Mexico's revolutionary government, true to its active political culture, implicates itself deeply and decisively in the process of creation and structuration of this organism, bringing a different perspective when establishing its internal mechanisms, its programs and goals. The Mexicans bring indeed a different demand that makes evident the need to move toward an international order with diversity and solidarity, in which peripheries have a place and a voice, quite apart from any form of condescension or paternalism. Torres Bodet's influential and polemic speech during the preliminary discussions in London sets the tone quite explicitly: "We will never know what devotion to freedom can do in man—he says from the outset—if we do not think about the enormous disproportion that civilized countries have allowed to prevail for centuries between the cultural development of a few of them and the abandonment of others." And continues:

> Some of the delegates present here, coming from nations in which illiteracy has disappeared, may find anachronic that there are countries in which, alongside an

educated elite and the remains of cultures with a great lineage, there are still millions of young persons and adults that do not have even a rudimentary knowledge of the alphabet. If the monopoly of certain industries and certain commercial procedures has been the source of continuous disagreements among men, how should we accept that improvements in technique, the means of scientific investigation and the conquests of knowledge should be monopolized also by the privilege of fortune alone? The duty that I invoke here must be understood in much broader terms, and therefore concerns the education of peoples subjected to protectorate, mandate, or colonial regime. The ignorance in which they have remained is a danger for peace and, even if this were not the case, an elemental principle of justice should compel us to demand for them, on behalf of the organism to be created, a preferential attention.[10]

From a diplomatic perspective Mexico understood that it was important to support Europe's reconstruction efforts after the Second World War, as the Old Continent was impoverished and dismembered; but not to restore a world order that would repeat the old unequal distribution of power and wealth and that would reinstitute the old relations of subordination between colonial peripheries and metropolitan centers. "It worried me," Torres Bodet writes in his memoires, "how the great powers, even when vexed and depressed, still talked as great powers ignoring the peoples that they called *insufficiently developed*."[11] For Mexico UNESCO should have served as an instrument not of conservation but of change and the main tool for this transformation should have been a planetary democratization of education, science, and culture. The perspective of Europe and the United States was, evidently, different. The latter saw the organization as an instrument to consolidate their political hegemony, whereas the former prioritized the objective of reconstructing Europe and securing world peace through an idealized return to the values of the West, recast as "universal values," without changing the prewar geopolitical hierarchies.[12] Unsurprisingly, and as part of this return to the origins, discourses on the importance of promoting the study of Latin and Greek and the necessity to restore the cult of Antiquity and to preserve the status of the Graeco-Roman civilization as a model proliferate in the French and British public sphere, as it is made vividly evident, for example, in UNESCO's logo. Joining this trend, the French conservative journal *Le Figaro* published in November 1952 the alarmist headline "Latin or Babel. . .," as if, precisely in this preamble to decolonization, life was under the imminent threat of international chaos and confusion.[13]

The program of the collection of translated works is, from early on, one of the stages of the confrontation between these opposed perspectives on the organization and its goals. Initially, the idea emerged with a proposal made by the delegation of Lebanon during the United Nations General Conference in December 1946. With the goal of promoting the understanding and peace among nations, the Lebanese delegation proposes "the translation of the world's classics into the languages of the Members of the United Nations" and sends a request to the Economic and Social Council to request UNESCO to examine the viability of the proposal.[14] In 1947 UNESCO's Executive Council created a Translation Office under the direction of the French university professor Jean-Jacques Mayoux, an English language and literature specialist, and instructed him to draft a plan to be presented at the Mexico conference.[15] The organization's internal documents inform us of the difficulties that arise from the beginning around the definition of a "classic," both in the sense of "universal work" and "representative work," and regarding the historical and conceptual scope of the concept, limiting it or not to the cultural pattern established by the study of the ancient civilizations of Greece and Rome. UNESCO's Director-General himself, the British Julian Huxley, feels compelled to intervene in June 1947 to remind those responsible for the plan that a classic is, above all, a national or regional work, and that it is only universal if it is representative of a given culture.[16] To shorten the debate and avoid polemics, it was decided to request from each member country a list of their "classic works," which they considered necessary to translate. But, in fact, this solution created new problems as the incompatibilities between the criteria used by the different countries to build their lists and the notion of "classic work" espoused by several European members of the organization quickly became evident. The preamble of the questionnaire requesting the lists is already an exercise in tightrope walking, as shown by the four features with which the classics are defined, namely:

> A classic, we submit, is any work in whatever intellectual field (literature, science, philosophy, religion, etc.) which is deemed representative of a culture or a nation and which remains as a landmark in the cultural history of mankind.
>
> Although it might express a particular culture, it is characteristic of a classic that it transcends the limits of that culture and is representative of it, not only within the nation itself, but also in the eyes of other nations.
>
> Length of life being one of the characteristics of a classic, we may regard as classics those works which have stood the test of time and have preserved their human value for generations. It may be agreed that only works published before 1900 shall be deemed classics.
>
> Classics which UNESCO proposes for translation will be such as no excessive difficulty of wording or meaning puts out of reach of a broadly educated and well-read public.[17]

Facing the obvious difficulties posed by such conceptualization, the Second Conference that meets in Mexico in 1947 decides to modify the original proposal and renames the program "Translation of Great Works," dividing it strategically and diplomatically into two collections: "that of reputed classical works, to which the Economic and Social Council refers" and "that of contemporary works from different fields, not only of literature but also of philosophy or social sciences, exact and natural sciences."[18]

The Conference also orders the creation of a commission of international experts whose mission is to examine regularly the list proposed by the member states and asks for resources to be released to assist the least affluent countries, so they can participate in the program. Behind these resolutions one can glimpse the discussion that took place in the Mexican capital, but which was curiously underreported by Mayoux in his article for *Le Courrier de l'UNESCO*, the organization's official publication. Celebrating the project's approval and launch in half a page, and featuring a photograph of the inauguration ceremony where one can see the Mexican president Miguel Alemán and his Minister of Education Manuel Gual Vidal, Mayoux's headline announces that UNESCO will promote "the translation of the classics" and reintroduces the disputed term when describing the nature and the corpus of the future collection.[19]

The first meeting of the Commission of Experts in May 1948 is the next moment of this silent battle. It is formed by fifteen members from thirteen different countries (France and Great Britain keep four seats for themselves). This body has the mission to examine the list of classics sent by the states after the consultation, to establish a list of qualified translators and another one of publishers interested in the project and, finally, to analyze the problem of the collection's distribution. Susanne Klengel summarizes well what the discussion was all about: "a veritable discord between the old and young nations that convinced all participants that the term 'classics' could not be applied to the texts that were to be translated."[20] The meeting's minutes attest to this. During the discussions, Brazil's representative Tavares Bastos revisits an observation by the Australian delegation and notes that the selection of 1900 as the temporal limit for the definition of the classics is discriminatory for many new countries. Meanwhile, Mexican delegate Jesús Silva Herzog emphasizes that the concept of "universality" used to define the classics is very relative and corresponds to works from the countries that historically have wielded the political and economic capital to promote their authors at the international level, which is not the case of many Latin American books and authors widely recognized in the region, such as Montalvo, Sarmiento, Martí, Sierra, and Rodó.[21] It should be noted that Silva Herzog, then a member of the governing board of the Fondo de Cultura Económica, the Mexican state publisher, was a man who knew well the international translation market with its asymmetries and inequalities and who also knew that the circulation of texts did not obey only aesthetic or literary criteria. His intervention redirects the debate and underlines the urgency to reformulate the program of translations from a more inclusive perspective by insisting on the multidirectional nature of circulation. For it is a matter not only of the dissemination of "the classics" from the metropolitan centers to the peripheries but of bringing the contemporary works of the peripheral literatures to the countries of the center. Such is the great turnaround that was imposed within the project in that year of 1948 with the first meeting of the Commission of Experts and which is later confirmed with the election of the Mexican candidate, Jaime Torres Bodet, as Director-General of UNESCO.

Jaime Torres Bodet and the Collection of Representative Works

Result of a compromise between the French and the Americans, or, better said, between the Anglo-Saxon and Latin branches of the organization, the appointment of a Mexican politician, poet, and diplomat as a head of the UNESCO marks a new direction that decisively reorients the programs and scientific, educational, and cultural activities toward more open and inclusive horizons.[22] In fact, stemming from the critiques of the European humanism and advocating for the emergence of a new humanism, more diverse and modern, with Torres Bodet, Mexico initiates the process of incorporating the peripheries into the debate about the state of world culture. The inauguration discourse of the new director in December of 1948 is unequivocal in this regard:

> The interdependence of the peoples, today a primordial necessity, is not confined to the fields of politics and economics; it also extends to the spheres of culture and the mind. In different parts of the world voices are heard announcing the advancement towards a new kind of humanism. That means that we cannot keep on accepting, unaltered, the idea of man and of culture that we inherit from classical humanism. (. . .) Classical humanism was circumscribed at one time to the Mediterranean region. Modern humanism should not acknowledge limits nor borders. The UNESCO's supreme task is to contribute to the arrival of this new humanism.[23]

This declaration should be recontextualized within the public debate in England and France where, as we saw earlier, the revindication of classicism goes hand in hand with Western ambitions of a status quo and a return to the international order of the prewar era. Torres Bodet ushers in a change, which, not without pushback, is reflected in various areas of the institution and which acquires a particular profile in that of literatures, through the reactivation of the aforementioned *Index Translationum* in 1948 and the celebration of Goethe's Centenary in 1949. That was the occasion to give new luster to the blazons of *Weltliteratur*, gathering, in a commemorative volume, the works of such diverse writers as Taha Hussein, Alfonso Reyes, Thomas Mann, Gabriela Mistral, Jules Romains, Léopold Sédar Senghor, and Stephen Spender, among others.[24] But doubtless the collection of great works in translation was the key piece of the project. Torres Bodet declares in his report before the delegates in 1949 that, as far as literature is concerned, no other seems more urgent nor more necessary to him.[25] At the end of that year, the second meeting of the Commission of Experts on Translation is called, this time presided by the Director of the National Library of France, Julien Cain, and the Vice Chancellor of the University of Cairo, Mostafa Amer Bey. Notably more balanced and egalitarian than the preceding one, this committee not only includes Latin American countries, represented by Brazil in the person of Sergio Buarque de Holanda, and by Mexico with its Ambassador Antonio Castro Leal. It also includes China, India, and the Arab states.[26]

Torres Bodet, whose leadership gives rise to noticeable tensions with the delegations of the United States, Great Britain, and France—three countries, which he calls in private "The Three Kings"[27]—tries to push forward rapidly the implementation of the project, providing its own funding formula. He wants to launch as soon as possible the two pilot collections which were to start the circulation of the selected and translated works in two vast linguistic areas: the Arabic and Latin American regions.

Notably, it is the same block of countries, which, at that point in time, allow him to secure a sufficient majority within the organizations to reorient the programs and budgets, transferring resources from North to South.[28] The key players of the diplomatic and financial strategy, the Arab League and the Organization of the American States, join the meeting, since according to the Director's plan, alongside the countries, the regional organizations were called to assure negotiation, financing, and logistics of book production and distribution. Reaffirming his commitment to the project, Torres Bodet personally inaugurates the work of the committee with a discourse that insists pragmatically on the necessity to follow a well-defined and circumscribed strategy.

> After lengthy preliminary work, UNESCO is now at last reaching the stage of practical results. The whole problem of translation has already been examined by the experts; but we could not come to grips with it on a world-wide scale; we had to select certain special fields for our first experiments. Arrangements have already been made with certain governments; these agreements will soon bear fruit and bring to readers in many countries translations in handy collections at a reasonable price.[29]

The second meeting of the Commission of Experts validates the launch of the two collections: the works of Avicena and Al Ghazali will be translated into French, English, and Spanish, while the works of Aristotle, Shakespeare, Cervantes, and Descartes will be translated into Arabic. At the same time, a list of Latin American titles is drawn to be considered as candidates for the program, a working document to be discussed at the regional meeting in La Havana in 1950, partly inspired in the old Latin American collection of the International Institute on Intellectual Cooperation.[30] Nonetheless, Torres Bodet's essential contribution consists in giving the project a specific body and shape under the rubric of "Collection of Representative Works," thus abandoning definitively the ambiguous notion of a "classic" that had been used previously, and clarifying the sense of the circulation and of the cultural areas that would be included in the program.

Further, Torres Bodet invites the French writer and editor Roger Callois to UNESCO, to be personally put in charge of following both series and coordinating the workflow between the different actors of the editorial process.[31] We have to underline that Callois is, above all, a specialist in Latin American literature. This is the man, who, upon his return from Argentina, had just signed with Gallimard the launching of his very famous collection La Croix du Sud, the first international collection of the authors from the continent.[32] Consequently, with his incorporation into the team at the Office of Translation and into the section of Letters and Arts of the UNESCO, the emphasis is made on the development of the series devoted to Latin America, which is at the same time an evident priority for Torres Bodet and the Mexican government. Numerous letters from the archives of the UNESCO furthered the work in this direction, as they were being sent to the various governments requesting incessantly the lists of titles and authors to be translated.[33] There is also the list of the provisional program of more than a hundred of books, which were to shape the corpus of the future collections and which constitutes a sort of a literary canon of Latin America on the global scale at that mid-century moment.

Periodized into four eras—the Pre-Columbian, the Conquest, the Colonial Period, and the modern times—the plan for the collections would have the common section, so to speak Latin-Americanist, where a series of anthologies and continental compilations would be featured, such as *Chroniclers of the Indies* or *The thought of the Founders of America*, alongside the properly national lists of nineteen countries, composed mostly of the works and authors from the nineteenth and the beginning of the twentieth centuries.[34] The rule to be respected was not to include still living authors. But the representation of the works is certainly not equally distributed between the different countries. Argentina counts twelve titles, among which we find works by Sarmiento, Echevarría, and Alberdi, in a line-up that concludes with Lugones and Güiraldes. Brazil is also represented by twelve authors, chronologically framed between the sermons of Father Vieira and Da Cunha's *Os Sertoes*. Mexico also belongs to this group with its dozen titles, starting with an anthology of the pre-Columbian poetry and ending with Antonio Caso. Most countries do not count, nonetheless, more than five or six titles, and at times must be content with just one author and just one title. Such is the case with Nicaragua (Rubén Darío) and Puerto Rico (Eugenio María de Hostos). Also, a crude error of confusing some Peruvian and Paraguayan authors, observed by Klengel, must be recognized.[35] With all this considered, this famous list constitutes a fair and unavoidable testimony of the political and diplomatic voluntarism of the Mexicans. Let us say that Mexico's vocation to practice a certain continental leadership takes this form, reclaiming a place for Latin America in the future map of visible literatures on the global scale.

Anthologie de la poésie mexicaine/Anthology of Mexican Poetry

The anthology evidently forms part of this list and, in some UNESCO documents, even appears as the title that was to be the first in the collection.[36] Prompted by Samuel Beckett's death in 1989, Octavio Paz remembers in a short notice that it was the Spanish essayist and critic Ricardo Baeza, who was working occasionally back then as secretary of the Office of Translations, who entrusted to him the job of editing the volume.[37] As is well known, Paz occupied in Paris a post of the Third Secretary of the Embassy of Mexico since 1945 and in his capacity as the "informal cultural aggregate," in Froilan Inciso's words, had woven an ample net of relations that connected different artistic, political, and intellectual groups active in postwar France.[38]

Baeza comes from one of those groups. According to Emilie Morin, he was part of the constellation of the Spanish Republican exile, a vast archipelago that gathered writers and poets of very different persuasions, from liberals to anarchists, and from Catholics to communists.[39] Paz, who had attended the famous International Congress of Writers for the Defense of Culture in Valencia in 1937, maintained close relations with many of the exiles and, in Paris, continued his work in support of the Republic. It is not to be forgotten that, in the beginning of 1946, just a few months after having arrived to the French capital, and thanks to the support of Ferdinand Verheren and Jean Cassou, he made possible the translation and edition of an anthology of contemporary Spanish poetry, which presented itself as a gesture of solidarity with the exiles and an act of resistance against Franquism.[40]

It is difficult to estimate today how much autonomy Baeza had to propose this work to Paz without asking authorization from Torres Bodet or even from Roger Callois. Neither is it clear who chose the two translators of the anthology. Eliot Weinberger asserts that it was Paz himself, but, in his notice, the Mexican poet suggests that it could have been otherwise.[41] Truth be told, while the genesis of the project is clearly outlined in the official documents available to us, there are, on the contrary, very confusing and contradictory versions about the process of text selection, following up on the translations and the final design of the volumes that were edited. In any case, the translators also come from the intellectual networks around Paz in postwar Paris: for the French version, Guy Levis Mano, and for the English, Samuel Beckett.

Editor, poet, graphic designer, and political and cultural activist, Guy Levis Mano was a survivor of the war and the Holocaust, and a central figure of the literary field at that moment. His relationship with Paz is woven through two distinct circles: on one hand, the aforementioned Republican exiles, with which Levis Mano maintained solid professional and personal ties, and on the other, the Surrealist movement, of which he had been a promoter and a fellow traveler since its beginnings in the 1920s. Born in Salonica and residing in France since his adolescence, Ladino was his native language and, as such, opened the doors for him to the Spanish Medieval, Classical, and contemporary poetry, which he read in the original.

We owe him an impressive catalogue of translations into French, among which can be found Góngora, San Juan de la Cruz, and the Romancero, up to Federico García Lorca, Rafael Alberti, and Juan Ramón Jiménez. But even more remarkable is his catalogue of Surrealist poetry, since, as an editor, he published and promoted the works of Tristan Tzara, Paul Eluard, Benjamin Peret, Antonin Artaud, René Char, Pierre Jean-Jouve, and even André Breton himself, among others. Such was his centrality and influence within the French literary field that, in 1939, Joë Bousquet wrote to him in a letter: "the writers of our time who have not seen at least one of their books published by your publishing house, will not be entirely writers of our times."[42] It is very likely that Paz had made his acquaintance through Breton's circle and through the Parisian Surrealists with whom he communed since his arrival to the city in 1945. At that moment, it was difficult to imagine anyone better prepared and more competent for the task of translating the anthology of Mexican poetry into French, predominantly featuring poets from the Baroque, Neoclassical, and Romantic periods.

To the contrary, Samuel Beckett does not seem, in principle, the best choice to render the poems into English. It is difficult to trace who entrusted him with such a task, although it is true that the Irishman had already worked for UNESCO on a translation from Spanish, which was nothing less than a poem by Gabriela Mistral for the Goethe commemorative volume in 1949.[43] According to Paz' version of events, he met Beckett in the entourage of the journal *Fontaine* and its director, Max-Pol Fouchet. Beckett cites him in a cafe at Trocadero Square at the end of 1949, and, somewhat uncomfortably, admits that he was offered the translation of the anthology that was being prepared. Then he adds that he needs the honorarium money, and that, although he does not know Spanish, he had studied Latin in Ireland and knows how to write in French; besides, he promises that a Hispanist friend and writer, Gerald Brennan, would review the final version of the translations.[44] The young Paz, whose economic situation was just as precarious despite his diplomatic post, finds this proposal acceptable and brings it to Baeza. Beckett's manuscripts and drafts, preserved in England and the United States, show that he kept his word and that he worked relentlessly on the translation of the poems during winter and spring of 1950.[45]

The correspondence between Reyes and Paz offers testimony of the revision process of both translations. Paz writes repeatedly to the old master from Monterrey asking for his philological insights on all kinds of words and names, which neither he nor the translators manage to decipher: *yerbaniz, parotas, ahuejotes, cipro, enceso*. . .[46] Reyes resolves some of the doubts, leaves others aside, and recommends to Paz, as far as his poetry is concerned, and particularly the poem "Yerbas de Tarahumara," one of the anthology's entries, that he should use the old version of Valery Larbaud.[47] But it was done otherwise. The version published in the French anthology is one by Levis Mano, which, in my opinion, does not detract nor is inferior. It seems that Paz complained about liberties that the French translator took with the originals, but the truth is that his work came out both creative and rigorous, especially in the transfer of numerous archaisms in the Baroque and Neoclassical poems.[48] On the contrary, Beckett's work provoked serious reservations among the British and US editors that welcomed the anthology: Thames & Hudson and Indiana University Press.[49] In the just quoted notice and in the posterior interview with Weinberger, Paz recounts his meetings with Beckett during the process of translation, their conversations, the back-and-forth of questions and answers, and remembers that, curiously, among the Mexican poets that interested Beckett the most, were those of the Baroque period—and especially Sor Juana—and three modern ones: Tablada, López Velarde, and Reyes.[50] Nonetheless, for the Irishman, just as he confesses in his correspondence, this was basically a job to pay the bills and a punctual intervention in a universe that was not his. It is enough to remember that, in one of his letters, Beckett goes as far as to label the poems he had translated as "execrable."[51] In this sense, it is difficult to see in his translations a sort of subtle or veiled anti-colonial struggle, or a denouncement of the injustices of the Spanish Conquest, as in Morin's interpretation.[52] Neither should we see in them the moment of apotheosis in the history of translations of Mexican poetry, as Weinberger suggests.[53] It is more precise to admit that the destiny of the English version of the anthology, still reissued today, is explained in a great measure not only by the quality of the poems therein but also by this unexpected participation of Beckett as a translator from Spanish.

Following up on the translations was, nonetheless, a less problematic affair for the anthologist than the selection of the thirty-five poets and their texts. A preliminary note, reproduced in French and English, recounts the tensions that plague all of the editorial process.⁵⁴ Paz emphasizes in it his dissatisfaction with the work entrusted to him, lamenting that the selection criteria obliged him to leave out pre-Columbian and popular Mexican poetry, perhaps two of the richest aspects of the national lyric. The supplementary rule of not including living authors, with the only exception of Alfonso Reyes, adds to this rosary of complaints as the most regrettable omission of all, since, according to the anthologist, it leaves out of the selection "one of the most representative groups of current Spanish language poetry."⁵⁵ Finally, the period in which the anthology is framed, 1521 to 1910, imposes on him the obligation to choose the most historically representative poets and poems and those who best lend themselves to translation into English and French, when his desire would have been to give priority to a purely aesthetic assessment. In his correspondence, Paz repeats practically the same jeremiad to Reyes, but, magnifying the problems of the selection, adds: "I confess to you that, if I only had listened to my taste, I would have only had included a dozen poets."⁵⁶

The insertion of this preliminary note seems to have been the result of a compromise in the face of the conflict that arose when, near the time of publication, two presentations by the French Paul Claudel and the British Cecil M. Bowra were added to the two versions of the anthology. According to Incizo, Paz threatened to abandon the project, withdrawing his introduction and his notes, if it was not clear what his part of the responsibility was in the edition of the anthology and what part was played by UNESCO.⁵⁷ His anger is understandable: Claudel was by then one of the most conservative and reactionary members of the French Academy, an intransigent Catholic who had flirted with Franco and Pétain before belatedly converting to Gaullism, and who was also leading French public opinion in a campaign in defense of Christian traditionalism and the cult of Graeco-Roman Antiquity. Anyone who scrolls through the pages he writes for the anthology cannot but confirm that, shamefully, he never read the poems of the selection and that he did not even mention the name of a single one of the Mexican poets that, in principle, he had to present.⁵⁸ His text is a regrettable and cumbersome disquisition on classical poetics as an insurmountable and eternal archetype of literary creation, an essentialist and universalist discourse that, in tune with the positions that T. S. Eliot defended at the time in Great Britain, sees in the ancients the only source of health for the modern civilization, and in Virgil, the only true classic.⁵⁹ From these Olympic heights, Claudel not only Olympically ignores Paz's anthology but also makes it invisible and makes dialogue with it impossible, solemnly marking an immeasurable distance and establishing an order of priority that, through the editorial order of the texts, reaffirms cultural hierarchies.

From the other shore, taking up the accents of *The Labyrinth of Solitude* (1950), Paz describes Mexican poetry in its introduction as a long battle between creation and history, punctuated by those decisive moments that were the Baroque, Independence, and Revolution, and accompanied by key figures such as the Virgin of Guadalupe, the fiesta, the mask, and the death. Thus, the Mexican Baroque style is, for him, a "Guadalupan" style,⁶⁰ the poetry of the early twentieth century is presented as a revelation because "the Revolution tears off the successive masks that covered the face of Mexico";⁶¹ and, finally, and with regard to contemporary poetry, it seems to him that "the nature of the poem is analogous to that of the fiesta" (Paz, 1952: 31).[62] The young Paz finds a place for himself within the Mexican literary field, rearranging his own national tradition in the continuity of his famous essay and also advancing as a mediator between Mexican poetry and its most cosmopolitan horizon: "a universality that does not betray us and a fidelity that does not isolate or drown us."[63] In fact, its introduction is like a hand stretched out toward that conciliatory horizon where Mexicans would eventually become contemporaries of all men, but where the postcolonial gap that constitutes the time of a peripheral culture and its "desires of the world" or "cosmopolitan desires," as Mariano Siskind says, are also visible: the external and imaginary space on which the shortcomings of our modern project are pictured.[64]

Claudel's text highlights the limits of this attempt at dialogue, which are also those of the openness and receptivity of the old metropolises, by imposing an ahistorical and essentialist perspective on poetry, authoritatively centered on the classical tradition and from which Paz's speech becomes simply unreadable, like Mexican poetry itself. The contrast is pathetic. Unfortunately, Bowra does not do much better when, in his presentation of the English version, he offers his readers a journey through the history of the European poetic tradition, from Homer to the French symbolists, and only about ten lines from the end remembers to mention Mexico.[65] Patricia Novillo-Corvalán summarizes this disaster:

> Without seeking to overstate their profound ignorance of Mexican culture and literature, neither Bowra nor Claudel made the minimum effort to acquaint themselves with the poems at hand. Instead, their ten-page introductions praised the universal essence of poetry, while myopically disregarding the subject matter of the anthology. Their careless dismissal of Mexico's rich poetic tradition violated the laudable principles of UNESCO's cultural program, based on inclusivity, egalitarianism, and the forging of cultural bridges between member nations.[66]

Perhaps it should be added that this ostensible gap between the anthology and those who were to promote it to the public of Anglophone and Francophone countries has, despite everything, the virtue of highlighting the frontal clash between two cultural policies that finds at UNESCO, in the Collection of Representative Works and in the effort to open the space of world literature, one of its most notable stages in the middle of the twentieth century. It is very likely that Paz's threat to withdraw from the project has led the organization's editors to add an explanatory note to the two versions of the anthology with which it tries to manifestly address the uncomfortable situation that has been created:

> This anthology is published by virtue of an agreement between UNESCO and the Mexican government within the framework of the translations of Representative Works that UNESCO has undertaken. The anthology is the work of Octavio Paz, who was also asked by UNESCO to write a study on Mexican poetry. On the other hand, and in a very different perspective, l'UNESCO has asked Paul Claudel to do everything possible to awaken the interest of the French-speaking public in this

collection and Professor C.M. Bowra to do the same with the English-speaking public. Their essays should not be considered as prefaces or introductions in the usual sense. They are intended rather to emphasize the essential solidarity of creative artists in different nations, languages, centuries and latitudes, and to point out the fundamental identity of emotions to which the genius of the poet can give form at once lasting and beautiful.[67]

Thanks to this compromise, Paz finally accepts that the two volumes would be edited, although, during many years, he would avoid speaking about the matter like one avoids a bad memory. In various articles and conversations of his last years, he does not hesitate to attribute to Torres Bodet, his sworn enemy, the initiative to request the contribution from Claudel and Bowra.[68] Nonetheless, in the UNESCO archives there is not one document that would prove this, just as there is no proof that it was Torres Bodet that provoked Paz's departure from Paris and his transfer to the Embassy of Mexico in India before the anthology got published.[69] There were other officials in the organization who well may have requested the famous presentations, and especially during that period of intense political crisis within UNESCO, which would culminate in an open collision between Mexico and the United States, and which would in turn result in the Mexican director's resignation in December of 1952.[70]

The End of the Game

With Torres Bodet's departure, the Mexican spring of the organization comes to its end and begins a period of open US hegemony under the successive directorships of John W. Taylor (1952–3) and Luther Evans (1953–8). But neither of them gets rid of the editorial project. During the fifties, the collection of the Representative Works, under the leadership of Roger Callois, continued to thrive, diversify, and amplify. Callois manages the Iberoamerican Series practically like a private feud, and administers it jointly with Gallimard's La Croix du Sud, placing the contemporary authors in the latter and the canonical ones in the former, as he recounts to Elena Poniatowska in an interview at the beginning of the 1960s.[71]

Although an evaluation of the global impact of the UNESCO collection demands, doubtlessly, a longer and more detailed study, it is nonetheless clear that the experience of the *Anthology of Mexican Poetry*, like other titles in the series, not only evinces the asymmetry and inequalities of such an unbalanced system as that of world literature but also demonstrates the difficulty to think of and implement a cultural politics that would escape from the logic of the hegemony reconstructed in the first years of the postwar era. Sarah Brouillette is right when she affirms that " it would be silly to separate the collection of the Representative Works of the UNESCO from the effort to ensure the guardianship and the dominant position of the old imperial powers in the process of fixing and orchestrating global development."[72] But it would be equally absurd to ignore the role played by Mexico in the emergence and configuration of the collection, revendicating a privileged place for Latin America. At that moment, as rightly observed by Klengel, "it was precisely the debate about the translations of the Latin American works that caused a new consciousness about the literary periods and traditions on the international level to emerge and to grow."[73] Let us add, to conclude, that the story that we have tried to summarize here clearly shows how the debate about the place of Latin American literature allows to circumscribe with greater precision the political and cultural arena where, from then on, in the times of revolution and decolonization, the fight for a place in the showcases of the world literature will play out.

Notes

1. Alfonso Reyes and Octavio Paz, *Correspondencia (1939–1959)*, edición de Anthony Stanton (México: FCE, 1998), 129.
2. *Anthologie de la poésie mexicaine*, choix, commentaires et introduction d'Octavio Paz, traduction de Guy Lévis Mano, présentation de Paul Claudel, UNESCO, Collection d'Œuvres Représentatives, Série Ibéro-américaine (Paris: Nagel, 1952).
3. *Collection UNESCO d'Œuvres Représentatives, Catalogue général* (Paris: Editions UNESCO, 1994).
4. Susanne Klengel, "El universo (que otros llaman la Biblioteca) y *l'Univers concentrationnaire*: la recepción de Borges en la segunda posguerra," *Variaciones Borges*, no. 36 (2013): 35–51; Céline Giton, *Le livre, instrument de paix et de démocratie mondiale ? La politique du livre de l'UNESCO, 1945–1975* (Paris: Harmattan, 2019).
5. Klengel, "El universe . . .," 36.
6. *Summer seminar on Education for mutual understanding. To what extent is the World literature used in school as means of promoting international understanding?* (UNESCO Archive SEM/SEC.I/5/ED 1947).
7. *Index Translationum*, http://www.unesco.org/xtrans/ (accessed January 27, 2020).
8. Nuria Sainz and Carlos Tejada, *México y la UNESCO, la UNESCO y México: Historia de una relación* (UNESCO, Oficina de México, 2016), 69–89.
9. Ibid., 27–8.
10. Jaime Torres Bodet, *Memorias, Años contra el tiempo* (México: Porrúa, 1969), 316–17.
11. Ibid., 106.
12. Chloé Maurel, "Les tensions politiques au sein de l'UNESCO," *Revue d'histoire diplomatique*, no. 1 (2011): 29–46.
13. Pierre Marzars, "Le Latin ou Babel . . .," *Le Figaro Littéraire* (Paris, 1 November 1952), 23.
14. *Traduction des classiques mondiaux* (UNESCO Archive Phil./7/1947), 4.
15. Giton, *Le livre, instrument de paix,* 350.
16. *Compte Rendu de la réunion du Comité des Traductions* (UNESCO Archive 803 A 064, 1947), 1.
17. *Traduction des classiques mondiaux*, 3–4.
18. *Rapport complémentaire sur les traductions* (UNESCO Archive PHS/CONF.1/2, 1948).

19　Jean-Jacques Mayoux, "Les classiques, patrimoine universel," *Le Courrier de l'UNESCO*, no. 1 (Février 1948): 7.
20　Susanne Klengel, "El derecho a la literatura (mundial y traducida). Sobre el sueño traslatológico de la UNESCO," in *Re-mapping World Literature*, ed. Gesine Mueller, Jorge J. Locane, and Benjamin Loy (Berlin: De Gruyter, 2018), 141.
21　*Rapport sur la réunion du Comité d'Experts sur la Traduction de Classiques, 18–22 May* (UNESCO Archive PHS/Conf.1/3, 1948), 2–4.
22　Maurel, "Les tensions politiques au sein de l'UNESCO," 36.
23　Jaime Torres Bodet, "We Must Raise the Moral and Intellectual Condition of the Masses," *The UNESCO Courier* (Paris, December 1948), 5.
24　*Goethe: UNESCO's Homage on the Two Hundredth Anniversary of His Birth* (Paris: UNESCO, 1949).
25　*Report of the Director-General on the activities of the Organization, September-October* (UNESCO Archive 4 C/3 + ADD. & ADD. 2, 1949), 58.
26　*Report of the meeting of the international committee of experts on translation problems, Paris, November 21–25* (UNESCO Archive PHS/Conf.5/3, 1949), 1
27　Gail Archibald, *Les Etats-Unis et l'UNESCO, 1944–1963* (Paris: Publications de la Sorbonne, 1994), 152.
28　Ibid., 152–3.
29　*Address by M. Torres Bodet, Director-General of UNESCO, to the Committee of Experts, Paris, November 21 1949* (UNESCO Archive DG/49, 1949), 2.
30　*Report of the Director-General on the activities of the Organization, September-October* (UNESCO Archive 4 C/3 + ADD. & ADD. 2, 1949), 59.
31　Giton, *Le livre, instrument de paix*, 353.
32　Gustavo Guerrero, "La Croix du Sud (1945–1970): génesis y contextos de la primera colección francesa de literatura latinoamericana," in *Re-mapping World Literature*, ed. Gesine Mueller, Jorge J. Locane y Benjamin Loy (Berlin and Boston: De Gruyter, 2018), 199–210.
33　*Correspondance du Directeur Général* (UNESCO Archive 802.03 099.5, 1950).
34　*Provisional list of Latin American Books to be translated into English and French* (UNESCO Archive XR/NC/Conf.reg. 1/12, Annex II, 1950).
35　Klengel, "El derecho a la literatura (mundial y traducida)," 146.
36　*Report of the Director-General on the activities of the Organization from April 1950 to March 1951* (UNESCO Archive 6 C/3 + ADD, 1951), 146.
37　Octavio Paz, "Samuel Beckett y la poesía mexicana" (*Vuelta*, no. 159, México: febrero 1990), 52.
38　Froylán Inciso, *Andar fronteras: el servicio diplomático de Octavio Paz en Francia (1946–1951)* (México: Siglo XXI, 2008), 127.
39　Emilie Morin, *Beckett's Political Imagination* (Cambridge: Cambridge University Press, 2017), 118.
40　Octavio Paz and Ferdinand Verhesen, *Petite anthologie de la poésie espagnole contemporaine*, préface de Jean Cassou (Gilly: Editions du Cercle d'Art, 1946).
41　Octavio Paz, "Samuel Beckett y la poesía mexicana," 52; Eliot Weinberger, *Oranges & Peanuts for Sale* (New York: New Directions, 2009), 64.
42　Laura Alcoba, "Guy Lévis Mano, traducteur de Gil Vicente," in *Le théâtre espagnol du siècle d'Or en France*, ed. Cristophe Couderc (Presses Universitaires de Nanterre, 2012) : 290.

43 Goethe: UNESCO's Homage, 75.
44 Octavio Paz, "Samuel Beckett y la poesía mexicana," 52.
45 Weinberger, Oranges & Peanuts for Sale, 65; Patricia Novillo-Corvalán, Modernism and Latin America: Transnational Networks of Literary Exchange (Routledge, 2017), 148.
46 Reyes and Paz, Correspondencia (1939–1959), 124.
47 Ibid., 127.
48 Inciso, Andar fronteras, 128.
49 The letters of Samuel Beckett, vol. III, 1957–1965, ed. George Craig, Martha Down Fehsenfeld, Dan Gunn, and Lois More Overbeck (Cambridge: Cambridge University Press, 2014), 509–10; 663–5; Morin, Beckett's Political Imagination, 121.
50 Octavio Paz, Eliot Weinberger and Samuel Beckett, The Bread of Days, Eleven Mexican Poets, trans. Samuel Beckett, Notes on the Poets by Octavio Paz, Commentaries by Octavio Paz and Eliot Weinberger, Etchings by Enrique Chagoya (the Yolla Bolly Press, 1994), 121–3.
51 The Letters of Samuel Beckett, vol. III, 1957–1965, 442.
52 Morin, Beckett's Political Imagination, 125.
53 Weinberger, Oranges & Peanuts for Sale, 66.
54 Anthologie de la poésie mexicaine, 35.
55 Ibid., 35.
56 Reyes and Paz, Correspondencia (1939–1959), 129.
57 Inciso, Andar fronteras, 128.
58 Anthologie de la poésie mexicaine, 9–15.
59 Klengel, "El derecho a la literatura (mundial y traducida)," 132.
60 Anthologie de la poésie mexicaine, 20.
61 Ibid., 29.
62 Ibid., 31.
63 Ibid., 30.
64 Mariano Siskind, Cosmopolitan Desires, Global Modernity and World Literature in Latin America (Northwestern University Press, 2014), 7.
65 Anthology of Mexican Poetry, compiled by Octavio Paz, trans. Samuel Beckett, preface by Cecil M. Bowra (Bloomington: Indiana University Press, 1958), 21.
66 Novillo-Corvalán, Modernism and Latin America, 126.
67 Anthologie de la poésie mexicaine, 5.
68 Paz, Weinberg and Beckett, The Bread of Days, Eleven Mexican Poets, 122.
69 Inciso, Andar fronteras, 132.
70 Archibald, Les Etats-Unis et l'UNESCO, 153.
71 Elena Poniatowska, Jardín de Francia (México: FCE, 2008), 407.
72 Sarah Brouillette, UNESCO and the Fate in the Literary (Stanford: Stanford University Press, 2019), 33.
73 Klengel, "El derecho a la literatura (mundial y traducida)," 143.

11

Juan Rulfo's World Literary Consciousness

Nuala Finnegan

Deep Vellum press's splendid translation of Juan Rulfo's *El Gallo de Oro* [*The Golden Cockerel & Other Writings*] by Douglas Weatherford rather grandly proclaims, not without hyperbole, that its publication "heralds a landmark event in world literature."[1] Published as part of a series of events and publications commemorating the centenary of Rulfo's birth in 2017, this claiming of Rulfo as a giant of world literature was not necessarily new.[2] However, the aforementioned description places one of Rulfo's lesser known works within a largely undefined world literary framework in which it seems to register a yearning for a Rulfian *oeuvre* that is open to new readers and positioned to appeal cross-culturally on different levels. Indeed this publication forms part of a wider process of re-appraisal of Rulfo that has been ongoing for some time and which involves the belated recognition of other facets of his work aside from the best known published texts, *El Llano en llamas* and *Pedro Páramo*, to consider also the large corpus of photographic work and other shorter pieces of writing of which *El Gallo de Oro* is an example.[3] Taking this as a starting point, this chapter considers the position of Rulfo through the lens of Ángel Rama's well-circulated ideas about the *letrado*, or a lettered elite in the Americas. From here, the chapter traces the way in which Rulfo moves beyond this concept by embracing an epistemology that is rooted in mobility and plurality. This in turn invites a reading that casts both Rulfo as writer, and Rulfian poetics more widely, as embodying a critical planetary consciousness. Following this, I suggest that his work exemplifies that school of thought that insists on world literature as a concept that registers the violent legacy of world capitalism as its "political horizon."[4] Materialist concerns are explicitly registered in many of Rulfo's texts and through my close reading of the story "Paso del Norte" with its critique of gendered capitalism and violent coloniality, it is possible to see that his is a body of creative work anchored in this world-historical stance. Finally, I briefly consider what might be termed the multidirectional impulses of his work, arguing that Rulfo's fractured approach to creative practice becomes a tool to think through the many ways in which world literature's more progressive impulses might be most effectively animated.

Rulfo as World Writer

Rulfo's fictional output has often had an uneasy relationship with many of the literary traditions into which it has been shoehorned and it has also proved resistant to many of the critical paradigms thrown at it—postcolonial; regional; magical realist—to name only a few.[5] The process through which both the celebrated short story collection *El Llano en llamas* (1953) and the novel *Pedro Páramo* (1955) were elevated and subsequently reified into national treasure status is well documented.[6] Seeking a literary phenomenon that might energize the cultural landscape of the decades that followed, the talismanic nature of *Pedro Páramo* in particular furnished an industry of speculation about why Rulfo didn't write anymore.[7] If Rulfo was at the absolute center of the national literary elite, he was, on the other hand, rather ambivalently positioned with regard to certain other literary currents of the wider region, most notably magical realism. Indeed, despite obvious points of convergence, Rulfo has always been an uneasy bedfellow among the so-called Boom writers. While sometimes mentioned as a precursor or a founding father figure, he rather infrequently appears in histories of the phenomenon; nor does he feature prominently in more recent reevaluations which scrutinize magical realism as part of a broader world literary panorama.[8] In fact, Rulfo very much defied the kind of conventional world literature trajectory as embodied emblematically by, say, Gabriel García Márquez.[9] What is more, Comala, Rulfo's fictionalized universe, was not woven into the kind of universalist discourse that totally subsumed the construct of Macondo (its suffocating legacy, of course, is another story).[10] It is well known that the opening of the category "world literature" to a world beyond Europe happens from the 1960s onward, through the double prism of the global success of magical realism and the emergence of the powerful theoretical framework of postcolonialism.[11] In this sense, Rulfo, whose major works are published before the key texts of this period, is already before and beyond these interpretative frameworks. As Ignacio Sánchez Prado astutely notes, he may be legible as a magical realist, but his fictional world always exceeded that category.[12] Taking this into account, Rulfo proves to be a test case, a writer who interrogates the very limits of the category "world" even in its most complex and elastic conceptualization.

If it is accepted that Rulfo's work is already ambivalently situated as some embodiment of the nation par excellence at the same time as its seemingly innate Mexicanness removes it from elucidation within a wider continental sensibility, then what does it mean to speak of Rulfo as a world writer? Perhaps an effective approach lies in rooting Rulfo within the archetypal framing of the *letrado*, as outlined by ángel Rama in his now-famous formulation. In a meticulous examination of the networks of cultural power in Latin America since the colonial period, Rama underlines the importance of the elite group of men called the *letrados* who inhabited that complex ecology of lettered culture and state power that he encapsulated as "La ciudad letrada" or The Lettered City.[13] In this sense Rama's envisioning of the role played by the intellectual communities of the Americas has a clear parallel with Pascale Casanova's spatial conceptualization of literature, outlined in the study *The World Republic of Letters*.[14] This parallel is highlighted by Sánchez Prado, who notes that her central theory, drawing on Bourdieu, advocates for a spatial conceptualization of literature anchored in an expanded notion of power relations embedded within an autonomous geocultural map.[15] Rama's study, in turn, while also insisting on the nexus of power relations governing cultural output and actors, illustrates just how pliable a category the *letrado* really was, bending in consonance with the fluctuating historical and political contexts and which saw writers occupying diverse roles as journalists, essayists, and political leaders. Indeed, this conjoining of political leadership and writing became one of the hallmarks of post-Independence intellectual formation in the Americas. Rulfo is easily mapped within this closed configuration of revered male figures and is also positioned as cultural practitioner in the wider sense as accomplished fiction writer undoubtedly, but also screenwriter, public intellectual, anthropologist, historian, editor, not to mention photographer.[16] Following Pierre Bourdieu, one can see how his authorship of *Pedro Páramo*, in particular, locates him as a fluid figure within the set of unstable power relations mapped by both Rama and Casanova. Furthermore, the novel's aura, understood in Benjamin's sense of the term,[17] ensured that his status as canonical writer remained unchallenged even as the decades passed with no obvious follow-up in the fictional domain.

In other ways Rulfo enacts a different conceptualization of Rama's *letrado*. Forging an uneasy relationship with the urban milieu of which he was only sometimes a part,[18] he ruptures the intrinsic connection between intellectual formation and the urban environment so central to Rama's thesis. Instead, and in place of cleaving to any fixed notion of the urban, Rulfo spends much of his life, quite literally on the move. Starting with the move to Mexico City from Jalisco at the age of fifteen, considerable periods of his adult life are passed traveling the more rural states of Mexico in various jobs. His work as a traveling salesman for the Goodrich Tire Company ensured a wide scope of travel opportunities, and he worked too for the Commission of the Cuenca de Papaloapan (1955–6), investigating the impact of the dam on the populations around the basin. In the latter third of his career, he was employed by the Instituto Nacional Indigenista (National Indigenous Institute), writing and editing an extensive selection of archaeological and historical studies. Through this work, then, he embraces a commitment to movement, to mobile epistemologies, or to knowledge generated by and on the move. It is as part of this dynamic that he parts company from writing in the strictest sense of the word to move toward what Paulina Millán describes as "writing with light" ["escribir con luz"].[19]

This movement finds expression too in his constant moving through mode, through genre, through medium, through space. Such a mobile trajectory allows us to see him symbolize the more planetary idea of the creator/artist in a process of constant discovery and openness. In this regard, through his embracing of multiplicity of form (short story, novella, photography, vignettes), he speaks to a deep investment in a consciousness shaped around plurality, a concept anchored in a different approach to the notion of world.[20] This is a consciousness that includes, however peripherally, indigenous subjects erased from the national imaginary as well as the dead.[21] In terms of literary form it is also plural, including travelogue-type texts like the masterful meditation on the ruins of Castillo de Teayo in Veracruz, as well as textual fragments and film-scripts.²² Only the short stories of *El Llano en llamas* remotely conform to generic norms as conventionally understood and, thus in formal terms, he remains essentially an enigma. The material conditions of life as a *letrado* are also of importance here. As has often been emphasized by Rulfo himself, he was first and foremost a worker within a complex ecology of labor made up of diverse cultural actors and gatekeepers. Cristina Rivera Garza, in her intimate (and rather controversial) reflections on Rulfo, insists on the materialist trace in Rulfo's creative trajectory, citing his need to work and his need for work.²³ Rulfo's oft-quoted response to the question of why he hadn't written another *Pedro Páramo*, "Lo que pasa es que yo trabajo"²⁴ [The thing is, I work], positions him within a world-system, an organization of labor relations that configures the intellectual at different nodal points along a geocultural spectrum. Roaming between these points, Rulfo refuses singular modes of creativity embracing a more plural and cosmopolitan approach.

Through this sustained investment in openness and movement then, Rulfo may be located within a different set of operating structures around the concept of world literature. Transferring these observations about his positioning to a consideration of the world-views espoused in his creative work, it is possible to establish a link with Frederic Jameson when he speaks of a mode of discourse "locked in a life-and-death struggle with first-world cultural imperialism . . . a cultural struggle that is itself a reflection of the economic situation of such areas in their penetration by various stages of capitalism."²⁵ Viewing the urban-rural tension generated by his work through this lens supports Kirsten Oloff 's fascinating reading of *Pedro Páramo* when she observes the presence in his work of the "intertwined processes of rapid urbanization, de-peasantization, and the increasing capitalization of the countryside."²⁶ Here, then, the registering of this dynamic in both the authorial trajectory and the interiority of his fictional world prompts the question of the capacity for his work to generate a renewed, shared consciousness of the longue durée of capitalism. I would argue that this consciousness is forcefully present in his creative output and that his work aligns with that view of world literature by the Warwick Research Collective, among others, as a concept that registers the violent legacy of world capitalism as its "political horizon." *Pedro Páramo* perhaps fits the bill most forcefully as Kirsten Oloff trenchantly points out in her reading of this figure as "capitalist agri-business-man-gone mad."²⁷ However, other elements of his creative output may also be located within this viewpoint, including the stories from *El Llano en llamas* or *El Gallo de oro* or the other writing fragments already referenced.

"Paso del Norte": World Literary Text

By way of extending this question, I would like to turn to a closer scrutiny of one of the short stories of *El Llano en llamas*, "Paso del Norte." Thus far, I have focused my analysis of Rulfo within a world framework of literature, characterized by a certain geocultural dimension much of which is heavily predicated on ideas by Pascale

Casanova and Franco Moretti. It may thus seem somewhat ironic to turn to a close reading of a fragment from a canonical text, given the well-documented opposition to this stance articulated by Moretti. We may recall that the same critic tells us that

> the trouble with close reading (in all of its incarnations, from the new criticism to deconstruction) is that it necessarily depends on an extremely small canon. This may have become an unconscious and invisible premiss by now, but it is an iron one nonetheless: you invest so much in individual texts only if you think that very few of them really matter. Otherwise, it doesn't make sense.[28]

There has been extensive critique of Moretti's position by Gayatri Chakravorty Spivak, John Arac, and others;[29] nevertheless, these comments are strangely apposite in the case of Rulfo's fictional *oeuvre*, which was, in Moretti's terms, "extremely small." What is more, "Paso del Norte" occupies a rather slippery position within his body of work and was the subject of much criticism by the author himself. For this reason, the story was omitted from the 1955 and subsequent versions and was reintroduced only in 1980.[30] In this regard, even within Rulfo's "extremely small" body of work, "Paso del Norte" struggled to find a space. "Paso del Norte" is also a text that is studied little when compared to either *Pedro Páramo* or other very acclaimed stories from *El Llano en llamas*, and it has never been assigned the master status frequently attached to stories such as "Luvina" or "Diles que no me maten" [Tell them not to kill me]. Notwithstanding these observations, I would still argue that it is a text that matters in Moretti's conceptualization of the term and in this section, I would like to continue to consider two topoi explored in detail in the story. These comprise gendered capitalism as seen through the father-son relationship conceived in markedly transactional terms, and border-crossing as examined within a broader narrative shaped by a violent colonial necropolitics.

The story in its revised form comprises two dialogues between father and son. These dialogues reveal the son's decision to leave his rural village where he can no longer support his family, to travel north across the border. His decision is fiercely opposed by the father, and the first dialogue is a bitter exchange between a son who feels his father has failed him, and a father—portrayed largely without empathy—as indifferent to the son's concerns for his young family. As the son reproaches his father for not handing him on a trade or, in fact, any useful skills, it is hard to argue with an interpretation of "Paso del Norte" as a staging of a failed masculinity linked to a political landscape engulfed by a toxic capitalism. Indeed, through its multivoiced narration, the story condenses in a few sparse lines the dystopian extremes of capitalist exploitation and extraction. As the son explains:

> —Pos que hay hambre. Usté no lo siente. Usté vende sus cuetes y sus saltapericos y la pólvora y con eso la va pasando. Mientras haiga funciones, le lloverá el dinero; pero uno no, padre. Ya naide cría puercos en este tiempo. Y si los cría pos se los come. Y si los vende, los vende caros. Y no hay dinero pa mercarlos, demás de esto. Se acabó el negocio, padre. (194)[31]

—Well there's hunger here. Not that you'd feel it. You sells our rockets and your throw bangers and fire-works and you makes enough to get by. So long as there's a show going on, you'll keep raking in the money, but not me, father. Times such as these there's nobody left rearing pigs now. And if anybody rears them, it's for eating purposes. And if they sell them, they charge high on the sale. And money's scarce for buying them besides. The business's gone bust, father. (115)[32]

The recurring presence of certain key tropes of the world capitalist system in this passage such as buying, selling, business, and money registers the story as part of an excavation of that system's destructive traces and effects. The story ultimately posits the father-son relationship as transactional in nature, with the son admonishing his father, "¿Qué me gané con que usté me criara?, puros trabajos" (195) [What did I get out of you rearing me? Jobs and more jobs] (116). He goes on to reproach him for never having shown him a trade or a skill, "ni siquiera me enseñó el oficio de cuetero" (195) [you didn't even teach me fireworks] (116), alleging that it was his duty to show him a path toward a viable future, "Pero usté me nació. Y usté tenía que haberme encaminado, no nomás soltarme como caballo entre las milpas" (195) [But you were the one brung me into the world. And the one ought to have steered me, instead of just letting me run off like a horse into cornfields] (117). This insistence on a transactional view of family life is sustained throughout and is vividly demonstrated in the closing lines when the father reminds his son that he owes him 30 pesos on the deeds of the house that has been sold: "Y tú vete buscando onde pasar la noche, porque tu casa la vendí pa pagarme lo de los gastos. Y todavía me sales debiendo treinta pesos del valor de las escrituras" (198) [So you head out now and find a place to spend the night, because I sold your house to cover bills. And you still owe me thirty pesos to settle what the deeds cost] (123).[33] The expectation of being shown the way by his father evidenced in the previous dialogue reveals a capitalist superstructure that is activated through a dynamic of mobility. Capitalism is thus imagined as the movement of both money and its agents, a movement that is mirrored in both Rulfo's own trajectory (involving multiple employers and varying salaries) and in the internal dynamics of his texts as they dart in multiple directions (of which more in the concluding section).

The text also comprises an indictment of the traditional patriarchal family, the graphic failure of which is revealed in various ways and, not least, through the almost complete absence of women figures. The story presents a triangulated configuration of female archetypes, from a dead mother, a dead sister, and an absent (whore) wife as evidence of the collapse of the traditional family as a viable unit under the capitalist world-system. Outwardly presented as the system drivers in their function as the re-producers of the children, they are also completely erased as subjects so that the only remnants of the family unit are the father-son relationship predicated almost entirely on use value. In this envisioning of the family unit, then, the women are dead (figuratively or literally) and the men are at war. The son goes on to rebuke the father further:

Ni siquiera me enseñó usté a hacer versos, ya que los sabía. Aunque sea con eso hubiera ganado algo divirtiendo a la gente como usté hace. (196)

You didn't so much as teach me how to make refrains, even though you knew how. At least that way, I could have made a bit of money entertaining people, like you do. (118)

Here, the reader learns of the father's immersion in the commercial world of verse-making, a profession that thrived well into the late twentieth century and that saw literacy as a valuable commodity within the wider contractual culture described. Historically, of course, and returning to Ángel Rama, we know of the literate nature of culture in the Americas. Aníbal Gonzalez writes that "this is a society founded on a pervasive utilization of writing and a deep respect for it. In spite of this foundation, or perhaps even because of it, writing was from the very beginning regarded in Spanish America with a mixture of mistrust and awe."[34] The respect alluded to in González's description is powerfully present in the son's exchange with his father. What is more, here the words have a value under a capitalist system that enables literacy itself to be commodified within a community that is desperately poor and uneducated. This representation of the craft of writing as an embedded component of an intricate and aggressive capitalist enterprise might be understood as a recognition of Rulfo's own complicity as (world) writer, a crafter of words and a maker of verses, just like the father of the story. In this sense, Rulfo locates himself within the wider web of commercial power relations that subtend the writing industry and the wider literary and paraliterary apparatus that so suffocated him. Thus a parallel is established between the writer exposing the ravages of a failed modernizing process through his work at the same time as he infers his complicity within a system in which spinning tales also represents a commercial opportunity.

Elliptical Narratives

As already outlined, there are two primary topoi laid bare in the short story, "Paso del Norte," that allow the reader to gain a sense of the planetary consciousness defined previously. Having analyzed the structural node of gendered capitalism at the heart of the story, I would now like to turn my attention to its central narrative axis, namely, the protagonist's journey north to the border and his attempt to cross the Rio Grande into Texas with his friend Estanislao. Set upon and shot at in the darkness, Estanislao falls and the protagonist seeks to rescue his friend, pulling him away from the danger they are facing. Away from the water, Estanislao dies in the protagonist's arms whereupon he is apprehended by a border guard and mercilessly beaten. Blaming the "Apaches" for the attack that left his friend dead and the protagonist injured, the border guard hands over a small sum of money to the protagonist ordering him to return home. It can be gleaned from this short summary that the story comprises the archetypal elements of violent white colonial power concentrated in a few lines involving an illegal land grab, a violent policing of movement, the apportioning of blame to innocent indigenous peoples, and a deportation masquerading as benign care. In this way, the second half of the story stages the eerily familiar tale of border-crossing set within the concomitant frames of militarized violence and necropolitics. Here, I will briefly examine the account of this border-crossing to examine the way in which it traces this pattern of movement within overlapping historical frames including that of the *Bracero* program, of the Apache wars in Texas, and as part of the neocolonial wound.

Looking more closely at the sequence of events narrated in the second dialogue, the protagonist appeals to the border guard to stop attacking him saying, "No me pegué que estoy manco" (197-8) [Don't hit me, I only got the use of one arm] (122). Brutally beaten, the reference to the arm serves as an oblique allusion to the *Bracero* worker program through which work permits were issued to Mexican men to fill the labor shortages occasioned in the US economy by the Second World War.[35] The *Bracero* program—with its etymological roots in the word, "brazo," meaning arm—partook in the crude system of labor relations whereby the only form of Mexican labor tolerated in the United States was manual. In this way, the protagonist's damaged arm is a rich signifier of his lack of value within the contemporary regime of economic exchange. The passage goes on to lay the blame for the attack on the protagonist at the feet of Apaches:

—Entonces han de ser los apaches.
—¿Cuáles apaches?
—Pos uno que así les dicen y que viven del otro lado.
—¿Pos que no están las Tejas del otro lado?
—Si pero está llena de apaches, como no tienes una idea. (198)

—So they must have been Apaches.
—What Apaches?
—Well that's what they call them, the ones living other side.
—Yeah, but isn't that Texas other side?
—Yes, but the place is thronged with Apaches like you couldn't imagine. (122)

This idea of Texas as full of marauding Apaches attacking Mexican border-crossers over the Rio Grande speaks to prevailing mythologies about the Apaches as war-like but, as the story infers, it is far more likely to be an excuse for yet more Anglo violence wrought on the bodies of the Mexicans and blamed on the native peoples of the Southwest. Reference was already made to the anthropological thrust of Rulfo's fiction; Claudio Esteva Fabregat writes about the anthropological hermeneutics that underpin Rulfo's world and the multiple realities that generate his text.[36] Here, these other realities are arranged palimpsestically in overlapping layers of cruelty including the Apache community in Texas with their history of violent conquest and submission,[37] the *Bracero* program with its racialized history of regulated manual labor, and the emergence of a militarized border patrol from 1924 onward. The confrontation with the border guard, addressed as "sargento" by the terrified protagonist, starkly illustrates the regime of necropolitical coloniality at work showing the guard's power to decide who dies, who lives, and who gets scapegoated. It is through this anthropological thick description, then, that the irrupting and competing discourses of coloniality, racial suppression, and labor exploitation converge.

It goes without saying that these interconnecting narratives are indelibly anchored in their geopolitical location of "Paso del Norte," one of the former names (until 1882) of Ciudad Juárez and which features explicitly in certain versions of the story and is excised from others. Cristina Rivera Garza traces connections between both the troubled border cities of Ciudad Juárez and Ciudad Mier, and Rulfo's fictional world of Comala. In this discursive re-imagining, she labels the latter a "protonecropolis"[38] within a broader dystopian imaginary that spans a series of spatial, temporal disjunctions. The disjunctions referenced by Rivera Garza are embedded within "Paso del Norte" and can be seen in the multiple discursive and temporal movements between histories of colonial oppression and extractivism (*Bracero* program; Apache) as well as the spatial movement undertaken by the protagonist between the border and an ambiguous homeplace. This movement of meaning between the *irreal* (Comala/homeplace) and the contemporary *hyperreal* (Ciudad Juárez as monstrous border site) leads me to Vittoria Borsò who detects within Rulfo's work what she terms "una ontología procesual," or an ontology in process, a process indelibly connected to environment and place formed as part of an infinite relationality.[39]

To test this question of relationality, it is important to examine an axis of David Damrosch's thinking about the world literary text. Damrosch presents three separate, but related, definitions, the third of which claims that "World literature is not a set canon of texts but a mode of reading: a form of detached engagements with worlds beyond our own place and time."[40] Scrutinizing my own position here, I need to ask what it means to read the violent border-crossing and resulting family death and breakdown in "Paso del Norte" from my perspective, from my own periphery. If, following Damrosch, this fiction points to a world beyond my own place and time, then it constructs yet another relation, a line to *my place* in which there is anxiety over the return of a militarized border threatened by the potentially sinister implications of a British withdrawal from the European Union and its associated impact on the island of Ireland where I live. Reading it thus, the moments of both Rulfo's story and my moment of interpretation, while temporally dislocated of course, are also sutured across time and place in the way imagined by Sarah Lawall when she talks of world literature as "the ability to read for a *new* world in relation to the *old*: to construct new worldviews by comparing other systems of reality, to imagine and bring about change by examining reciprocal reflections and their intervening space of exchange."[41] Exchange and reciprocity then constitute the hallmarks of the vision espoused by Lawall and here Rulfo's world text offers me, writing from a troubled European periphery at a particularly vulnerable historical moment, a space through which to recognize myself.[42] This is not to suggest in any banal (not to mention problematic) way that we can collapse historical and racial difference nor to suggest that all postcolonial trauma is experienced the same way but, rather, it is to suggest that this staging of colonial cruelty speaks absolutely to a multiplicity of current moments, our place, our time experienced in the plural, on the move, and not just on the Mexico-United States border. In this sense too, and to return to Lawall, we might speak of world literature as a "process of global discovery."[43]

Loose Ends

Thus far, it has been possible to see that the text has subscribed to a critical planetary consciousness in terms of a blistering critique of both the extremes of neocolonial necropolitical power as well as advanced capitalism. In these concluding comments, I would like to focus on what I see as a certain multidirectional pull discernible within "Paso del Norte," a ripple away from the other foci already discussed, to other narrative and interpretive planes, other dimensions. The text is thus complicated at times by a language that draws inward and away to other textual elements, oddities that are seemingly out of place. The reader gains a glimpse of this in the ambiguous opening of the second father-son dialogue when the son intones the words, "Padre, nos mataron" (197) [Father, they slaughtered us] (120). Unclear as to whether this is already a dialogue from the grave, a foreshadowing of the graveyard community of *Pedro Páramo*, or a kind of coalitional solidarity set up with the dead Estanislao, there is no further reference to it and such spectral ambiguity forms a leitmotif throughout Rulfo's troubled poetics. There are other elements that seem out of place too, including the pathos discernible in the protagonist's relationship with Estanislao. This is communicated through the poignant refrain "sácame de aquí, paisano" (197–8) [get me out of here, *paisano*] (121), which resonates three times in different forms throughout the short account. Similarly, if the elemental drive of hunger forced the protagonist northward, within this aesthetic of hunger there is also a kind of softness, even love, which is channeled primarily toward the protagonist's wife, Tránsito, who, as her name suggests, constitutes another line of focus, another of the connecting bridges that thread through the story. How else to explain the seemingly irrational ending whereby having arrived home to find his children alive and well with his father, the protagonist immediately takes off to try and find his wife who has disappeared with a mule driver? Is this, then, a romantic sensibility coming to the fore in line with the kind of sentimentality pervasive in the crazed love for Susana San Juan evinced by Pedro Páramo? Or is this another manifestation of the kind of appropriative logic central to the normative family unit that propels him to recover that which he owns? What is the reader to make of this puzzling attachment when, following Damrosch, "we read in the field of force generated between these two foci"?[44] If the emotional investment in the individual is yet another sign of the text's imbrication within the world-system of gendered capitalism, then the humanity shown between the protagonist and his friend during the border scene along with his enduring love for his wife surely reveals some of that system's fissures. What is more, the father, thus far unsentimental and resentful of his son, has more than fulfilled his obligations, taking his grandchildren in and informing his son that they are sleeping peacefully. So is this a redemptive glimmer, a severing of the ancient script of father-son alienation? Or is it further evidence of the transactional relationship moving into a new phase of greater indebtedness (we recall the father letting his son know that he now owes him 30 pesos and that his house has been sold). There are no easy answers to these "loose ends" in the Rulfian text. Perhaps they, more than any other details, are evidence of the way in which the story is less accomplished in the narratological sense than some of the other better known stories, an opinion proffered by the author himself. Or maybe they signal further elliptical refraction, in Damrosch's sense of ellipsis as the multiplication of centers of meaning, the darting of the text in unexpected ways that generate a light that refracts but that is unable to clarify. It is, of course, this je ne sais quo aesthetics that has for so long haunted and enthralled readers of Rulfo across the globe however much it finds itself in antithesis to Casanova's ideas that literature emerges only from a set of discursive productions rendered legitimate by the systemic practices of the "World Republic" of letters, as Sánchez Prado notes.[45] In this sense again, Rulfo tests the very limits of the world literary construct in its many iterations. Ultimately, I would argue that it is through a set of interpretive pathways that seek to preserve and even celebrate this multidirectional poetics that we might best approximate the real "world" essence of Rulfo's work.

Notes

1 Juan Rulfo, *The Golden Cockerel & Other Writings*, trans. Douglas Weatherford (Dallas: Deep Vellum, 2017).
2 For example, Susan Sontag called *Pedro Páramo* "one of the masterpieces of twentieth-century world literature" and called its translation into English "an important literary event." Foreword to *Pedro Páramo*, trans. Margaret Sayers Peden (New York: Grove Press, 1995), ix–x.
3 Roberto García Bonilla makes reference to hundreds of introductory texts as well as approximately sixty others between prologues, conference presentations, some four hundred more on architecture, almost all of them unedited. "Juan Rulfo: Escritura y sobrevivencia," *Letras Libres*, May 9, 2013. Available online: https://www.letraslibres.com/mexico/juan-rulfo-escritura-y-sobrevivencia (accessed August 28, 2020).
4 The Warwick Research Collective borrow this term from Nicholas Brown, *Utopian Generations: The Political Horizon of Twentieth-Century Literature: Combined and Uneven Development* (Princeton: Princeton University Press, 2005), 76.
5 There is a vast body of scholarship on the work of Juan Rulfo and a basic search of key bibliographic databases yields more than 2,000 entries ranging from monographs, biographical pieces, journal articles, and book chapters. It is estimated that there are more than seventy monographs on Rulfo, and his work and the centenary celebrations of his birth in 2017 yielded a plethora of studies such as, *El Llano en llamas, Pedro Páramo y otras obras en el centenario de su autor*, ed. Pedro Angel Palou, Francisco Ramírez Santacruz (Madrid/Frankfurt am Main: Iberoamericana Editorial Vervuert, 2017), and Cristina Rivera Garza, *Había mucha neblina o humo o no sé que* (Mexico: Literatura Random House, 2017).
6 Jorge Luis Borges contends that *Pedro Páramo* is "una de las mejores novelas de las literaturas de lengua hispánica, y aun de la literatura." Juan Rulfo, *Pedro Páramo in 1954* (Mexico: UNAM, Fundación Juan Rulfo, Editorial RM), back matter. The Nobel laureate Gabriel García Márquez affirmed that he could recite the book by heart and that it influenced *One Hundred Years of Solitude*. Irene Caselli, "The Great Latin Writer you may want to know about," May 16, 2017. Available online: https://www.bbc.com/news/world-latin-america-39921471 (accessed August 28, 2020). See also

García Márquez, "Breves nostalgias sobre Juan Rulfo," in *Inframundo. El México de Juan Rulfo*, ed. Frank Janney (México: Ediciones del Norte, 1980), 23–5. Chris Power reminds us that "At the turn of the millennium, the Uruguayan daily *El País* asked writers and critics to vote for the greatest Latin American novel. The winner, by a clear margin, was Juan Rulfo's *Pedro Páramo*." "A brief survey of the short story part 52: Juan Rulfo," August 27, 2013, *The Guardian*. Available online: https://www.theguard ian.com/books/2013/aug/27/juan-rulfo-brief-survey-short-story (accessed August 31, 2020). Emily Hind provides a brilliantly forensic scrutiny of Juan Rulfo's position at the heart of the Mexican literary establishment, see *Dude Lit: Mexican Men Writing and Performing Competence 1955-2012* (Arizona: University of Arizona Press, 2019).

7   García Bonilla gives a sense of how the Rulfo enigma challenged cultural commentators. See "Juan Rulfo: Escritura y sobrevivencia," *Letras Libres*, May 9, 2013.

8   See for example *América Latina y la literatura mundial: Mercado editorial, redes globales y la invención de un continente* (Madrid and Frankfurt am Main: Iberoamericana/Vervuert, 2015); *Teaching the Latin American Boom*, ed. Lucille Kerr and Alejandro Herrero-Olaizola (MLA, 2015); Christopher Warnes, *Magical Realism and the Postcolonial Novel: Between Faith and Irreverence* (Basingstoke: Palgrave Macmillan, 2009); Deborah N. Cohn, *The Latin American Literary Boom and U.S. Nationalism During the Cold War* (Nashville: Vanderbilt Press, 2012). There are many studies of Rulfo that locate his work within the critical model of magical realism; see, for example, Julia King and Stephen M. Hart, "The Earth as Archive in Bombal, Parra, Asturias and Rulfo," in *A Companion to Magical Realism*, ed. Stephen M. Hart and Wen-Chin Ouyang (Woodbridge: Tamesis, 2005), 55–66; Marta Gallo, "Realismo mágico en *Pedro Páramo*," in *Otros mundos otros fuegos: Fantasia y realismo mágico en Iberoamérica*, ed. Donald A. Yates (East Lansing: Michigan State University, Lat. Amer. Studies Center; 1975), 103–11; Alicia Llarena, *Realismo mágico y lo real maravilloso: Una cuestión de verosimilitud* (Ediciones Hispamérica, 1998).

9   For a useful discussion on this, see Gesine Müller, "Remapping World Literature from Macondo," in *Re-mapping World Literature in Writing, Book Markets and Epistemologies between Latin America and the Global South / Escrituras, mercados y epistemologías entre América Latina y el Sur Global* (Berlin: De Gruyter, 2018).

10 Mariano Siskind writes that "Macondo is the mediation between the idiosyncratic hyper-localism of the Colombian tropical forest and the general situation of the continent. Macondo is the village-signifier that names the difference of Latin America, and later, perhaps of the Third World at large." "Magical Realism," in *The Cambridge History of Postcolonial Literature*, ed. Ato Quayson (Cambridge: Cambridge University Press, 2012), 854. The McOndo movement emerged in the 1990s as a reaction against the Magical Realist school and the European reception of Latin American literature through this interpretative lens. See Dierdra Reber, "From Macondo to McOndo: Tracing the Ideal of Latin American Literary Community from Magical Realism to Magical Neoliberalism," in *Teaching the Latin American Boom*, 197–207.

11 Ignacio Sánchez Prado, "'Hijos de Metapa': un recorrido conceptual de la literatura mundial (a manera de introducción)," in *América Latina en la "literatura mundial"* (Pittsburgh: University of Pittsburgh Press), 17.

12 "La literatura mundial como praxis: apuntes hacia una metodología de lo concreto" in *World Literature, Cosmopolitanism, Globality: Beyond, Against, Post, Otherwise*, ed. Gesine Müller and Mariano Siskind (Berlin: De Gruyter, 2019), 62–75.

13 In this important study, Ángel Rama discusses the currents and countercurrents in turn-of-the-century literary life, showing how the city of letters was finally "revolutionized." *La ciudad letrada* (Hanover: Ediciones del Norte, 1984).
14 Pascale Casanova, *The World Republic of Letters* (Cambridge, MA: Harvard University Press, 2004).
15 For further discussion, see Sánchez Prado, "Hijos de metapa," 26. For an outline of Bourdieu's ideas, see *Field of Cultural Production* (New York: Columbia University Press, 1994).
16 There are an estimated 6,000 photographic negatives in Rulfo's archive. See Paulina Millán, "A Journey through Juan Rulfo's Photography," in *Rethinking Juan Rulfo's Creative World: Prose, Photography, Film,* ed. Dylan Brennan and Nuala Finnegan (Oxford: Legenda 2016), 51–65.
17 "Aura" is understood here as the integral quality of an artwork discussed by Walter Benjamin in his famous essay, first published in 1936. Walter Benjamin, "The Work of Art in the Age of Mechanical Reproduction," in *Illuminations,* ed. Hannah Arendt (New York: Schocken Books [1968] 2007). For a good insight into this book's particular aura, see *Pedro Páramo en 1954,* published as part of the 2017 centenary of Rulfo's birth and which discusses at length the various "leyendas" that surround the book's publication.
18 García Bonilla writes about the peculiar pressures felt by Rulfo at being part of an emergent literary elite following the publication of *Pedro Páramo*: "Después de la salida de *Pedro Páramo* vinieron muchas fiestas, muchos cocteles, muchas desveladas." "Juan Rulfo: Escritura y Sobrevivencia."
19 Cited in Judith Amador Tello, "Juan Rulfo entre Antropólogos," May 26, 2017, *Proceso.* Available online: https://www.proceso.com.mx/488200/juan-rulfo-antro pologos (accessed August 28, 2020). See also, Millán, "A Journey through Juan Rulfo's Photography."
20 This view is further strengthened if we consider also the plurality and unorthodox character of his literary universe, populated with writers from Germany, the United States, and Nordic countries, though rarely with writers associated with any conceptualization of a literary center. This dimension is lucidly analyzed by Ignacio Sánchez Prado in "La literatura mundial como praxis: apuntes hacia una metodología de lo concreto."
21 Much has been written about Rulfo and his relationship with the indigenous communities he referenced in his literature and also in his photographic work. It is worth underlining Rulfo's own words in this regard, "nunca empleo a los indios porque para mi es imposible entrar y llegar a profundizar en la mentalidad indígena" [I never feature Indian characters because for me, it is impossible to enter or to understand the indigenous mentality in any depth]. Stephanie Merriam, "The Existential Juan Rulfo: *Pedro Páramo,* Mexicanness, and the Grupo Hiperión," *MLN* 129, no. 2 (2014): 308–29, 319. doi:10.1353/mln.2014.0019.
22 Castillo de Teayo, *Mapa: Revista de Automovilismo y Turismo* 14, no. 194 (January 1952): 8.
23 During the celebration of the centenary of Rulfo's birth in 2017, the Fundación Juan Rulfo led by Víctor Jiménez cancelled its support of an event at the Universidad Nacional Autonóma de México because of its inclusion of Rivera' Garza's book presentation. Accusing the book of being defamatory against Rulfo, the scandal received much coverage in the press.

24 Cited on back matter, Rivera Garza, *Había mucha neblina o humo o no sé qué*.
25 "Third-World Literature in the Era of Multinational Capitalism," *Social Text*, no. 15 (Autumn 1986): 65–88, 68.
26 "The 'Monstrous Head' and the 'Mouth of Hell': The Gothic Ecologies of the Mexican Miracle," in *Ecological Crisis and Cultural Representation in Latin America: Ecocritical Perspectives on Art, Film, and Literature*, ed. Mark Anderson and Zelia M Bóra (Lanham: Lexington, 2016), 79–80. See also, Ericka Beckman, "Unfinished Transitions: The Dialectics of Rural Modernization in Latin American Fiction," *Modernism/Modernity* 23, no. 4 (2016): 813–32.
27 "The 'Monstrous Head' and the 'Mouth of Hell'," 88.
28 "Conjectures on World Literature," *New Left Review* 1 (January–February 2000). Available online: https://newleftreview.org/issues/II1/articles/franco-moretti-conjectures-on-world-literature (accessed August 31, 2020).
29 See, Rachel Serlen, "The Distant Future? Reading Franco Moretti," *Literature Compass* 7, no. 3 (2010): 214–25. Available online: https://warwick.ac.uk/fac/arts/english/currentstudents/undergraduate/modules/fulllist/special/en264/serlen_reading_franco_moretti.pdf (accessed August 31, 2020). Spivak takes issue with Moretti on a number of levels in *Death of a Discipline* (New York: Columbia University Press, 2003). See also Jonathan Arac, "Anglo-Globalism?" *New Left Review* 16 (July–August 2002): 35–45.
30 Sergio López Mena talks about the suppression of parts of the short story, *Los caminos de la creación en Juan Rulfo* (Mexico: UNAM, 1993), 512. For additional information on sections excluded, see Roberto García Bonilla, "El llano en llamas, una historia de su escritura y su publicación," *Espéculo: Revista de Estudios Literarios*, 25, 2003. Available online: http://webs.ucm.es/info/especulo/numero25/llano.html (accessed August 31, 2020).
31 Quotations from the story are from Juan Rulfo, *Pedro Páramo y El Llano en llamas* (Barcelona: Planeta, 1990), and page numbers will appear immediately following in parentheses.
32 All translations are from Juan Rulfo, *El Llano in flames*, trans. Stephen Beechinor (Structo Press, 2019). All page numbers following the translations in parentheses are from this edition.
33 Alberto Ribas-Casasayas offers a compelling analysis of the way in which necrocapitalist ideas of debt shape and structure Rulfian narratives. "El tirano indigente: Pedro Páramo, deuda y necropolítica," *A Contracorriente* 14, no. 3 (Spring 2017): 49–75.
34 Aníbal Gonzalez, *Killer Books: Writing, Violence and Ethics in Modern Spanish American Narrative* (Austin: University of Texas Press, 2001), 4.
35 The Bracero program (1942–64) was the first large-scale bilateral labor agreement between the United States and Mexico and fundamentally changed the previously existing migratory models based mostly on indentured labor. During the period, some five million worker permits were issued to Mexicans. For an excellent overview, see Jorge Durand, "El programa bracero (1942–1964). Un balance crítico," *Migración y Desarrollo* 9 (segundo semestre, 2007): 27–43. Available online: https://www.redalyc.org/pdf/660/66000902.pdf (accessed August 31, 2020). The radio documentary series *Yo fui bracero* offers a fascinating insight into the program, including a testimony from ex-Bracero workers. Available online: http://imryt.org/radio/yo-fui-bracero (accessed August 31, 2020).

36 "En realidad, es el texto que escribió Rulfo el que sugirió otras realidades." Claudio Esteva Fabregat, "Juan Rulfo: creación literaria y percepción antropológica. Ámbitos de una antropología literaria," in *Nuevos Indicios: Sobre Juan Rulfo: Genealogía, estudios, testimonios,* ed. Jorge Zepeda (Mexico City: Fundacion Juan Rulfo. Juan Pablos Editor, 2010), 181–218, 184. It is also important to recall that Rulfo was immersed in the anthropological environment of the National Indigenous Institute (INI) and had extensive contact with anthropologists, including Gonzalo Aguirre Beltrán, Guillermo Bonfil Batalla, and Rodolfo Stavenhagen. Judith Amador Tello maintains that Rulfo had a better relationship with anthropologists and historians than with literary critics or even literary figures. "Juan Rulfo entre Antropólogos."

37 Apache tends to be used as a shorthand to reference what are in reality several native American communities based in the Southwest. As the result of centuries of misrepresentation, they are often portrayed as warlike and aggressive, hence the plausible presence in the story as the source of the hostility against the Mexican protagonist. For an earlier historical overview, see Elizabeth A. H. John, *Storms Brewed in Other Men's Worlds: The Confrontation of Indians, Spanish, and French in the Southwest,* 1540–1795 (Norman: University of Oklahoma Press, 1996), also, Stan Hoig, *Tribal Wars of the Southern Plains* (Norman: University of Oklahoma Press, 1993).

38 *Los muertos indóciles,* 36.

39 Borsò, "Orientalismo y realismo mágico al revés. Juan Rulfo y Salman Rushdie o los desafíos del Sur global para la literatura mundial," in *Re-mapping World Literature Writing, Book Markets and Epistemologies between Latin America and the Global South / Escrituras, mercados y epistemologías entre América Latina y el Sur Global,* ed. Gesine Müller, Jorge J. Locane, and Benjamin Loy (Berlin: De Gruyter, 2018), 247–64, 261.

40 *What Is World Literature?* (Princeton: Princeton University Press, 2003), 281.

41 Sarah Lawall, *Reading World Literature: Theory, History, Practice* (Austin: University of Texas Press, 2010), 48.

42 It should be recalled here that Irish literary modernism is central to Casanova's thesis in *The World Republic of Letters,* in which she argues that the structural conditions in the Irish context may be applied to other "world" contexts too, including sites in the Global South.

43 Lawall, *Reading World Literature,* 48.

44 Damrosch, "World Literature Today," *Symploke* 8 (2000): 7–19: 18–19.

45 As Sánchez Prado explains, "Casanova apuesta frontalmente por un concepto de literatura que no corresponde a un *je ne sais quoi* estético, precisamente al plantear que el término 'literatura', en el fondo, denomina al conjunto de producciones discursivas legitimadas por el sistema de prácticas de la 'república mundial'" [Casanova opts directly for a concept of literature that does not correspond to a *je ne sais quoi* aesthetics, by suggesting that the term "literature", names a set of discursive productions rendered legitimate by the "World Republic's" system of practices]" ("Hijos de Metapa," 25).

12

Uno se sale de uno para verse viendo
Mexican Countercultural Literature as Psychedelic Interventions of World Literature

Iván Eusebio Aguirre Darancou

Mexican countercultural literary production is—in both its sources and intended audiences—a prime example of world literature, in spite of the limitations of Mexico's symbolic position in the world literary market, reinforced by the marginality of this particular mode of cultural production. Understanding world literature beyond the critical tools that describe literary fields and spheres outside the confines of nation and language, this chapter uses countercultural literature as a particular mode of writing and reading to foreground the ways in which world literature can function as a critical paradigm able to navigate the tensions between a complex and lengthy history of cosmopolitanism and a strong national literary sphere through the act of world-building in the texts themselves.[1] Written between the years 1965 and 1975, the novels analyzed in this chapter are exemplary of a literary tradition with strong cosmopolitan and worldly roots, engaging with the Global Sixties during the decade of love and peace, the use of psychedelics, and anti-colonial struggles. In order to resist the reimposition of world literature as the paradigm that replicates political and economic structures onto cultural production, reading these novels as such will require tracing the ways in which they engage not only with the greater global processes of capitalist expansion but also with the literary traditions considered as stalwarts of world literature by virtue of their position in the global literary spheres and their proximity to the paradigmatic centers. This chapter follows Hector Hoyos in thinking of Latin American novels as global in order to preserve and underline the tensions and differences that make up the world of world literature, by focusing on how these particular novels intervene in the definition of world and seek to propose alternatives from their geographic but also symbolic locations.[2]

To better understand the interventions of Mexican countercultural literature into world literature debates and spheres, Pheng Cheah's notion of *worlding* is useful. Defined as a temporal process that orders the world through the imposition of a teleological time and a strict adherence to the temporal normativity emanating from the metropolitan centers, worlding brings to the forefront the ways in which the "world" in world literature is above all a (normative) temporal one.³ Engaging this particular aspect of world literature, psychedelic literature appears as a subset of counterculture saturated with global commodities and experiences being re-signified into Western modernity during the Global Sixties. These novels in particular use psychedelics and other substances as literary and cultural devices with which to intervene on a global front, first by questioning the foundations of the world through art or politics and second by proposing alternative worlding strategies created by individuals who therapeutically engage with psychedelics to face the multiple violence, traumas, and dispossessions enacted by capitalist worlding. These personal/political actions are shared by other cultural and political actors of the Global Sixties, a common language that allowed for the better integration of national cultures into a world-system. The current psychedelic research being carried out in medical and research laboratories globally allows for the refocusing of the strong political injunctive in countercultural literature, specifically in the ways in which worlds are resisted and redefined.⁴ As such, this chapter will focus on three of the main novels of the Mexican countercultural moment: Parménides García Saldaña's *Pasto verde* (1968, untranslated, *Green Grass*), Margarita Dalton's *Larga sinfonía en d* (1968, untranslated, *Long Symphony in D*), and Fernando del Paso's *Palinuro de México* (1977, translated 1989, *Palinuro of Mexico*) as distinct examples of the various strategies through which world literature is intervened from the particularities of a national culture.

As a sociocultural phenomenon, counterculture is particularly interesting for world literature due to its material and symbolic erasing of national/cultural differences and tensions; alongside the strictly sociological definition of counterculture as a series of urban youth movements, counterculture can also be defined as a paradoxical positioning against culture as a sociability or habitus. Mariano Siskind proposes world literature as a critical discourse on modernity bringing together the multiple worlds created in the greater expansion and integration of cultures, albeit through the violent histories of colonialism and capitalism.⁵ Countercultural literature emerged from the spaces and moments when cultural and economic markets, generational differences, political revolution, racial (in)equalities, and sexual liberation come together. It is marked by a use of literature itself as a medium through which to destabilize the primacy of literature as an ideology, and most particularly the form of the novel tied to histories of capitalist expansion and colonial imperialism. In doing so, it offers to the critical discussion on world literature an answer to the troubling reimposition of the "redeeming power of culture" and the reiteration of colonial hierarchies that erase cultural differences that critics such as Siskind have pointed out.⁶ Counterculture is a space from which to imagine world(s) different or outside of the capitalist-colonialist space-time compression.

Second, whether playfully or philosophically complex, countercultural literature centralizes the heterotemporality that Pheng Cheah has described as world literature's contribution to critical theory.⁷ The emergence of non-Western temporalities coexisting with modern progress that Cheah observes in postcolonial world literature is mirrored concretely in the cosmo/metropolitan centers (such as Mexico City), where the tensions between different processes of worlding emerge without having to "leave" modernity. Psychedelic literature engages this particular aspect through the effects of psychedelics and entheogens on understandings of time and space. Another way of visualizing the multiple temporalities that coexist in counterculture as a culmination and rupture of modernity is through the notion of plural temporalities, contained in the necessary contingency of durations between things and ideas.[8] Countercultural aesthetics and ethics actively move toward the decentralization of Western ideologies in all their forms, the incorporation and reciprocal engagement with non-Western ideologies, and the continuous resistance toward any form of centralization, in other words the awareness and permanence of the plural temporalities already contained within normative culture.

In the spatial reconfigurations that counterculture provided, lysergic acid (LSD) trips became rites of passage into youth culture of the Global Sixties, marking the limits of a generational shift that not only "landed the youth in a country of the mind few adults had any idea even existed" but also potentially—especially when accompanied by a politicized position-taking in the literary and cultural fields—left them aware of the different power dynamic and economic histories that ordered what they understood as "world," from the university campus of California to the mountains of Oaxaca, the burning jungles of Vietnam, the political unrest crowding the streets of Europe, the civil rights movements in the United States, and the various anti-colonial struggles taking place in the Global South.[9] In this sense, countercultural literature provides a prime example of knowledge as the production of a concrete-in-thought, a process that takes an always-already imaginary material (the histories of colonialism and capitalism, in this case) and produces differing knowledge through a radical discontinuity with it.[10] As a literary endeavor to make sense of the multiple cultural modes being used to define the normative world—since "if the global unity created today is one of mass cultural homogenization through sign systems and chains of images that are not of literature, when why is the study of literature still relevant in an age of global mass culture?"—countercultural literature explores the production of knowledge through the embodied experiences of worldliness.[11] In its playfully serious bringing together of cultural registers, it is a modality of world literature that mobilizes the institutional powers available to their writers in order to signal the limitations of the institution itself, and provide alternatives grounded in embodied experiences as global (and worldly) subjects.

A Short History of Mexican Countercultural Literature

Mexican countercultural literature as world literature is not simply as the transnational circulation of specific works in institutional and market networks but rather as the circulation of forms (literary and cultural) that determine the conditions of possibility of world literature as practice.[12] The jazz and rock music emerging in mid-century as rebellious positionings not only against the institutional authorities of music but also against normative definitions of culture (both "high" and "low") is the direct historical antecedent of countercultural production. Historian Eric Zolov has signaled rock's often contradictory reception in the Spanish-speaking continent, both as an indubitable mark of modernity and a sign of progress according to the ideals and values of the West, and as a challenge to the traditional boundaries of gender, race, class and language associated with normative constructions of nation, also a product of "uneven development."[13] In the literary sphere, the multiple voyages and expeditions of authors such as Jack Kerouac, Neal Cassady, Allen Ginsberg, and William S. Burroughs attest to this complex cultural circulation.[14] Their Orientalization of Mexico notwithstanding, these authors transform the geopolitical proximity into a cultural continuum, their uniquely worldly literary forms (engaging with issues like the atomic bomb, racial inequalities as products of colonialism, and gender oppression) become templates for Mexican countercultural authors to engage with in their own writings.

The novel that begins this engagement is Parménides García Saldaña's *Pasto verde* (*Green Grass*), first published in 1968.[15] As part of the loose literary group retroactively named "La onda" (The Wave), García Saldaña is a key figure in the self-fashioning (both within literary works and in the greater literary sphere of their interactions) of writers as cosmopolitan based less on high modernism aesthetics and more on the multiple shared experiences that begin to characterize life in the West in this decade.[16] As such, language is the medium through which to reformulate the construction of youth, sexuality, and the consumption of legal and illegal substances; counterculture as an ethical (albeit symbolically violent at times) genre that allows for the resignification of these new paradigms of modernity.

The novel narrates the experiences of Epicuro Aristipo Quevedo Galdos del Valle Inclán as he smokes cannabis, drinks excessive amounts of alcohol, listens to jazz and rock albums, and cruises the streets of Mexico City with his friend Pepcoke Gin and others. Using slang from the streets of Mexico City, New York, New Orleans, and San Francisco, the characters exemplify the way in which language is a hybrid construction that inserts Mexico into the World as well as the World in Mexico precisely through the emergence of a youth culture mediatized in music, film, and television much more than in its literary spheres.[17] For García Saldaña, this material world blurs linguistic and national boundaries emerging from the geographies of a global countercultural youth and carries the potential of radical subversion. A prime example of this experience can be seen in Epicuro's listening to radio songs throughout the novel as mediatization of his feelings of love and loss: "Heartbreakhotelestoyoyendo en elradioporquérocíomiamor porotromehacambiado" [I'mlisteningtoheartbreakhotel on theradiobecauserociomylove haschangedmeforanother].[18] Epicuro listens to both English and Spanish sob-story songs (boleros) on the radio that speak of heartbreak and patriarchal modes of relations between men and woman dictated by ownership. Alongside a critique on the construction of "woman" under capitalism as a commodity to be traded among men, this moment in Epicuro's stream signals the awareness of the power of media (radio, in this case) to give shape to gendered subjects and the potentiality within media itself to resist these processes.

During the course of the novel, the various characters consume enormous quantities of the psychoactive plant cannabis. The use of cannabis first marks the characters as global subjects, and second, modifies the character's behavior (sudden dancing, popular slang, etc.) to show how the substance is widening the generational gap, while also changing the narrator's stream of consciousness, making explicit the global counterculture that informs this particular mode of cannabis consumption: "everybody must get stoned! Alucinación alucinación visión visión introspección retrospección, tepasadación pasadación pasadoción pasadoacción" [everybody must get stoned! Hallucination hallucination vision vision introspection retrospection, tooktoomuchtion, toomuchtion, muchtion, pastaction].[19] Bob Dylan's musical quote is fused with the effects of the substance, and both become a way for Epicuro to navigate his consciousness outside the limits of cultural and, ultimately, national imaginaries. In this way, the past is infused with action, and the present is an arena where Epicuro and the youths that he prefigures and foreshadows can reshape. Dylan's injunction to global youth is read literally, but the order goes beyond the consumption of cannabis to point directly at one of the alternate mental states it induces where the limits of nation are superseded. The worldly reader that García Saldaña demands is not precisely one that consumes the same substances or music, but rather one that visualizes the nation/world as he does, populated by an emerging generation that is already global, already worldly.

The novel uses these common experiences to underscore national subjectivities as one more layer in the emerging global subjectivities that populate countercultural spaces. When his best friend Pepcoke Gin visits him, Epicuro literally transforms himself from a (always-already inter)national *mestizo* to an erudite worldly citizen:

"Antes de abrir me quito mi tunica de sacerdote olmeca y mi penacho y mi traje de rolling stone y me meto dentro de mi traje Quevedo y luego me calzo en las narices mis antiparras Quevedo Ya vestido adecuadamente para recibir al Maese Pepcoke Gin abro la puerta"

[Before opening the door I remove my Olmec priest tunic and my headdress and my rolling stone suit and I get into the Quevedo suit and then I slip on the Quevedo eyeglasses Once I'm dressed adequately to receive Maester Pepcoke Gin I open the door].[20]

In his embodied existence, Epicuro navigates world spaces not by rejecting the nation, but by donning and removing it when the circumstances require it. The emerging global subjectivities are multilayered and multitemporal. Epicuro is both Olmec AND rock'n'roller when he changes, and he is informed by both Bob Dylan and the myriad of heartbreak boleros he listens to. In this first iteration of countercultural literature, however, the characters experience these emerging global realities with a violent clash of cultural identities and normativities.

The second novel in this short history is Margarita Dalton's *Larga sinfonía en D (y había una vez)* [*Long Symphony in D (and once upon a time)*], also published in 1968. The novel narrates a day in the life of three youths as they consume lysergic acid (LSD) and walk the streets of London. Ana, an Australian painter named Martin, and a self-exiled Mexican student activist named Roberto form a microsociety that brings together a series of issues relating directly to increasingly globalized societies, from questions of pop art in commodity capitalism and media industries to the definition and limits of revolutionary action in the wake of Cuba and the anti-colonial struggles of Africa and Southeast Asia. While the novel went by practically unnoticed in the national literary sphere—mostly due to the patriarchal norms ruling literary institutions, and the radical feminist interventions it makes—*Larga sinfonía* is a text that constructs itself as world literature not only in the audience and reader it calls for but more interestingly in the reconstruction of alternative worlds and temporalities. Similar to *Pasto verde*, the textual innovation required to create the representational space for the psychedelic experience makes of the novel a prime example of avant-garde experimentalism: each chapter covers an hour of the day but they are not in chronological order, each hour of the day allows for the representation of a particular effect of LSD as well as a change of space, and the text itself is modified in narrative voice and other stylistic changes to better illustrate the radical subjective changes LSD may generate (i.e., the page dividing into three columns of stream of consciousness that ultimately come together, capitalized words sprinkled through the novel that compose an alternative story, various narrative voices and temporalities in a single paragraph). These countercultural innovations engage the constructions of world in spatial and temporal dimensions, in both textual and political terms.

The alternative that *Larga sinfonía* proposes is a radical act of reimagining. It is up to the global subject to reject the normative structures of appropriation that characterize Western culture's contact with other cultures. For this reason, the first words of the novel are a "recommendation":

>Ante todo este libro debe leerse con los ojos abiertos
>todo este libro debe leerse con los ojos abiertos
>este libro debe leerse con los ojos abiertos
>debe leerse con los ojos abiertos
>leerse con los ojos abiertos
>con
>los
>ojos
>abiertos.
>[Above all this book must be read with open eyes
>all this book must be read with open eyes
>this book must be read with open eyes
>must be read with open eyes
>read with open eyes
>with
>open
>eyes].[21]

First, this technical repetition anticipatorily places the reader in the synesthetic space seeing the sounds. The recommendation recreates a record-player needle skipping, while underlining the specific mode of reading the text is demanding as a worldly novel worlding through counterculture. Later in the novel, Martin vocalizes this countercultural ethic by stating "existe la posibilidad de *desaprender*" [the possibility of *unlearning* exists] and describes it as being born into and living in a room with no doors until one day a door appears, but the reality outside (which does not deny but rather expands and complements the reality inside) cannot be appreciated unless one opens their eyes.[22] Characteristic of the psychedelic experience as studied by psychologist William James (the noetic quality of the mystical experience) or neuroscientist Robin Carhartt-Harris (the diminution of the Default Mode Network in the mind/brain), Dalton emphasizes the agential position of the worldly subject during this moment of mystical neurodiversity, a subject who intentionally unlearns the norms imposed by the hetero-colonial-capitalist society that surrounds them.[23]

This particular position-taking underscores the intervention in world-building the novel enacts, particularly when read under the heterotemporality that Cheah describes in postcolonial world literature.[24] The trio's psychedelic experiences are inserted in a history of Western psychedelic knowledge that dates back to Plato and the mysteries of Eleusis and passes through the histories of the flesh of the gods (a term used to describe the hallucinogenic mushrooms consumed throughout Europe during the Middle Ages).[25] It is precisely here that countercultural literature allows for an understanding of the heterotemporal nature of Western modernity itself. The normativity imposed by the Greenwich Meridian is questioned in the activation of these alternative timelines, and the normative space of an empire's capital city is subverted. It is important to underline, however, that this heterotemporality is activated by the character's own self-reflection and is not inherent to the psychedelic experience itself.

The psychedelic experience in a worldly setting becomes a momentary rupture in the fabric of space and time imposed by the normative force of literature.[26] During the seventh hour after ingesting LSD, the trio begins to integrate their singular and shared experiences and calls attention to the limits of rational thought expressed in writing: "solo los que no han sentido la necesidad de despojarse del pensamiento, son los que se sienten tranquilos y repasan la palabra escrita" [only those who have never felt the need to relinquish thought, are the ones that feel ease and go over the written word].[27] This paradoxical critique of the written word, including literature, ultimately points to the powerfully decolonial move to explore other modes of knowledge-construction. Vittorio Morfino, speaking from the plural temporality that characterizes Western modernity, describes knowledge as neither the production or reflection of the real object (in this case, the lettered word in relation to the world), but as the production of a "concrete-in-thought, starting from the transformation of an imaginary material which is always-already given as structured, then generating a radical discontinuity with it."[28] An ethical discontinuity with the histories of representation and a momentary unworlding provokes in the reader an imagination of other worlds. Through the epigraphs that mark each chapter, the novel is situated between Lewis Carroll, the Beatles, and *New York Times* clippings, signaling the cultural use of the psychedelic experience as a radical democratization of Western culture.[29]

A central theme of this endeavor is the questioning and redefinition of revolution in the global context of postcolonial actions throughout capitalist geographies. *Larga sinfonía* proposes first an interior re-evolution of the psyche as the paramount political action, and it does so in the representational space constructed through signification that Cheah signals.[30] London as a capitalist capital of the world and Mexico City as a revolutionary capital (in the context of student movements, labor strikes, and state violence that marked 1968) are spatially remade through the active experiences and remembering of the trio *in* both of these metropolises. During their psychedelic experience the artist, the revolutionary and the feminist realize they "do not merely inhabit social space as passive subjects but can actively participate in making it."[31] The nine hours documented in the novel insert the characters (and the readers with them) in a globalized space where their presence impacts the space around them as much as the space impacts their own imaginings.

I close these briefs notes on the short-lived history of Mexican countercultural literature by emphasizing how, in spite of the limitations of language (these two novels remain untranslated) and circulation (*Pasto verde* was only recently republished in a small press and *Larga sinfonía* remains unedited since 1968), the authors conceive of their work as literature speaking of and to the world. Through the shared experiences of youth culture, rock music, psychedelic substances, global advertising, and postcolonial/revolutionary action, the authors conceive of globalized subjects existing in worldly spaces. However, the limitations of this particular moment in countercultural history are important. The experiences of Epicuro in *Pasto verde* and the trio in *Larga sinfonía* remain temporally curtailed by their lack of integration into life and politics. Though they signal to the reader the need to reflect on these, the novels themselves function as snapshots, brief glimpses of the powerfully decolonial and anti-capitalist potentials of psychedelic experiences under a countercultural framework.

Palinuro of Mexico: A Mexican Trip Treatment for the World

Published first in Spain in 1977 and written between 1968 and 1974, Fernando del Paso's *Palinuro de México* began circulating in English upon its translation in 1989.[32] The novel draws from English satirical tradition (Lawrence Sterne, Jonathan Swift) to narrate the adventures of Palinuro, a student of medicine, and his girlfriend and cousin Estefania as they live in downtown Mexico City during the summer of 1968. Through references and reinterpretation of classic characters and canonical literary styles of Western cultures (Palinurus, Charon), and an intertextual dialogue with authors across the Atlantic as much as national history, the novel is an extension of countercultural literature into explicit world literature, constructing itself

> through a strategic performance of a series of canonical discursive formations in ways that parody their cultural authority and that ultimately rely on elements of the archive preserved on the fringes and interstices of Western culture.[33]

During the course of the novel, the two main characters consume LSD and cannabis in various moments, and their mental, geographic, and political explorations are key in their assembling with Western culture and global developments. Following the recent developments of psychotherapy assisted with psychedelics (PAP), I propose a reading of *Palinuro of Mexico* as a countercultural reenactment of a series of psychotherapy sessions focused on the tensions between nation-world that emerge in a global capitalist system as well as the inner workings of capitalist subjectivation increasingly imposed on global subjects.[34] In doing so, the novel recovers and builds on the tenets of countercultural literature as described earlier, establishing a world literature space from which to understand Mexico (or any nation) as one more geography in a shared world-system (cultural, economic, political, and social). The centrality of nation functions as a blurry delineation of the extensiveness of this world-system and the need to visualize it precisely from these "peripheral" positions in order to better understand its psychic, subjective and interpersonal relations and their implications.

Read alongside current research on the neuroscience and psychotherapeutic uses of psychedelics in carefully structured therapeutic sessions,[35] the novel's "sessions" cover Mexico's literary and cultural past re-created in and through the characters from their singular and singularized positions as already global countercultural citizens. Thus, through the adventures of Palinuro on the streets of Mexico City, the Advertising and Other Imaginary Islands, the morgue of the Hospital (as institution of modernity), the catacombs under national cemeteries (repositories of the bones of the Nation), and, above all, the room in the Plaza of Santo Domingo (that ends up functioning in much the same way the highly controlled and safe space of a therapy room functions in contemporary psychotherapy), the novel reveals and dwells on the patterns of individual and collective self-destructive behavior that our current capitalist, colonial, heteronormative, and anthropocentric world-system imposes onto the temporal and spatial fabrics of the world. Furthermore, by developing the crucial element of the moment of integration and incorporating the politically and socially disruptive experiences of the global counterculture as well as the responses from the capitalist consumer culture that was solidified in those years, *Palinuro of Mexico* uses counterculture to imagine and generate other ways of being in the world—and other ways of being worlds—that are becoming ever more socially and ethically relevant.

Recent neuroscience and psychotherapy research demonstrate the effects of psychedelics such as LSD or psilocybin (mushrooms) on the mind by mapping the effects they have on the human brain. The Default Mode Network (DMN) has been defined as a "network of brain structures that light up with activity when there no demands on our attention and we have no mental task to perform."[36] First described by neurologist Marcus Raichle in 2001, the DMN functions among the complex series of specialized systems within our brain tasked with specific activities as the network that in some way conducts order and establishes connections between regions of the brain. By working at a remove from the sensory processing of the outside world as well as from concrete task-based operations, the DMN allows for the formation of an individual self/ego able to conceive of itself through time and space, touching and connecting all the different aspects of what it means to *be*. The network becomes solidified in the neural networks in the passage from childhood to adulthood, and research has shown it to activate especially during specific higher-level metacognitive processes such as self-reflection, mental time travel, mental constructions (such as the self or ego), moral reasoning, and "theory of mind" – the ability to attribute mental states to others, as when we try to imagine 'what it is like' to be someone else.[37]

As such, it first of all is the part of the brain that "grows" and keeps us alive through learning social norms and habits that better allow for our survival in our immediate environment, and second, it is the part of our brain that controls the processing of information we are constantly receiving from our various sensorial stimuli. In regulating these stimuli, the DMN also activates the capacity for "predictive interpretation," the ability to take as less stimuli as possible and make a series of inferences and logical predictions based on previous experiences.[38] This neurological framework allows us to understand how exactly a world is created not only in literary or cultural terms but ultimately in shared social contexts that literally shape the mind. One of the main effects of psychedelics on the human brain is the temporary diminution of activity in the DMN and the increase in activity between other parts of the brain, for example, directly between regions that process emotion and memory.

This temporary diminution of DMN activity explains what mystics, neuroscientists, medical and religious scholars, and psychonauts have referred to in decades of research as "ego dissolution."[39] However, while the idea of an ego/self dissolves in the blurring of boundaries between subject/object that occurs during a psychedelic experience, consciousness remains, thus illustrating that it is precisely in the relations between the individual and the world around them (be it other humans or the rest of the environment) where consciousness may lie. The decolonial, anti-capitalist, antipatriarchal, and feminist implications of these consciousnesses redefined through interrelational embodiments run deep and provide explicit counterpoints to the various modes of symbolic and psychological violence mobilized by normative world-constructions. Furthermore, the DMN's dual operations of repressions (controlling access to certain memories or emotions in various regions of the brain) and filtering (reducing the flow of sensory information) again have deep political implications if the contemporary individual is shaped not so much by an evolutionary need to survive harsh environmental conditions as by an individual's position in a society ordered by hierarchical structures (class, race, gender, etc.). As such, the temporary deactivation brings forth the opportunity for radical empathy in the direct access to past and current sensory information. More importantly for my purposes here, the psychedelic/mystical experiences constructed in the Mexican and global counterculture are moments where, without disappearing into potentially empty categories such as "citizen of the world" or "cosmopolitan" or the more mainstream ideology of "we are all one," the characters interact with each other and the environment around them in ways that radically challenge the dominating economic and political orders precisely through the use of literary devices and techniques that re-create these psychedelic moments for the reader rather than re-present them.

In a therapeutic context—as opposed to the recreational ones observed in previous novels, valuable as they are—this particular effect of the temporary diminution of the DMN and increase in other neural networks becomes functionalized through the careful control of external stimuli. The basic structure being used today in therapeutic contexts builds on the tenets of set (the mindset with which a psychedelic is consumed) and setting (the physical environment where the psychedelic is consumed) developed in the early years of psychedelic research. Today, psychedelic-assisted psychotherapy (PAP) consists of three moments. First, a series of sessions without the use of substances where the therapist learns about the client's past and the client establishes trust with the therapist; these moments appear in *Palinuro of Mexico* in the introductory chapters and sections of the book dedicated to learning about Palinuro's family background and their global lineage. Second, a session generally between 4 and 8 hours where the client consumes a high dose of a psychedelic in a safe and controlled environment (usually a furnished hospital room resembling a relaxed lounge area) and generally using eyeshades to control visual stimuli and headphones with a carefully curated music playlist designed to complement the arc of the psychedelic experience.[40] These moments are found in the novel during the chapters that focus on the experiences of Palinuro and Estefania in their small apartment, physically isolated from the stimuli of the world while they engage with the worlds within. Third and finally, a series of integration sessions where client and therapist "make sense" of the experiences had; this moment is crucial in creating a supportive context to understand the psychedelic experience and regarded by therapists and researchers as *the* essential component of PAP. In the novel, the final chapters focalize the psychedelic experience on the state violence lived in Mexico during the later 1960s and place it in the context of global political and social struggles, providing a visual and literary language that accounts for the personal and historical experiences of the 1960s generation beyond Mexico itself.[41] Interspersed throughout the novel as well are moments of self-reflection that continuously integrate the psychedelic experiences into their existence as subjects of global capitalism living the histories of colonialism, while also citizens of Mexico.

Although similar to the effects reported in re/creative contexts with lower doses, the concrete effects of this particular form of therapeutic uses are profoundly revealing and highlight the political potentiality of *Palinuro of Mexico*, particularly in the world-system we inhabit—and that inhabits us. First, the barriers between self/other and subject/object are lowered; while much philosophical, cultural, and medical research has worked within normative and hegemonic constructions of self and subject, the decolonial and anti-capitalist implications of this lowering of barriers run deep. Palinuro and Estefania, as center protagonists through which all of the narration and world-building passes, establish a series of reciprocal relations between themselves, and then between them two and the rest of objects, things, and words that populate their world. Second, PAP functionalizes the specific psychedelic effect of changes in thought patterns and brain functions, particularly in the visualization of thoughts that characterize the trip (i.e. hallucinations). Thus, Palinuro literally "sees" the history of Mexico as a particular development of Western culture, streets are populated by the national/fatherland's "heroes" they are named after, and Palinuro begins to think/see the literal substitution of this masculinist nation's bones with the iliac crest of the motherland.[42] Third, there are momentary ruptures of the mental patterns generated by living (and surviving) in a capitalist society built on the histories of violent colonialism and state violence. In the novel, Palinuro in the Imaginary Islands escapes the subjectivation imposed by consumer capitalism through a Swiftean parody of the advertising machinery.[43] Palinuro and Estefania rupture the violent objectivation and sexualization that underpins capitalist (visual) economies in the representation of female sexualities and bodies, and the novel achieves that by exploiting-exploding the structure of voyeuristic gaze of pornographic discourse with the centralization female pleasure *without* fetishizing. And, finally, in the act of reading the lengthy novelization of these alternative sociopolitical relations the reader momentarily leaves the normative relations that fix individuals to each other, to objects, to temporality, and, ultimately, to existence. This power of imagination, springing from a psychedelic-mystical-countercultural experience then activated in the reader, cannot be underscored in the context of world-building and political action, as underlined by Morfino.[44]

From their room in the Plaza de Santo Domingo, where multiple temporalities and spatialities of Western culture coexist—from antiquity to pop art—the novel unfolds as a series of psychotherapy sessions where the traumatic moments of national history are integrated into the subject's position as a global citizen with a common history. Without seeking to impose a fixed structure on the text—or the psychedelic experience it textualizes—it is possible to identify specific psychotherapeutic moments that are not escapist or recreational in the representation of psychedelic substances, particularly as Palinuro and Estefania consume them in their room.[45] As the primordial couple giving shape to the new world that emerged in the Global Sixties, their genealogy with Abuelo Francisco directly situates the Mexican Revolution (and the histories of state violence it ideologically legitimates) as the ideological framework being challenged; nation is a fiction that silences the histories of violence underpinning normative Western culture.[46] The work of Palinuro in the Advertising Agencies assembles his global subjectivity into the networks of global desire-production.[47] Palinuro's passing through the schools and histories of medicine culminates in the final "house of the sick," where both characters and reader are resituated as subjects of biopower in its utmost reaches—no more than a body on which to practice an autopsy as the ultimate categorization of life.[48] And, finally, the stairs in Palinuro's building where they (and the reader) are singularized as objects of necropower and state violence; not simply a representation or memorialization of the bloody massacre of Tlatelolco, but a critical reflection on the inherent and structural violence of the modern state. Palinuro has been interpreted as a "gathering of subjectivities that unfolds in both a personal and collective unconsciousness," responding to the complex and multiple realities of the Global Sixties.[49] Understanding this gathering as multitude anchored in the character of failure/surrender the mythical Palinurus embodies, this first moment of establishing a set and setting for the reenactment of a national-Western psychotherapy reveals the "weaving" of temporalities-spatialities "that constitutes the ineluctable horizon of all political action."[50]

Placed in this sociohistorical context, the brief mention of substances helps make the novel literature of and to the world(s). The ideological limit that has been signaled in the text's utopian promise can be reinterpreted as an expression of the ineffability and paradoxicality that characterizes the mystical/psychedelic experience.[51] During the subjective displacement that occurs between Palinuro and the Palinuros, between the I and the multiple I's that appear, the "epiphanies" that characterize the mystical-psychedelic experience are explicitly politicized: the liberation of desire, the poetic use of language/imagination as a decolonial act, the relational construction of subjectivity—an ontology of relation—and the fragility of the lineal-teleological temporality that underpins Nation and World.[52]

Perhaps the segment that most condenses the political valiance in liberating desire is Palinuro's voyage into the Advertising Agencies and other Imaginary Islands. Publicity is experienced as the historical antecedent of what is now being described as the tyranny of common sense that neoliberalism (economically rooted in the liberalizations of 1970s) establishes as the basis for a global governmentality.[53] Against this capitalist individualism constantly generating production/consumption desires, *Palinuro* mobilizes the psychedelic experience to literally see the publicity barons in their systemic role. For Palinuro, it is necessary to face the "danger of depalinurizing (what would most depalinurize Palinuro would be a good depalinurizer)" and subvert the perfect flexibility of the neoliberal subject from within.[54] Rupturing commodity fetishism allows for a radical discontinuity grounded in the explicit revealing of the absurd by "declaring that he did not buy all these products in order to do all these things but that he did all these things in order to be able to buy all these products."[55] The Swiftean voyage is coupled with the psychedelic effects of visualizing the most abstract thought to reveal first the affective manipulation carried out by advertising and mediatization in general, and furthermore a politically effective tool: laughter.

Alongside laughter, *Palinuro of Mexico* emphasizes the decolonial potential of language in its poetic function under a countercultural ethos. In "The death of our mirror," the couple solve their problems with "intellijence," and though this word-play leads them to the profound unhappiness of a pre-linguistic existence condemned to an absolute silence when facing the chaos of the significant-signifier separation, it is in this space where things (and words) cease to be simply objects/merchandise or symbols to be used, and enter into reciprocal relations of meaning. Integrating these visual experiences is an act of countercultural knowledge-construction emerging from embodied knowledge, and thus Palinuro and Estefania develop relational subjectivities.[56] Emerging from their immanent existence, this ontology of relation radically subverts the capitalist ethos that underpins hegemonic constructions of World. Limited by the subject-object/consumer-product relation, capitalist logic is discarded in favor of a countercultural ethos with profound decolonial implications. If the objects in the room (but let us imagine as well so-called natural resources, animals bred as food sources, objectified and otherized bodies, etc.) are the real source of subjectivity in the relations established between the individual and the "outside" world, relations that not only signify but ultimately sustain and nourish, then the exploitation of these objects and bodies as consumer products is ultimately unthinkable, radically unimaginable.

It is from these immanent and ontological relations that the transcendence of time/space is understood as political, that parodoxicality that has been a trademark of the psychedelic/mystical experiences studied since pioneers William Richards and Walter Pahnke first proposed a taxonomy.[57] The momentary collapse of a lineal temporality forces Palinuro (and the reader) to inhabit the revolutionary history of Abuelo Francisco *alongside* the state violence unleashed in 1968 against student groups.[58] Though he will die—murdered by this state violence due to his political activism—*Palinuro of Mexico* resists the teleological base of modernity that would transform Palinuro (and other students) into martyrs and heroes in favor of a more ethical political discourse that seeks to incarnate rather than memorialize.[59] Of all the mental effects psychedelics have on the Default Mode Network—particularly in a therapeutic context—this radical destabilizing of a lineal temporality is the most politically provocative since it situates the character in a temporary "outside" modernity and capitalism. Capital's power to remove temporal barriers in its constant circulation, to control and appropriate time in a continuous reproduction of the extraction-commodification-consumption process, is exploded by the pluralization of temporalities, multiple and postcolonial, that reject the normative world order and establish connections with the other temporalities emerging in other global countercultural contexts across the globe.[60] In specific national contexts, but reaching to the world constructed through the histories of colonialism/capitalism, counterculture thus provides a non-teleological way of temporalization that historicizes without memorializing, of a world-building that depends on the making explicit of these plural temporalities we inhabit.

By way of concluding this approach to Mexican countercultural literature functioning as world literature, the third stage of a successful PAP serves as an image and model of integration. In its historical moment, counterculture emerged as a gathering of experiences where psychedelics played a central role; today, almost fifty years later, research on these substances is rescuing and developing the therapeutic potential behind them (for the Western establishment, at least). The insights these countercultural literary interventions provide within a world literature framework are many, from redefinitions of self/subject without recurring to indigenous models (a path that too quickly leads to exoticization, especially in cultural products emerging from and circulating in global markets) to the increasingly pressing need to recognize the multiple temporalities we inhabit in order to imagine an outside not only to the economic crisis looming ahead but to the environmental crisis we are experiencing already. As the characters of García Saldaña, Dalton, and del Paso propose, national and global histories must be *re-created* and, in their reordering as part of a Western History (the history of Capital), offer us other ways of being individuality in community, alternate forms to the logics of Colony and Capital. Countercultural literature pushes us to think of our embodied existence, not only to make visible the legacy of Colony and Capital on our mind and our bodies but to use our experiences to create embodied knowledge, a world literature where many worlds abound.

Notes

1 Ignacio Sanchez Prado, *Strategic Occidentalism. On Mexican Fiction, the Neoliberal Book Market, and the Question of World Literature* (Chicago: Northwestern University Press, 2018), 8.

2 Hector Hoyos, *Beyond Bolaño. The Global Latin American Novel* (New York: Columbia University Press, 2015), 29.
3 Pheng Cheah, *What Is a World? On Postcolonial Literature as World Literature* (Durham: Duke University Press, 2016), 8–10.
4 Eduardo Ekman Schenberg, "Psychedelic-Assisted Psychotherapy: A Paradigm Shift in Psychiatric Research and Development," *Frontiers in Pharmacology* 9, no. 733 (2018).
5 Mariano Siskind, *Cosmopolitan Desires. Global Modernity and World Literature in Latin America* (Chicago: Northwestern University Press, 2014), 17.
6 Ibid., 55–6.
7 Cheah, *What Is a World?*, 12.
8 Vittorio Morfino, *Plural Temporality: Transindividuality and the Aleatory Between Spinoza and Althusser* (Chicago: Haymarket Books, 2014), 44.
9 Michael Pollan, *How to Change Your Mind: What the New Science of Psychedelic Teaches Us About Consciousness, Dying, Addiction, Depression and Transcendence* (New York: Penguin Books, 2018), 3.
10 Morfino, *Plural Temporality*, 4.
11 Cheah, *What Is a World?*, 78.
12 Sanchez Prado, *Strategic Occidentalism*, 15.
13 Eric Zolov, *Refried Elvis: The Rise of the Mexican Counterculture* (Berkeley: University of California Press, 1999), 10.
14 Rachel Adams, "Hipsters and Jipitecas: Literary Counterculture on Both Sides of the Border," *American Literary History* 16, no. 1 (2004): 72.
15 Parmenides Garcia Saldaña, *Pasto verde* (Mexico: Wdiciones El Viaje, 2008).
16 Adams, "Hipsters and Jipitecas," 60.
17 Ibid., 79.
18 Garcia Saldaña, *Pasto verde*, 72.
19 Ibid., 67.
20 Ibid., 61.
21 Margarita Dalton, *Larga sinfonía en d (y había una vez)* (México: Editorial Diógenes, 1968), 7.
22 Ibid., 108.
23 Pollan, *How to Change your Mind*, 322–3.
24 Cheah, *What Is a World?*, 12.
25 Dalton, *Larga sinfonía*, 150.
26 Cheah, *What Is a World?*, 10.
27 Dalton, *Larga sinfonía*, 14.
28 Morfino, *Plural Temporality*, 4.
29 Hugo M. Viera, "Intoxicated Writing: Onda Writers and the Drug Experience in 1960s Mexico," *Studies in Latin American Popular Culture* 33 (2015): 152.
30 Cheah, *What Is a World?*, 85.
31 Ibid.
32 Fernando del Paso, *Palinuro of Mexico*, trans. Elisabeth Plaister (Normal: Dalkey Archive Press, 1996).
33 Ignacio Sánchez Prado, "Dying Mirrors, Medieval Moralists and Tristram Shandies: The Literary Traditions of Fernando del Paso's *Palinuro of Mexico*," *Comparative Literature* 60, no. 2 (2008): 146.

34 Alexander B. Belser, Gabriel Agin-Liebes, et al. "Patient Experiences of Psilocybin-Assisted Psychotherapy: An Interpretative Phenomenological Analysis," *Journal of Humanistic Psychology* 57, no. 4 (2017): 354–88.
35 Pollan, *How to Change Your Mind*, 331–96.
36 Ibid., 302.
37 Ibid.
38 Ibid., 308.
39 Ibid., 304.
40 Belser et al., "Patient Experiences of Psilocybin-Assisted Psychotherapy," 373.
41 Sánchez Prado, "Dying Mirrors, Medieval Moralists and Tristram Shandies," 150.
42 Del Paso, *Palinuro of Mexico*, 472–85.
43 Sanchez Prado, "Dying Mirrors, Medieval Moralists and Tristram Shandies," 154.
44 Morfino, *Plural Temporality*, 164, 175.
45 Del Paso, *Palinuro of Mexico*, 42, 48, 290, 315.
46 Ibid., 232–3.
47 Frederic Lordon, *Willing Slaves of Capital: Spinoza and Marx on Desire*, trans. Gabriel Ash (London: Verso, 2014), 44, 51.
48 Del Paso, *Palinuro of Mexico*, 376.
49 Sanchez Prado, "Dying Mirrors, Medieval Moralists and Tristram Shandies," 149.
50 Morfino, *Plural Temporality*, 15.
51 Del Paso, *Palinuro of Mexico*, 156.
52 Morfino, *Plural Temporality*, 44.
53 Irmgard Emmelhainz, *La tiranía del sentido común. La reconversión neoliberal de México* (Mexico: Paradiso Editores, 2016), 19.
54 Del Paso, *Palinuro of Mexico*, 191.
55 Ibid., 214.
56 Ibid., 123.
57 Walter N. Pahnke and William A. Richards, "Implications of LSD and Experimental Mysticism," *Journal of Religion and Health* 5, no. 3 (1966): 175–208.
58 Del Paso, *Palinuro of Mexico*, 138.
59 Sanchez Prado, "Dying Mirrors, Medieval Moralists and Tristram Shandies," 158.
60 Cheah, *What Is a World?*, 69.

13

Carlos Fuentes and World Literature

Pedro Ángel Palou

Can we label Carlos Fuentes's representation of himself and the world postcolonial exotic, as Graham Huggan's use of the term? Huggan[1] describes this type of author as one that uses strategies like *staged marginalities, otherness,* and *the cult of authenticity* to gain global readership. Huggan analyzes African and Asian writers mostly and has some blind spot when thinking of other writers of the so-called Global South. He is very clear, however, when thinking that the so-called Boom generation and magical realism have become "hypercommodified." In such a way that they have constructed, a "blatantly commercial alterity industry based on 'exoticist spectacle, commodity fetishism and the aesthetics of decontextualization.'"[2] The writers of the Boom employed many strategies to enter the world stage. They were diverse and complex, since they came from different nations from Latin America. Carlos Fuentes was regarded as the ambassador of Mexican culture. During the entire creation of his literary persona—along with a huge body of work—he made Mexico his main topic. He, of course, interpreted Mexico in his own terms. His own, *Tiempo Mexicano*, to paraphrase a famous book of him. His interpretation, in fact, seemed to work well—even as a public literary performance of *Mexicanness*—so long as Mexico was a state that based its public policies on the construction of a political subject, namely, the *mestizo*. Neoliberalism, however, broke the illusion within Fuentes's work that the coexistence of past and present could be resolved through his notion of Mexican Time. Perhaps this is why the tone of his book of essays entitled *A New Time for Mexico* is so different.[3] Published in November 1994, Fuentes makes clear from the prologue that this book was meant to be both prophetic and radiographic; both lofty and firmly grounded. The mestizo has been replaced here by the citizen. No longer simply a drag on the present, Fuentes envisions the past as a Chac-Mool threatening to seize incipient modernity; a guarantor of historical responsibility. He advocates "democracy with memory, progress with culture, future with past."[4] The first essay in the book returns to the pre-Hispanic world that inhabits Mexico's battered modernity. The suns of ancient cosmogony—water, earth, wind, and fire that returns to the water—are here envisioned as tradition, identity, history, and culture; and the blind spots, curiously enough, are the Indians. I say *curiously* because in the second essay, Fuentes actually pulls back from that representation, citing the declaration of his friend Fernando Benítez in the monumental ethnographic encyclopedia, *The Indians of Mexico*: "To forget them is to condemn ourselves to oblivion."⁵ Fuentes's problem, just like Paz's, was that he could not envision the state outside of the very terms that created it. There was no state before the Mexican Revolution; this was before the *Es Thus* of Hegel's *Ces't comme sa*. It is what it is.

In order to reimagine the significance of the historical events of twentieth-century Mexico, we must first extract them from all official (post-revolutionary) metaphysics and the workings of bourgeois memory. This could be done by exploring the identity narrative of the national, auto-ethnographic unit, modeling an approach pioneered by Marie Louise Pratt.⁶ What Fuentes misses in his reading of neoliberalism is that Mexican modernity was born of the postcolonial search for a police state capable of creating a sovereign entity that would allow the establishment of bourgeois order (a la Porfirio Díaz and later the Constitutionalists, but not the Agrarianists, of 1917).

Because Fuentes's book of essays returns to the topic of the Mexican Revolution, it seems—but only *seems*—to revise his earlier interpretative framework. Fuentes does here envision three Mexican revolutions: the agrarian (of Villa and Zapata, conservative in its land-based worldview); the bourgeois (of the Maderistas and then the followers of Obregón and Calles, forward-looking in its creation of a modern nation-state); and the proletarian (the workers' movement that most clearly lost the war). It is this defeat, in fact, which seems to me most indicative of the continuity between the triumphant, modernizing Revolution and the signing of the North American Free Trade Agreement (NAFTA) that Fuentes discusses in the essay entitled "So Far from God." The central question that Fuentes grapples within that chapter, and not without some optimism, is how to combine nationalism with liberal reform. Reality will intervene to shatter that illusion. The year 1994 was a dangerous year, and yet Fuentes dared to tell the story—in diary format—of the Zapatista uprising.

There is a problem with Carlos Fuentes's *late* style; and it stems from his internationalization—not only as a Mexican commodity but as a liberal intellectual. The problem is the nature of the new *factor* in his analysis. The bio-political construction of the *mestizo* gives way to the *citizen* and its collective entelechy of *a civil society*—both concepts being political by-products, precisely, of the implementation of the global economic system. The correlates of neoliberalism dilute, rather than articulate, all that is syntagmatic. Fuentes's later novels (from *The Years with Laura Diaz* to *The Will and Fortune* and from *The Eagle's Chair* to *Adam in Eden*) lack significant lessons. Rather than structured, they present oscillating pendulums of meaning that yearn for the memory of the sacred as the path to inclusive modernity. "The unfulfilled promise of all our modernizing projects," writes Fuentes, "has been democracy . . . we also have to resume an economic development that can no longer be deprived of its political shield, which is democracy; its social shield, which is justice; or its mental shield, which is culture." Fuentes even sees democracy as the core of an identity that will allow the wound to be closed from within, using its own resources. "I do not seek in nationalism the defense of the nation . . . But I do seek, again and again, the defense of society, of culture and of who we are."⁷ The citizens, as I noted earlier, have now taken the place of the mestizos. The master signifier is not new but does require changing its paradigmatic axis if the new syntax is going to be able to articulate something. Pages later Fuentes is able to say it clearly: Mexico did the right thing in joining NAFTA: for "we would have won nothing by isolating ourselves in a world of possible autarchies"[8]

In short, Fuentes's view of a solution continues to insist that the growth and development of Mexico be built from within, through the work of Mexicans and the exercise of Mexican sovereignty. At the same time, however, his perspective on NAFTA can sometimes take a sudden, social-democratic turn, as when he argues that the Free Trade Agreement should be Europeanized, meaning given greater social content.

What Fuentes's analysis misses, however, is the data from the 1990s, and it is chilling. By 1995, despite the so-called *structural reforms*, Mexico entered a deep recession and the government devalued the peso by 77 percent (reserves were reduced from 30 to 6 billion pesos). Privatization occurred at a rapid pace; by 1992, only 15 percent of the 1,115 state-owned companies that had existed at the beginning of the Salinas administration (1988–94) were still state-owned. A handful of people were enriched by this wave of privatization. It was less an exercise of free-market economics than a distribution of wealth among a circle of friends. The World Bank also pressured the Mexican government to abolish the 1917 Constitution's historic Article 27 that had recognized the collective landholding rights of rural communities under the *ejido* system. Although admittedly there were problems with the system, *ejido* lands began being sold, broken apart, and privatized as of 1992. The signing of NAFTA further complicated survival for the rural inhabitants of the countryside for whom subsistence was no longer possible. Indeed, just as this disaster was occurring, the Mexican government was deciding the terms for a massive import of corn from Canada and the United States to meet domestic needs. Modernity can be all things, except inclusive.

In his famous interview with Francoise Truffaut, Alfred Hitchcock described a scene he'd envisioned, but didn't end up shooting, for his film *North by Northwest*:

> I wanted to have a long dialogue scene between Cary Grant and one of the factory workers as they walked along the assembly line. They might, for instance, be talking about one of the foremen. Behind them a car is being assembled, piece by piece. Finally, the car they've seen being put together from a single nut and bolt is complete, with gas and oil and already to drive off the line. The two men look at each other and say: "Isn't it wonderful!" Then they open the door to the car and out drops a corpse.[9]

The body that falls from the assembly line of neoliberalism is the mestizo. Using the insights of Joan Copjec in her brilliant *Read My Desire*,[10] one could attempt to use Foucault's classical interpretation in order to understand the mestizo corpse: that is, the fact that his presence goes unnoticed while the car is slowly being assembled is only a paradox because it disappoints the panoptic power; the corpse in that case would be a necessary fiction for the discreet operation of the law. However, as Copjec suggests, a Lacanian solution to the enigma of the closed space in Hitchcock's imagined scene would be different.[11]

From a Lacanian perspective, the paradox is the belief that what is hidden must be even more veiled, even more hidden. According to Lacan, nothing exists but the surface; at the same time, however, the corpse would not be fictional (as in Foucault), but real. The great revelation is that there is nothing to reveal; there is nothing behind the curtain. The body was there the whole time, decomposing before the naked eye, in clear view even of the earlier Fuentes who evidently saw it in Andrés Aparicio's son. Turning to a mathematical metaphor a la Frege to underscore the point, we know that the very act of counting—arithmetic—depends upon there being a category in the series of numbers into which no object falls. The number of objects subsumed by the category of "non-identical-to-itself" would be zero. The body that falls out from the car once the door is opened is the element of surplus value that stalks every symbolic structure and allows the articulation of its parts. The mestizos's corpse is zero. It is not even a body, but rather that which allows the body to exit the apparently closed space. It is the element added to the structure to mark what the structure lacks. The paradox is that the added element is only ever on the surface; it manifests itself in its own functioning. The limit of Fuentes's interpretation of nationalism is itself that excess body that falls dead from the assembly line; the corpse that neoliberalism presents in all its superficiality.

A longtime client of the legendary literary agent Carmen Ballcels, Carlos Fuentes was widely translated into many languages. He also believed in the power of literary consecration. He devoted much time to making sure that the entire collection of his work in English be published in the Dalkey Archives. For the forewords of his books, he personally chose such prestigious authors as Salman Rushdie, Milan Kundera, and Jorge Volpi. Similarly, while the special issue of Cahier L'Herne was designed by Claude Fell (one of Fuentes's translators into French) and Jorge Volpi, it was Fuentes himself who decided upon most of the collaborations for the volume.[12] He believed this particular publication would be instrumental to his final consecration as a cosmopolitan intellectual. The same Claude Fell and Volpi, along with Gabriel García Márquez, Milan Kundera, Tomás Eloy Martínez, Juan Goytisolo, Julio Ortega, Sergio Ramírez, Daniel-Henri Pageaux, Edmundo Paz Soldán, and me, contributed to the volume. In a brilliant analysis, Sarah Brouillette states that:

> The suggestion that postcolonial literature, as it circulates in the Anglo-American marketplace, exists only as evidence of Western fetishization of the rest of human experience, or that reception of postcolonial texts is always or only a kind of market colonization, ignores a number of factors. Attention to the material organization of the current literary marketplace does not reveal a single market, but rather a fragmenting and proliferating set of niche audiences, which are admittedly united by a set of general rules dictated by the major transnational corporations.[13]

For his part, García Márquez praised Fuentes's esprit de corps, claiming that it was actually Fuentes who created and sustained the Boom—through his sponsorship of the work of some of its writers in Mexico, his contacts with Spanish publishing houses, the backing of his own agent, the aforementioned Carmen Ballcels, and his garnering of support from a variety of other institutions. Kundera's contribution was the publication in French of the Afterword he wrote for Dalkey's English edition of *Terra*

Nostra. Nadine Gordimer praised the magician in Fuentes's writing style. As the French *homage* is traditionally political as well, there were also contributions from former Chilean president Ricardo Lagos; from Juan Ramón de la Fuente, the ex-president of the UNAM, Latin America's largest public university; and from Fuentes's friend Jean Daniel, the French journalist, who celebrated the "glory of *mestizaje*" in Fuentes's work and the hybrid nature of his use of culture and language. Further description of all the articles in the volume would take too much time and would only serve to underscore the main goal here, which is to recognize this specific publication as a key moment in Fuentes's drive to transcend his own mortality, and, more importantly, to gain and sustain an international readership for his work.

This is also why he agreed to help organize and attend an international conference in his honor in the French town of Aix en Provence. Just as with a previous conference in Mexico called "Geography of the Novel," he himself decided on the list of participants. Whereas the invitees to that Mexican conference were mostly his friends (Nadine Gordimer, Coetzee, Rushdie, Julian Barnes, Susan Sontag, and others), for the Aix en Provence conference he made a different choice, deciding to invite members of a younger generation of Latin American writers whose works he had previously endorsed. After each of these two conferences, Fuentes compiled his thoughts on the writers he had admired (Mexico conference) and endorsed (Aix de Provence conference) in order to produce two important essay collections: *Geography of Novel* and *The Great Latin American Novel*. In both volumes, he offers astute readings of the traditions to which he belongs and of the works of the heirs to whom he is passing the torch.

At the 2011 conference at Aix en Provence, there were two round tables with his friends (including Daniel and Goytisolo), two days of Buñuel films that Fuentes introduced and later critiqued, and two days devoted to younger Latin American writers. To these younger writers (myself included), Fuentes gave explicit instructions: there was to be no discussion of Fuentes's life or his writings (he'd given the same gag order at a conference in Mexico in honor of his eightieth birthday); rather, we were to concentrate on contemporary trends in Colombian, Argentine, Chilean, Mexican, and Central American literatures, or on the Latin American novel in general. This seems to have been his way of saying goodbye and anointing the authors he cared about. Of course, the conference did include a showing of a film by Valeria Sarmiento and Guy Scarpetta on Fuentes's life and work. The group of younger Latin American authors Fuentes invited to the occasion included Juan Gabriel Vázquez, Jorge Volpi, Ignacio Padilla, Santiago Gamboa, Carlos Franz, and Arturo Fontaine. Although the absence of women writers was a noticeable limitation, the geographical coverage of Latin American countries was expansive. Fuentes performed readings of the younger writers' works with adeptness and admiration, amply demonstrated in the subsequent essays he devoted to each of them.

One group who lacked any representation in this event, as if Fuentes had erased them entirely from the Latin American literary map, was the generation between the Boom and the so-called Crack. César Aira is a prominent writer from that generation. In a short novel of his entitled *The Literary Conference*, Aira's first-person narrator,

César, is a writer who makes a living doing translations, but also leads a secret life as a mad scientist. He has become a millionaire by solving a centuries-old enigma about the origins of a strange man-made phenomenon known as the Macuto Line. After receiving an invitation to a literature conference in the small town of Mérida in Venezuela, César decides to go to the conference disguised as a harmless writer, but his real intention is to execute a master plan: to clone Carlos Fuentes and create an army of powerful intellectuals who will then dominate the world. Things do not go quite as planned, however. The cloned wasp he sent out to capture some of Fuentes's DNA had done something wrong and the resultant worms were not at all what César had expected. As Aira writes, through the voice of his narrator:

> As I have already mentioned, the worms' color and texture were their most noticeable characteristics. They are also what led me to the heart of the matter. Because that color, that very peculiar brilliant blue, immediately reminded me of the color of Carlos Fuentes's cell, which my wasp had brought me . . . Though when I saw that color in the cell, it did not evoke what it was evoking now that I was seeing it extended over vast undulating surfaces. I now realized that I had seen that color somewhere else, the very same day the cell had been taken, one week before. Where? On the tie Carlos Fuentes was wearing that day! A splendid Italian raw silk tie, over an immaculate white shirt . . . and a light grey suit . . . (one memory led to another until the picture was complete). And this horrendous piece of evidence revealed the magnitude of the error. The wasp had brought me a cell from Carlos Fuentes's tie, not his body! A groan escaped my lips:
> "Stupid wasp and the accursed mother who made you!"
> "What?" Nelly asked, surprised.
> "Don't pay any attention to me, I understand myself."
> The fact is, I couldn't blame her. It was all my fault. How could that poor disposable cloned tool knows where the man stopped, and his clothing began? For her it was all one, it was all "Carlos Fuentes".[14]

An author dies, but their work persists. No matter how diligently a particular author works to determine their "afterlife," their readers will remain loyal only if the subject matter appeals to them. The wasp's mistake was that of all those attendees at Aira's "literary conference" who confused Fuentes with Fuentes's writings. My hope is that hundreds of blue worms do not start emerging like the ones who came out of his silk tie. I hope we can still read Fuentes, despite the petrification of death and the mausoleum of literary consecration.

If we read now his obituaries as a late-life appraisal, we will be shocked. Anthony DePalma begins his obituary for *The New York Times* with an interesting set of adjectives to describe Fuentes's main accomplishments: he was not only a public intellectual but an *elegant* one; not just a man of letters but a *grand* one; his novels are *panoramic* and capture the *complicated essence* of his country's history "for readers around the world."[15] The choice of adjectives used to begin the obituary immediately raises questions worth considering. What does it mean to be elegant and grand, to have panoramic vision, and even to be able to grasp the "essence" of one's own country's history? Why does being elegant, grand, and complicated matter? These are apparently the credentials that make it possible for a local author to gain an international readership. Reading between the lines of DePalma's opening paragraph, what he really is saying is that Fuentes did not write for his Mexican readers, but in order to *travel* outside his country as an ambassador, a well-dressed and well-mannered one.

In the following lines of the obituary, DePalma notes that it was Julio Ortega, Brown University professor and Fuentes's biographer, who confirmed Fuentes's death to the press, further locating Fuentes as a citizen of the world (since he taught in places like Brown and Princeton). DePalma adds that Fuentes's doctor, Arturo Ballesteros, gave official notice of the death to the Associated Press, a clear indication that this was world news. Such references raise yet another important question: for whom is an obituary written? In the case of *The New York Times* obituary, it seems to have been intended for people unfamiliar with Fuentes's *oeuvre*. It introduces Fuentes as a prominent Latin American author in the same literary genealogy as García Márquez and Vargas Llosa, both of whom have been and continue to be even more widely read in English than Fuentes. Fuentes, then, is recognized as forming *part* of the Boom, yet DePalma offers no information about this literary movement beyond its being an "explosion of Latin American literature."

It is the following paragraph, however, where DePalma *translates*, so to speak, Fuentes's writing for the English-speaking audience, pointing to the "wide recognition" that his 1985 novel *The Old Gringo* enjoyed in the United States. DePalma states directly, "It was the first book by a Mexican novelist to become a best seller north of the border, and it was made into a 1989 film starring Gregory Peck and Jane Fonda." What he fails to mention is that it became a best seller only after the release of the film and largely because of the film.

The obituary goes on to suggest yet another key credential for a Latin American writer: "In the tradition of Latin American writers, Mr. Fuentes was politically engaged, writing magazine, newspaper and journal articles that criticized the Mexican government during the long period of sometimes repressive single-party rule that ended in 2000 with the election of an opposition candidate, Vicente Fox Quesada." Political engagement, then, is lauded here, although not in terms of any particular affiliation; for DePalma is careful to add that Fuentes was also critical of Venezuela's leftist leader Hugo Chávez, calling him a "tropical Mussolini." In fact, DePalma then contradicts his earlier statement about political engagement, claiming that Fuentes was more ideological than political: "He tended to embrace justice and basic human rights regardless of political labels. He supported Fidel Castro's revolution in Cuba but turned against it as Mr. Castro became increasingly authoritarian." These observations cement even further Fuentes's credentials as a Top 10 ambassador of world literature; a liberal intellectual more in tune with broad Western traditions than with the particular struggles of Latin America or Mexico. To underscore the point, DePalma adds that, like his father, Carlos Fuentes was a diplomat, and in fact was appointed ambassador to France in 1975—a post from which Fuentes resigned as soon as former Mexican president Díaz Ordaz was named ambassador to the neighboring country of Spain.

After this long "ideological" description, the obituary finally returns to Fuentes's literature, but presents it here again as the means to an end. DePalma writes that Fuentes believed that through his fictional works, "he could make his voice heard, and he did so prolifically and inventively, tracing the history of modern Mexico in layered stories that also explored universal themes of love, memory and death." With this sentence, DePalma downplays Fuentes's descriptions of modern Mexico, insisting that what is most worthwhile in his work is his ability to intersect those descriptions with *universal* themes. In its attempt to paint Fuentes as a *grand* man of letters, this obituary has effectively de-territorialized Fuentes and de-historicized his work, erasing one of Fuentes's most salient traits: his political and historical vision. DePalma does recognize that right to the end of Fuentes's life, "His novels remained ambitious and topical." Yet here is another contradiction; for aren't these the same *topics* that DePalma had just downplayed?

Perhaps this is why DePalma ends the obituary on a biographical note. He claims that Fuentes wrote in every genre except the autobiographical (ignoring several pieces that Fuentes published in English and that Enrique Krauze would later use to criticize Fuentes during the height of the campaign to secure the Nobel Prize for Octavio Paz). In any case, what aspects of Fuentes's biography does DePalma find worthy of mention in the obituary? The answer is his international credentials: that he was born in Panama, since his father at that time was a member of Mexico's diplomatic corps; that he moved from one country to another for that same reason; and that he "learned to speak English fluently while enrolled in a public school" in Washington DC, where Fuentes's father had been appointed ambassador. For an aspiring writer with such a cosmopolitan upbringing, the literary language choice was vitally important. DePalma quotes from a 1985 *New York Times* interview when Fuentes admitted that he had to decide: "whether to write in the language of my father or the language of my teachers." He claimed he chose Spanish for the "flexibility" of the language, and for a practical reason: English, he said, with its "long and uninterrupted literary tradition, did not need one more writer." This rhetorical response by Fuentes might have satisfied his global readers, but it flies in the face of the main purpose of his work, which was to contribute to the uninterrupted tradition of Spanish Literature, including, in particular, Mexican Literature. In fact, his literary masterpiece, *Terra Nostra*, is a tribute to that language, to his native language. Clearly, in his statement to *The New York Times*, Fuentes had embellished his remarks on the language decision for his English-speaking readers. As Sarah Brouillette clearly points out: "The more literature associable with specific national or ethnic identity enters the market, the more the market, despite increasing concentration and globalization, can make the claims to inclusivity and universality that justify its particular form of dominance. Expanding markets for literatures in English have depended on the incorporation of a plurality of identities for global export."[16]

DePalma's obituary does at least mention Fuentes's quarrel with Octavio Paz and the entire Nobel Prize affair, pointing to the article that destroyed the longtime friendship: "[I]n 1988, the literary magazine *Vuelta*, which Mr. Paz directed, published an article fiercely critical of Mr. Fuentes, accusing him of lacking true Mexican identity." This was a very strange accusation coming from a cosmopolitan journal, but DePalma does not question its validity, focusing instead on the "often public feud." But the corollary he offers is the real gem: "Neither man apologized, diminishing the reputation of both." DePalma offers absolutely no evidence to support this statement nor could he; for neither Paz's nor Fuentes's reputation suffered from the feud.

It was after Paz's death, reads the obituary, that Fuentes became the "elder statesman of international letters." Here DePalma needs no additional adjectives; for the noun *statesman* carries its own powerful charge. What does it mean to go from being an internationally acclaimed author to a statesman? Who appoints a writer to this post? Does the field of world literature resemble a State or a Nation, or is the position simply a function of how one wields their fame? The only evidence that DePalma offers for this transition to elder *statesman* is that upon Fuentes's eightieth birthday, hundreds "gathered at the Metropolitan Museum of Art in New York to celebrate his life and work." He fails to mention that Fuentes also received international acclaim that year within his own country, at a three-day conference held at the Castillo de Chapultepec. The inaugural dinner for this event was presided over by Felipe Calderón, then-president of Mexico, and the invitees included celebrated writers from around the world, including his friend García Márquez. Among those seated at the head table were Nadine Gordimer and the former president of Spain Felipe González. Also in attendance was Juan Ramón de la Fuente, the president of Mexico's National University (UNAM). I also had the privilege of attending the dinner, having been chosen by Fuentes himself to represent the younger generation of Mexican writers. The three-day conference that followed was not actually focused on Fuentes's work (he refused to have his writing be the focus) but dedicated to reflections on the continued vitality of Latin American literature.

For its part, the obituary written by Nick Caistor for the British newspaper *The Guardian* announced the death of Carlos Fuentes in different terms, with a byline that reads "Mexico's most celebrated novelist."[17] Here Fuentes is presented as an author who "published more than 60 works," as a writer of fierce political engagement, a polemicist, and again as the author of the first Mexican book on *The New York Times* bestseller list. Like DePalma, Caistor also emphasizes Fuentes's international upbringing in terms of his birth and education. In general, however, this obituary pays greater attention to Fuentes's political engagement and the content of his literature. Caistor praises Fuentes as a brilliant polemicist, able to be critical of leftist countries while also maintaining a critical distance from the United States. "He was a sharp, incisive speaker," writes Caistor, "who loved to shine and dominated his audience. He was full of often malicious wit, conveyed in the very Mexican spirit that every conversation or argument is a duel that is to be taken completely seriously -and then forgotten over a drink." There is some essentialism at play here regarding the *Mexicanness* of Fuentes's skill as a polemicist, but the point is well taken. What truly differentiates this obituary from that of the *New York Times* is Caistor's recognition that "Throughout his life, wherever he lived, Mexico was the center of Fuentes's artistic preoccupations." Caistor even includes a quote from Fuentes describing Mexico as a "very enigmatic country, and that's a good thing because it keeps us alert, makes us constantly try to decipher the enigma of Mexico, the mystery of Mexico, to understand a country that is very, very baroque, very complicated and full of surprises." Based upon those aspects of Fuentes's *oeuvre* highlighted in *The Guardian* obituary, it would appear that Fuentes's popularity in Europe is tied to his being a Mexican author. *The New York Times* obituary, on the other hand, suggests that within the United States—a country that publishes a mere 7 percent of its books in translation—it is the universalist themes of Fuentes's work that most appeal to readers.

But was Fuentes really into universalism, or into nation building narratives? Debjani Ganguly has discussed this topic at length while contesting Benedict Anderson. For Ganguly, the problem lies on thinking that the idea of a novel based on nation themes can turn into a world novel. She even declares that the novel "ceases to be an analogue of a limited sovereign community like the nation," because the world cannot be a "sum of nations."[18] Reading Fuentes as a "global novelist" can alter, then, our perception. He was a Mexican novelist writing for a specific moment of the publishing industry when being global meant being very nation bound. This is probably the reason why it is not as read or recognized now as he hoped and struggle to be. This is why the Latin American novel and the magical realism as a trope has become outdated for the industry that only looks for the novel of violence while promoting the new "Latin American."

Notes

1 Graham Huggan, *The Postcolonial Exotic: Marketing the Margins* (London: Routledge, 2001).
2 Ibid., 71–2.
3 Carlos Fuentes, *Nuevo tiempo mexicano* (Mexico City: Taurus, 1994).
4 Ibid., 11. There is an English edition, *A New Time for Mexico* (Berkeley: University of California Berkeley, 1998).
5 Ibid., 39.
6 Mary Louise Pratt, *Imperial Eyes: Travel Writing and Transculturation* (London: Routledge, 1992). Her take could be of great use while considering, for example, *A Distant Family*, one of the underrated novels of Fuentes.
7 Ibid., 128.
8 Ibid., 240.
9 François Truffaut, *Hitchcock* (New York: Simon and Schuster, 1983), 257.
10 Joan Copjec, *Read My Desire* (New York: Verso, 2015).
11 Ibid., 171.
12 Claude Fell and Jorge Volpi, "L'Herne Fuentes," *The Guardian*, May 15, 2012. https://theguardian.com/
13 Sarah Brouillette, *Postcolonial Writers in the Global Literary Marketplace* (New York: Palgrave Macmillan, 2007), 24.
14 César Aira, *The Literary Conference*, trans. Katherine Silver (New York: New Directions Book, 2010), 78–9.

15 Anthony DePalma, "Carlos Fuentes," *New York Times*, May 16, 2012. https://www.nytimes.com/
16 Brouillette, *Postcolonial Writers in the Global Literary Marketplace*, 58.
17 Nick Caistor, "Carlos Fuentes Obituary," *The Guardian*, May 15, 2012, https://www.theguardian.com/
18 Ganguly Debjani, *This Thing Called the World: The Contemporary Novel as a Global Form* (Chapel Hill: North Carolina University Press, 2016), 90.

14

Neoliberalism, Distinction, and World Literature in Mexico in the Twenty-First Century

Oswaldo Zavala

On November 28, 2018, Mexican author Paco Ignacio Taibo II made national news after a controversial statement regarding his appointment as head of the Fondo de Cultura Económica (FCE), the governmental institution managing the prestigious publisher of the same name and a network of bookstores and cultural centers in numerous cities across Mexico and abroad. A celebrated author of detective fiction and historical novels, Taibo II was offered the post by the leftist president Andrés Manuel López Obrador, who won the July 1, 2018, general election in a landslide and with a strong mandate in Congress. Circumventing the legal requisite of being born in Mexico to become director of the FCE (Taibo II was born in Spain), the federal government effectively maneuvered to ultimately modify the existing law and allow Taibo II to occupy the post after the presidential inauguration of December 1. "As a last resource, if it's still not passed by Monday (Nov. 31), there will be a presidential order to appoint me as acting chief while the new law is approved," said Taibo II during a public reading at the Guadalajara International Book Fair, Latin America's largest literary event. "In any case, we fucked them really hard, comrades."[1] The vulgarity of the original expression in Spanish—"se las metimos doblada," literally "we put it inside folded"—was criticized in social media by intellectuals, political pundits, and social media influencers as representative of alleged aggressive masculinity and homophobic tendencies in the Mexican left. (A widely used colloquial phrase, it even merited a small discussion thread in the online resource site wordreference.com, among puzzled researchers seeking for an effective translation into English.[2])

In a very different social and political context, another controversy involving a Mexican author drew attention in social media the year before, bringing to the fore what could be understood as the other pole of the Mexican literary field. On February 12, 2017, Valeria Luiselli, an internationally acclaimed young novelist and essayist based in New York City, wrote a column in the Spanish newspaper *El País* about recent feminist currents in the Western world. After criticizing the replacement of "the free exercise of complex thought for the boring right to take to the streets with poster boards," Luiselli wrote: "The current feminism, gullible and reactionary, makes me really yawn" ("El feminismo actual, simplón y reaccionario, me produce largos bostezos").[3] The daughter of a career diplomat, Luiselli was criticized for her apparent elitism as a privileged writer who attained a rich international education and life experience growing up in South Africa, India, and South Korea.[4] With the polemic that ensued, Luiselli altered the line chastising not feminism in general but instead the type that, according to her, stubbornly replays social struggles from the 1960s by mobilizing activists in the streets.[5]

These controversies and their conditions of possibility are representative of what I argue to be the two main currents of "Mexican literature" within the national and transnational fields of cultural production in the first two decades of the twenty-first century.[6] The first one is directly related to domestic political processes and the function of the engaged writer as a public and organic intellectual often with the support of an official institution. The second one questions the political role of public intellectuals seen from the perspective of a writer disengaged from social movements and outside of public institutions, attaining an apparent higher degree of autonomy for the literary field. These currents are divergent as they embody mutually exclusive intellectual postures, but both positions are in fact constitutive of the general structure of the same unifying field. The mediation of class, race, hegemonic private and public institutions, along with consumer practices of mass media and social networks, brings the two stances in horizontal proximity. They are simultaneously at the national and transnational levels because they are articulated in a literary field that can longer be separated from the neoliberal transformation of the country—and, for that matter, the entire hemisphere—and the very logics of symbolic capital accumulation. In Pierre Bourdieu's words, writers "occupy a dominated position in the dominant class, they are owners of a dominated form of power at the interior of the sphere of power."[7] In consequence, my approach is indeed deliberately reductive of the otherwise complex and vibrant literary productions in Mexico because it looks at the construction of the literary field and its dominant writers, but only as that field and those writers are in turn dominated by neoliberalism as the main principle of sociopolitical organization.

These two currents are representative of "Mexican literature," in quotation marks, because this is not the designation of all literary productions in Mexico, but only of its dominant minority. Writers of "Mexican literature," nationally and abroad, articulate the most commercially successful stances in the domestic *and* the global editorial market, in both print and digital formats, with translations to numerous languages—especially into English—and the consistent recognition of literary awards in Western cultural capitals such as New York, Paris, and London. They are, in fact, as I will discuss in what follows, at the center of what is known in recent academic debates as "world literature." Similarly, the conceptualization of "world literature," also in quotation marks, will be understood here as a set of critical models of analysis produced within the cultural logic of neoliberal thought and social distinction in current debates about non-English-language literary productions circulating in globalized editorial markets. As it "moves through stages of recognition, commodification, consumption and conversion," "world literature" must be studied as an expression of interiorized sociopolitical practices of power and exclusion codified as a mechanism of exchange value.⁸ As such, "world literature" is politically inscribed in consumerist practices of elite cultural and academic institutions primarily in the United States and Europe, and not just ethereally "by circulating out into a broader world beyond its linguistic and cultural point of origin," as David Damrosch famously defined it.⁹ In this context, as "Mexican literature" has become available in the English-language book market with record numbers of translations of novels, short stories, essays, and poetry in the last two decades, its place and pertinence to various models of "world literature" must be examined in relation to the epistemic mediation of neoliberalism in the hemisphere.

The present essay proposes to understand Mexico's two central currents of "world literature" as the direct result of the sociopolitical transformation triggered by the gradual adoption of neoliberal policy in the decades of 1980 and 1990. The transition from a welfare state to neoliberal governance and governmentality exacerbated inequality and class distinction along with a process of depoliticization within the cultural fields of production. As the Mexican government dismantled the political, economic, and cultural institutions that defined the country's modernization project in the twentieth century, the privatization of natural resources (gas, electricity, minerals, and oil) became key public policy at the cost of rising poverty and social disparity. The precarization of Mexico's society was particularly noticeable in the states of the north with a dramatic surge in violence related to drug trafficking, femicide, police abuse with impunity, and the general dysfunctionality of basic city services such as healthcare, education, and urban infrastructure.¹⁰

In this context, the two literary currents that I will analyze in the present essay derive from a divergent, but anticipated, reaction to Mexico's neoliberal transformation. On the one hand, there are the writers who adopt an engaged position through seemingly political narratives in direct relation to the country's problematic present. Regardless of the genre, these authors place their literary project in proximity to a recurrent national state of crisis, echoing the strong political legacy of Mexican fiction studied by critics such as Maarten Van Delden and Seymour Menton. On the other hand, there are the writers who have sought a place outside of the sociopolitical demands of an engaged intellectual to pursue a seemingly freer position in the transnational expansion of the literary field. This may be understood through Bolívar Echeverría's concept of modern "whiteness" ("blanquitud") to describe the cultural practice in which national identity is in tension with a cosmopolitan claim that replicates the Western *habitus* of writers in the cultural capitals of the editorial market.¹¹

The hegemony of foundational authors and intellectuals of the mid-twentieth century (Alfonso Reyes, Octavio Paz, Carlos Fuentes, Juan Rulfo, among the most visible) was gradually claimed by a wave of writers born after 1968, that is, after the political convulsion of the Tlatelolco massacre of October 2 that marked a defining fissure in the authoritarian regime that controlled Mexico since 1929 and until the 2000 presidential election.¹² In this, key cultural institutions were transformed as well alongside what anthropologist Claudio Lomnitz has named the "privatization of culture,"¹³ the process of reorientation of the literary field toward a consumeristic society, the (self-)representation of the middle and upper classes, and the general narrative of social mobility within and outside of neoliberal Mexico.

But my central contention is that the circulation of symbolic capital in translation has become the *same paradigm* for hegemonic national productions in their original language. There is the narrative in dialogue with transnational literary fields (high culture novels by Álvaro Enrigue, Jorge Volpi's and Pedro Ángel Palou's "crack" novels, the fantastic and sci-fi narratives by Alberto Chimal and Bernardo Fernández "BEF" come to mind). On the obverse side, there are those who fictionalize the problematic past and present of the Mexican national project vis-à-vis a general failure of Western modernity (the narco-literature of Yuri Herrera and Juan Pablo Villalobos, the narratives of extreme poverty and undocumented migration of Antonio Ortuño, Emiliano Monge, and Julián Herbert, the detective noirs of Élmer Mendoza and Martín Solares, the gender and subjective critiques of Cristina Rivera Garza and Guadalupe Nettel, for example). I argue that these trends are constitutive of "Mexican literature" *before* and *after* translation as they are by-products of the process of neoliberalization that has profoundly modified the literary field and its institutions toward a horizon of expectations appealing to a middle- and upper-class readership in Mexico and abroad. Both in its original language and in translation, this "Mexican literature" may be read as a condensing metaphor for the country's entire literary field mediated by the effect of neoliberalism as the epistemic grounding of general Mexican culture and society in the twenty-first century.

"World Literature" as the Neoliberal Literary Field in Mexico

Critical insights on Western theories of "world literature" often adhere to what is rightly seen as a methodological flaw at the moment of inscription of a corpus of study. From the influential works of David Damrosch, Pascale Casanova, and Franco Moretti, the circulation of literature in English translation within capital centers of cultural power, what is termed "world literature," is necessarily an institutionalized and reductive expression of national literary productions as they struggle for global visibility. As Stefan Helgesson and Pieter Vermeulen observe, "world literature" has been criticized justifiably as "a flattening paradigm, all too enamoured of the ways in which literature *does* travel instead of studying the multifarious ways in which it *does not*."[14] This critique is also applicable to influential interventions written by Latin American scholars working within the US academic mainstream, in particular from those institutions articulating the hegemonic formulations of "world literature" relocating American and comparative literature studies as the disciplinary *loci* for this discussion.[15] To this contention, there have been visible efforts to restitute and trace the complexity and peculiarity of the non-English-language fields vis-à-vis the dominant approaches to "world literature." As Ignacio Sánchez Prado argues, "world literature" scholarship has often perpetrated a systemic erasure of Latin America as a region due to a "pervasive inattention to the specificities of each national literary and cultural field."[16]

Scholars such as Lois Parkinson Zamora, Silvia Spitta, Emily Apter, and Sánchez Prado himself have written convincing critiques of "world literature" by turning instead to a detailed study of the specific material conditions of cultural production independently from its transnational circulation, expanding the all-too-predictable canons of Latin American literature in translation. Drawing on the work of Djelal Kadir, Zamora and Spitta have posed the question of Western hegemony to argue that "the positioning of the United States *as elsewhere* with respect to the rest of the hemisphere—whether we live and work in the US or in other parts of the world—necessarily conditions, and complicates, our efforts."[17] Following Barbara Cassin's notion of the "untranslatable," Apter questions in turn the circulation of books in translation by demonstrating how the literatures of the world, as an unreachable totality, "mess with world literature, turning it into a process of translating untranslatably."[18] More recently, Sánchez Prado's *Strategic Occidentalism* proposes to shed light on "the construction of a national world literature" in order to "decenter narratives on the circulation of literary aesthetics that are naturalized by global approaches."[19]

While these critical examinations of "world literature" compellingly point at the insufficiency of the model to grasp the complexity of the literary production of any given country, I look at the radical transformation of the literary fields in Latin America, in particular in those countries where writing practices are deeply mediated by class and racial conditions between the *criollo* elites and hegemonic cultural institutions.[20] While there are evident historical differences in the structures of each literary field, there has been a clear shift in the circulation of literature both in the original Spanish and in English translation that links them on the same epistemic grounding.

This leveling effect comes from the interiorization of neoliberalism as the organizing principle in the literary fields of Mexico, Colombia, Chile, and Argentina, predominantly. As a result, young writers emerge with very similar projects and analogous editorial expectations for their novels and short stories. Sarah Pollack has noted how the works of young writers such as Alejandro Zambra (Chile), Antonio Ortuño (Mexico), Juan Gabriel Vásquez (Colombia), and Pola Oloixarac (Argentina), among others, share the same conditions of possibility as they are framed within dominant politics of representation that are no longer limited to those expected in translation for the US editorial market, but also for each of those literary fields at the moment of their inscription in the original language. By analyzing various anthologies of recent Latin American fiction translated into English, Pollack finds that they advance two complementary and reductive visions of Latin America as the sociopolitical object of contemporary "Latin American literature": "they either project themselves as reiterative variations of a precarious and marginal Latin American society, or they narrate an experience of a decadent middle and upper-class that has lost all sense and suffers irreversible existential angst."[21] In this, Pollack shows an emptying of historical and political markers embedded in Latin American literature during the twentieth century, leaving the anthologies *outside* of the symbolic territory where the question of *latinoamericanismo* posed by the region's intellectuals (Martí, Rodó, Reyes, Mariátegui, Retamar) has been explicitly renounced by the most recent generations of writers.[22]

"Are we perhaps a region destined to be anthologized?" wonders Liliana Weinberg as she examines the political and cultural role of the anthology in the neoliberal market.[23] As writers face a crisis of Latin American modernity and the viability of the nation-state, Weinberg laments what she calls a "text drain" in the region's literary fields, that is, "a shrinking of public spaces for dialogue, discussion, and joint construction and sharing, as well as a loss of the sense of specificity in artistic and literary practices."[24] Weinberg draws in turn from Josefina Ludmer's notion of "post-autonomous literature," through which the latter signaled the deep neoliberal transformation after which "everything cultural (and literary) is economic and everything economic is cultural (and literary)."[25] Pointing at a sort of post-foundational condition, Ludmer saw in her early examination of neoliberalism and culture (originally published in 2006) that literary works at the beginning of the twenty-first century resisted basic social categorizations defining their representational status to the point that even the grounding notion of the literary seemed disavowed:

> Post-autonomous literatures of the present would leave "literature," they would cross the borders, and they would enter a milieu (into a matter) real-virtual, without an outside, the public imagination: in all that is produced and circulates and penetrates us and is social and private and public and "real".[26]

The definition of this new "public imagination" announced some of the essential conditions for the Mexican literary field in the following decade. The controversies surrounding Taibo II and Luiselli are symptomatic in this context: they are inscribed in media debates about government institutions and social movements in direct tension with a personal stance that destabilizes the division between the private and the public. While Taibo II and Luiselli may be located in different, even opposing, poles of the political spectrum, their interventions may, and should, be considered as effects of the same structure of signification in which the Mexican literary field is leveled with those of the United States and Europe. This occurs in part because they also function as extensions of those fields abroad in an expansive "public imagination" where the economic blends with the artistic and as such it is always interconnected through a consumerist experience of mass media, social networks, and the transnational immediacy of books, newspaper columns, interviews, and public literary events. This is how, in the neoliberal era, the national is dispersed, exteriorized, in the simultaneously public and private transnational agora of the neoliberal present.

The Transnational Literary Field and Social Distinction

David Harvey locates a radical shift in Western modernity with the 1968 movements across the world, when counterculture and an effervescent reaction to a standardized understanding of the state as bureaucratic, authoritarian, and repressor of social change inadvertently accompanied a sentiment of rebellion against modernist values associated with a radical rejection of government structures and all institutions of power.

It was almost as if the universal pretensions of modernity had, when combined with liberal capitalism and imperialism, succeeded so well as to provide a material and political foundation for a cosmopolitan, transnational, and hence global movement of resistance to the hegemony of high modernist culture.[27]

Following Harvey's analysis (and for that matter Fredric Jameson's), the question about postmodernism is without doubt a precedent to the hegemony of neoliberalism as the current logic of cultural production. But the concept of postmodernism as a keyword, while it maintains certain validity in PhD programs of American studies and comparative literature in the United States, must be explained through the history of neoliberalism as it became the central signifier of Western societies in the 1990s, as Harvey's work shows us. Connected with the individualistic search for freedom and expression, first with the irruption of the rebellious 1968 movements, then with the fall of the Berlin Wall in 1989 announcing the end of the Cold War, neoliberalism was consolidated as the dominant paradigm along with the assumed decline of polarizing states with competing ideologies or "master narratives." In this respect, Harvey signals the historical process brought about by a mentality that originated in that global call for individual freedom:

> the promoters of the new gospel found a ready audience in that wing of the 1968 movement whose goal was greater individual liberty and freedom from state power and the manipulations of monopoly capital [...] capitalism reorganized to both open a space for individual entrepreneurship and switch its efforts to satisfy innumerable niche markets.[28]

Within this sociopolitical framework, dissident intellectuals are not only expected but actually utilized as mediators of the neoliberal rationale because, in its conceptual foundation from the works to Friedrich Hayek to Milton Friedman, neoliberalism is primarily the platform for individual protest against presupposed governmental and monopolized market tyranny and in favor of action "against the grain," of consumer diversity, in short, for rebellion and individual choice.

Harvey's point is perhaps better understood for the case in point with a critique of neoliberalism written from a Mexican perspective, as sociologist Fernando Escalante Gonzalbo explains:

> The result is a displacement of the axis of discussion in the public space, in the entire world. Individualism, a preference for market solutions, economic freedom, are the undebatable starting point. And there remains, on the other hand, a residual left, nostalgic, that adopts precisely the attitudes foreseen in the script offering the best imaginable support for neoliberalism: a left denouncing all that is new, content with labeling it "neoliberal" as if that were enough, cornered in the defense of the past. That is, a left that serves to confirm that there is no alternative.[29]

It is not difficult to see how neoliberalism and counterculture currents share basic values such as independent thinking, unrestrained freedom—in particular from official institutions—minority identity politics, and even the opposition to the "war on drugs." This is perhaps the most complex aspect of neoliberalism as the central signifier of the social and the cultural, for it guarantees the articulation of elite discourse as much as that from its opposing challenges.

In Mexico's literary field, this explains the simultaneous visibility of writers like Luiselli and Taibo II. Both are propelled by the same market of symbolic goods that caters to cosmopolitan high culture and populist nationalism alike. Luiselli's works have earned numerous awards and recognitions in the United States and abroad, frequently showcased by elite publications such as *The New Yorker* and *The New York Times*. On a different zone of the neoliberal market, Taibo II has a cult following as the author of popular detective fictions (competing with celebrity detective writers such as Henning Mankell) and one of the bestselling biographies of Ernesto "Che" Guevara (challenging the *auctoritas* of acclaimed US journalist Jon Lee Anderson's own biography of the iconic revolutionary figure), and more recently with highly popular documentaries on Mexico's history and political events streaming online through Netflix.

This is the radical difference from Latin America's long bipolar history between national and cosmopolitan literatures. Pedro Henríquez Ureña famously noted the reiterative inscription of these two currents as they replayed their expected differences across the twentieth century, from the regional novels of Ricardo Güiraldes and José Eustasio Rivera in tension with the stylized fiction of Macedonio Fernández and Jorge Luis Borges, to Mexico's fierce debates between the avant-garde group of Contemporáneos and its critics from the nationalist literary establishment. Henríquez Ureña observed in his 1949 study: "The quarrel, then, narrows itself to whether—as would happen if either faction had its way—no artist or writer is to be allowed to introduce social and political questions in his work or whether every artist and writer is to be compelled to introduce them."[30]

This same discussion was apparently extended to the 1990s with the emergence of the "crack" writers (Jorge Volpi, Pedro Ángel Palou, and Ignacio Padilla most notably) who denounced the outdated and redundant demand for the lucrative "magical realism" formula by editors in Mexico and abroad, symbolically breaking away from the imitators of "boom" writers like Gabriel García Márquez, Carlos Fuentes, and Mario Vargas Llosa. But in what John Beverly termed the "neoconservative turn," "crack" writers in fact reactivated the cosmopolitan debates of the 1920s and 1930s as a reaction to the flattening of the Mexican literary field entering the neoliberal transformation of the social and cultural space, blurring the lines between high and low culture, and between the lettered city and the commercially successful circulation of recycled Latin American fiction.[31]

The bipolar tension between these century-old currents was, thus, bridged by the full neoliberal turn of the 2000s. As Mexico's editorial scene became dominated by transnational conglomerates such as Penguin-Random House or diversified by specialized, boutique, independent publishers such as Almadía and Sexto Piso, "Mexican literature" became an increasingly predictable corpus. Instead of the symbolic space for disputing hegemony between the two competing narratives of the national vs. the cosmopolitan, the neoliberal literary field opened up significant places for both currents to coexist without the need for struggle. Since the 1990s, not only are both currents comfortably legitimized, but they actually correspond to matching interchangeable audiences domestically and abroad. That is the reason why international literary festivals like the book fairs of Guadalajara and Frankfurt are environments encouraging intense political discussion but also the uninterrupted meeting grounds of choice to negotiate translation deals and film rights, guaranteeing the continuity of the global editorial marketplace in either side of the planet.

The process of "privatization of culture" in Mexico since the 1980s, as studied by Lomnitz, has instigated the construction of a separate space of sociopolitical significance for writers and intellectuals who no longer identified with the national project and that instead form clusters of legitimacy through independent publishing companies and audiovisual monopolies.[32] Here we find precisely the milieu from which writers such as Valeria Luiselli emerged, in connection with the center-right leaning collectives formed around magazines like *Nexos* and *Letras Libres*. But this distinction of high culture no longer means an exclusive operation for the privatized literary field, but only one of its multiple expressions. This explains why Taibo II came in as a replacement choice for the post of director of the Fondo de Cultura Económica after Margo Glantz, a writer and critic often associated with Mexico City's cultural elites, in many ways in the opposite political spectrum. Seen from the perspective of the transnational literary field, it is logical that even as a public official managing the government's publisher, bookstores, and cultural centers, Taibo II assertively announced that he would not "renounce his life as a writer," that is, his *private* position as a public intellectual.[33]

According to Pierre Bourdieu, the autonomy of the literary field meant "to give primacy to that of which artist is master, i.e., form, manner, style, rather than the 'subject', the external referent."[34] In the neoliberal literary field, however, both form and content are no longer the active choice of the writer, but a wide range of possibilities always already codified, expected, rewarded. Even the very work of those critical of the history of neoliberalism in the Western world (David Harvey, Naomi Klein, Wendy Brown, and Paul Krugman, for example) is also conveniently promoted by the same platforms that allow for independent, counter-hegemonic discourse, namely, mainstream corporate media like *The New York Times*, editorial conglomerates such as Farrar, Straus and Giroux, and even the online streaming platform YouTube. Consequently, "Mexican literature" does not fall short from reflecting and denouncing class divisions, xenophobia, and segregation, with part of the intellectual class expressing leftist positions welcomed and published in the same presses where the reader may find radical opposing views.

I locate in this point my main contention against scholarship seeking to study the singularity of Latin American writing and its place with national literatures facing the transnational editorial market. In his book, Sánchez Prado explains, for example, that "strategic Occidentalism" names "the way in which specific writers, particularly from a 'semiperipheral' tradition like Mexico's, adopt a cosmopolitan stance to acquire cultural capital within their national tradition." Leading Mexican writers, he argues, deploy this deliberately assumed form of Occidentalism "through the translation and vindication of marginal traditions and authors and the formulation of literary aesthetics, poetics, and politics that do not replicate hegemonic waves of influence, but instead seek to reconstruct networks of cosmopolitan works through practice."[35] While Sánchez Prado's erudite understanding of the Mexican literary field may be applicable to most of the twentieth century's productions, it implies that in the twenty-first century there remains a national *interior* that somehow stays untouched by hegemonic forms of Occidentalism, waiting in what seems to be a hypothetical *exterior*, that writers strategically appropriate to engage "world literature" transnationally. Conversely, I contend that, less than a carefully adopted strategy, the transnational condition of "Mexican literature"—at least in the first two decades of the twenty-first century—is present from the first inscription in the original language. It is the resulting effect of being the *only* mode of articulating a legible literary work. If other writers in this field working within either of the two currents are not translated and lack the visibility of their celebrated peers, it is not because the latter managed to be "more strategic" than the former, but because they would be redundant iterations in an editorial market sufficiently stocked—of the proverbial three percent of books in translation in the United States—of "Mexican literature."[36]

Rebuilding a National Literary Field

On February 7, 2018, *The New York Times* published a profile of Valeria Luiselli that recalled a performance of a musical version of Cervantes's "Don Quixote" with children from a Brooklyn-based educational center singing in Luiselli's living room in her New York City apartment. This event followed Luiselli's attention to the crisis of unaccompanied undocumented children from Mexico and Central America processed by the complex and dysfunctional immigration courts of the United States. Her involvement as court translator for the children led to the writing of her acclaimed essay *Tell Me How It Ends. An Essay in Forty Questions* (2017) and ultimately to her novel *Lost Children Archive* (2019), a fictionalized account of a road trip to the US Southwest region, written "as a loudspeaker for all my political rage."[37] In what may be the final stage of the neoliberal integration of the transnational literary field of Mexico and the United States, Luiselli chose to write this novel directly in English. In a first instance, this book could be studied as an example of what Deleuze and Guattari called "minor literature," that is, literary works written by a writer from a linguistic minority that embarks in a process of "deterritorialization" by writing in a dominant language in order to subvert its symbolic coordinates and to populate it with other subjectivities, disrupting vocabulary and a vindicated alternative world view.[38] But a closer look may reveal the logical consequence of the transnational literary field that makes writing in the original language simply unnecessary. Perhaps this anticipates that even the question of translation may become secondary to the neoliberal circulation of symbolic capital between elite writers who adopt English not just as the desirable platform for social mobility, but as the *only* platform.

Also in 2019, Paco Ignacio Taibo II's documentary *Patria,* based on a novel trilogy about the nineteenth-century wars between Mexican conservatives and liberals, became available for streaming on Netflix. It shows Taibo II narrating those events by traveling to historical sites and interviewing local experts with a strongly committed political angle, reproducing the narrative structures of globalized serial shows such as Anthony Bourdain's *Parts Unknown* or Morgan Freeman's *The Story of God,* where both hosts travel the world interviewing experts and shedding light on various cultures and traditions. On a first analysis, these documentaries may be understood as effective political interventions to democratically alter what Jacques Rancière's calls the "partition of the sensible," the regime that legitimates new subjects and objects as they become visible and audible so that they may be considered to exercise a self-assigned right to speak and to be heard.[39] In these accounts, however, we must pay attention to the reinvigorated transnational literary field that is not only uncontested by the irruption of the supposedly democratic "part of those without a part," but it is in fact *enriched* by it. The same phenomenon has carved a place for the alternative, community-driven production of the editorial "cartoneras" in various cities of Latin America and Europe. The low-cost production of artisanal books handmade with recycled cardboards, printing texts by emerging and consolidated authors who ceded all copyrights, is nonetheless an expression of the same flexibility and malleability of the neoliberal book market. While the original project conceived by Argentinean *provocateur* Washington Cucurto was aimed at challenging the pernicious "savage capitalism" in the region, most "cartoneras"—including the Mexican version—often "operate in different niche and with a more selective public than its Argentinean predecessor. They integrate themselves to the socioeconomic, demographic and culturally idiosyncratic context."[40]

What is the route, if any, out of the neoliberal entrapment of the literary field? Following a close reading of Roberto Bolaño's works, I have argued elsewhere for the possibility not only of a counter-hegemonic, post-Occidental, Latin American literature but also for the truly disruptive articulation of literary practices that could lead to an alternative experience of the region's modernity.[41] Considering the key decolonial interventions of Anibal Quijano and Enrique Dussel, among others, Bolaño joined a minority of Mexican writers such as Daniel Sada, Juan Villoro, Cristina Rivera Garza, and Sara Uribe who open different avenues to craft, in fact to *imagine,* literary writing emanating from forms of community that allow for a second life of the nation-state *after* neoliberalism.[42] But placing such demand, as we have frequently done with our critical scholarship, on one or several singular literary projects (Borges, Arguedas, Lezama Lima, Guimarães Rosa, Rulfo, Bolaño), misses again the gravity of the neoliberal impasse and can hardly account for the emancipation of an entire literary field.

This is where the institutions of "world literature" can teach us a final lesson. Their consistent organization of a coherent subfield allows for the deployment and mobilization of hegemonic interpretations of literary productions that generate the symbolic power of the very institutions enunciating their chosen literary productions on those terms. They in fact *invent* their objects and the rules for their interpretation first and foremost because they have the material foundations to do so with the constant work of university research centers, publishers, conferences, awards, and recognitions, and, most importantly, the close collaboration of writers themselves. Harvard's Institute for World Literature; editorial conglomerates like Penguin-Random House and HarperCollins; independent publishers such as New Directions, Coffee House Press, and Deep Velum; cultural festivals such as Pen World Voices; influential magazines like *The New Yorker* and *Los Angeles Review of Books*; and distinctions like the National Book Award and the Pulitzer Prize all build collectively what James F. English calls "the economy of prestige."[43]

Far from the active construction of a national literary field, Mexican cultural institutions, publishers, research centers, and certainly Mexican writers operate as extrapolated franchises of the US and the European editorial and media markets. In this context, the 2018 election of left-leaning president Andrés Manuel López Obrador may renew a discussion about how to rebuild our literary field independently of the neoliberal principle of sociopolitical organization. Taibo II's plan to reprint classics of Mexican literature at reduced prices may be a humble first step, but cultural independence can occur only with a greater effort to generate national industries in all sectors, as Frantz Fanon urged in his seminal work *The Wretched of the Earth* (1961). As it is known, Fanon diagnosed Latin America's subalternization as the result of a greedy bourgeois class that functions primarily as the mediator for colonial exploitation, providing raw materials for immediate gains without any interest in promoting national industries and production. Fanon's critique extends to the creative class, which he saw dominated by the same colonizing foreign imaginary to which the Latin American intellectual passively directs his attention:

> The colonized intellectual, at the very moment when he undertakes a work of art, fails to realize he is using techniques and a language borrowed from the occupier. He is content to cloak these instruments in a style that is meant to be national but which is strangely reminiscent of exoticism. The colonized intellectual who returns to his people through works of art behaves in fact like a foreigner.[44]

If we consider the two currents that I have discussed in these pages, we may attest to the profound interiorization of the neoliberal imaginary as Mexican writers maintain their attention directed to the strategies of representation that are most likely to gain recognition in what I have called the transnational literary field, domestically and abroad. While they demonstrate extraordinary skill and talent, this is the case for most of the commercially successful writers of "Mexican literature" today. Emiliano Monge's *Las tierras arrasadas* (2015, *The Arid Sky*, 2018) and Antonio Ortuño's *La fila india* (2016), for example, dramatize the tragedy of undocumented migration, the failure of the Mexican state, and the overall precarization of Mexican society, confirming the typical assumptions of the reader of "Mexican literature" in capital cities like New York or London. The same may be said of Martín Solares's detective novel *No manden flores* (2018, *Don't Send Flowers* 2018) and Fernanda Melchor's stylized crime thriller *Temporada de Huracanes* (2017, *Hurricane Season* 2020). On the other hand, recent novels by young writers like Aura Xilonen's *Campeón* Gabacho (2015, *The Gringo Champion* 2017) or by established authors like Álvaro Enrigue's *Ahora me rindo y eso es todo* (2018) seem to be "born in translation," following Rebecca Walkowitz's term, as they work directly with US cultural, historical, and political referents.[45]

As with the creative class, academic scholarship faces a similar challenge for the immediate future. Mexicanists, whether in Mexico or elsewhere, should engage in the same effort to rebuild a national literary field. This is the process, described again by Fanon, of intellectual emancipation: "Whereas the colonized intellectual started out by producing work exclusively with the oppressor in mind—either in order to charm him or to denounce him by using ethnic or subjectivist categories—he gradually switches over to addressing himself to his people."[46] Our work as critics begins similarly in the exact moment in which, from a national perspective, we *name* our own objects of study and the horizon of intelligibility on which they should be studied, This was, of course, the essential operation of the landmarks of our century-old *latinoamericanismo*. José Enrique Rodó's "Arielism," Ángel Rama's "transculturation," Oswaldo de Andrade's "antropofagia," Roberto Fernández Retamar's "Calibán," and José Lezama Lima's "baroque expression," among many others, served as central signifiers to explain the main cultural processes of the twentieth century. It ought to be considered our intellectual problem as Latin American scholars in the United States and elsewhere that, at the beginning of the new century, one of our most recurrent academic debates still revolves around the question of how "marginal" Latin American writers may be visible by the institutions of "world literature." It is time to renounce it for a renovated Latin Americanist agenda in our own terms.

Notes

1 Redacción, "Taibo II, de 'fusilamientos' a 'meterla doblada,'" *El Universal*, December 4, 2018. https://www.eluniversal.com.mx/cultura/letras/taibo-ii-de-fusilamientos-meterla-doblada.
2 See https://forum.wordreference.com/threads/se-las-la-metimos-doblada.3525805/.
3 Valeria Luiselli, "Nuevo feminismo," *El País*, February 13, 2017. https://elpais.com/elpais/2017/02/12/opinion/1486916548_132338.html. The newspaper website indicates that it modified the controversial line at the request of Luiselli.
4 Oswaldo Zavala, "'La libertad de pasar por alto lo innecesario': Valeria Luiselli, Gilberto Owen y el giro neoliberal," in *Volver a la modernidad. Genealogías de la literature mexicana de fin de siglo* (Barcelona: Albatros, 2017), 151–73.
5 "El feminismo actual me produce bostezos: Valeria Luiselli," *El Informador*, February 22, 2017. Blogger Esther M. García saved a screenshot of the original article published online: http://lobasuncuartopropio.blogspot.com/2017/02/respuesta-valeria-luiselli-parte-1.html.
6 I am drawing here from Pedro Henríquez Ureña's concept of "literary current" describing long-term genealogies of literary groups, trends, and movements, as they are disrupted by transforming sociopolitical events. I will later come back

to this point. See: Pedro Henríquez Ureña, *Literary Currents in Hispanic America* (Cambridge, MA: Harvard University Press, 1949).

7   Pierre Bourdieu, *The Field of Cultural Production* (New York: Columbia University Press, 1993), 164.
8   Djelal Kadir, "Literature, the World, and You," in *The Common Growl. Towards a Poetics of Precarious Community*, ed. Thomas Claviez (New York: Fordham University Press, 2016), 78.
9   David Damrosch, *What Is World Literature?* (Princeton: Princeton University Press, 2003), 6.
10 Edel Cadena Vargas, "El neoliberalismo en México: saldos económicos y sociales," *Quivera* 7, no. 1 (Enero-Junio, 2005): 198–236.
11 Bolívar Echeverría, *Modernidad y blanquitud* (México: Era, 2010).
12 Ryan F. Long, *Fictions of Totality. The Mexican Novel, 1968, and the National Popular State* (West Lafayette: Purdue University Press, 2008).
13 Claudio Lomnitz, *La nación desdibujada. México en trece ensayos* (Barcelona: Malpaso, 2016). I will return to this argument as I advance my critique of the contemporary Mexican literary field.
14 Stefan Helgesson and Pieter Vermeulen, eds., *Institutions of World Literature: Writing, Translation, Markets* (New York: Routledge, 2016), 1.
15 I have argued this point in length in the works of scholars such as Héctor Hoyos and Mariano Siskind. See Oswaldo Zavala, "The Repolitization of the Latin American Shore: Roberto Bolaño and the Dispersion of 'World Literature,'" in *Roberto Bolaño as World Literature*, ed. Nicholas Birns and Juan E. De Castro (New York: Bloomsbury, 2017), 79–98.
16 Ignacio Sánchez Prado, *Strategic Occidentalism: On Mexican Fiction, the Neoliberal Book Market and the Question of World Literature* (Evanston: Northwestern University Press, 2018), 12.
17 Silvia Spitta and Lois Parkinson Zamora, "The Americas, Otherwise," *Comparative Literature* 61, no. 3 (Summer 2009): 195.
18 Emily Apter, *Against World Literature: On the Politics of Untranslatability* (New York: Verso, 2013), 18.
19 Sánchez Prado, *Strategic Occidentalism*, 13.
20 The long history of racism resulting from the practices of racial distinction constructed since colonial times in Mexico and most of Latin America explains the hegemony of the *criollo* class (white Mexicans with close migrant predecessors from European countries, in particular Spain). See Federico Navarrete, *México racista. Una denuncia* (México: Grijalbo, 2016).
21 Sarah Pollack, "Sin Macondo, sin futuro, sin política: las antologías de narrativa latinoamericana contemporánea en traducción," in *En camas separadas. Historia y literatura en el México del siglo XX*, ed. David Miklos (México: Tusquets y CIDE, 2016), 228. My translation.
22 See, for example, the prologue to the anthology *The Future Is Not Ours*, edited by Peruvian author Diego Trelles Paz. While he highlights that historical past may still be a "literary theme," Latin America as a sociopolitical space is no longer of central interest to those writers included: "Not the roots, not the traditions, much less outdated concepts such as nationality or the homeland, pose a limit now to our unconditional pact with fiction." Diego Trelles Paz, *El futuro no es nuestro*. Nueva

narrative latinoamericana (Oaxaca: Sur+ 2011), 21–2 (my translation). Significantly, this anthology was published in various Latin American countries and in English translation, mostly including established writers publishing in transnational publishers, such as Daniel Alarcón, Santiago Roncagliolo, Juan Gabriel Vasquez, and Samanta Schweblin.

23 Liliana Weinberg, "The Oblivion We Will Be: The Latin American Literary Field after Autonomy," in *Institutions of World Literature: Writing, Translation, Markets*, ed. Stefan Helgesson and Pieter Vermeulen (New York: Routledge, 2016), 76.
24 Ibid.
25 Josefina Ludmer, "Literaturas postautónomas 2.01," *Propuesta Educativa Número 32* 2 (November 2009): 42.
26 Ibid., 45.
27 David Harvey, *The Condition of Postmodernity: An Enquiry into the Origins of Cultural Change* (Cambridge: Blackwell Publishers, 1990), 38.
28 David Harvey, "Neoliberalism as Creative Destruction," *The Annals of the American Academy of Political and Social Science*, Vol. 610, NAFTA and Beyond: Alternative Perspectives in the Study of Global Trade and Development (March 2007): 22–44, 31.
29 Fernando Escalante Gonzalbo, *Historia mínima del neoliberalismo* (México: Turner, 2016), 189–90.
30 Henríquez Ureña, *Literary Currents in Hispanic America*, 194.
31 John Beverly, *Latinamericanism after 9/11* (Durham: Duke University Press, 2011).
32 Lomnitz, *La nación desdibujada*, 225.
33 Noticieros Televisa, "Paco Ignacio Taibo II encabezará FCE en lugar de Margo Glantz," *Televisa.com*, October 5, 2018.
34 Pierre Bourdieu, *Distinction: A Social Critique of the Judgment of Taste*, trans. Richard Nice (Cambridge, MA: Harvard University Press, 1984), 3.
35 Sánchez Prado, *Strategic Occidentalism*, 18–19.
36 I refer here to Chad Post's popular website *Three Percent*, based at the University of Rochester, committed to the promotion of literature in English translation as it represents, according to his calculation, about three percent of all published works in the United States. See: http://www.rochester.edu/college/translation/threepercent/.
37 Concepción de León, "Valeria Luiselli, at Home in Two Worlds," *The New York Times*, February 7, 2019.
38 Gilles Deleuze and Félix Guattari, *Kafka: Toward a Minor Literature*, trans. Dana Polan (Minneapolis: University of Minnesota Press, 1986).
39 Jacques Rancière, *The Politics of Literature*, trans. Julie Rose (Cambridge: Polity, 2011).
40 Jania Kudaibergen, "Las editoriales cartoneras y los procesos de empoderamiento en la industria creativa mexicana," *Cuadernos Americanos* 152, no. 2 (2015): 127–46, 135.
41 Oswaldo Zavala, *La modernidad insufrible. Roberto Bolaño en los límites de la literatura latinoamericana contemporánea* (Chapel Hill: University of North Carolina Press, North Carolina Studies in the Romance Languages and Literatures Series, 2015).
42 See, for the case of Sada, my article: "La genealogía *otra* de la modernidad latinoamericana: Daniel Sada y la literatura mundial," *Latin American Literary Review* 40, no. 79 (2012): 23–44.

43 James F. English, *The Economy of Prestige: Prizes, Awards, and the Circulation of Cultural Value* (Cambridge, MA: Harvard University Press, 2005).
44 Frantz Fanon, *The Wretched of the Earth*, trans. Richard Philcox (New York: Grove Press, 2004), 160.
45 Rebecca L. Walkowitz, *Born Translated: The Contemporary Novel in the Age of World Literature* (New York: Columbia University Press, 2015).
46 Fanon, *The Wretched of the Earth*, 173.

15

Planetary Poetics of Extinction in Contemporary Mexican Poetry

Carolyn Fornoff

The turn to world literature asks what happens when we stop equating Mexican literature with the delimited confines of the nation-state. Such a turn necessitates a methodological pivot. Rather than read literature written by Mexican authors for what it tells us about the nation or *mexicanidad*, we might look for how it maps alternative geographies or timescales that are smaller, larger, or more scattered than the spatial-temporal bounds of the nation. Such a pivot can be tricky, since the field of Mexican cultural studies has long articulated its importance within the US academy as based on its ability to shed light on cultural objects and themes that are distinctively Mexican. An unwitting result of such an approach is that cultural products that are not explicitly concerned with autochthonous issues are often excluded from dominant conversations in the field. In part this is because stepping outside of the here and now is perceived as a move that is problematically apolitical. Detachment from the local context can slide dangerously into what Donna Haraway has critiqued as "the view from nowhere," a disembodied stance that elides accountability for the blind spots of one's situated perspective.[1]

Nonetheless, the assumption that Mexican works of literature are primarily valuable insomuch as they speak about Mexico rather than about "universal" or deterritorialized themes is a demand with troublingly colonial echoes. It recreates the stakes of the battle waged by the *modernistas* at the end of the nineteenth century, who combated the pigeonholing of Latin American writers as interpreters of local difference, and instead laid claim to the ability to write about anything or anywhere. Even now, in the twenty-first century, the act of writing the world from Mexico is an assertion of the legitimacy and value of Mexican interpretations of processes that do not originate in the national context. The invocation of the world also combats insularity by bringing far-flung events and processes into localized literary conversations, encouraging readers to draw connections between the past and present, the local and the remote.

Reading for the world also means reading for the planet in the material sense. According to Wai Chee Dimock, such an approach takes its "measure from the durations and extensions of the human species itself," rather than the arbitrary temporal and geographic coordinates of the nation.[2] This method questions the totalizing project of the nation by reframing it within the broader context of the human experience as a species—a species that is only one among many. At the close of *Against World Literature*, Emily Apter similarly advocates that a shift from world to planet is necessitated by the swelling urgency of "earthly extinction."[3] Most recently, Jennifer Wenzel put forth the concept of "world-imagining" to refer to a type of environmentalist literary engagement with the world geared toward "forging new modes of relation among humans and with nonhuman nature."[4] Following these efforts to center the earthly realm in approaches to world literature, this chapter considers how Mexican poets broach matters of planetary concern in ways that reach beyond national borders and even the bounds of species. These spatial, temporal, and ontological jumps are a defining characteristic of contemporary Mexican poetry concerned with environmental themes, which I term *planetary poetics*.

This chapter explores one subtheme within contemporary Mexican planetary poetics: extinction. Anxiety about the futurity of life and the irreversibility of death on a planetary scale has become an increasingly visible topic in art throughout the world. Extinction impends on the horizon, no longer solely understood as a historical or natural process, but something that is ongoing, accelerating, and a distinct possibility for our own species. The temporality of extinction is multiple; it is a common thread that conjoins the deep past with the present and the far-off future. Extinction has become what Joanna Zylinska describes as "a looming affective fact" that circulates "not just as a concept but also as a set of material conditions."[5] This chapter analyzes the planetary poetics of extinction of two contemporary Mexican poets: Karen Villeda and Isabel Zapata. Villeda and Zapata write respectively about the extinction of the dodo in *Dodo* [Dodo, 2013], and the thylacine (or Tasmanian tiger) in *Una ballena es un país* [A Whale Is a Country, 2019]. The extinctions that these poets highlight did not occur in Mexico, but on the islands of Mauritius, off the southeast coast of Africa, and Tasmania, to the south of Australia. Brought about by the arrival of settlers, these extinctions operate as cautionary historical examples of the irreparable impact of settler colonial violence on the human and more-than-human planet. Read together, Villeda and Zapata signal the imperative that Mexican poetry write the world in order to make visible the brutality of extinction and interrogate what comes after the end of life.

Planetary Fragility

The turn to broader temporal and spatial paradigms is especially resonant as processes of climate change affect the world on a global scale. The revelation that humans have geological impact has blurred the distinction between human history and the history of the planet, previously conceptualized as distinct temporal regimes. Humans are no longer just biological agents, but geological ones, with a collective force capable of altering the planet. In response to this collision of human and natural history, Dipesh Chakrabarty has famously argued that it is imperative to scale up: to think at the level of species or deep time.[6] This recognizes our shared inheritance of the transforming planet and our fragility on it. Indeed, the term *Anthropocene*, while polemical for its incorrect implication that this crisis has somehow been evenly engendered, is nonetheless evocative in linking the current geological era with the fate of the human species. As Richard Grusin darkly concludes, "to periodize the Anthropocene is already to assume a future world in which human presence on Earth has been reduced to a lithic layer."[7] Extinction is thus central to how the Anthropocene is narrated.

While the climate crisis is shared, it was not uniformly produced, nor are its effects evenly distributed. Consequently, scaling up to think at the level of the planet does not mean abandoning our skepticism of universal categories or dehistoricizing the processes of colonization and capital that brought us here. Rather it requires a balancing act that Chakrabarty describes as "a global approach . . . without the myth of global identity" that subsumes particularity.[8] Gayatri Spivak likewise argues that it is more useful to think at the level of the planetary than the global. Whereas the global suggests the abstract homogeneity of capitalism, the planetary decenters human design dreams and instead configures us as "planetary accidents."[9] The planet is the ultimate symbol of alterity for Spivak because it is out of reach of human mastery; it is a "determining experience," "mysterious and discontinuous—an experience of the impossible."[10] Foregrounding the planet moves past not only national borders but also the taxonomic lines of species that have been deployed since the Enlightenment to elevate the human above other forms of life, and some humans above others. Planetary ethical orientation is thus not limited to cosmopolitan unity across nations, but across species and life forms. Within such a framework, extinction signals the life-and-death stakes of anthropogenic world-making and world ending.

Extinction has a particular hold over the imagination because it marks a definitive end, an irremediable loss, and a point of no return. When a species becomes extinct it no longer exists in the biosphere; there are no remaining known members of that group. This loss ripples into the ecosystem with cascading consequences that are destructive or generative for the multispecies community. The effects of species loss are cumulative in ways that are not self-evident; the disappearance of one species might prompt the flourishing or unraveling of another. The decline of species richness—the diversity of taxonomic species—puts the stable functioning of the ecosystem into jeopardy.

Before now, the Earth has experienced five mass extinction events in its 600-million-year history. We are in the midst of a sixth mass extinction, which, unlike previous events, is tied to past and present human activities. Extinction is the direct result of capitalism, a system whose pursuit of continuous growth and ceaseless accumulation is premised on the commodification of the finite planet.[11] The sixth extinction is predicted to be the worst since the asteroid that wiped out the dinosaurs; current extinction rates are 1,000 times that of background levels considered "normal."[12] The International Union for Conservation of Nature Red List estimates that more than 27 percent of all assessed species are threatened with extinction.[13] This is a conservative appraisal, given that many species are data deficient: they have not been fully assessed, nor are all species known. Anthropogenic drivers of extinction include habitat destruction, overexploitation, pollution, and the introduction of non-native species. Occasionally extinction is immediate, like in the wake of site-specific land clearing. Usually it is a belated process that culminates decades or centuries after the initial habitat disruption. This temporal lag is referred to as "extinction debt": the future liability of present or past habitat destruction.[14] So while we often think about extinction as a single moment—the death of the last individual—these breakdowns are slow processes that are difficult to track, a gradual temporality Thom Van Dooren evocatively calls "the dull edge of extinction."[15]

While extinction holds great sway in the cultural imagination because of its decisiveness, it is not necessarily the best metric for assessing biodiversity loss. The focus on total eradication distracts from more ambiguous, yet insightful, conservation indicators like population diversity, which refers to the geographical distribution of species. Ursula Heise observes that if bees disappeared from most places in the world but survived in Italy, they would not technically be extinct, yet the results would be catastrophic for agriculture.[16] In other words, a species could be in gradual decline or persist in small numbers in zoos or laboratories ("functionally extinct"), and still considerably impact the ecosystem. Gerardo Ceballos, an ecologist at the Universidad Autónoma de México, and his co-authors at Stanford warn that regardless of extinction metrics, we are experiencing an era of "biological annihilation."[17] Wildlife abundance has decreased by more than 50 percent since 1970, and nearly a third of all vertebrate and mammal species are experiencing significant declines in population size and range.

Even though the focus on extinction might seem overly narrow to biologists, it is a highly effective narrative and aesthetic cue for communicating the urgency of environmental decline. Extinction is unambiguous; it marks a definitive loss. Its apocalyptic implications heighten its affective impact in cultural products aimed at awakening environmental consciousness. Like elsewhere in the world, in Mexico endangered species have become ubiquitous in popular cultural products, popping up in street murals, documentaries, food packaging, or as *alebrijes*. Particular attention is given to endangered flagship species whose habitat is rooted in Mexico, like the vaquita porpoise, leatherback sea turtle, and axolotl salamander. In contrast with less charismatic endangered species, like the totoaba fish, Cofre de Perote salamander, or Jico deer mouse (to name just a few endemic critically endangered species), these iconic animals are relatable and recognizable; their anthropomorphic features make them more endearing, and thus more effective affective tools. Their repeated cultural circulation makes extinction more visible, an important task given that most extinction processes take place at a remove from urban areas, out of sight, not noticeable until it is too late.

Two key precursors to contemporary Mexican planetary poetics of extinction are José Emilio Pacheco and Homero Aridjis. As early as 1976, Pacheco published a book of poetry, *Islas a la deriva* [Islands Adrift], that included a section of poems titled "Especies en peligro (y otras víctimas)" [Endangered Species (and other victims)]. There Pacheco interpreted extinction in the broadest of senses, as the possible foreclosure of everything from birds to whales to the work of art and the mermaid. Extinction is for Pacheco sign and symptom of broader societal ruin. His poem "Zopilote" [Vulture] concluded that the disappearance of the Californian condor, critically endangered at the time, would trigger a world awash in trash. Similarly, the poetic voice in "Augurios" [Auguries], included in the collection *Desde entonces* [From Now On, 1980], hypothesized that the recent disappearance of birds in Mexico City was due to air pollution. Or, he speculated, the birds sensed the city's imminent demise and fled.[18] In these poems Pacheco collapses nonhuman and human ruination, conceptualizing extinction as both allegorical of and the material consequence of the excesses of modernity.

Homero Aridjis likewise responded to the heightened visibility of ecological damage in Mexico in the eighties through poetry and activism. The foremost intellectual dedicated to conservation in Mexico, Aridjis founded in 1985 the Grupo de los Cien [Group of 100], a group of intellectuals united around the goal of greater environmental regulation. Among the many causes promoted by the Grupo were the protection of the Monarch butterfly from logging in 1986, the push to improve air quality in Mexico City through the "Hoy no circula" [Not Running Today] campaign in 1987, and the ban on the commercial sale of marine turtles in 1990.[19] In tandem with this localized activism (aimed at changes at the state level, achieved through collaboration with international conservation groups), Aridjis's poetry tackled extinction by highlighting flagship species like the whale and imperial woodpecker.[20] Compared with the tenacity of his activism, Aridjis's poetry is fatalistic, saturated in restless melancholia akin to what Apter terms "planetary dysphoria."[21] It frequently invokes apocalyptic, biblical images of the last members of the human race surrounded by silence and destruction, or anticipates this outcome as inevitable. For instance, in "Paraíso negro" [Black Paradise], the poetic voice pleas with "Our Lady of the Dead Planets" to "make sure we shall never lament the absence / of the whale from the sea, the elephant from the land, / or the eagle from the sky."[22] Extinction in this dirge is looming threat, a "Black Paradise" juxtaposed in implicit opposition to an idealized Eden.

In contrast with the melancholic, apocalyptic register of Pacheco and Aridjis's poems, contemporary Mexican poetry of extinction pivots away from speculative doom and gloom. This turn is somewhat surprising given that scientific evidence of ongoing biological annihilation is now more robustly alarming than it was in the eighties. We might hypothesize that this move away from melancholy and despair in part is a conscious effort to avoid abrasive modes associated with environmentalism, which has been perceived as preachy, judgmental, and sanctimonious. Rather than convince the public, these affective modalities have heightened distrust of environmentalist messaging, counteracting its intended impact.[23] In Mexico, environmentalism has also been wielded to advance neoliberal policy agendas like energy privatization, or in ways that unfairly impact or place blame on poor and racialized communities.[24] Within this context, Karen Villeda and Isabel Zapata's choice to narrate extinction through historical events that are temporally and geographically distant is a way of depoliticizing the issue while still retaining its planetary ethical implications. The dodo and the thylacine do not instinctively raise readers' hackles in same way the recently canceled Texcoco airport, the planned Tren Maya, or recent disputes between fishermen and conservationists in the Gulf of California do. These national polemics are already associated with specific political projects; readers approach them with preconceptions. By contrast, the extinction of the dodo and the thylacine does not carry this affective baggage. By narrating through distant, historical cases of extinction, Villeda and Zapata use case studies that are less politically charged and yet whose lessons are applicable to the ongoing sixth extinction, an event that is affecting the world on a global scale, while unfolding at the hyper-local level.

Second, the two extinction cases interpreted by Villeda and Zapata are historically proven. This differentiates them from the vexed task of tracking ongoing extinctions, which can be hard to decisively report. Even in cases of flagship species endemic to Mexico that are considered functionally extinct (no longer living in their natural habitat), like the axolotl or the imperial woodpecker, the open-ended nature of the species' survival makes them rhetorically slippery for thinking about the end of a world. Villeda and Zapata use definitive, historical cases of extinction to explore the vulnerability of life, and the swiftness with which an entire species can be wiped out. They approach extinction as a planetary question of ethical concern that is also a specific historical process, rather than a vague horizon of ruination.

Planetary Poetics of Extinction

The first living animal acknowledged, in writing, as eradicated by humans, the dodo is synonymous with extinction. Its disappearance in the mid-seventeenth century was a pivotal event in the nascent historical awareness of the irreversible impact of colonizers on the environments they traversed. It was the first categorical biological loss to be narrated in a way that implicated humans "causally, perhaps emotionally, and certainly ethically."[25] The dodo's extinction is thus a foundational cautionary tale of the destructiveness of planetary connectivity. Karen Villeda's poetry collection *Dodo* (2013) lingers on the brutality of extinction processes. Villeda weaves the dodo's reduction to a fragmented, lifeless body into the broader spectacle of patriarchal imperialist violence, foregrounding the brutality that is normally minimized in adventure narratives. *Dodo* underscores that violence against animals is not a unique expression of power, but inextricable from other exercises in dominance, be they sexual, racial, or geopolitical.

Dodo is narratively and thematically unified around the Dutch arrival to the island of Mauritius in the Indian Ocean in the late sixteenth century.[26] There sailors encountered the dodo, an unusual, large bird that proved easy to hunt given its inability to fly and unfamiliarity with predators. They also inadvertently introduced rats to the island. Although this latter fact goes unmentioned by Villeda, this new predator accelerated the dodo's decline by consuming its young, straining its ability to reproduce.[27] Less than 100 years after the arrival of the Dutch, the dodo was extinct.

Divided into seven sections, *Dodo* is chronologically structured around this encounter. It begins with Dutch Admiral Wybrand Van Warwijck's expedition to the island of Mauritius and culminates with the dodo's disappearance by the mid-seventeenth century. Each section contains seven paragraph-length prose poems; each poem is composed of seven clauses. In addition to the formal rigor of a structure disciplined around the number seven—including seven human characters—each prose poem is individually presented on the page, chunking the work into digestible pieces. This is an effective presentational strategy given Villeda's tendency toward challenging abstraction, manifest through the frequent absence of proper nouns, verbs, or identifiable subjects, signposts that typically facilitate the reader's ability to follow the text.

Dodo's structure resembles an epic or adventure travel narrative. It follows the seven sailors as they embark on their voyage, discover the island of Mauritius, encounter the dodo, explode into interpersonal sexual violence, hunt the bird to extinction, and depart the island. Yet while the book's chronology is linear, a complex repertoire of formal strategies scramble its discursive ease. Each poem is primarily narrated from an objective or omniscient third-person point of view, which provides fragmented images of a scene. This narration is interrupted by italicized lines that indicate that a subjective, first-person narrator is speaking. These first-person accounts interject emotions, memories, or observations that enrich or complicate the retelling. It is unclear who is speaking in these italicized moments, giving the sensation of a murky chorus of voices in a dark room. Similarly disorienting, in spite of the poem's linear chronology—from arrival to extinction—the narration is frequently severed from temporal cues. This effectively detaches this tale of extinction from its historical and spatial coordinates and suggests that extinction is not a linear phenomenon, but elliptical or cyclical.

Villeda is one of Mexico's foremost poets under forty. She is prolific and has published two children's books, four collections of poetry, and two books of essays. A notable characteristic of her work is its experimental use of multimedia. Villeda views poetry as an interactive art that should engage audiences beyond print. On her website, poetronica.net, Villeda blends verse with new media and digital technologies; she presents her poems as interactive games or Wikipedia-like collaborations. As she writes in her online manifesto, poetry is not anachronous to the digital age: "The poem is a programming language, is a hypermedia environment, is a meme that can [be made] popular in the Internet. . . . I seek a device poem that circulates and can be consumed in multiple readings. I want to pass from text to hypertext. I want to pass from the hypertext to hypermedia."[28] As part of this praxis, each of her collections is available in some multimedia format.[29] This approach expands Villeda's audience; it reaches readers who might not be local and provides multiple entry points to her projects.

Dodo is accompanied by a stop-motion adaptation. Freely available on YouTube, the film contains an abbreviated version of *Dodo*'s events.[30] Viewers are first introduced to the book's characters, crafted out of colorful felt. Next, verses appear on screen, followed by stop-motion sequences that animate them (Figure 15.1). The use of stop-motion, craft materials, and Fischer Price toys evokes a juvenile quality, which references the dodo's prominent role in classics of children's literature, like *Alice in Wonderland* and *Robinson Crusoe*.[31] These naive touches and the handmade appearance of the puppet-like characters contrast jarringly with the poem's violent content. The most explicit scenes of sodomy, cannibalism, and murder are not included in the stop-motion adaptation. This absence suggests that language is capable of communicating the severity of violence in a way that stop-motion recreations would only trivialize.

Figure 15.1 *Dodo*, Karen Villeda, 2014. Printed with Villeda's authorization.

The use of stop-motion—which stitches together individually photographed frames to create the sensation of motion—formally echoes Villeda's fragmented narrative style, which provides glimpses of images or events that are not fully fleshed out, but seemingly jerkily assembled, porous scenes filled with absences that the reader must fill in or gloss over. Likewise, stop-motion's use of inanimate objects brought to life by an unseen external hand reinforces Villeda's discursive presentation of the sailors as passive, fragmented bodies, rather than historical agents. This deindividualization is discursively achieved in *Dodo* by doing away with grammatical cues that clarify who is speaking or acting. The sailors are infrequently referenced by name, and instead referred to as a collection of body parts: hands, lips, armpits, and genitalia. The first mention of the men introduces them as prepositional objects: "siete barriles como pretexto para catorce brazos" [seven barrels, a pretext for fourteen arms].[32] This presentation of the sailors as pairs of arms reinforces their status as labor, rather than the enlightened subjects of reason associated with the epic. Acknowledged by their armpits, lips, or thumbs, the sailors are a moving conglomeration of parts, an indeterminate pack of sexual and violent creatures.

Like the crew, the dodo is not identified as an individual or as a species, but as a physical, fragmented body defined by the shape of its body and beak. In spite of its titular protagonism, Villeda's dodo is barely sketched in, outlined through the briefest of mentions to its plumage or naked head. It is never brought fully into view as a whole being. It is accessible only through the trace, as the included image of its footprint generated with Villeda's fingerprints suggests halfway through the poem.

Two main exceptions to this erasure of agency are the Admiral and the island of Mauritius. One of the few characters referred to by name, the Admiral is a grotesque character that licks, sodomizes, punishes, and "jamás resbala" [never blunders].³³ The invocation of his name indexes the Admiral's power: his ability to act and determine the crew's fate. Analogously, Mauritius Island is personified and endowed with the agency of a protagonist. "Mauricio" is a subject that dances, belches, blooms—and is ultimately broken. As a result, the normal grid in which the human is aligned with subject, and nonhuman with object, is put into question.

Dodo maps a web of synecdochal associations in which most characters are not referred to by name, but through other repeatedly invoked physical characteristics. The Admiral is referred to as "manos toscas" [rough hands], and the dodo as the "pelona enamorada" [besotted bald one].³⁴ This strategy of synecdoche that describes through parts effectively places bird, man, and island on equal discursive footing. Veering between subjects and across species, the narrative disorients the reader—making us aware of our desire to reinstate a hierarchy of order that parses subjects (humans) from objects (birds/land). Resisting this hierarchical taxonomical ordering, in *Dodo* species intermingle as a kaleidoscope of parts. This is exemplified in a poem in Part IV that narrates the sailors' first encounter with the dodo:

Catorce sobacos que sudan la gota gorda. Un cuerpo abombado, pico larguísimo en gancho. Una hinchazón de párpados y siete trompas. Siete narices chatas y dos manos toscas. Un pulgar curvo. *Un cuerpo abombado, vertimos miel sobre él.* Moscas por moscas, docena de labios resecos.³⁵

[Fourteen armpits that sweat buckets. A convex body, a long-hooked beak. A swelling of lids and seven snouts. Seven flat noses and two rough hands. A curved thumb. *A convex body, we pour honey over it.* Flies and more flies, a dozen parched lips.]

Although this poem narrates the first encounter between the men and the dodo, there is no action. The near-total absence of verbs crafts a photographic still life. In spite of the lack of verbs, Villeda's use of fragmented lists accelerates the pace of reading. As Alejandro Higashi has observed, the recurrent inventories that appear throughout the poem "literalmente obligan a leer sin reposo y muy rápido dejan sin aliento" [literally oblige one to read quickly, without stopping, without taking a breath].³⁶ At the same time, the reader must resist this acceleration, and slow down to determine who each part references through context clues: the Admiral's hands, the Redhead's thumb, the dodo's beak. Similarly, the use of ambiguous words like "trompas" [snouts] abstrusely indexes species; we only know that the aforementioned snouts are human because of their quantity. This rhetorical opacity undermines human exceptionalism and flattens the divide across species.

Another effect of the absence of identifying nouns is that it becomes difficult to perceive whether the dodo or the men are the target of the narrated violence; a blurring of species that purposefully confuses the dodo's vulnerability with our own. As the book progresses, the violence grows in crescendo: the sailors kill the dodo at the Admiral's urging. The slaughter is recounted through a list of fragmented parts: a snapped neck, a bloody heart. The dead body is refashioned into an aesthetic adornment: the feathers into a wig and the intestine into a choker. The Admiral forces the crew to kiss the dead animal while flaunting their genitalia, urinating on the island in declaration of ownership. The abject intensity of this episode signals the inextricability of extinction and colonization, acts of extreme violence wrapped up in rituals of masculinity and dominance that fragment the human and nonhuman into pieces.

The language used to describe the dodo's killing reappears verbatim in a subsequent scene that narrates the death of the Mongol, a character who was previously the target of sexual and physical abuse. He mysteriously shows up dead, in the form of an "ovillo" [ball], "dead as a dodo," and, like the dodo, is eaten up by the crew.[37] With these rhetorical repetitions, Villeda links the violence of extinction with other forms of violence exercised by humans against other humans, violence that is sexually and racially coded. The dodo thus stands in for the vulnerability of life writ large. At the same time that we might identify with the dodo's fragility, as Malva Flores has noted, *Dodo* indexes that the senseless violence of the Admiral and crew is equally intrinsic to contemporary human behavior.[38] The book's conclusion with a taxonomical page in Latin reduces the record of the dodo, no longer a body or a footprint, to a scientific entry. The cold brevity of the dodo's final record obscures the violence of its demise.

Whereas Villeda's dodo is barely sketched in, Isabel Zapata is principally concerned with the representation of extinction and its afterlife. Zapata's poem "Miembro fantasma" [Phantom Limb] centers on the extinction of the thylacine, otherwise known as the Tasmanian tiger or wolf. The poem is included in her debut book of poetry, *Una ballena es un país* [A Whale Is a Country, 2019], a twenty-first-century bestiary in the tradition of precursors like Pacheco's aforementioned *Álbum de zoología* and Juan José Arreola's *Bestiario* [Bestiary, 1972]. In the collection, Zapata explores the human obsession with other species, a fascination with alterity that inevitably folds back in on itself, revealing more about human nature than about other creatures. In "Miembro fantasma," she proposes that fictions about the thylacine led to its eradication. Even in the face of extinction's conclusiveness, traces of the animal continued to haunt the cultural memory, circulating as an idea detached from material reality. These representational specters index, for Zapata, the violence of representation—its willful ignorance and neglect—but also its endless possibility. Representation in the wake of extinction illustrates the power of fiction to be both world-making and world destroying.

The last known thylacine died in Tasmania in 1936; however, there have been some credible sightings reported since. "Miembro fantasma" collates an archive of the animal's slide toward extinction with a collection of photographs, films, testimonies, and scientific records that kaleidoscopically veil and unveil the carnivorous marsupial. This curated record suggests that extinction perversely heightens our interest; it is only upon the disappearance of an animal that we regret not having better known it. This retrospective thirst is contrasted with the impassivity with which the animal was treated while it lived. Zapata suggests that what is left in the wake of the thylacine's absence is a series of failed attempts to discern it—including her poem—an afterlife that underscores that humans are interested in nonhuman animals as imaginative constructs, and not as material bodies.

The poem opens with a photograph from the late 1860s by an unattributed photographer, which Zapata notes in the acknowledgments she found on the internet. The photograph depicts a seated man looking at a trapped and killed thylacine, which hangs directly opposite him, suspended by its back paws (Figure 15.2). Man and prey are symmetrically configured less than a foot apart. In the bottom half of the frame, the dead animal's outstretched limbs almost touch the man's relaxed legs. Rather than look at the camera to show off his trophy to the photographer, the man appears in profile, staring impassively at the thylacine's underbelly. The choice of this particular image—rather than a photograph of the thylacine by itself, or while it was living—establishes the poem's thematization of the human fascination with the extinct animal body.

The inclusion of the photographed thylacine at the outset of the poem lends the animal a tangible materiality. Over the course of the poem, the thylacine becomes progressively less corporeal, and more a shared figment of the human imagination, or,

Figure 15.2 Studio portrait of Mr. Weaver and bagged thylacine, 1869, unknown photographer. Public Domain.

as Zapata puts it in the poem's concluding line, the "síndrome colectivo del miembro fantasma" [collective phantom limb syndrome].[39] The representational archive that Zapata gathers indexes the failed human ambition to objectively know other species. This is underscored in the first section of the poem, which recounts how the last living thylacine, named Benjamin, was alternatively described as like the kangaroo, tiger, cat, wolf, demon, hyena, and lion. Difficult to categorize, the thylacine occupied a space of taxonomical excess. Representational practices attempted to paper over this aporia through fictionalization, projection, and even deception. Zapata locates this excess in the very first human depictions of the thylacine: prehistoric rock art in Australia's Kakadu National Park endowed it with wings. The mention of rock art is the only non-settler account of the thylacine included in "Miembro fantasma." This inclusion suggests that for Zapata the distance between representation and reality is a universal human problem, shared by aboriginal cultures.

Nonetheless, the thylacine's extinction is indisputably linked to the colonization of Tasmania. The forced removal and genocide of aboriginal peoples throughout the nineteenth century paved the way for the territory to be refashioned by settlers, who perceived the thylacine as an existential threat. This myth was perpetuated by representational practices that framed the animal as a predator that needed to be eradicated. Zapata opens the second section of the poem with a description of Henry Burrell's photograph of a thylacine holding a chicken in its mouth. This image, which was staged with a trained thylacine, spread the idea that the animal was a threat to farmers, which led to its active extermination, encouraged by the state through monetary rewards.

"Miembro fantasma" asks where the memory of the thylacine resides if the human archive is riddled with such inaccuracies and fictions presented as truth. To compensate for these faulty or nonexistent mediations, Zapata adds one of her own: the speculative transcription of its coughing bark. Yet even these imagined speech acts—"*fiu fiu fiu fiu*," "*cofcofcofcof*"—are ultimately deemed insufficient by the poetic voice, which concludes that in the absence of recordings the memory of the thylacine is best preserved by the grass that experienced its step.[40] In other words, the thylacine's memory is captured not through mediation, representation, or reanimation—like imaginative transcription or archeological excavation—but by the living repository of the environment. Hence Zapata posits the memory of the thylacine exists, but out of human reach. Human attempts to reanimate the extinct are propelled by discomfort with finality, and preference for the fantasy of return.

The denial of the conclusiveness of extinction is underscored in the third section of the poem, which gathers seven accounts by people who claimed to have seen a thylacine between 1984 and 2017, after the species was officially deemed extinct. Transcriptions of these accounts are included in italics, and detail encounters with traces of the thylacine: its tracks, smell, a glimpse of its tail. These sightings formulate the afterlife of extinction, the echoes that hold sway in the collective imaginary long after material absence. This collective delusion—the assertion that the thylacine lives, the denial that it has been snuffed out—is what Zapata deems the "phantom limb" of extinction. Phantom limb syndrome is the sensation that an amputated limb is still attached. The phantom limb causes pain; it itches, twitches, or moves. The brain does not recognize that the body part is gone; it takes up mental space, even though it is not physically present. Zapata uses this metaphor to map the societal response to extinction: the unshakable feeling that something must still exist even when it has been lost. The fantasy that the thylacine continues to persist—in secret, just barely out of sight—is more digestible than the painful irreversibility of its violent eradication by human hand.

Extinction is an end, and yet it has an extended tail of remembrance, denial, and fantasy, a cultural memory that lingers long after the specie's material absence. Zapata does not see this enduring legacy as a hopeful sign of permanence in spite of extinction, or of the power of representation to capture and preserve something that is lost. Rather she finds the long afterlife of extinct species to be a symptom of human delusion and attachment to animals as concepts rather than material reality. In the final section of the poem, Zapata likens continued sightings of the thylacine to the human belief in phenomena without biological basis, like the Loch Ness monster or the goblin. The thylacine, in other words, has become fully detached from its material embodiment and assumed the status of a legend. Zapata concludes in the final lines of the poem, "Celebramos la vida que no existe. / La sombra que avanza sin un cuerpo." [We celebrate life that does not exist. / The shadow that advances without a body].[41] In extinction, the real body of the animal has been lost; it no longer is locatable. All that remains are traces, echoes, testimonies: the fantasy of the animal's endurance and eventual return.

Narrating from the historical archives of extinction Karen Villeda and Isabel Zapata illustrate that species loss is grounded in geophysical space and time. While these processes play out in localized ways, they are the result of global histories of human migration, encroachment, and domination. By looking at classic cases of extinction that occurred outside of Mexico, Villeda and Zapata reflect on the brutality of extinction and its aftermath: how disappeared species are remembered and circulate in the cultural imaginary. Both are troubled by representational practices that keep these lost creatures alive as curious relics or fantastical figures, but gloss over the violence of their eradication. *Dodo* and "Miembro fantasma" revisit extinct figures without nostalgia, foregrounding the horrific consequences of global connectivity and human brutality.

By casting back to spaces and times far away, Villeda and Zapata take readers to the aftermath of extinction. They note that these historical extinctions did not mark the end of our planet—they did not bring about the apocalypse implied by previous extinction narratives. In fact, far from apocalyptic implications, these poets suggest that we do not feel the consequences of extinction enough. Villeda and Zapata ask readers to grapple with the violence of these absences. Their poetics of extinction thus remap the planet, rewriting planetary history in ways that link human histories of imperialism with the histories of nonhuman life. Such planetary recastings only obliquely reference national contexts; they frame looking beyond nation and species as an ethical imperative in the age of the sixth extinction. Ecological orientation should not be limited to local attachments, Villeda and Zapata imply, because extinction is an integral fold in the fabric of our history as a species, a reminder of our collective responsibility to the web of life in which we are contingently enmeshed.

Notes

1. Donna Haraway, "Situated Knowledges: The Science Question in Feminism and the Privilege of Partial Perspective," *Feminist Studies* 14, no. 3 (1988): 581.
2. Wai Chee Dimock, "Introduction: Planet and America, Set and Subset," in *American Literature as World Literature*, ed. Wai Chee Dimock and Lawrence Buell (Princeton: Princeton University Press, 2007), 5.
3. Emily Apter, *Against World Literature: On the Politics of Untranslatability* (New York: Verso, 2013), 353.
4. Jennifer Wenzel, *The Disposition of Nature: Environmental Crisis and World Literature* (New York: Fordham University Press, 2020), 1.
5. Joanna Zylinska, "Photography after Extinction," in *After Extinction*, ed. Richard Grusin (Minneapolis: University of Minnesota Press, 2018), 51, 53.
6. Dipesh Chakrabarty, "The Climate of History: Four Theses," *Critical Inquiry* 35 (2009): 197–222.
7. Richard Grusin, Introduction to *After Extinction* (Minneapolis: University of Minnesota Press, 2018), vii.
8. Chakrabarty, "The Climate of History," 222.
9. Gayatri Spivak, "Imperative to Re-Imagine the Planet," in *An Aesthetic Education in the Era of Globalization* (Cambridge, MA: Harvard University Press, 2011), 339.
10. Ibid., 341.
11. Ashley Dawson observes that capitalism paradoxically "tends to degrade the conditions of its own production." *Extinction: A Radical History* (New York: OR Books, 2016), 42.
12. Jurriaan M. De Vos, Lucas N. Joppa, John L. Gittleman, Patrick R. Stephens, and Stuart L. Pimm, "Estimating the Normal Background Rate of Species Extinction," *Conservation Biology* 29, no. 2 (2015): 452–62.
13. IUCN Red List, "Summary Statistics 2019," https://www.iucnredlist.org/resources/summary-statistics (accessed July 9, 2019).
14. David Tilman, Robert M. May, Clarence L. Lehman, and Martin A. Nowak, "Habitat Destruction and the Extinction Debt," *Nature* 371 (1994): 65–6.
15. Thom van Dooren, *Flight Ways: Life and Loss at the Edge of Extinction* (New York: Columbia University Press, 2014), 13.
16. Ursula K. Heise, *Imagining Extinction: The Cultural Meanings of Endangered Species* (Chicago: University of Chicago Press, 2016), 25.
17. Gerardo Ceballos, Paul R. Ehrlich, and Rodolfo Dirzo, "Biological Annihilation Via the Ongoing Sixth Extinction Signaled by Vertebrate Population Losses and Declines," *PNAS* 114, no. 30 (2017): E6089–96.
18. José Emilio Pacecho, "Augurios" and "Zopilote," in *Nuevo álbum de zoología* (Mexico: Era, 2013), 45; 50–1. For more on animals and environmental crisis in Pacheco, see Randy Malamud, "José Emilio Pacheco: 'I saw a dying fish,'" in *Poetic Animals and Animal Souls* (New York: Palgrave, 2003), 77–92; Scott Devries, *Creature Discomfort* (Leiden: Koninklijke Brill, 2016), 158–66; Micah McKay, "'Pasto sin fin del basurero': Trash and Disposal in the Poetry of José Emilio Pacheco," *Latin American Literary Review* 47, no. 93 (2020): 49–58.
19. Homero Aridjis and Betty Farber, *Noticias de la tierra* (Mexico: Debate, 2012): 22.
20. For more on extinction in Aridjis, see Devries, *Creature Discomfort*, 151–8; Heise, *Imagining Extinction*, 46–8; and Adam Spires, "Homero Aridjis and Mexico's

Eco-Critical Dystopia," in *Blast, Corrupt, Dismantle, Erase: Contemporary North American Dystopian Literature*, ed. Brett Josef Grubisic, Gisele M. Baxter, and Tara Lee (Waterloo: Wilfred Laurier University Press, 2014), 339–54.
21 Apter, *Against World Literature*, 353.
22 Homero Aridjis, "Paraíso negro / Black Paradise," trans. George McWhirter, *ISLE* 5, no. 2 (1998): 107–8.
23 See Nicole Seymour, *Bad Environmentalism: Irony and Irreverence in the Ecological Age* (Minneapolis: University of Minnesota Press, 2018), 2.
24 See Mikeal D. Wolfe on how putatively environmentalist bodies like Comisión Nacional del Agua deploy environmentalist rhetoric but pursue developmentalist policies, all while displacing blame on campesinos for the "irrational use of water." *Watering the Revolution: An Environmental and Technological History of Agrarian Reform in Mexico* (Durham: Duke University Press, 2017), 225. Matthew Vitz also discusses how "a technocratic urban environmentalism amenable to capital accumulation" has resulted in policies that purportedly protect forests by razing squatter settlements in Mexico City, "while luxury suburbs were left intact." *A City on a Lake: Urban Political Ecology and the Growth of Mexico City* (Durham: Duke University Press, 2018), 232.
25 Van Dooren, *Flight Ways*, 3–4.
26 Prior to the arrival of the Dutch the island was uninhabited; it had been visited by Arab traders in the Middle Ages and the Portuguese in the early sixteenth century, but neither settled there, nor did they leave written records of the dodo bird. Van Dooren, *Flight Ways*, 2.
27 Julian P. Hume, "The History of the Dodo Raphus cucullatus and the Penguin of Mauritius," *Historical Biology* 18, no. 2 (2006): 69–93.
28 Karen Villeda, "About," http://www.poetronica.net/about.html (accessed July 9, 2019).
29 For analysis of Villeda's digital experimentation, see Daniel Escandell Montiel, "Twitter y poesía no creativa por Karen Villeda y Denis Audirac en su obra POETuitéame," *Literatura Mexicana* 31, no. 1 (2020): 179–204.
30 Karen Villeda, *Dodo*, 2014. https://youtu.be/xDbPSs7vqFI (accessed July 9, 2019).
31 Karen Villeda, "*Dodo*, poetry stop motion," http://www.poetronica.net/poetryand stopmotion.html (accessed July 9, 2019).
32 Karen Villeda, *Dodo* (Mexico: Fondo Editorial Tierra Adentro, 2013), 11.
33 Ibid., 43.
34 Ibid., 54; 77.
35 Ibid., 42.
36 Alejandro Higashi, "Karen Villeda habla sobre *Dodo*," *Ancila: Crítica de Poesía Mexicana Contemporánea*, June 1, 2014. See also: Julio E. Ruiz Monroy, "*Dodo* la supervivencia de la poesía extinta," *Luvina* 76 (2014).
37 Villeda, *Dodo*, 67. Emphasis in original.
38 Malva Flores, "Todavía respira," *Letras Libres*, July 11, 2014.
39 Isabel Zapata, *Una ballena es un país* (Mexico: Almadía, 2019), 51.
40 Zapata, *Una ballena es un país*, 47–8.
41 Ibid., 51.

Contributors

Iván Eusebio Aguirre Darancou is Assistant Professor in Hispanic studies at the University of California-Riverside. His research focuses on the intersections between nation, sexuality, and consumption as critical practice, foregrounding dissident sexualities, the use of substances, and humanimal subjectivities mobilized to challenge anthropocentric modernities. He has published articles on authors Augusto Monterroso, Guillermo Cabrera Infante, Parménides García Saldaña, and José Agustín in journals such as *Hispanic Review*, *Tierra adentro*, *Revista de Literatura Mexicana Contemporánea*, and *Romance Notes*. He also published on film directors such as Nicolás Echevarría and Sergio García Michel.

Nuala Finnegan is Professor of Spanish and Latin American studies at University College Cork, Ireland, and Director of the Centre for Mexican Studies. She has published in the areas of contemporary Mexican literary and visual cultural studies with a particular focus on gender. Interested in multidisciplinary approaches and community engagement, she has worked collaboratively as curator on many exhibitions, for example, *Entre Mundos/Between Worlds: Images from Life between Mexico and Ireland* in 2019, and *OUTPOSTS: Global Borders and National Boundaries* in 2017–18. Publications include the essay collection *Rethinking Juan Rulfo's Creative World: Prose, Photography, Film* (2016), with Dylan Brennan.

Carolyn Fornoff is Assistant Professor of Latin American cultures at the University of Illinois at Urbana-Champaign. Her work examines responses to climate change in Mexican and Central American literature and film. She is co-editor of *Timescales: Thinking across Ecological Temporalities* (2020), and *Pushing Past the Human in Latin American Cinema* (2021).

Shelley Garrigan is Associate Professor of Spanish at North Carolina State University. Her research so far has centered on the politics and economic underpinnings of nineteenth-century Mexican national art and art collecting; the formation of Mexico's foundational cultural institutions; and the institutions' intersections with literature, women, and science in nineteenth-century Mexico, Jewish/Mexican identities, and border art. Her book *Collecting Mexico: Museums, Monuments and the Creation of National Identity* (2012) explores the intersections of patrimony and commerce during the era of national consolidation and modernization in Mexico.

Gustavo Guerrero is Professor of contemporary Latin American literature and cultural history at CY Cergy-Paris University and at the Saint-Germain-en-Laye Institute of Political Studies. He is Gallimard's editor for Spanish, Portuguese, and Latin American books. He has edited numerous scholarly works and critical editions on Latin American literature. As an essayist, he has published *Teorías de la lírica* (1998), *La religion del vacío* (2002), *Historia de un encargo:* La catira *de Camilo José Cela* (2008), with which he won the XXXVI Anagrama International Essay Prize, and *Paisajes en movimiento, literatura y cambio cultural entre dos siglos* (2018), among other books.

Manuel Gutiérrez Silva is Lecturer in the Department of Spanish and Portuguese at UCLA. He is editor of *The Films of Arturo Ripstein: The Sinister Gaze of the World* (2019) and has published articles and reviews in the *Revista de Estudios Hispánicos*, *A Contracorriente*, and *Mexican Studies/Estudios Mexicanos*. He is currently co-editing a volume of essays dedicated to the *Revista Moderna* (1898–1903) (2021).

Stephanie Kirk is Professor of Hispanic studies at Washington University in St. Louis. She is the author of two books: *Sor Juana Inés de la Cruz and the Gender Politics of Knowledge in Colonial Mexico* (2016) and *Convent Life in Colonial Mexico: A Tale of Two Communities* (2007 and 2018), and the editor of *Religious Transformations in the Early Modern Americas* (2014, with Sarah Rivett) and *Estudios coloniales en el siglo XXI* (2011). She has published numerous articles on gender and religious culture in colonial Mexico, and on Sor Juana Inés de la Cruz.

Pedro Ángel Palou is Fletcher Professor of oratory at Tufts University. A prolific novelist, he is the author of thirty-three books, including the acclaimed *Con la sangre en los puños* (Xavier Villaurrutia Prize in 2003) and an historical trilogy, *Zapata, Morelos* and *Cuauhtémoc*, on three important heroes of Mexican history. Palou was honored with the Francisco Xavier Clavijero Prize in History for his cultural sociology of Mexican literature between 1900 and 1940, *La casa del silencio, aproximación en tres tiempos a Contemporáneos*. His latest scholarly book is *Mestizo Failure(s), Race, Film and Literature in Twentieth Century Mexico* (2016).

Adela Pineda Franco is Lozano Long Endowed Professor in Latin American Literary and Cultural Studies at the University of Texas at Austin, where she directs the Teresa Lozano Long Institute of Latin American Studies. She has written on modernismo, Latin American literature and film, and US-Mexico cultural relations. Her recent books, *John Steinbeck y Mexico. Una mirada cinematográfica en la era de la hegemonía norteamericana* (2018) and *The Mexican Revolution on the World Stage: Intellectuals and Film in the Twentieth Century* (2019), explore the role of cinema and intellectual thought in the shaping of inter-state cultural relations during the twentieth century.

Sara Potter is Associate Professor of Spanish at the University of Texas at El Paso who specializes in contemporary Mexican and Latin American literature. Her book project *Disturbing Muses: Reconfiguring National Bodies and Histories in Post-Revolutionary Mexico* examines representations of gender, technology, and urban space in avant-garde narrative from the post-Revolution to the present. Recent publications include "Of Monsters and Malinches: Signifying Violence in Edgar Clément's *Operación*

Bolívar and Tony Sandoval's *El cadáver y el sofá*" in the *Revista de Estudios Hispánicos* and "Postcolonial Pandemics and Undead Revolutions: Contagion as Resistance in *Con Z de Zombie* and *Juan de los Muertos*" in *Alambique. Revista académica de ciencia ficción y fantasia*.

Ignacio M. Sánchez Prado is the Jarvis Thurston and Mona Van Duyn Professor in the humanities at Washington University in St. Louis. He is the author of numerous books and articles, and the editor of over a dozen scholarly collections. These include his monograph *Strategic Occidentalism: On Mexican Fiction, The Neoliberal Book Market and the Questions of World Literature* and the edited book *Mexican Literature in Theory* (2018). He has served as President of the Association for the Study of the Arts of the Present and as Kluge Chair of Cultures of the South at the Library of Congress.

Karen Stolley is Professor of Spanish in the Department of Spanish and Portuguese at Emory University. Author of *Domesticating Empire: Enlightenment in Spanish America* (2013), she coedited with Mariselle Meléndez a special issue of the *Colonial Latin America Review* on Latin American Enlightenments (2015). Her essay "Other Empires: Eighteenth-century Hispanic Worlds and a Global Enlightenment" is included in *The Routledge Companion to the Hispanic Enlightenment* (2020). Current projects include a co-edited volume with Catherine M. Jaffee on *The Black Legend in the Eighteenth Century: National Identities under Construction* (forthcoming with Oxford Studies in the Enlightenment).

Jorge Téllez is Assistant Professor of romance languages at the University of Pennsylvania. His research and teaching focus on colonialism in Latin America, past and present. His work studies how colonial legacies have shaped modern and contemporary cultural institutions and practices. His forthcoming book with Notre Dame University Press, titled *Precarious Narratives: The Picaresque and the Writing Life in Mexico, 1690–2013*, studies the emergence and development of the Mexican literary field through the lens of the picaresque. He has published articles about print culture, book history, and poetics in colonial Latin America. He is currently working on a new book, tentatively titled *Colonial Collections: Value, Objects, and Narratives of the Past in 21st Century Latin America*, that delves into the relationship between art and politics by analyzing contemporary cultural productions and institutions that engage the colonial past as sources for literary, artistic, and historical value. His first book, *Poéticas del Nuevo Mundo* (2012), was awarded the Siglo XXI-Editores International Essay prize in 2011.

Laura Torres-Rodríguez is Associate Professor at the Department of Spanish and Portuguese at New York University. Her research stresses the importance of the Pacific Ocean in the making of Mexican and larger Latin American histories, as well as in the historical configuration of the US-Mexico borderlands. She is the author of *Orientaciones transpacíficas: la modernidad mexicana y el espectro de Asia* [Transpacific

Orientations: Mexican Modernity and the Specter of Asia] (North Carolina Studies in the Romance Languages, 2019). The book won the 2020 LASA Mexico section prize for best book in the humanities.

Oswaldo Zavala is Professor of contemporary Latin American literature and culture at the College of Staten Island and at the Graduate Center of the City University of New York (CUNY). He is the author of *La modernidad insufrible. Roberto Bolaño en los límites de la literatura latinoamericana contemporánea* (2015), *Volver a la modernidad. Genealogías de la literatura mexicana de fin de siglo* (2017), and *Los cárteles no existen. Narcotráfico y cultura en México* (2018). He has published more than fifty articles on contemporary Latin American narrative, the US-Mexico border, and the link between violence, culture, and late capitalism.

Index

1917 Constitution
    Article 3   110
    Article 27   205

Academia de Letrán   71–80, 82
Académie Française   137
Acapulco   7, 30, 58
Actual No. 1 (Maples Arce)   118, 122
Adorno, Rolena   45
Aesop's Fables   8
Against World Literature (Apter)   232
Age of Silver: The Rise of the Novel East and West, The (Ma)   58–60, 62–3, 67
Ahora me rindo y eso es todo (Enrigue)   227
Aira, César   207–8
Alatorre, Antonio   109
Alberti, Rafael   162
Álbum de zoología (Pacheco)   240
Alemán, Miguel   141, 158
Alighieri, Dante   12, 18, 24
Almadía   222
Almanaque surréaliste du démi-siècle   145
Altamirano, Ignacio   74
Alzate y Ramírez, José Antonio   46
América Latina en la literatura mundial (Sánchez Prado)   82
American literature   24, 55, 59, 66
Americas   8, 9, 10–14, 25, 26, 28, 32, 39, 40, 45–7, 5–9, 62. *See also* United States
Ancient Greek Literature (Bowra)   109
Andamios interiores: Poemas Radiográficas (*Interior Scaffolding: Radiographic Poems*, Cisneros)   124
Anderson, Benedict   41, 212
Anderson, Jon Lee   222
Andrade, Oswaldo de   227
Andries, Lise   73
Ángel Palou, Pedro   128, 222
Antarctic Academy   11, 13
Anthropocene   233
anthropological hermeneutics   178
Antonio Campos, Marco   72, 73
A pesar del oscuro silencio (*In Spite of the Dark Silence*, Volpi)   128
Apollinaire, Guillaume   124
"Apollo, or About Literature" (Reyes)   105, 107, 108
Appadurai, Arjun   81
Apter, Emily   47, 76, 218, 219, 232, 235
Arab League   160
Arac, John   175
Aragon, Louis   144
Araucana (Ercilla)   9
Arenal, Electa   31
Aridjis, Homero   234, 235
Ariosto, Ludovico   18
Aristotle   18, 160
Around the World in Eighty Days (Verne)   112
Arredondo, Inés   127
Artaud, Antonin   162
art galleries   141
Art Mexicain du précolumbien à nos jours   140
Arts, The   93
art writing   141, 142, 145
Ashton, Dore   148
Asia   4, 7, 55, 57, 58
Asia-Mexico relationship   55, 57
Associated Press   209
Asturias, Miguel Angel   119
Atala (Chateaubriand)   74, 75
Auerbach, Erich   109
"Augurios" (Auguries, Pacheco)   235
avant-garde   4, 93, 105, 110, 117–27, 129, 147, 192

Avicena   160
Azcárraga, Emilio   142
Aztec civilization   43
"Aztec-Spanish Dialogues"   24

Baeza, Ricardo   161–3
Baja California   43, 56, 127
Bakhtin, Mikhail   62
Balbuena, Bernardo de   7, 8, 15–18
Balderston, Daniel   126
Ballcels, Carmen   206
Ballesteros, Arturo   209
Barnes, Julian   207
Baroque   15, 18, 25–9, 163, 164
Barrera, Trinidad   11
Barrera Enderle, Víctor   72, 73
Barroco de Indias   18, 23, 27, 28
Bartolache, José Ignacio   46
Basto, Tavares   158
Beatles, The   193
Beckett, Samuel   5, 137, 161–3
Beckman, Ericka   91
Beecroft, Alexander   4, 8, 9, 107
"BEF". *See* Fernández, Bernardo
Béguin, Albert   109
Bembo, Pietro   10
Benítez, Fernando   203
Benítez Rojo, Antonio   83
Benjamin, Walter   173
Bestiario (Bestiary, José Arreola)   240
Beverley, John   45, 47, 222
Bey, Mostafa Amer   159
Biblioteca Mexicana (Eguiara y Eguren)   46, 82
Bibliothecas   42
biological annihilation   234, 235
Bjork, Katharine   58
Bleichmar, Daniela   45
Boîte-en-valise (Duchamp)   146
Bolaño, Roberto   117, 127–9, 225
Bologna earthquake   45
Books Abroad   145
Boom writers   106, 134, 172, 203, 209, 222
Borges, Jorge Luis   2, 83, 119, 222, 225
Borsò, Vittoria   179
Boscán, Juan   11, 18
Bosch Fonserré, José   143

Boturini Benaduci, Lorenzo   43
Boullosa, Carmen   2
Bourbon dynasty   40, 42, 44
Bourdain, Anthony   225
Bourdieu, Pierre   135, 173, 216, 223
Bousquet, Joe   162
Bowra, Cecil Maurice   109, 137, 138, 164–6
Boyer, Pascal   30
Bracero program (1942–64)   178, 179, 184 n.35
Brading, David   42, 43
Braque, Georges   124
Brennan, Gerald   163
Bretón, André   140, 162
Bretón de los Herreros, Manuel   75
Brevísima relación de la destrucción de las indias (Brief History of the Destruction of the Indies, Las Casas)   9
Brouillette, Sarah   134, 138, 166, 206, 210
Brown, Wendy   223
Buarque de Holanda, Sergio   159
Buffon, Louis Leclerc   42, 44
Buñuel, Luis   146, 207
Burrell, Henry   242
Burroughs, William S.   190
Buscaglia-Salgado, José   62, 66, 67

Cacho Casal, Rodrigo   13
Cahier L'Herne   206
Cain, Julien   159
Caistor, Nick   211
Calderón, Felipe   211
Calderón y Beltrán, Fernando   76, 79
Callois, Roger   160, 162, 166
Campeón Gabacho (*The Gringo Champion*, Xilonen)   227
cannabis   190–1, 194
Cannes' International Film Festival   146
Cantinflas   112
"Canto a un dios mineral" (Song to a Mineral God, Cuesta)   128
capitalism   28, 63, 66, 91, 97, 171, 174–6, 180, 188, 198, 200, 221, 233
Cárdenas, Lázaro   107
Carhartt-Harris, Robin   193
Caribbean-Atlantic system   64
Caribbean islands   62, 63, 65, 67

Carroll, Lewis   193
Cartas de relación (Letters from Mexico, Cortés)   9
Carter, Boyd   137
Casanova, Pascale   9, 14, 15, 25, 29, 90, 106, 134–8, 172–5, 181, 218
Cassady, Neal   190
Cassin, Barbara   219
Cassou, Jean   140, 162
Castoriadis, Cornelius   144
Castro, Fidel   209
Castro Leal, Antonio   159
Catherine of Siena   24
Ceballos, Gerardo   234
Cervantes, Freija I.   109
Cervantes, Miguel de   9, 12, 58, 79, 160, 224
Chakrabarty, Dipesh   232
Char, Rene   162
Charles Elliot Norton Lecture Series   147
Chatrian, Alexandre   98
Chávez, Hugo   209
Chávez Castañeda, Ricardo   128
Cheah, Pheng   1, 187, 188, 193, 194
Chiampi, Irlemar   109
Chimal, Alberto   218
Chimalpahin (1579–1660)   7, 8
China   4, 58
China illustrata (Kircher)   30
China-Mexico relationship   56, 57
Chroniclers of the Indies   161
Cien del Mundo   112
Cisneros, Odile   124
citizenship   66, 67, 105
Clásicos Verdes   111–12
classical tradition   12, 14, 165
Classical Tradition, The (Highet)   109
classicism   108, 159
Claudel, Paul   137, 138, 164–6
Clavijero, Francisco Javier   42, 43, 47
climate crisis   233
Coetzee, J. M.   207
Coffee House Press   226
Cohen, Walter   8, 9, 12, 16
Colección Cvltvra   109, 110
Colegio de Letrán   74
The Collection of Representative Works   137, 138, 158–61, 165, 166

Collège de France   108
College of Santa Cruz Tlatelolco   43
colonial Latin America   7, 18, 26
colonial literature   4, 13, 16, 24, 55, 59, 65–6
colonial Mexico   7, 28, 57–9, 67
colonial poetry   7, 9, 13, 14, 16
colonial textualities   60, 66
colonization/colonialism/coloniality   25, 28, 31, 39, 67, 90, 91, 171, 179, 197, 198, 200, 233
  American   7
  Spanish   8
"The Columbian Exchange"   10
Columbus, Christopher   9, 24
Commission of Experts on Translation   158–60
Commission of the Cuenca de Papaloapan   173
Comparative Literature   25
Conn, Robert T.   105
Conservatory of Music   82
Constant, Benjamin   77
Constitution of Chipalcingo (1814)   78
Contemporáneos   117–29
contemporary Mexican poetry   231–43
Cook, Noble David   10
Cooper, James Fenimore   60, 65
Copjec, Joan   205
Córdova, Arturo de   112
Cortés, Hernán   7, 9
Corte Velasco, Clemencia   126
Cosmic Generator (2017)   56
Cosmopolitan Desires (Siskind)   117
cosmopolitanism   1, 4, 8, 39, 47, 71, 72, 74, 78, 79, 81, 82, 84, 90–4, 99, 106, 112, 117, 120–3, 127, 128, 154, 165, 187, 223, 224
cosmopolitan literature   75, 122
Count of Montecristo, The (film)   112
Crack Generation   127–9, 207
"crack" writers   222
criollos   18, 25, 28, 30, 40–6, 219
Criollo patriots/patriotism   42, 43, 46, 47
Cruz, Anne J.   14
cubism   124, 125
Cucurto, Washington   225
Cuesta, Jorge   94, 95, 119, 121, 128

Cultural Center for Contemporary Art   142
culture
    campaigns   139, 149
    consumption   74, 75, 77, 79
    exchange   137
    history   4, 33, 157
    institution   105, 107, 109, 133–5, 149, 217
    production   1, 18, 28, 187, 216, 219, 221
    system   26, 28
Curtius, Erns Robert   109

Dalkey Archives   206
Dalton, Margarita   5, 188, 191, 193, 200
Dama de corazones (*Queen of Hearts*, Villaurrutia)   122, 125
Damrosch, David   1, 11, 15–18, 81, 107, 108, 134, 145, 146, 179–81, 217, 218
Daniel, Jean   207
D'Annunzio, Gabrielle   110
Darío, Rubén   89, 95, 121
Davidson, Peter   28, 29
Death without End (Gorostiza)   126
Deep Vellum press   171, 226
defamiliarization   146, 147
Default Mode Network (DMN)   195–6, 200
Defense of Culture   161
Defoe, Daniel   58, 60, 64
de la Fuente, Juan Ramón   207, 211
Deleuze, Gilles   224
del Paso, Fernando   5, 188, 194, 200
del Valle, Ivonne   41, 43
democratization   108, 110, 156, 193
DePalma, Anthony   208–11
De Pauw, Corneille   42, 44
Derrida, Jacque   61
Descartes, Rene   160
Descripción histórica y cronológica de las dos piedras (León y Gama)   42
Desde entonces (From Now On)   235
D'haen, Theo   40
Díaz del Castillo, Bernal   9
Díaz Mirón, Salvador   94

Diccionaire de la Conversation et la Lecture   75
Digital Humanities Center, Stanford University   41
Dimock, Wai Chee   32, 33, 55, 61, 65, 66, 231
Discurso en loor de la poesía (Speech in Praise of Poetry)   11
Distant Reading (Moretti)   8
Dodds Pennock, Caroline   26, 27
dodo   232, 235, 236, 238–40
Dodo (Dodo, Villeda)   232, 236–40, 243
Domínguez, César   120, 122
Dominguez Michael, Christopher   133, 142–4
Don Quixote (Cervantes)   58, 224
Dos Passos, John   119
Duchamp, Marcel   145–9
Dussel, Enrique   47, 225
Dylan, Bob   191

Early American Literature   24
East Asian world-system   58
Echeverría, Bolívar   217
Ecology of World Literature, An (Beecroft)   8
Economic and Social Council   156, 157
economy and ecology   56, 57
education   108, 110, 112
ego dissolution   196
Eguiara y Eguren, Juan José de   46, 47
Egyptian pyramids   31–2
ejido system   205
El año nuevo   75
El bachiller (Nervo)   96
El Bernardo o Victoria de Roncesvalles (The Bernardo, or Victory of Roncesvalles, Balbuena)   7, 17
"El cinematógrafo" (Urbina)   98
El Colegio de México   107
El Colegio Nacional   108
El domador de almas (Nervo)   96
Eliot, T. S.   164
El Mosaico Mexicano   75
El Mundo Ilustrado (Urbina)   92, 93, 99
Eloy Martínez, Tomás   206
El País   215

El Partido Liberal 94
"El periódico-teléfono" (Nervo) 99
El periquillo sarniento (*The Mangy Parrot: The Life of Periquillo Sarniento Written by Himself for His Children*, Fernández de Lizardi) 60, 64
El recreo de las familias 75, 78, 79
El Renacimiento 74
El siglo XIX 80
"El soldado de la libertad" (Calderón y Beltrán) 76
Eluard, Paul 162
El Universal 98
El Universal Ilustrado 123
El voto nacional 78
Emergent Worlds: Alternative States in Nineteenth- Century American Culture (Sugden) 59, 60, 66
Enciso, Froylán 136
endangered species 234
En esto ver aquello: Octavio Paz y el arte (2014) 142
England 24, 40, 159, 163
English, James F. 226
Enlightenment 23, 29, 40-2, 46, 154
Enrigue, Álvaro 218, 227
Enríquez, Mariana 2
environmentalism 235
Epístolas (Martí) 46
Erasmus 24
Ercilla, Alonso de 9
Erckmann, Émile 98
Escalante, Evodio 126, 127, 133
Escalante Gonzalbo, Fernando 221
Escuela Nacional Preparatoria (National Preparatory School) 119
"Especies en peligro (y otras víctimas)" (Endangered Species (and other victims), Pacheco) 234
Espronceda, José de 76
Essay politique sur le royaume de la Nouvelle-Espagne (Humboldt) 45
Esteva Fabregat, Claudio 178
Estridentismo 119, 125
Estridentistas 117-29
Euripides and His Age (Murray) 109

Eurocentrism 1, 3, 4, 24, 26, 28, 29, 31, 57, 58, 84, 90, 92, 107, 121
Europe 7, 8-10, 24-6, 28, 29, 33, 39-41, 45, 47, 64, 78, 90-2, 97, 109, 118, 122, 154, 156, 172, 217, 220
  art 141
  culture 75, 77, 124, 154
  history 23
  humanism 159
  libraries 80
  literature 8, 14, 73, 75, 90, 95, 98
  poetry 14, 165
  societies 27
European Literature and the Latin Middle Ages (Curtius) 109
Evans, Luther 166
Ex-Convent of Saint Augustine 80
"extinction debt" 234
extinction events 233, 235, 236, 242, 243

Fanon, Frantz 226, 227
Farrar 223
Fell, Claude 206
female sexualities 198
"feminine boom" 129
feminism/feminization 57, 68 n.8, 96, 215, 216
Fernández, Bernardo 218
Fernández, Macedonio 222
Fernández de Lizardi, José Joaquín 60
Fernández Retamar, Roberto 83, 227
Ferrari, Guillermina de 81
Féval, Paul 112
Figaro Litteraire 143
First World War 109, 110
Flores, Malva 240
Flores, Tatiana 123
Fonda, Jane 209
Fondo de Cultura Económica (FCE) 108, 109, 158, 215, 223
"Fonógrafos" (Phonographs, Villaurutia) 123
Fontaine 163
Fontaine, Arturo 207
Foucault, Michel 205, 206
Fouchet, Max-Pol 163
Fox Quesada, Vicente 209

France   24, 40, 73, 96, 111, 135, 136, 145, 154, 158, 159, 161
Francocentrism   106
Franqui, Carlos   144
Franz, Carlos   207
Freeman, Morgan   225
French Academy   164
French Editions d'Art Albert Skira   147
French literature   90, 106, 162
French Revolution   78
Frenk, Margit   109
Friedman, Milton   221
Fromm, Erich   144
From Paris to Tlön: Surrealism as World Literature (Ungureanu)   134, 146
Fuchs, Barbara   15, 16
Fuentes, Carlos   3, 5, 47, 105, 106, 203, 204, 206, 208–12, 217, 222
   Adam in Eden   203
   Aix en Provence conference (2011)   207
   Eagle's Chair, The   203
   Geography of Novel   207
   Great Latin American Novel, The   207
   New Time for Mexico, A   203
   Old Gringo, The   209
   "So Far from God"   203
   Terra Nostra   206–7, 210
   Tiempo Mexicano   203
   Will and Fortune, The   203
   Years with Laura Diaz, The   203
"Fundación del manierismo hispanoamericano por Bernardo de Balbuena" (Foundation of Hispanic American Mannerism by Bernardo de Balbuena, Rama)   14
Furet, François   144
Further Adventures of Robinson Crusoe, The (Defoe)   60, 64
futurism   124, 125

Gabriel Vázquez, Juan   207
gachupines (peninsular Spaniards)   41
Galerie des Beaux-Arts   139
Gallego, Nicasio   75
Gallimard   134, 160, 166
Gallo, Rubén   119, 122, 123
Gamboa, Santiago   207
Ganguly, Debjani   212
Garciadiego, Javier   108, 111
García Lorca, Federico   128, 162
García Márquez, Gabriel   2, 172, 206, 209, 211, 222
García Ponce, Juan   127
García Saldaña, Parménides   188, 190, 191, 200
Garcilaso, Inca   11
Garcilaso de la Vega   76
Garibay, Ángel María   107
Gavaldón, Roberto   112
Gazeta de literatura de México   46
gendered capitalism   171, 175, 177, 180
Al Ghazali   160
Ginsberg, Allen   190
Giton, Céline   154
Gladios   109
Glantz, Margo   223
global capitalism   4, 92, 195, 197
global civil society   65–7
global cosmology   26, 27
globalism/globalization   4, 23, 26–8, 30, 31, 35 n.35, 47, 57, 89, 90, 96
global literary system   8, 9
Global Sixties   187–9, 198
Glorias de Querétaro (Glories of Querétaro, Sigüenza y Góngora)   29
Goethe, Johann Wolfgang von   39, 40, 77, 79, 108, 111
Goethe's Centenary (1949)   159, 162
Gondra, Isidoro Rafael   75
Góngora y Argote, Luis de   162
Gongoristic revolution   17
Gonzalez, Aníbal   177
González, Felipe   211
González Martínez, Enrique   94
Goodrich Tyre Co   173
Gordimer, Nadine   207, 211
Gorki, Maxim   110
Gorostiza, José   119, 126, 155
Goytisolo, Juan   206
Graeco-Roman civilization   156, 157

Grandeza mexicana (Mexican Greatness, Balbuena)   7, 8, 15
Great Britain   158, 159, 164
Green Wave, The (Rukeyser)   145
Grupo de los Cien (Group of 100)   235
Grusin, Richard   233
Gruzinski, Serge   7, 8, 26, 28
Guadalajara International Book Fair   215
Gual Vidal, Manuel   158
Guardian, The   211, 212
Guattari, Félix   224
Guérard, Albert   108
Guerrero, Gustavo   5, 139
Guevara, Ernesto "Che"   222
Güiraldes, Ricardo   222
Gutiérrez Nájera, Manuel   94, 95, 99, 121
Gutiérrez Silva, Manuel   93

Hamsun, Knut   107
Haraway, Donna   231
HarperCollins   226
Harvard's Institute for World Literature   226
Harvard University   147
Harvey, David   220, 221, 223
Hayek, Friedrich   221
Hayot, Eric   1
hegemony   1, 3, 14, 15, 27, 55–7, 64, 67, 71, 91, 121, 140, 156, 166, 217–19, 221, 225
Heise, Ursula   234
Helgesson, Stefan   218
Heller, Ágnes   144
Henríquez Ureña, Pedro   14, 222
Henry IV (king)   8
Herbert, Julián   218
Hernández Palacio, Esther   126
Herodotus   18
Heroides (Ovid)   10
Herrera, Fernando de   77
Herrera, Yuri   218
Higashi, Alejandro   239
Higgins, Antony   43, 46
Highet, Gilbert   109
Hispania   145
Hispanic American Historical Review, The   145
Hispanism   14, 17, 47
Histoire natural (Buffon)   42
Histoire philosophique des . . . deus Indes (Raynal)   42
Historia Antigua de México (Clavijero)   42
History of America (Robertson)   42
History of European Literature, A (Cohen)   8
History of Mexican Literature, A (Sánchez Prado, Nogar and Ruisánchez Serra)   73
Hitchcock, Alfred   205
Hollywood   112
Homer   18, 165
homoerotic aesthetics   96
Horace   76, 77
Horizon   145
Howe, Irving   144
"Hoy no circula" (Not Running Today) campaign   235
Hoyos, Héctor   59, 118, 187
Huggan, Graham   203
Hugo, Víctor   73, 75
"Hugo" (Janin)   75
Huidobro, Vicente   119
Humboldt, Alexander von   45, 46
Hunchback, The (Féval)   112
Hussein, Taha   159
Huxley, Julian   157

Iberoamerican Series of the UNESCO Collection of Representative Works   153, 166
Icaza, Xavier   125
imitatio   16
imperialism   65, 89, 174, 188, 221
  Atlantic   67
  Spanish   64, 67
Impressions du Mexique et de France: Impresiones de México y de Francia (Andries and Suárez de la Torre)   73
Inciso, Froilan   161
Index Translationum   155, 159
Indiana University Press   163
Indians of Mexico, The (Benítez)   203
indigenous civilizations   24, 39, 42, 43

258   *Index*

indigenous people   10, 12, 26, 40, 41, 45, 93, 110, 177, 242
industrial cinema   98
Inéditos del siglo XIX (Vieyra Sánchez)   72
Infortunios de Alonso Ramírez (The Misfortunes of Alonso Ramírez: The True Adventures of a Spanish American with 17th-Century Pirates, Sigüenza y Góngora)   30, 60–7
Infrarrealism   4
infrarrealistas (infrarealists)   127
Instituto Nacional Indigenista (National Indigenous Institute)   173
international art market   141
International Congress of Writers   161
International Institute for Intellectual Cooperation   155, 160
international literary festivals   223
International Reunion of Poets   148
International Studio   93
The International Union for Conservation of Nature Red List   233
Irving, Washington   60, 66
Islas a la deriva (Islands Adrift, Pacheco)   234
Italian humanism   10
Ixtlilxochitl, Fernando de Alva   43

Jaeger, Werner   109
Jakobson, Roman   109
James, William   193
Jameson, Fredric   62, 174
Janin, Jules   75
Japan   24, 58, 92
Jean-Jouve, Pierre   162
Jesuits   41, 43–5
Jimenez, Juan Ramón   162
Jorullo earthquake   44, 45
José Arreola, Juan   127, 240
"Joshua Electricman y sus máquinas" (Joshua Electricman and His Machines, Gutiérrez Nájera)   99
journalism   90, 93, 99
Juárez, Benito   80, 81

Kadir, Djelal   219
Kakadu National Park   242
Katayama Toshihiro   147
Kellerman, Bernhard   110
Kerouac, Jack   190
Kircher, Athanasius   29–32
Kirk, Stephanie   4
Klein, Naomi   223
Klengel, Susanne   154, 158, 161, 167
Koselleck, Reinhardt   154
Krauze, Enrique   210
Krugman, Paul   223
Kundera, Milan   206

La alcoba de un mundo (*In the Bedroom of a World*, Ángel Palou)   128
La Biblioteca Nacional   71, 80–3
Lacan, Jacques   205
La Casa de España   107
La ciudad letrada (The Lettered City, Rama)   15
La Croix du Sud   160, 166
Lacunza, Juan Nepomuceno   72, 77
Lafaye, Jacques   42
La fila india (Ortuño)   226
Lagerloff, Selma   107
Lagos, Ricardo   207
Laird, Andrew   44
"La Lunette de Hans Schnaps" (Erckmann and Chatrian)   98
Lamartine, Alphonse de   75
La Nave   109
Landívar, Rafael   44, 45, 48
La Nef   145
La novela quincenal   110
"La onda" (The Wave)   190
Larbaud, Valery   163
Larga sinfonía en d (*Long Symphony in D*, Dalton)   188, 191–4
La ruptura   140
Las Casas, Bartolomé de   9
La Señorita Etc. (*Miss Etc.*, Vela)   123, 125
Las tierras arrasadas (*The Arid Sky*, Monge)   226
Latin America   1, 2, 4, 14, 15, 18, 25, 35 n.35, 40, 47, 56, 73, 75, 82,

83, 90, 91, 105, 106, 110, 126, 161, 166, 172, 203, 218, 222
colonial studies   60
countries   59, 91, 207
literature   55, 57, 74, 106, 107, 111, 160, 167, 219
theories   120
writers   2, 106, 121, 207, 209, 227, 231
Lawall, Sarah   179
Lebanon   156
Le Courrier de l'UNESCO   157
Lecturas clásicas para niños   111
Le Figaro   156
Legrás, Horacio   108, 110
Lengua y Estudios Literarios   109
León de la Barra, Francisco   94
León-Portilla, Miguel   43
León y Gama, Antonio de   42–3, 46
Les Lettres Françaises   144
Les Temps Modernes   144
Le Surrealisme   145
letrados   84, 171–4
Letras Libres   223
Levis Mano, Guy   162, 163
Lezama Lima, José   18, 225, 227
liberal humanism   154
liberalism   67, 143
Liberal Party (1810–80)   4
Liceo Hidalgo   74
Liceo Mexicano   74
Life of an Amorous Man (Saikaku)   58, 60
Limeñan academy   11
List Arzubide, Germán   119, 127
(il)literacy   110–12
literary autonomy   91, 94, 135, 149
Literary Conference, The (Aira)   207
Literary Currents in Hispanic America (Henríquez Ureña)   14
literary legacy   118, 125–9
literary purism   94, 95
Lizardi, José Joaquín Fernández de   17
Llanos y Álcaraz, Adolfo   73
Loa for The Auto-Sacramental of the Divine Narcissus (Sor Juana Inés de la Cruz)   24
Loera y Chávez, Agustín   109

Lomnitz, Claudio   217, 223
Longman Anthology of World Literature   24, 25, 29
López Obrador, Andrés Manuel   215, 226
López Velarde, Ramón   94, 163
Lord Byron   76, 77, 79
Los Angeles Review of Books   226
Los detectives salvajes (*The Savage Detectives*, Bolaño)   127
Los ingrávidos (*Faces in the Crowd*, Luiselli)   128
Los olvidados (film, 1950)   146
Lost Children Archive (Luiselli)   224
Loti, Pierre   92
Lowe, Lisa   67
Loyo, Engracia   110
Lucan   18
Lucena Giraldo, Manuel   27
Ludmer, Josefina   220
Luis de León, Fray   76, 77
Luiselli, Valeria   2, 3, 117, 127–9, 215–16, 220, 222–4
Luis Suárez, Juan   26
Lukács, Georg   62, 64
lysergic acid (LSD)   189, 191, 192, 194

Ma, Ning   58–62, 64, 66, 67
Maciel, Olivia   128
McKee, Robert   96
MacSweeney, Christina   128
Macuto Line   208
magical realism   172, 203, 212
Malaquais, Jean   143
Manila Galleon   30, 31, 58, 64
Mankell, Henning   222
Mann, Thomas   159
Maples Arce, Manuel   117–19, 122–5, 127
María, José   72
Marín, Gloria   112
Martí, José   91, 121
Martí, Manuel   46, 219
Martínez de Castro, D. Antonio   81
Martínez-San Miguel, Yolanda   15, 16, 27–8, 45, 61, 62, 64, 65, 67
Marx, Karl   148
Marxism   139, 143, 148

Materia y sentido: El arte mexicano en la mirada de Octavio Paz (2009) 142
Mauritius Island 232, 236–9
Mayoux, Jean-Jacques 157, 158
Medina, Cuauhtémoc 140
Melchor, Fernanda 3, 226
Melville, Herman 60, 65
Même 145
Memorias de mis tiempos (Prieto) 74, 78
Méndez de Cuenca, Laura 97
Mendoza, Élmer 218
Menton, Seymour 217
Mercurio Volante (Bartolache) 46
Merimée, Prosper 110
Merleau-Ponty, Maurice 144
Merrim, Stephanie 27, 28
Meruane, Lina 2
mestizo 7, 8, 18, 40, 110, 203–5
Metropolitan Museum of Art 142, 211
Mexía, Diego 7, 10–17
Mexicali 56
Mexican Belle Époque 95
Mexican countercultural literature as world literature 187–8
  history 189–94
  trip treatment for world 194–200
Mexican Foreign Service 135
Mexican Muralism 139, 140
Mexicanness 33, 106, 120, 121, 122, 172, 203, 211
Mexican Revolution (1910–20) 92–3, 105, 110, 117, 119, 120, 123, 129, 139, 198, 204
Mexican *situado* 62
Mexico 1, 3–4, 7, 8, 16, 17, 23–6, 31, 32, 40, 43, 47, 48, 55, 57–9, 63, 71–5, 83, 84, 91–5, 97, 105–9, 112, 122, 136, 141, 154–9, 166, 197, 204, 205, 216, 217, 224, 231
  art 136, 139, 140, 141
  culture 77–9, 81–3, 106, 107, 136, 139, 141, 218, 231
  embassy 136–9, 144, 166
  films 112
  independence 71, 72
  letters 41, 74, 75, 79, 83, 84, 129

literary institutions 105, 108
poetry 3, 94, 95, 137, 138, 161–6
post-revolutionary 123, 124, 126
women writers 95–7, 129
Mexico City 4, 7, 11, 14–16, 25, 27, 29, 32, 42, 48, 118, 119, 123, 124, 126, 127, 140
México Moderno press 110
Mexico: Thirty Centuries of Splendor (1990) 142
Mid-Century Generation 127, 129
"Miembro fantasma" (Phantom Limb, Zapata) 240–3
Mier, Fray Servando Teresa de 75
Mignolo, Walter 32
Millán, Paulina 173
Milosz, Czeslaw 144
Mimesis (Auerbach) 109
Ministry of Education 111
Mistral, Gabriela 159, 162
modern art 140, 141
modernismo 89–91, 93–99, 102 n.33, 105, 109, 121
Modernista movement 4
modernistas 90–4, 96–9, 121, 124, 231
modernity/modernization/modernism 8, 14, 28, 35 n.35, 39, 47, 48, 55, 58, 60, 62, 64, 66, 67, 71, 84, 89, 90–3, 96–8, 106, 110, 117, 118, 123–5, 129, 138, 141, 188–90, 193, 200, 204, 205, 217–20
modern literature 90
modern poetry 7, 147
Modotti, Tina 119
Molina, J. Michelle 30
Molloy, Sylvia 96, 121
Monge, Emiliano 218, 226
Monroy, Luis 75
Monsiváis, Carlos 120
Montero, Oscar 96
Mora, Pablo 75, 76
Moraña, Mabel 26, 61
More, Anna 63, 64, 67
Moretti, Franco 4, 8, 9–11, 39, 61, 175, 218
Morfino, Vittorio 193, 198

Morin, Emilie   161, 163
Moulton, Richard G.   2
Müller, Gesine   2
Mundial Magazine   93
Murray, Gilbert   109
Museo de Arqueología, Historia y Etnografía   75
Museo Nacional de Arte   75
Museum of National Art   142

Naciones intelectuales (Intellectual Nations, Sánchez Prado)   121
Nagel   153
Nahui Olin   119
Namur, P.   81
"Nao de China"/"Nao de Acapulco"   30
National Book Award   226
National Commission of Free Textbooks   112
National Council for the Culture and the Arts   112
national culture   73, 77, 82–4, 106, 110, 128, 188
national identity   122, 129, 217
nationalism   4, 9, 74, 92, 95, 106, 112, 117, 120, 121, 128, 141, 204
National Library   80, 82, 83
national literature   9, 11, 16, 25, 71, 79–80, 94, 105, 106, 108, 117, 120, 122, 129, 223–7
National Preparatory School   82
nation building   84, 212
Navarro, Joaquín   77
necropolitics   175, 178, 180
Negrete, Jorge   112
neo-Aztecism   42, 43
Neoclassical poems   163
neoliberalism   199, 203–6, 216–23, 225, 226, 235
Neruda, Pablo   119
Nervo, Amado   92–4, 96, 99
Netflix   225
Nettel, Guadalupe   218
New Directions   226
New Museum, New York City   56
New Spain   3, 4, 7–9, 12, 16, 25, 27, 29–31, 39, 40–3, 45–8

New World   8, 10, 11, 14, 16, 17, 25–8, 40, 42, 44
New World Baroque   23, 24, 27, 28, 29
New Yorker, The   222, 226
New York Review of Books   148
New York Times, The   93, 142, 193, 208–12, 222–4
Nexos   223
Nicholls, Peter   124
Niven, David   112
Nobel Committee   143
No manden flores (*Don't Send Flowers*, Solares)   226
North America   41, 155
North American Free Trade Agreement (NAFTA)   204, 205
North by Northwest (film)   205
Norton Anthology of World Literature   24, 25
Novela como nube (*Novel Like a Cloud*, Owen)   121, 125
Novillo-Corvalán, Patricia   137, 138, 165
Novo, Salvador   95, 119, 123

Occidentalism   84, 223, 224
Olid-Peña, Estefanía   26
Oloff, Kirsten   174
Oloixarac, Pola   219
Ordaz, Díaz   209
Orfila Reynal, Arnaldo   109
Organization of the American States   160
Orientaciones transpacíficas: la modernidad mexicana y el espectro de Asia (Transpacific Orientations: Mexican Modernity and the Specter of Asia, Torres-Rodríguez)   58
Orientalism   92, 93
Orientalist European literary trends   57
Orozco, José Clemente   139
Ortega, Julio   206, 209
Ortuño, Antonio   218, 219, 226
otherness   24, 121, 203
Othón, Manuel José   94
Outram, Dorinda   40
Ovid   7, 10–14, 18
Owen, Gilberto   119, 121, 125, 128

pacean scholarship 134
Pacheco, José Emilio 234–5
Pacheco, José Ramón 76, 240
"Pacific Elegy" 60, 65
Pacific islands 64, 65
"Pacific literary archive" 59
Padilla, Ignacio 128, 207, 222
Pageaux, Daniel-Henri 206
Pagni, Andrea 73
Pahnke, Walter 199
Paideia (Jaeger) 109
Palencia-Roth, Michael 47
Palinuro de México (*Palinuro of Mexico*, del Paso) 188, 194–200
Palou, Pedro Ángel 218
Panchito Chapopote (Icaza) 125
Papaïoannou, Kostas 143
Pappe, Silvia 126
"Paraíso negro" (Black Paradise, Aridjis) 235
Paris 89, 90, 98, 135
Parnassus 93
Parts Unknown (Bourdain) 225
Pasto verde (*Green Grass*, García Saldaña) 188, 190–2, 194
Patria (2019) 225
Paz, Octavio 3, 5, 105, 106, 109, 119, 120, 125–7, 133–5, 153, 161–6, 204, 210, 211, 217
 ¿*Aguila o sol?* (*Aigle ou Souleil?*) 145
 Anthologie de la poésie mexicaine (*An Anthology of Mexican Poetry*) 5, 136–40, 148, 153–4, 161–6
 in Casanova's *World Republic of Letters* 134–7
 Children of the Mire 133, 147
 "David Rousset and Soviet Concentration Camps" 136, 143
 El laberinto de la soledad 145
 In Light of India 134
 In Search of the Present: Nobel Lecture, 1990 133–5
 and international left 142–5
 Itinerary 133, 135, 143
 Labyrinth of Solitude, The 106, 133, 134, 136, 138, 139, 148, 164
 Las peras del olmo (*The Pears of the Elm*) 125
 Marcel Duchamp: Appearance Stripped Bare 141
 Marcel Duchamp o el castillo de la pureza (*Marcel Duchamp or the Castle of Purity*) 133, 141, 146, 147
 "Mexico: The XIX Olympiad" 148
 and Parisian literary field 137–9
 "The Poet Buñuel" 146
 Privileges of Sight, The 133, 142
 Rousset Affair and *The Experience of Liberty* 142–5, 148
 Rufino Tamayo 140
 "Rufino Tamayo in Mexican Painting" 136, 139–42
 Selected Poems 145
 Sun Stone, A Tree Within 133
 surrealism, Marcel Duchamp and world literature 145–9
Paz Soldán, Edmundo 206
Peck, Gregory 209
Pellicer, Carlos 119
Penguin-Random House 222, 226
Pen World Voices 226
Peret, Benjamin 162
peripheral literature. *See* colonial literature
Periquillo Sarniento (Lizardi) 17
Petrarch (Francesco Petrarch) 10, 12, 17
"Petrarchist epidemics" 10, 11
Peza, Juan de Dios 94
Phelan, John Leddy 43
Philadelphia Museum of Art 147
Philippines 7, 8, 58, 63, 64, 67
photographic images 93, 94
Picasso, Pablo 124
Pineda Franco, Adela 4
Pitol, Sergio 112, 127, 128
planetary consciousness 171, 177, 180
planetary fragility 232–6
planetary poetics of extinction 231–43
planetary subject 31, 33, 36 n.53
Plum in the Golden Vase, The 58
Plural 141, 144

poetics as literary history 16–18
poetronica.net 237
Poetry of the Revolution (Puchner) 124, 129
political economy 40, 67, 71, 134, 138, 217
political institutions 133–5, 149
Pollack, Sarah 219
Pollack, Sheldon 122
Polonsky, Naomi 56
Poniatowska, Elena 166
Porfiriato 4, 91–4
Porfirio Díaz 93, 123
Portuguese Arcadia 112
post-autonomous literature 220
postcolonialism 2, 172
post-Kafkian Austrian literature 112
postmodernism 221
Power, Amanda 26, 27
Pratt, Marie Louise 204
Praz, Mario 109
Preface to World Literature (Guérard) 108
Prendergast, Christopher 40, 47
Prieto, Guillermo 72, 74, 77, 78, 82
Primera parte del parnaso antártico de obras amatorias (First Part of the Antarctic Parnassus: Love Poetry, Mexía) 11, 13
Primero Sueño (*First Dream*, Sor Juana Inés de la Cruz) 31, 32
privatization 205, 217, 223, 235
psychedelic-assisted psychotherapy (PAP) 195, 197, 200
psychedelic literature 187–9
psychedelics 5, 187–9, 192–200
public relations campaigns 136
Puchner, Martin 124, 129
Pulitzer Prize 226

Quetzalcóatl and Guadalupe (Lafaye) 42
Quijano, Aníbal 28, 35 n.35, 225
Quintanilla, Luis (Kyn Taniya) 119, 123, 126

radical modernism 129
radio broadcasts 123
Radio: Wireless Poem in Thirteen Messages (Quintanilla) 126
Raichle, Marcus 195
Rama, Ángel 14–16, 82–3, 121, 171–3, 177, 227
Ramírez, Ignacio 73, 77
Ramírez, Sergio 206
Ramos, Samuel 155
Rancière, Jacques 225
Rashkin, Elissa 126
Raymond, Marcel 126
Raynal, Guillaume-Thomas 42, 44
Read My Desire (Copjec) 205
Rebolledo, Efrén 94
Recherches philosophiques sur les Americains (De Pauw) 42
Renaissance 8–10, 15, 23, 26, 28
Renard, Jules 110
reproductive aesthetics 57
Republic of Letters 25, 40–2, 46
Revel, Jean-Francois 144
Revista Azul 92, 94
Revista Hispánica Moderna 145
Revista Moderna 92, 93, 96
Reyes, Alfonso 1, 82, 83, 105–9, 112, 137, 140, 153, 159, 163, 164, 217, 219
Richards, William 199
Rivas Mercado, Antonieta 119
Rivera, Diego 119, 139
Rivera, José Eustasio 222
Rivera Garza, Cristina 2, 3, 174, 179, 218, 225
Robertson, William 42
Robinson Crusoe (Defoe) 58, 60, 63, 64, 67
Roces, Wenceslao 109
Rodó, José Enrique 227
Rodriguez, Antonio 140
Rodríguez, Simón 75
Rodríguez Galván, Ignacio 75
Rojo, Vicente 146, 147
Romains, Jules 159
Romancero 162
Romeo and Juliet (film) 112
Roo, Quintana 77
Rosenberg, Harold 118, 148

Rottenberg, Mika   56, 57
Rousset, David   143–5
Ruelas, Julio   96
Ruiz de Alarcón, Juan   24
Rukeyser, Muriel   145
Rulfo, Juan   3, 5, 105, 106, 217, 225
   El Gallo de Oro (*The Golden Cockerel & Other Writings*)   171, 174
   elliptical narratives   177–9
   El Llano en llamas   171, 172, 174, 175
   "Paso del Norte"   171, 174–80
   Pedro Páramo   171–5, 180
   as world writer   172–4
Rushdie, Salman   206, 207
Rusticatio Mexicana (Landívar)   44, 45

Sada, Daniel   225
Saikaku, Ihara   58, 60
Salazar, Eugenio de   7, 17, 18, 27
Salinas de Gortari, Carlos   142, 205
Salvador, Jaime   112
Sánchez de Lima, Miguel   17
Sánchez Prado, Ignacio   11, 40, 43, 60, 82, 83, 94, 121, 127–9, 172, 181, 218, 219, 223, 224
Sánchez Vázquez, Adolfo   144
San-Ev-Ank   109
San Francisco   58, 97, 190
San Juan de la Cruz   162
Santa Cruz de Tlatelolco School   8
Sanz, Nuria   155
Sarmiento, Valeria   207
Sartre, Jean-Paul   144
Scarpetta, Guy   207
Schnapps, Hans   98
Schweblin, Samantha   2
Schwob, Marcel   110
Secondary School for Ladies   82
Second World War   140, 154, 156
Secretaría de Educación Pública (SEP)   110
Segovia, Tomás   109
Senghor, Leopoldo Sedar   159
Sepan Cuantos collection   112
Serge, Victor   143
Sexto Piso   222
Shakespeare, William   9, 12, 78, 79, 160

Sigüenza y Góngora, Carlos de   14, 29, 30, 31, 43, 60, 61, 64, 66, 67
Silva Herzog, Jesús   158
silver trade   57–60, 62, 64
Simbad el mareado (film)   112
simultaneism   124
Siqueiros, David Alfaro   139
Siskind, Mariano   90, 117, 121, 165, 188
"Sobre la imitación" (On Imitation, Pacheco)   75–6
social distinction   220–4
Society of Jesus   30
Solares, Martín   218, 226
Sontag, Susan   207
Sor Juana Inés de la Cruz   3, 4, 23–33, 163
Soviet Communism   143, 144
Spain   25, 29, 30, 32, 33, 62, 73, 78, 94
Spanish America   40, 41, 45, 60, 89, 91, 177
Spanish language   73, 107
Spanish literature   77, 127, 143, 210
Spanish poetry   164
Spender, Stephen   159
Spitta, Silvia   218, 219
Spivak, Gayatri   25, 31, 36 n.53, 175, 233
Stam, Robert   90, 103 n.40
Steiner, George   109
Sterne, Lawrence   194
Stevenson, Robert Louis   110
Stolley, Karen   4
stop-motion sequences   237, 238
Storia della California (Clavijero)   43
Story of God, The (Freeman)   225
Strategic Occidentalism (Sánchez Prado)   2, 94, 219
"strategic occidentalism"   110
Straus and Giroux   223
Stridentism   4
structural reforms   205
Suárez de la Torre, Laura   73
Sugden, Edward   59, 60, 65, 66
Suma del arte de la poesía (Summary of the Art of Poetry, Salazar)   7, 17
Sur   136, 143
surrealism   56, 125, 126, 145–9, 162
surrealist poets/poetry   126, 134, 145, 146, 148

Suskind, Mariano   74
Swedish Academy   142, 145
Swift, Jonathan   194

Tablada, José Juan   92–4, 163
Tagore, Rabindranath   110
Taibo II, Paco Ignacio   215, 220, 222, 223, 225, 226
Tamayo, Rufino   139–41, 145, 147, 148
Taylor, John W.   166
Teatro de virtudes (Theater of Political Virtues, Sigüenza y Góngora)   29
Teatro Ulíses (Ulysses Theater)   119
technology   122–3
Tejada, Carlos   155
Televisa   141, 142, 144
Tell Me How It Ends. An Essay in Forty Questions (Luiselli)   224
Temporada de Huracanes (Melchor)   226
Tenochtitlan   7, 27
Tenorio, Martha Lilia   13, 14, 17, 18
Thames & Hudson   163
Thought of the Founders of America, The   161
"Thoughts on the American Mind" (Reyes)   1
Three Musketeers, The (film)   112
Through Other Continents (Dimock)   65
thylacine (Tasmanian tiger)   232, 235, 240–3
Tin Tan   112
Tintansón Crusoe (film)   112
Tlatelolco massacre   217
Torres Bodet, Jaime   119, 155, 156, 158–62, 166
Torri, Julio   109
Tossiat Ferrer, Manuel   72
"Toward a History of World Literature" (Damrosch)   16
Tower of Babel   32
transatlantic exchange   25, 26, 29
Transculturación narrativa en América Latina (Narrative Transculturation in Latin America, Rama)   15
translation   72–7
Translation Office   156, 160, 161

"Translation of Great Works"   157
transnational culture   73
transnational humanism   39, 48
transnational literary field   220–4
transpacific circuit   55, 63, 92
transpacific commerce   55–8, 64
Treaty of Guadalupe Hidalgo   59
Truffaut, Francoise   205
Tzara, Tristan   162

Ulíses   119
Últimos momentos de Atala (Last moments of Atala, Monroy)   75
Una ballena es un país (A Whale Is a Country, Zapata)   232, 240
UNESCO and The Fate of the Literary (Brouillette)   134
Ungureanu, Delia   126, 134
United Nations Educational, Scientific, and Cultural Organization (UNESCO)   3, 5, 105, 137–9, 153–8, 160–2, 164–6
  Executive Council   156
  Letters and Arts   160
  Second General Meeting (1947)   155, 157
  and world literature   154–8
United Nations General Conference (1946)   156
United States   58, 59, 91, 97, 118, 122, 156, 159, 166, 217, 219, 220, 224, 227. *See also* Americas
Universal Baroques (Davidson)   28
Universal: diario de la mañana   80
universalism   40, 47, 91, 105, 108, 143, 158, 212
universal literature   108, 129
Universidad Autónoma de México   234
University of Köln   2
Unruh, Vicky   118, 126
"untranslatability"   76, 219
Urbe (*Metropolis*, Maples Arce)   119, 124, 125
Urbina, Luis G.   93, 94, 98, 99
Uribe, Sara   225
Urroz, Eloy   128
Urueta, Chano   112
Usigli, Rodolfo   119

Valero, Pedro 110
Van Delden, Maarten 144, 217
Van Dooren, Thom 234
Van Warwijck, Wybrand 236, 238–40
Vargas Llosa, Mario 209, 222
Vasconcelos, José 110, 111, 122
Vásquez, Juan Gabriel 219
Vela, Árqueles 119, 125, 127
Veladas literarias 74
Verani, Hugo 120
Verdadera historia de la conquista de la nueva España (True History of the Conquest of New Spain, Díaz del Castillo) 9
Verheren, Ferdinand 161
Vermeulen, Pieter 218
Verne, Jules 73, 112
Veyne, Paul 109
Vicente Melo, Juan 127
Viceroyalty of New Spain 27, 58, 59, 61, 62, 64
Vieyra Sánchez, Lilia 72
Vigil, José María 81–3
Villalobos, Juan Pablo 218
Villaurrutia, Xavier 119–21, 123, 125, 128
Villeda, Karen 5, 232, 235–40, 243
Villoro, Juan 225
Virgil 44, 76, 77, 164
Virgin of Guadalupe 42, 46, 164
visual arts 110, 134, 140, 142
visual culture 139, 141
Voigt, Lisa 24
Volpi, Jorge 128, 206, 207, 218, 222
Vuelta 144, 210

Walkowitz, Rebecca 227
Wallerstein, Immanuel 44
Warwick Research Collective (WReC) 106, 125, 174
Weatherford, Douglas 171
Webb, James L. A., Jr. 10
Weinberg, Liliana 219, 220
Weinberger, Eliot 162, 163
Weltliteratur 39, 40, 48, 81, 159
Wenzel, Jennifer 232
Western art 142

Western culture 17, 73, 74, 79, 81, 83, 91, 93, 105, 110, 192–4, 197, 198
Western literature 72, 74, 76, 77
Weston, Edward 119
What Is World Literature? (Damrosch) 107
Where the Air Is Clear (Fuentes) 106
White, Blanco 77
Wilde, Guillermo 41
William Tell 74, 75
Wimmer, Natasha 127
Wing, George G. 137
women modernista 96
World Bank 205
world consciousness 41, 72, 173, 174
worldliness 1, 11, 15, 17, 91, 189
world literary space 134, 135
world literature
  conceptualization 216–17
  criticism 89, 90, 91
  as neoliberal literary field 218–20
  status 125–9
  system 39
  theory 1–4, 7–11, 15, 16, 18, 23, 39, 55, 56, 82, 106, 133, 134
"world-making" 3, 39, 40, 47, 233, 240
World Republic of Letters, The (Casanova) 25, 134–7, 172
world-system(s) 59, 64, 65, 91, 174, 176, 180, 188, 195
  East Asian 58
  Eurasian 67
  theory 44
Wretched of the Earth, The (Fanon) 226
Xilonen, Aura 227
Xirau, Joaquín 109
Yiwu market 56, 57
youth culture 189, 190, 194
YouTube 223, 237
Yunkers, Adja 148
Zambra, Alejandro 219
Zamora, Lois Parkinson 218, 219
Zapata, Isabel 5, 232, 235, 236, 240–3
Zapatista uprising 204
Zolov, Eric 189
"Zopilote" (Vulture, Pacheco) 234
Zylinska, Joanna 232

www.ingramcontent.com/pod-product-compliance
Lightning Source LLC
Chambersburg PA
CBHW062123300426
44115CB00012BA/1784